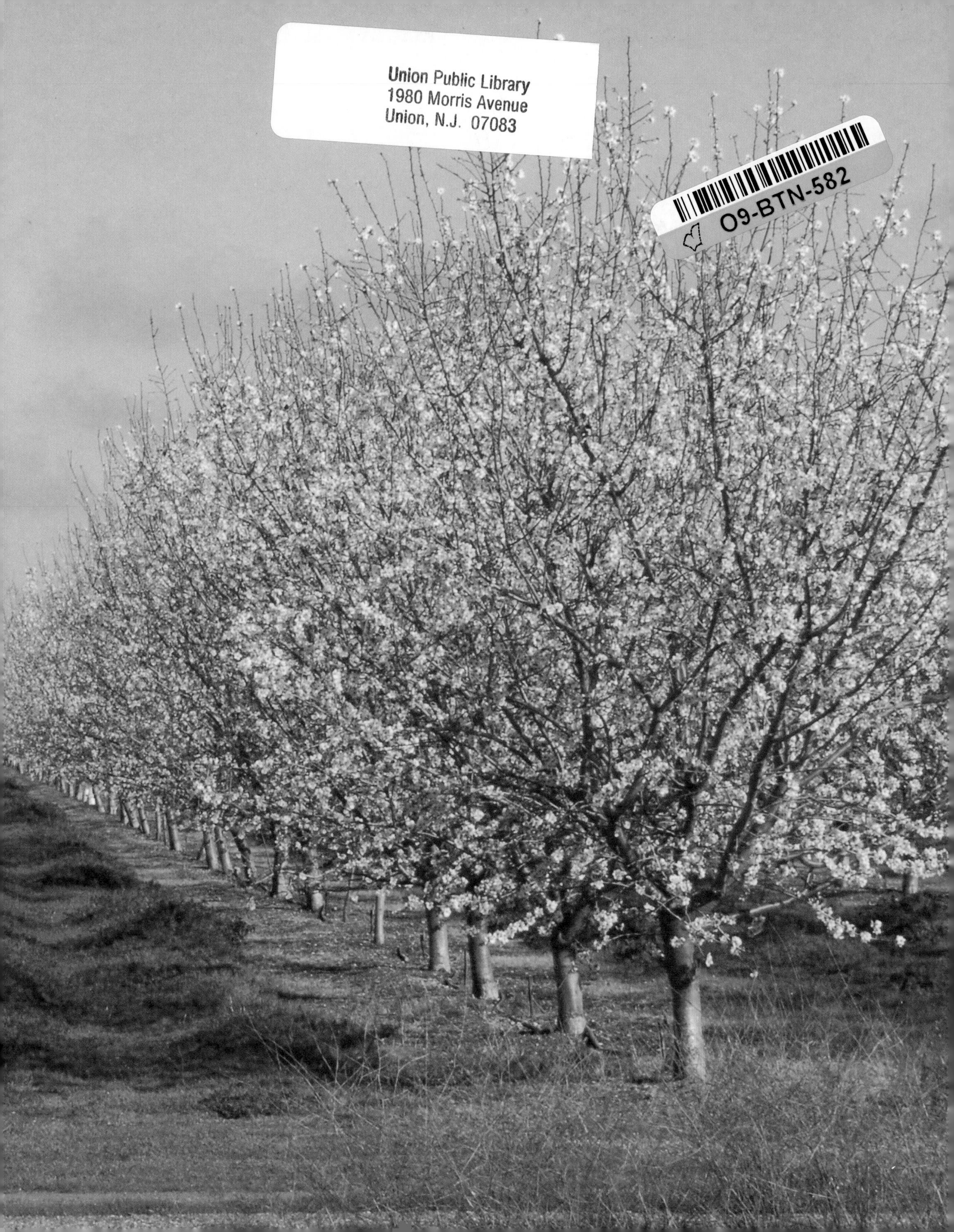

edible

A CELEBRATION OF LOCAL FOODS

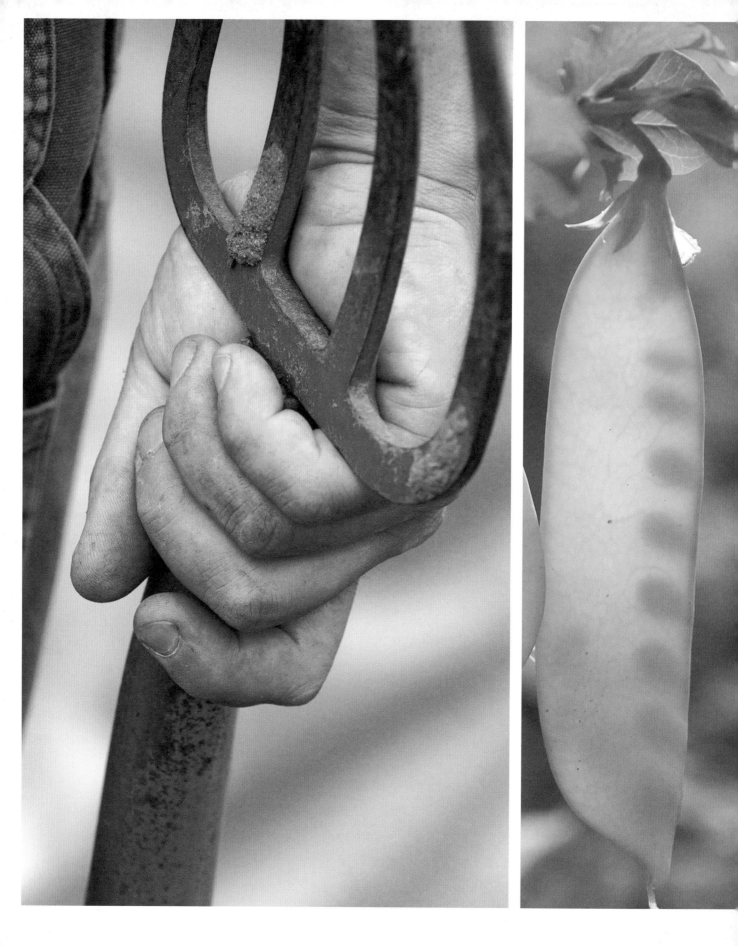

edible

A CELEBRATION OF LOCAL FOODS

TRACEY RYDER *and* CAROLE TOPALIAN

cofounders of Edible Communities Publications

WILEY

John Wiley & Sons, Inc.

Design and layout by Ed Anderson

Library of Congress Cataloging-in-Publication Data

Ryder, Tracey.
 Edible : a celebration of local foods / Tracey Ryder.
    p. cm.
 Includes index.
 ISBN 978-0-470-37108-4 (cloth)
 1. Cookery, American. 2. Local foods—United States. 3. Sustainable living—United States. I. Title.
 TX715.R9933 2010
 641.5973—dc22

                          2009023912

Manufactured in China

10 9 8 7 6 5 4 3 2 1

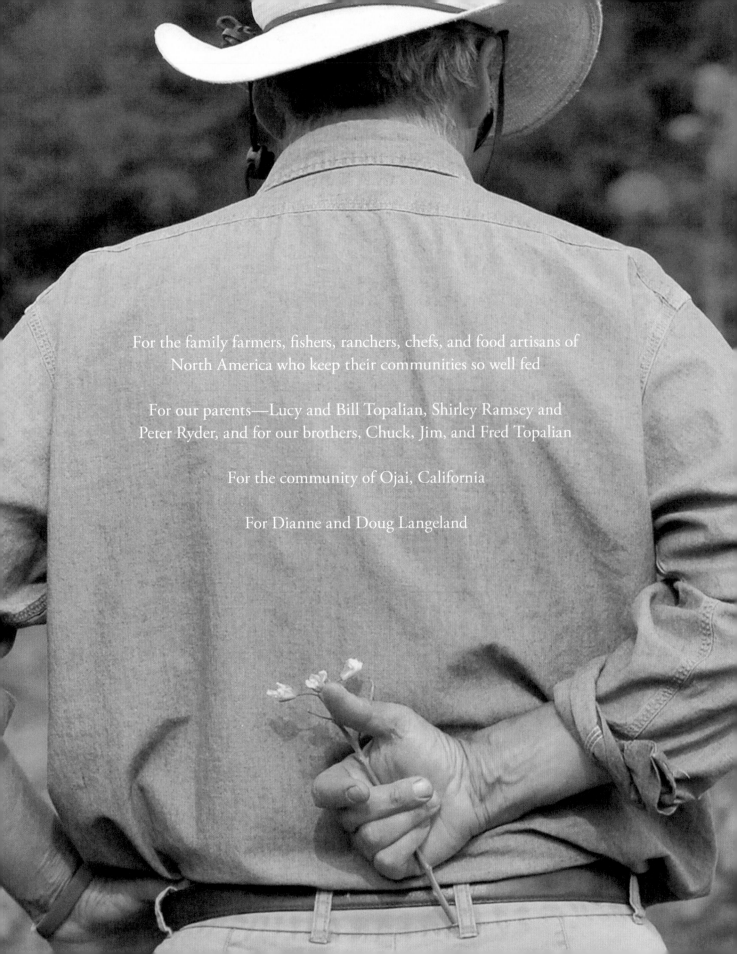

For the family farmers, fishers, ranchers, chefs, and food artisans of
North America who keep their communities so well fed

For our parents—Lucy and Bill Topalian, Shirley Ramsey and
Peter Ryder, and for our brothers, Chuck, Jim, and Fred Topalian

For the community of Ojai, California

For Dianne and Doug Langeland

contents

Foreword *by Michael Ableman*   ix

Acknowledgments   xi

Introduction   1

EDIBLE STORIES   6

Northeast   9

Southeast   55

Southwest   81

California and the West   115

Pacific Northwest   153

Midwest   179

EDIBLE RECIPES   206

Spring   208

Summer   232

Fall   256

Winter   284

Recipes by Region   312

Edible Communities Publications   313

Index   316

FOREWORD

I plow my field, I plant my seed, for kings or emperors what use have I?

Chinese proverb

In 1973, I joined a commune in southern California that was based on agrarian principles. We had three different parcels of land totaling some 4,000 acres on which we raised row crops and orchards, operated a complete goat and cow dairy, and produced grain and fiber. We supplied our own natural food stores, bakery, juice factory, and restaurant as well as feeding ourselves. We even made our own clothing, backpacks, and shoes.

After only four months living in that community I was given the responsibility of managing the 100-acre pear and apple orchard located in a high desert valley east of Ojai, California. At the time this was one of just a handful of commercial orchards in the country that was farmed organically. Here I was at the age of eighteen with no orcharding experience, having never managed anything, directing a crew of thirty people, most of whom were older than I.

The orchard had been abandoned for fifteen years; the branches between the trees had become so intertwined that you couldn't find the alleys down the middles of the rows. I had a 1930s copy of modern fruit science, the journal from the guy who ran the place the year before and gave up in frustration, plus, attached to the door of my twenty-foot unheated trailer, a copy of Johann Wolfgang von Goethe's famous quote: "Whatever you can do or dream you can, begin it. Boldness has genius, power, and magic in it."

Now this could have ended up really poorly, and under most similar situations I would have probably spent the rest of my life working in some high-rise office building. But there was something that took place down those rows of apple and pear trees, something very different from what was happening in most agricultural fields and orchards in North America.

I went to work each day with thirty of my friends, and while we worked we joked and talked and discussed our dreams. We tried out our latest theories and philosophies on each other, speculated on the fate of the earth, and ate our lunch together under the shade of the trees. In the winter we pruned every day for four months straight; in the spring we thinned fruit for weeks on end; and in the fall it was a ten-week harvest marathon.

It was repetitive work, but at the end of each day instead of feeling I had been chained to some mind-numbing drudgery, I felt like I had attended an all-day party. The work got done, the orchard thrived, and those apples and pears gained a reputation around the country. And while the cold nights and hot days of that high desert provided ideal growing conditions, I am sure that the fruit was equally infused with the energy of that group of people and the pleasure they found in each other and in that land.

This was my introduction to agriculture. This community experience has informed all of my agricultural endeavors since: It demonstrated that good food is more than just the confluence of technique and fertile soil, that it is the result of men and women who love their land, and who bring great skill and passion to working with it.

These are the people whom you will find in the pages of this book. They are farmers and ranchers, they are fishermen and cooks and activists, and they are changing our relationship with the land and with food.

Amid the incessant drumbeat of bad news permeating our lives these days are glimmering signs of hope, manifested at the weekly gathering at the farmers' markets, in neighborhood food gardens, in fields and orchards well tended, and on home and restaurant tables where people have once again discovered the deep satisfaction of food well grown and prepared. In the midst of dramatic world change it is amazing to witness how something as simple as a dry-farmed apricot or a tangerine picked at the perfect moment can transform lives.

Every major social movement throughout history has started with a handful of adventurous folks who have dared to reimagine their world and had the energy and courage to create new models. This time they come to us with soil and flour and garlic and seeds on their highly skilled hands. They are our postmodern pioneers, our "quiet" revolutionaries, and this revolution begins in the soil and ends up on our plates.

I've been involved with this movement my whole adult life: as a farmer, as a passionate eater, and as a teacher sharing with others the power of food as a pleasurable force for change.

When I started farming it was for very simple reasons: I wanted to eat well and to work on the land. I didn't realize at the time how good farming could bring together so many aspects of our lives: ecology, community, economy, health, education, and so on. I didn't know that growing food could become such a powerful force in people's lives, reconnecting them with nature's cycle, with the law of cause and effect, and with that deep and soulful pleasure that comes from eating fresh foods cultivated in living soil by people who care.

When you're young and you've just "discovered" a new path, you want to convert others. I spent years thinking that if I could just tell folks why it was important to consider another way, if I could be more eloquent in my expression, if I could just convince them, beat them into submission, then things would change.

Now I think, if I could just grow the best tomato.

I've realized that pleasure is a much greater motivator for change than guilt.

From the West Coast to the Great Plains to the rocky shores of New England, countless others have discovered that same pleasure, and they are changing their world one handful of seeds, one bucket of compost, one tomato at a time. Edible Communities has been bringing their stories to life, weaving diverse foods and traditions and individuals together in their magazines and introducing them to millions of readers. Their work in creating an edible network, bringing regions across North America together around food, has been remarkable.

For too long a potato was just a tasteless medium to convey ketchup and salt to your mouth; it was a food item, necessary but somewhat inconvenient, to be prepared and consumed quickly, and those who were growing or cooking it were not terribly well respected. We are emerging from that time, emerging into a renaissance of food and agriculture.

The folks in this book are building this renaissance; they are bringing respect and honor to farming and cooking, raising those professions up to a level of high art and refined craft, and returning food to where it belongs: at the center and the heart of our families and communities. They are also working in very creative grass roots ways to reduce the gap between those who can afford good food and those who cannot.

I used to like to say chefs had received almost mythical rock-and-roll status and that it was time for farmers to receive that same attention. But the real shift we need cannot take place when only 1 percent of us is doing the work to grow the food for the rest, while everyone else is cheering us on. All of us love the attention, but farming is not a spectator sport.

So make friends with a cook, but don't forget to make friends with a farmer as well—you're going to need him or her. For I am certain that as the current global industrial experiment continues to unravel, agriculture will once again become a central part of our lives.

What will be missing when we can no longer rely on industry and technology and someone somewhere else to provide us with basic transportation and food and shelter is the knowledge, the wisdom, the basic skills required to live on this earth.

The rich edible journey so intimately and beautifully portrayed in this book honors all those who have been preparing for that time, reeducating themselves, rediscovering their place in nature, developing and refining their skills, and diligently working to re-create a world where the power of good food can change our lives. I am sure that the day will come when they will be sought after, looked to for leadership and guidance, when their farms and gardens and kitchens will be the repositories that kept a sacred and essential knowledge alive.

MICHAEL ABLEMAN *is a farmer, photographer, and author of* From The Good Earth, On Good Land, *and* Fields of Plenty. *He currently farms at the Foxglove Farm on Salt Spring Island in British Columbia, Canada, where he also directs the Center for Arts, Ecology, and Agriculture. Please visit www.fieldsofplenty.com and www.foxglovefarmbc.ca.*

ACKNOWLEDGMENTS

Many people have helped in the preparation of this book. First and foremost, we would like to thank all of the Edible Communities publishers, board of directors, and staff members for their hard work, collaboration, and guidance, particularly Doug Langeland, Pamela Hamilton, Ilene Bezahler, Phil Solman, Mary Ogle, Jean Roth, Doug Adrianson, Jennifer Cliff, Stephen Munshin, Bruce Cole, and Kelly Day.

We wish to thank our agent, Lisa Ekus, whose enthusiasm and support of this book have been our guiding light throughout the entire process. To Kristi Hart, our editorial manager, we send a heartfelt thank-you for pulling all the pieces together in perfect order. And to our editor, Linda Ingroia, we are grateful to you for shepherding this project from the moment you asked Tracey to pass the butter during an awards dinner in 2006 until the day we held the book in our hands for the first time. Without your patience, wisdom, and expertise, this book would not exist.

Thanks also go to those behind the scenes at Wiley, including: Natalie Chapman, the publisher; Ava Wilder, the dedicated production editor; Jeff Faust, the cover art director; and David Greenberg in publicity. Also, thanks to Ed Anderson for his beautiful design.

A giant thank-you goes to Gail Gordon Oliver for her exceptional skill and talent as a recipe developer, tester, and writer, and to our dear friend Michael Nicola for bringing such a good eye (and great props) to the styling of our recipes. The book is more beautiful and delicious for your efforts. Thank you to Joel Coleman and Robert Starr, two great Santa Fe chefs, who cooked up a storm when we needed extra help testing recipes.

We owe an enormous debt of gratitude to Cheryl Koehler and Carol Penn-Romine for research, writing, and gathering content, and to all of the contributing writers who so carefully brought these honest, authentic stories and recipes to the page—your dedication to this movement has the power to create real change.

To all the freelance writers, designers, photographers, interns, sales reps, and editors who work with our publishers each and every day, we send our wild applause.

We extend a big hug all the way from Santa Fe to Ojai as we thank our friends who were there at the beginning and who still keep *Edible Ojai* shining brightly: Jane Handel and Ramona Bajema, Claud Mann and Perla Betalla, Jim Churchill and Lisa Brenneis, Anna Thomas and Larry Yee, and all of the incredible contributors, past and present, who put such love and care into the words that appear on its pages.

Love to Doug and Dianne Langeland for jumping in and making it a foursome way back then, and thus, a real community (and for lobster rolls and bubbles!), and to Andy Huppert for being there from the start and for teaching us the art of herding chickens. To our mom, Shirley Ramsey, for coming to Santa Fe whenever we needed her to and for taking such good care of Calvin, Alice, and Nick every time we had to travel.

Finally, to the local heroes whose stories come alive on these pages and whose daily work in the fields, waterways, and kitchens of North America make our lives richer, healthier, and more delicious than we ever dreamed possible—we thank you with all our hearts.

INTRODUCTION

Whenever I have doubts about whether all of this effort has been worth it, I go out into the wilds behind my backyard and taste a fruit or flower freshly plucked from a tree or vine. My mouth, my tongue, and my heart remind me what my mind too often forgets: I love the flavor of where I live, and all the plants and creatures I live with.

Gary Paul Nabhan, Coming Home to Eat

PREPARING THE SOIL

Edible Communities started small and, at its heart, remains so today. Our very first publication came to life in the spring of 2002 and was a sixteen-page, sepia-toned newsletter called *Edible Ojai* that was published quarterly, with the seasons. For two years, we published the small but sturdy journal with the help of some amazingly talented and generous friends, and with the enthusiastic support of our entire community.

Before the premiere issue of *Edible Ojai* debuted that spring, Carole and I had spent the previous fall and winter asking ourselves those meaning-of-life-type questions that indicated a change was at hand for us, both personally and professionally. Carole had been enjoying a career as a professional photographer for well over twenty years, both in the fine art world and commercially, and was looking to do more of both, but she also wanted her commercial work to focus on more meaningful subject matter than the random corporate clients she had been serving. In November, my father, whom I adored, died of a sudden heart attack. This drove me to take a long inward look to try and figure out what I really wanted to do with my life. I had been a writer and graphic designer for years but felt, as Carole did, that a more fulfilling subject matter was in order. As is typical with me, I read to find answers.

During my quest, one book provided the spark that changed everything. *Coming Home to Eat: The Pleasures and Politics of Local Foods* by Gary Paul Nabhan, is a personal journey for Nabhan as he spent a year eating only the foods that came from within a 250-mile radius of his home in Arizona, yet is broad in its telling of the larger story of the current local foods

movement today. The book compels and captures. It raises questions and offers solutions. I wept while reading certain passages and cheered over others. "Obsession" is probably too strong a word to describe how I felt about this book, but the book quickly became a personal manifesto for what eventually distilled in my mind and came to life as *Edible Ojai* and, subsequently, Edible Communities.

In upstate New York, where I'm originally from, my family ate locally and in season. We simply knew no other way to eat—it was our way of life. The closest supermarket was more than twenty miles from our home, so no one went out to the store to quickly pick up milk if we ran out. Canning and preserving the late-summer harvest was an annual ritual for us. My father hunted deer and small game each fall so he could fill our freezer with meat that would last all winter. We tapped our maple trees and boiled the sap until it became the dark sweet syrup we used on pancakes and to sweeten baked goods and to top our ice cream. My nana was a legendary cook who came from a large farm family that had lived on, and farmed, the same land for generations. We feasted on trout, caught from mountain streams and cooked on site in a cast-iron skillet more times than I can remember or count.

So, with the grief over the loss of my father and the discovery of Gary's inspiring story living side by side in my heart and mind, it was time for a new direction and a new desire to help people everywhere come home to eat.

From that moment on, I started each day with a newfound energy. I woke up feeling inspired and ready to take on a new project. After dozens of "edible" conversations with Carole, where we would drink coffee and daydream about story ideas, photo shoots, and page designs, we decided to enlist the help of our friends who were cooks and writers and to get started on the first issue of *Edible Ojai*. Then, one evening while we were having cocktails with our dear friend Jane Handel and her daughter, Ramona Bajema, in front of the fireplace at Jane's home, everything seemed to come together. Jane's experience as a seasoned writer, editor, and publisher, along with her heartfelt encouragement, gave us the confidence to forge ahead.

Sometime during the first two years, and after some early success with *Edible Ojai,* Carole and I started harboring the hope that we might expand our little "edible idea" into having a few more publications and imagined ourselves traveling up and down the California coast, writing stories and taking photographs for the other community-based newsletters we wanted to publish.

Of course, the plans you think you want to put into action have a way of changing on you before you even realize it, so when *Saveur* magazine included *Edible Ojai* on its "Top 100" list in January of 2004—less than two years after our first issue—things changed. The blurb that appeared called *Edible Ojai* "a concept we wish would crop up everywhere." We now refer to this mention as the two inches of ink that forever changed our lives.

Within a day of *Edible Ojai's* being mentioned in the national press, phone calls and e-mails started pouring in, and that first week brought over four hundred people our way who wanted the concept to "crop up" in their community, too. Clearly, we had struck a chord.

From our earlier desire to have multiple publications, we had chosen the name Edible Communities for our publishing venture, so to try to capture all the attention coming our way, we immediately posted a Web site at www.ediblecommunities.com that said, "If you are interested in starting your own *Edible* publication, send us an e-mail and we'll get back to you." Of course, at that point in time, we didn't have much of an idea as to how we could expand into all of those communities, but we knew we wanted to try.

From January to early May 2004, we searched to find a business consultant who could help us implement the kind of business model we wanted to use, but no one we spoke with seemed to understand what we had in mind. What we were looking for (especially since we realized we could not do all the publications ourselves if they were all over the country) was a way to train individuals who lived in and knew their own communities well enough that they could create their own publications with our support.

Fortunately for us, one of our dear Ojai friends, Larry Yee, had an idea of who could help us. He introduced us to an attorney whose father had invented VISA and who knew how to help young companies grow and scale using the VISA model, which basically operates democratically and considers its affiliates members of the company. This sounded so much in line with what Carole and I envisioned that we spent several days with a team of attorneys in Missoula, Montana, who helped us create the foundation for Edible Communities. Today, one of those attorneys, Andrew Huppert, remains as in-house counsel and is one of our most trusted friends and advisers.

By the time we left Missoula, we had a contract in hand that we could use to start enrolling new publishers in what we were then calling a "pilot project" since we still weren't sure how this new company would ultimately flesh out. We knew there would be evolution and change as we grew and had more experiences with getting new publishers off the ground, so even though we wanted a functional business model and structure to work within, we wanted that structure to remain fluid until we tested it out and could see where it was headed.

THE FIRST SEEDLING

My childhood summers were spent visiting Cape Cod with my grandparents. It was there that I tasted my first lobster, dug my first clams, and established a lifelong love of oysters and melted butter, so it only made sense that our first magazine outside of Ojai would be on Cape Cod. From that week of the four hundred phone calls and e-mails from folks wanting an *Edible* publication in their own community, one in particular stood out. It came from Doug Langeland, who wrote saying that he and his wife, Dianne, were semiretired and were looking for a food-related business to buy, and he wondered if we might consider a publication on Cape Cod, where the two had a home and where Dianne's family had been for decades. Carole and I talked it over and decided that without a doubt, this was the place to start. It was a decision made purely by gut instinct but one we've never regretted for a single moment.

After a lengthy six-way conference among Carole and me, the Langelands, and our respective attorneys, a contract was signed (in spite of some bickering by the lawyers over which of their ideas should be incorporated into the document), and Carole and I loaded up my old SUV, affectionately named Eleanor, and headed from Ojai to Cape Cod. We had no real idea of what to expect once we got there and had to produce *Edible Cape Cod* in partnership with our new "members," whom we knew only from a few e-mails and phone calls. Traveling with us was our eleven-year-old golden retriever Kiva, two laptops, four cameras, a desktop computer with a huge monitor, a scanner, printer, a ton of paper, ink cartridges, and a mountain of various office supplies. We felt like a modern-day version of Lewis and Clark, but rather than searching for an inland waterway to the West Coast, we hoped to find new food routes through the distinct culinary regions of North America.

Not knowing how long it might take to figure things out, we rented a house next door to the Langelands and hunkered down for the duration. Fortunately for all four of us, we immediately hit it off and worked well together. Within two weeks and countless delicious meals together, we had not only created the first issue of *Edible Cape Cod,* we had become friends as well. To this day, the Langelands remain two of our closest friends and still are an integral part of the core team that guides and shepherds this company as we head into the future.

CULTIVATING A LARGER GARDEN

In one of our initial goal-setting meetings, we fantasized that we might one day get to a level where we could expect to add six new publications to our roster each year. We feel incredibly fortunate that to date we have been adding over ten new titles each year. From Vermont to Hawaii, Vancouver to South Florida— Edible Communities' magazines are enjoyed by readers who value the taste and healthfulness of local foods, as well as the importance of keeping local economies vibrant and family farmers thriving.

For me, the stories that live on the pages of these beautiful, earthy, intelligent publications are alive. They are compelling and celebratory. They are heartfelt, honest, and sincere without being sentimental. They go well beyond the two dimensions of the printed page. They withstand the test of time and are unforgettable. I think of them more as vintages, like wine, rather than editions. They are better in many ways, too, since you can open and enjoy them again and again, unlike wine that is opened and consumed, never to be tasted again in exactly the same way. Like good wine, *Edible* magazines have clarity, *terroir,* and depth of character.

I can't tell you how many times we hear from readers saying that they read each and every issue from cover to cover, and then read it again. This is simply how

it is with these agricultural, culinary, and community-affirming jewels. You cannot leave them alone. They demand ongoing attention. They breathe. Sometimes I half expect to reread an account from an older issue— perhaps one about a farmer who is in the process of starting seeds for a new season—and then expect those seeds to have become plants that are ready for harvest the next time I read the story. I'm often stunned that the stories are frozen in time when they seem so alive on the pages. I hope you find this to be true of the book you now hold in your hands, which is a harvest, so to speak, picked fresh from the pages of our magazines.

THE HEROES OF OUR LOCAL COMMUNITIES

The stories that follow are a tribute to some of the local heroes we've met and spoken with along the way. It is their stories that keep our forward momentum strong and our hearts and minds energized. The only downside for us in doing a book like this is that there is no way for its pages to contain all the stories we want to share with you. Our most difficult challenge was the editing process. For every story on these pages there are a hundred more we could easily have included. In the end, we went for balance among the six regions we publish in (and hope for several more future books to fill!).

This book is also a tribute to those who put their hearts and souls into creating *Edible* magazines for their communities. It is for the fifteen hundred writers, photographers, and editors who fill our pages every year, and who celebrate the local food heroes in their region by telling their stories. It is for the readers, subscribers, and advertisers who spend their hard earned dollars to help keep each magazine strong and who believe the presence of such a publication is a vital component of their community. It is for all of you along the way who have supported our efforts to create a collaborative, cooperative business model that operates by a set of guiding principles that bring out the best in people and that operates at the opposite end of the spectrum from that of most traditional corporations.

Mostly, however, this book is for our publishers, who live and work in the communities they publish in and who volunteer countless hours toward creating better local food systems. Because of the work they do, 15 million readers from all over North America and other parts of the world have a better understanding of why it's so important that we eat locally and in season. Edible Communities is a company built on handshakes, poetry, and promises. Its strength is in the people who have chosen to be part of it.

Even though this book celebrates the stories and successes of some of the local heroes we've encountered along the way, it doesn't mean that there aren't still challenges to be worked through. Farming, for example, is the only profession where you buy retail and sell wholesale, making the ability of small family farmers to earn a decent living from their hard work quite difficult. In addition to tending their fields or livestock, they now have Web sites that need constant updating, e-mails to answer, and more sophisticated business plans to generate and follow. The family who chooses to farm today has personal challenges as well. I can't tell you how many times a farmer has told me how different life is now that one member of the family, usually the mother, has to work "in town" at a job where she can get health insurance so that her family is covered. Otherwise, the cost of health insurance is too great a financial burden for a farm family.

The local foods movement has other issues inherent as well. The inner cities of urban communities still struggle to gain access to a consistent supply of fresh foods. Obesity and other health issues continue to take their toll on our children, who have become far too used to eating quick meals from a box picked up at a drive-through window.

The local heroes featured in this book have gone from being ordinary individuals on one day to being extraordinary change makers on another. They are quiet activists who have either overcome, or are working to overcome, the challenges this movement still faces. They start new farmers' markets where there were none, they sit on boards of directors for organizations helping to bring fresh food to inner-city communities, they lobby to change policy, and they never waver in their belief in a better food system or in their efforts to make it so.

ABOUT THIS BOOK

Edible celebrates the local foods movement through the eyes of those who are so deeply involved and those of others who have been touched by it through our publications. It does this in two ways, with essays about local heroes—the best of the many wonderful features in the *Edible* magazines—and with a collection of recipes that showcases both classic and modern dishes with foods grown in our own backyards. (Some locally produced products are mentioned in some instances, but general versions are always given.) The recipes are arranged seasonally and then by course to make it easier to use them. There's also a list at the end of the book of the recipes by region, in case you want to see what recipes represent your region or a region in which you have family, or which you love to visit.

The essays are presented by region and are organized to showcase the farmers (ranchers and fishermen, too), food artisans, retailers, chefs, and organizations, in that order—basically tracing the way that food travels, from land (and sea) to table.

We're also pleased to share highlights of the particular local communities in our magazine group, which you'll see in a recurring sidebar feature that includes the top five or six People, Places, and Things of each locale—it will be fun to see how many you know of and which are new for you to explore. The lists are not meant to be comprehensive and may even catalyze debates, but that's fine. We're happy to inspire conversations that discuss the best of local foods; they can only help us all to explore our communities more. For those of us in the food business, they help us continue striving for excellence.

Of course, as in depth as this book is, we can only scratch the surface of all the good things happening on a local level; we recognize that this is simply a celebratory snapshot of what is happening in local communities now. Although we focus on many people who have been around for years or even decades, circumstances shift and chefs may change restaurants, businesses close, or people move. As the local movement grows, newer, more prominent advocates may rise—and that is all for the good. We would hope that communities would keep adjusting to address the needs of the people who live there.

So if our goal is to have people think, act, and eat locally, why did we create a book that covers the entire territory of our publications—the United States and beyond? Because so much wonderful local activity is happening around the country that we should all know about, even if it is not happening in our own backyard. It is compelling to learn the challenges that others face;

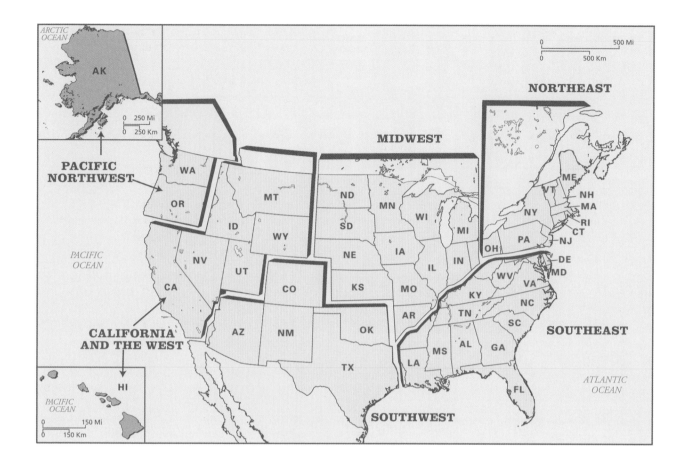

it is inspiring to see how people rise creatively and passionately to the occasion.

If you can't currently enjoy foods available in another part of the country, perhaps reading about them will prompt a trip to that region in the future, or perhaps you have family or friends who would love to take advantage of things they may not know about. Please share our stories!

We hope you find inspiration and comfort in this book, either from the stories of the true local heroes who are changing the way their neighbors eat or from trying the delicious recipes from each region. Whether you are a lifelong advocate of local foods or are just beginning to step into that garden, we wish you many abundant celebrations around the table of your family and friends.

—Tracey Ryder
Cofounder, Edible Communities

EDIBLE STORIES

Each January, during the Edible Communities Annual Meeting, our publishers announce the winners of their Local Hero Awards, which are nominated by the readers of each magazine. Winners are selected in multiple categories including: Farm/Farmer (a category that also expands to include the parallel efforts of ranchers and fishermen), Chef/Restaurant, Food or Beverage Artisan, Retailer, and Nonprofit Organization. The local heroes from each community are given an award certificate, and their stories are published in the magazines and promoted through our Web sites.

It is by getting to know these iconic yet down-to-earth heroes of the local foods movement that informs and guides our work on a daily basis. When we first started the company, we often said we did so because we loved farmers. This is even truer today; however, the statement would now include the fishers, ranchers, artisans, retailers, chefs, and others who have worked so hard to make this movement grow and thrive to the degree it has in recent years.

Choosing which stories to include in this book was our biggest challenge. There is not a single local hero story we felt could be left out, yet with literally hundreds of them to include, our pages filled and boiled over quickly, like a pot left over a high flame. So as you explore the following pages, we hope you are touched by the hard work, humor, history, and humility exhibited by this sampling of heroes. Remember that communities everywhere are filled with people just like these—we hope you meet those from your own community soon. Or, perhaps you are they—we hope you feel inspired to continue doing what you're doing for all the joy and despite the challenges.

NORTHEAST

The growing season may be short and the topsoil thin and rocky in the Northeast region, but food histories and traditions here run long and deep.

While it goes without saying that the food traditions of any region begin in the land-scape, it's especially interesting to consider the effects in the northern parts of the North American continent of those huge sheets of glacial ice that rampaged over the land during the Pleistocene Epoch. The retreating ice scraped out depressions in the bedrock that are now filled with magnificent lakes that provide generations of Northerners with good fishing. The glaciers also chipped away at the coast to create notably irregular, rocky shore-lines. They dropped off piles of rubble (moraines) that are now such recognizable geologic structures as Long Island, Cape Cod, and various barrier islands. All of these contribute to the access that food gatherers have to the huge variety of seafood for which the Northeast is so famous.

While we may love our clams and lobsters, we are not as happy about the way the retreating glaciers scraped away our topsoil and left behind all those rocks and boulders,

>>>

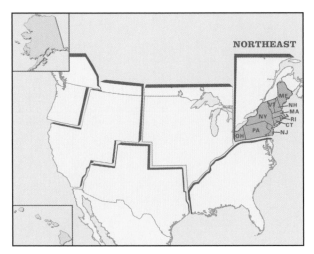

NORTHEAST

strewn like toys in a child's playpen over the exposed bedrock. The rocks were quite the curse when the new European colonist tried to clear his fields and till the thin soil to produce grains and row crops like he had in the Old World, where farmers had been at work for many generations before him. It's only in recent years, with the emergence of organic and biodynamic farming, that growers have learned the wisdom of the Native American farmers: They tilled the soil in small forest clearings, taking advantage of the fertility of decaying leaf litter, and then allowed the forest to return and rejuvenate the soil.

While the would-be farmer/colonists felt dismay with the growing conditions present in their new environs, many of them found a silver lining by raising livestock such as cows instead of crops. The result today is, for example, all that great Cheddar cheese, bearing the appellations of Vermont and New York. Cheddar is only the most notable product of the Northeast's long-lived dairy industry. The settlers found as well that rocky soil does little to deter fruit trees, and so apples are a major product throughout the region—leading to, of course, cider, hard cider, and applejack.

The immigrants brought a knowledge of brewing and distilling, along with a healthy thirst, and it didn't take long before they were producing distinctively New World versions of their favorite spirits using the things that grew best in the rocky ground—notably, apples, corn, and rye—as well as the molasses that came in with the slave trade. Wine production in the Northeast is quite the latecomer, but it's now a growing industry, and grapes are indeed native to the region.

To be perfectly fair, in this chapter we discuss a large area, north to south, and the glaciers did not assail the southern parts of the territory. As a result, we have the "Garden State" of New Jersey, where an extensive and celebrated farming region was a cornucopia for the burgeoning Northeast population centers through several generations. Oddly enough, it was "progress" in the form of the new interstate highway system that brought down the bounty. Here is how *Edible Jersey* publisher Nancy Painter describes it:

One of the most traumatic moments in food production for our community occurred in the 1950s. Two major highways—the Garden State Parkway and the New Jersey Turnpike—were built, effectively cutting a wide, high-speed swath directly through the state's core from north to south. Not only did it result in the displacement and loss of countless farms, especially in the northern part of the state, but it also caused an explosion of suburbanization, as farmlands turned into cookie-cutter residential and commuter communities. New Jersey's food dynamic was monumentally altered, and the state's identity was diminished by the polarizing pull of New York City to its north and Philadelphia to its south.

In fact, fertile pockets exist throughout the Northeast. Most are river valleys that accumulated sediments for centuries before drawing people to their fertile flood plains. Examples are the Hudson Valley of New York, the Pioneer Valley of Massachusetts, and the long and winding Connecticut River Valley. Lesser-known spots, such as Long Island's East End and Toronto's Holland Marsh, are noted for productivity of great significance to their large, nearby urban populations, and production in such places often exceeds the local demand.

When Native Americans first trudged into the Northeast from what are presumed to have been western migration routes, they found the fertile Connecticut Valley much to their liking. Just as they did in other temperate spots all over the continent, the tribeswomen planted beans, corn, and squash—that sacred triumvirate known as the Three Sisters for the way they are cultivated together. These vegetables remain important in our North American diet.

The early native peoples, with their small numbers, did not need to rely solely on agriculture. In the Northeast there was an incredible abundance of wild foods. Game, large and small (yes, including turkeys), could be trapped, and a profusion of crabs, clams,

oysters, and lobsters could be scooped from the seashore. From the lakes, rivers, and oceans there were finfish, and the seas offered water mammals, prized for their pelts and precious fat. In the bogs and thickets the people found a wealth of wild berries: blueberries, cranberries, gooseberries, blackberries, elderberries, raspberries, and strawberries, as well as beach plums and grapes. From the ground they gathered various herbs and roots, and from the extensive forests they harvested beechnuts, butternuts, hickory nuts, and walnuts, as well as the sap that when boiled down became the New Englander's sweet delights, maple syrup and maple sugar.

Some of these native foods have remained quite significant to Northeastern food economies—think Maine lobsters, New Hampshire pumpkins, Massachusetts cranberries, and, of course, maple syrup—but there is also a lasting influence from native cooking in regional fare. When we bake corn bread or a pot of beans, roast a turkey, or hold a clambake on the beach, we are emulating Northeast Native American cuisine. Our storied and traditional Thanksgiving menu offers a prime example of foods that were available to the first settlers, but it's also important to consider the overlay of old-world cooking styles in parsing out those dishes. For instance, the Indians did not sweeten their cranberries, squash, or sweet potatoes; that penchant came from the European settlers.

The first immigrants, the English and Dutch, put an indelible stamp on what we think of as standard "American" fare, where boiled meat might be paired with little more than cabbage and potatoes. Fortunately, many immigrant groups that followed have added nuance and spice: Go to the tip of Cape Cod and you'll find a seafood stew that descendants of the original Portuguese settlers still enhance with their spicy *chouriço*. Stop into an Italian joint just about anywhere and you'll find dishes laced with garlic and Mediterranean herbs—ingredients that do not easily grow in the Northeast. In more recent times, as New York became a primary entry point for immigrants from all over the world, there has become no limit to the flavors you'll find in one of its neighborhoods' food offerings.

Traveling around the Northeast today, as you can do simply by perusing the essays that follow, you will find a highly educated and industrious society that is familiar with the advantages of cooperative effort. Farming as a community enterprise goes back to colonial settlements in the Northeast, when tools and oxen were shared and everyone got together to raise a farmer's new barn as a weekend effort. The meat from one man's slaughtered cow was shared while it was fresh, and excess produce was always traded with neighbors. So when the concept of Community Supported Agriculture (CSA) came to America from Europe in the 1980s, it easily took root in Massachusetts, resonating with traditional notions of community-based industry. Likewise, the revival of local artisan food crafting was built on an image among Northeasterners of themselves as a society of craftspeople taking great pride in their work.

Like everywhere across our continent and in many parts of the developed world, the post–World War II lure of food production made easy through large-scale industrial practices diminished the perception of value to the Northeast's local agricultural landscape and "cottage" food industries. This came about just as the perceived need for more housing, highways, shopping centers, and office parks loomed, promoting a revaluing of land that gave rise to the harmful notion that food can (or even should) be produced at great distances from where it is consumed. The people you'll meet in these essays believe otherwise. Even in the crowded Northeast, the land can again support the needs of its residents for wholesome food. Sustainable production is key to that effort.

If, after reading these stories, you want to gain more firsthand knowledge of the past and future of sustainable food production, visit one of the Northeast's agricultural learning centers, such as Stone Barns Center for Food and Agriculture or Hawthorne Valley Farm, both north of New York City, or Shelburne Farms in northwestern Vermont. Better yet, just go to a local farmers' market and let your taste buds and the farmer offering samples at his stand tell you what we have to gain from supporting these efforts.

Allandale Farm

....

Boston's Last Working Farm

I had lived in Boston for over a decade when a friend asked me whether I'd ever visited Allandale Farm. I recall wondering why I had never heard about this place. Could there really be a farm in Boston? I realized, during my first visit, that I had discovered Boston's best-kept secret. Several years later when I had the pleasure of working at Allandale, my feelings about how very special a place Allandale is were confirmed.

Allandale Farm, located seven miles from downtown Boston, straddles the Boston and Brookline town lines and is nestled among houses, a private school, and a hospital. The property has streams, hills, woodlands, greenhouses, residences, and the original stables. Considered large for a New England family farm, it is approximately 130 acres and, like most New England farms, the land is not flat. It has shallow-to-bedrock soil, making only 30 or so acres useful for growing crops.

William Fletcher Weld purchased the property in the mid-1800s, and since then five generations of his family have lived on it, farming and maintaining it and being sustained by it until well into the mid-1950s.

Food was grown, harvested, and stored for year-round consumption. Chickens were raised for their eggs and pigs for their meat. Orchards provided apples, pears, and plums. Ponds were dug to produce ice for the icehouses. Stables were filled with horses, and workhorses plowed the fields. For a short period a small timber mill recycled the trees that fell on the property.

The property remained in the same family for over 200 years and was a well-run, relatively self-sufficient family estate. To this day it is one of the oldest privately held family farms in the United States.

Then, in the mid-1960s economic realities changed: Property taxes were rising rapidly, and the price of heating oil was skyrocketing. The family realized that in order to keep their property, the land needed to generate income. It could no longer remain a gentleman's farm. The next generation, James, Martina (Lee), Edward, and Robert, who were all in their twenties, stepped in and took control. Although none of them was trained in or planned for a future in farming, they had both the desire and determination to keep the land in the family.

When they started out, they learned a lot by trial and error. Corn was one of the first crops grown for the commercial venture. Edward Lawrence tells stories of coming home from work and heading to the fields to harvest the corn that would be sold the next day. They set up a stand by the roadside, and in the morning the corn would be laid out for sale. Business was conducted under the honor system—customers would leave money in a tin can. Corn proved to be the most successful and lucrative crop grown and sold up through the 1990s.

Other farming endeavors followed, none as successful as the corn. For example, a plan to grow Christmas trees failed when they found themselves replanting the small trees, not having realized that you needed to space them out at the outset. For many years land was leased out for farming, barely producing enough income to cover the expenses of the property.

In 1973, Massachusetts tax laws changed and Chapter 61A went into effect. Chapter 61A: Assessment and Taxation of Agricultural and Horticultural Land enabled small farms to be taxed at a lower rate than the residential rates they had been paying. This change in the tax law enabled Allandale and many other small family farms to remain intact rather than being forced to sell their land to developers.

With the family's realization that they could afford to keep the land, the farm was formally established and named Allandale Farm. As I learned only recently, the name does not have any familial significance. Its source is the name of the road where it is located. Making the legal commitment to maintain the land as a commercial farm meant that it was time to get serious about the use of the land. Coming home from work and picking corn for sale the next day would not longer suffice for running the farm; it was time to employ a full-time farmer.

Hiring a farmer to manage one's land is like dating to find a spouse. The farmer at Allandale needed to be a good grower and competent at managing a retail business as well as maintaining the balance of land use that had existed for generations. Over a period of ten years farmers came and went. The retail business expanded from a roadside stand to a small store that still works on the honor system.

During the 1970s, changes in the family's structure threatened to adversely affect the farm but fortunately didn't. The property was no longer the primary residence for the entire family. Two siblings moved away from Boston, leaving Edward and Lee to oversee the day-to-day operations. Despite not living on the site, they all agreed that they wanted the property to remain intact and, most important, agreed that they would not draw any personal income from the farm. As long as the farm was able to support itself, it would remain as is.

In the mid-1980s, Allandale Farm ended the "dating" process when the owners found a farmer who would ultimately prove to be the perfect match. John Lee had run the Codman Community Farm and owned his own farm in Lincoln. He was well respected in the local farming community. Raised in a farming family in Vermont, he was representative of the farmers of his generation—well educated, with more than an agricultural degree. When John heard about the job at Allandale, he jumped on it, only to learn that Edward had already been checking up on him. As it turned out, John discovered he was also a distant relative of the family. From the very beginning, the relationship worked. Although a one-year contract was drawn up, twenty-four years later John still manages the farm.

One of the first tasks undertaken was to develop a business plan for the farm incorporating new business ventures such as apple cider production, which John,

from his prior experience, knew would be successful. A cider mill was built, and Allandale's fresh cider was an immediate success. Cider continued to be a main commodity until 1998, when the laws changed, mandating that all commercially sold cider be pasteurized. The cost of buying the necessary equipment to meet these new regulations was prohibitive, so cider production ceased.

Expanding the farm stand was another project that John tackled early on. The building that exists today was built by connecting and rebuilding greenhouses that were dilapidated and in disrepair. Prior to his employment, the farm stand would close down after Halloween and open again for Christmas tree sales in December. With the new building, John expanded the season, opening in April with bedding plants and continuing straight through until Christmas, when the last tree was sold.

Through the mid-1990s the farm continued to grow slowly. All salaries, maintenance, improvements, and equipment purchases were paid for by the income generated from the land. The owners continued their original agreement not to take any income from the farm. The farm needed to be self-sufficient, and it was.

Over the years, John slowly continued to make changes in the methods of farming and the operations of the farm. He looked at what crops were the most productive as well as what his customers wanted. At the same time, he and his field crew considered ways to optimize the use of the land and what were the best practices in order to sustain the land. Organic farming practices were emerging, and Allandale embraced the movement. John and his crew wanted to ensure that the farm would remain a viable, sustainable entity to be passed on to future generations, much as it was given to them. Ultimately it was decided not to pursue organic certification but to continue practicing organic farming methods.

The change to organic farming had an impact on the types of crops that could be grown. Corn, a guaranteed, money-in-the-bank crop, could no longer be grown. Most customers desire that their corn be pristine, without worms, and in order to achieve this the crop must be sprayed, which goes against organic practices. John began buying corn from another local farm, along with apples and other fruits no longer grown on the farm. Over time, the self-serve farm stand was expanded to a full-service store; the varieties of crops increased and the farm developed a loyal customer base. Many of the farm's loyal customers were the parents of students at the Apple Orchard School, founded on the property in 1972 by Lee Albright.

The Apple Orchard School is for children ages three to six years. Their Web site summarizes their philosophy: "We use the environment extensively for learning and development. The wild animals (geese, ducks, rabbits, hawks, etc.) and domestic animals (chickens, a goat, a donkey, and a miniature horse) along with the growing and harvesting of crops play a large role in our teaching. The children are encouraged to learn and grow in a farm environment, rich with opportunities for exploration and discovery. The teachers are able to expand upon the natural curiosity and excitement of 'teachable moments' ever present in such a unique learning atmosphere."

Exploring the land and knowing one's environment had always been important to John and some-thing he believed needed to be reinstituted into a child's education. In 1995, with the farm running smoothly, Allandale started a summer program offering the experiences of the Apple Orchard to a greater number of children. Every summer, children ages four to ten may be seen exploring the woods, wading in ponds, and weeding the camp garden.

So what makes Allandale Farm such a special place? For me it is the amazement I feel every time I drive up Newton Street and see acres of green crops growing where there might be row houses or the pleasure I get when tomatoes are in season and I find thirty or more varieties arrayed on the tables waiting to be purchased.

As James, Edward, Lee, Robert, and John grow older, one might worry about the ability and the will for Allandale Farm to remain. Have they instilled in the next generation, twelve individuals versus four, the same love and respect for the land? Fortunately for Boston, the answer is yes.

ILENE BEZAHLER *is the publisher and editor of* Edible Boston. *Prior to that, Ilene was fortunate to have worked at Allandale Farm and experienced the pleasures that the property brings to the family and community.*

Coonamessett Days, Jamaican Nights

Gosh darn, the sky is falling . . . we are all doomed . . . news at 11.

This is the opening line of a typical newsletter from a nontypical farmer—perhaps a farmer with too much radon in his soil, perhaps not. More likely it's a farmer who just likes to give a good time. He continues . . .

The economy is collapsing and there is nowhere to turn for help—except Mars—but they're having a dry spell as well. Hopefully ours won't last as long. So what now? Do we tune in to CNN's Sunday Night Special "Surviving the Apocalypse"? Do we start hoarding essentials such as toilet paper, canned food, and beer—and safe drinking water, such as beer? Golly gee whiz, where can you turn at this time of crisis?

The final answer to this question ends up being *Coonamessett Farm.* Ron Smolowitz is the man behind the mouse, as well as the plow, and the 2,000 plus recipients of such bizarre e-mail newsletters are the members of Cape Cod's beloved farm in East Falmouth, the farm that's prepared to save us all—or at least its members.

This Friday, the last Jamaican Grill Night of the season, celebrating Cape Cod's Cape Land and Sea Harvest weekend, is the opportunity to start the Fall

Visitors to Coonamessett Farm

right. Bring the family, bring beer. If the temperature is below 50 or rain is falling, bring rum. Summer is gone—don't dwell on the past. Start anew!

Jamaican Grill Night and rum? I come from a family tree blooming with farmers and on occasion have visited their farms, where the only grill to be had was on the front of a retired '58 Ford pickup, and the only Morgan was a horse—Captain Morgan was more the seafaring type. The farmers I know aren't typically into cranking Bob Marley and marinating jerk chicken, and if they *were* partaking in any similar activities, you could be sure that the party would be over by 7 P.M.; 5 A.M. cow milking comes on brutally fast.

What Ron Smolowitz has done with Coonamessett Farm is like what the Swiss Army did to a knife. You'll realize this the first time you step foot in its fields. First of all, on your way to the fields, you might first wander through their store, where one can purchase anything from alpaca yarn and bolga baskets to locally made soaps and gourmet items. There is a laundry list of kids' farm-themed games and toys, locally made jewelry, hand creams and lotions, and, of course, the farm's own sauces and dressings.

Just off the store is the café, and although I've heard rave reviews over the years about its vegetarian chili, fresh wraps, omelets, and breakfast burritos, it's hard for me to eat in a café where the egg I'm salting probably came from the chicken who's glaring at me through the window. I realize that this is the kind of sustainable dining that foodies drive hours to experience . . . I just happen to find that creepy.

From the café you might walk outside and circle around barbecue smokers the size of hybrid cars. During the summer these smokers see more action than a Bruce Lee triple feature, and their greasy scars and

Photos by Doug Langeland

tattoos tell the calorie-filled tales of convivial gatherings under starry skies. The Jamaican Grill Nights of Coonamessett Farm are legendary on Cape Cod, and I've personally stood in the gravelly parking lot at dusk to witness hordes of carnivores slowly descend on the farm's tent like a scene out of a George Romero film. . . . All the while in the background, the steel drums sing out over the valley like a pied piper luring people away from the chockablock parking lots of the four-walled restaurants.

More recently the nightly celebrations at the farm have expanded with Vegetarian Buffet and Local Grill Nights, which include anything from artichoke creole and farm-fresh vegetable pot pie, to giving the smokers a serious workout with grilled leg of wild boar and pulled-pork BBQ. On any given evening the music of live fiddlers and guitarists swirls around the farm's twenty acres until the last splat of barbecue sauce hits the picnic table.

The tent also happens to house a dance floor, *and why not?* What good is a farm without a dance floor? The farm has hosted many weddings and rehearsal dinners and can create menus ranging from vegetarian to pig roasts and Cape Cod clambakes (wouldn't it be great if the bride's family were completely vegetarian and the groom's family was eagerly drooling over a pig on a spit? Great visual there.) Speaking of visuals, there are at least a half dozen backdrops throughout the farm that would be perfect for the ceremony.

Another newsletter awaits . . .

Anyone finding a 12-foot boa constrictor named Henry, lost on the farm last week, please notify farm staff. A small reward is offered for his return. Henry was reportedly last seen under some plants in one of the fields, but the reporter, last seen running out the farm gate, did not identify the location.

Apparently Farmer Ron is feeling overly enthusiastic about picking fruits and vegetables here and seems overwhelmed by the unfathomable possibility that someone in the world *(could it happen?)* wouldn't want to partake of the farm's natural bounty. And if such a person could actually exist, what could possibly be his reasoning? Hence "Henry the Boa" slithers out of Ron's imagination and into e-mail inboxes—leading to the panic of a few farm members, the morbid curiosity of Montessori Middle School volunteers, and the head-scratching of Animal Control officers. The e-mail finishes . . .

Blueberries are just about gone. Blackberries are starting up. Cherry and main crop tomatoes are ready. Flowers are in abundance for cutting. Try the Cape Gooseberries and the many varieties of peppers, eggplants, beets, and radishes. Lettuce, arugula, herbs, cabbage, onions, summer squashes, cucumbers, green beans—Wow! You can practically survive on the food available here!

Before continuing, it's time for a confession—and possibly an apology. The truth is, this story was added into this book about forty-eight hours prior to your picking it up, so if your sofa is stained with wet ink, I apologize. When approached to write about Cape Cod's favorite farm, I was soon informed that Ron was believed to be "out to sea." "What does that *mean?*" I asked a Coonamessett Farm staffer. I was told that before Ron and his wife, Roxanna, bought the then dairy farm in 1984, Farmer Ron was a marine engineer who graduated from New York's Maritime College and spent twenty years as a commissioned officer for NOAA's (National Oceanic and Atmospheric Administration) Fisheries Service, as well as a captain aboard Woods Hole's celebrated vessel the *Albatross*. Over drinks at the local watering holes between long trips at sea, Ron would proclaim to friends that he was going to give up the sea and become a farmer. Those trips at sea had delivered him from the seducing breezes of the South Pacific to the ridged glaciers of Alaska and beyond, but he finally kept that promise to himself. Ron continues to be involved in conducting research to benefit commercial fisheries. "Just my luck," I replied. "Deadline's a couple of weeks away and I get the only farmer who doubles as Jacques Cousteau." I waited idly for our farmer to return to *terra capea*.

Ron's commitment to research goes well beyond the whitecaps. It pools into just about everything he digs, waters, and plants, and he'll pass on his knowledge to any budding farmer-to-be who will listen. In the spring and fall there are tours at Coonamessett Farm just about every day—up to 5,000 a year. The farm hosts school groups, has opened its doors to the likes of the Montessori Middle School for "learning beyond the classroom," and partnered with Cape Cod Children's Museum for a hands-on Little Sprouts program for children ages four to ten. During the twelve-week program the kids plant, maintain, and harvest their own veggies, herbs, fruits, and flowers, and learn about organic gardening methods and composting. One could say that the Smolowitzes' roots in the Cape Cod community are stronger than any under their soil.

I am planning to buy baby chicks to rotate our flocks. If anyone is interested in purchasing a few, give me a call. I'm also going to Foxwoods Casino next week if anyone is interested in staking me. In one case—chickens—you put grain in and sometimes eggs come out. In the other—slots—you put in quarters and sometimes you get more back. I think I have a better chance on making my money back at the casino.

Farmer, gambler . . . what's the difference?

It is by no accident that this piece contains only e-mails to loyalists, as opposed to direct quotes from the farmer. When I finally caught up with Ron Smolowitz, I found he is a man of few words, in spite of his colorfully offbeat e-mail newsletters. We talked for a while, but during that time I kept looking down to find farm brochures and fliers magically appearing in my lap: "Yoga on the Farm" . . . "Storytelling and Pumpkin Painting Day" . . . "Artisan's Fair" . . . "Earth Day Celebration" . . . "Fiber Festival" . . . "Coonamessett Eco Cross Cycle Race." It was obvious that Ron preferred that the farm and his work with the community do the speaking for him. And so they have.

His last e-mail raises an interesting point. Thanks to Ron and Roxanna, Coonamessett Farm has evolved into five greenhouses with demonstration hydroponic and aquaculture systems, a wide range of vegetables, herbs, and berries, a general store, a café, an ice-cream stand, a menagerie of animals (both domestic and exotic), and most recently a wind turbine. It would seem that an undertaking of this magnitude would have to most definitely be backed with not just a great passion for farming but also a gambler's heart—and the gambles seem to keep paying off. Not just for Ron Smolowitz, but also for the thousands of residents of Cape Cod who know that when the sky occasionally seems like it *is* falling, they can always turn to their beloved Coonamessett Farm.

. . . .

TOM DOTT *has been co-owner of the Lamb and Lion Inn in Barnstable, Massachusetts, since 1999. Before moving to Cape Cod, he and his partner, Alice Pitcher, ran a four-diamond restaurant in New York's Hudson Valley that specialized in all things local. Tom promotes "culinary adventures" to inn guests and works part-time at The Wine List in Hyannis. In 2007, he received an Eddy Award for feature-length editorial for "The Vines That Bind," which appeared in the winter 2007 issue of* Edible Cape Cod.

. . . .

FARMER ~ *EDIBLE EAST END* (NEW YORK)

Organic Farming's Guru

. . . .

Scott Chaskey and His Quail Hill Farm

It was lunchtime in a little café in Amagansett, New York, a few years back and the actor Alec Baldwin, now a star of *30 Rock*, was sitting across from organic farmer Scott Chaskey. A woman hesitantly approached the two men in the booth, recognition lighting her face. She looked from the actor with the contagious smile to the bearded farmer then breathed, "Aren't you . . . *Scott Chaskey*?" That's how a very close friend of Scott's tells the story.

Chaskey, the director of Quail Hill Farm, one of the oldest CSA farms in the country, is almost instantly identifiable by his bushy, flaxen-softened white beard. "My wife has never seen me without the beard," he grins. When Megan and Scott, both studying abroad, met in London in 1978, the beard was red.

Driving along Deep Lane by the farm you often see the bearded and lean-framed Chaskey silhouetted against the light, driving his tractor along the top of

Scott Chaskey on Quail Hill Farm

the hill. You easily spot him among the thousand people attending the January Northeast Organic Farmers Association conference in upstate New York. He's board president of the 1,700-member group. He's everywhere, mentoring growers on organic farms, coaching five farm apprentices, teaching in local elementary schools, guiding children's hands as they learn to seed, and touring graduate students over Quail Hill fields. At last July's potluck supper in the apple orchard, yes, there was the soft-spoken, bearded farmer reading one of his poems, for, as his passport indicates, his profession is "farmer-poet."

While he may look like he stepped out of a nineteenth-century daguerreotype, Chaskey personifies the new breed of highly educated, highly motivated farmers who are leading America's Community Supported Agriculture movement. "Farming is my passion," says Chaskey, who received a master's in writing from Antioch University and studied for two years at Oxford University.

In the early 1980s, Scott and Megan married and moved to Mousehole, Cornwall, on the English coast. There he heard of the Cliff Meadows on the south-facing slope, known locally as "the earliest ground in Britain," which once grew the first new potatoes and first daffodils sent to Covent Garden. Soon, an old Cornish farmer was tutoring him in an ancient understanding of organics and soil. It fits Scott's persona that he managed to rent Cliff Meadows land to farm, bought an acre he still owns, and single-handedly built a frame house. The Cornishman visited daily. Scott learned.

He and Megan, an accomplished flutist, traveled with the first of their three children to Amagansett in 1989 for an extended visit. There they attended a meeting of a CSA to which Megan's parents belonged. Unexpectedly, Chaskey found himself planting the first crops for Quail Hill Farm, which would open in spring 1990 as a CSA project of Peconic Land Trust.

In Amagansett his passion for protecting the soil—its structure, its health, the life that thrives in it—grew. It took him several years to nurture the land back to vitality. He began to teach everyone who would listen—CSA members, schoolchildren, chefs, other farmers—about the critical need to save diversified organic seeds and the need to farm sustainably. "I don't think anyone realizes how central education is to what we do," he says.

There is his other passion, writing and poetry. His second book of nonfiction, *Seed Time*, its title from a Wordsworth poem, is about the relationship between farming and writing. "It follows a seed from its development until it blossoms and goes back to seed, just as a writer needs seed time," says his literary agent, the former editor Paul Bresnick. A charter member of Quail Hill, Bresnick says, "I'd always admired the letters Scott wrote to farm members, which always began with some beautiful writing about nature, about land, about wildlife." Almost a decade ago, Bresnick, now in a new career as a literary agent, persuaded Scott to write a book inspired by the newsletters, *This Common Ground—Seasons on an Organic Farm*.

Though the well-reviewed book speaks of nature, fifty-eight-year-old Chaskey doesn't consider himself primarily a nature poet, though he supposes many do. His real subject is "the mystery of self and others in relationship to the world. The big picture."

Chaskey reflects on his time at Oxford. "I had a reader's card at the Bodleian Library, the *Bodleian*," he says, his voice still rising in amazement. "It's an unusual thing to stay active as a writer and to teach without being an academic. So while I've done some teaching, I've been lucky enough to have a whole different profession, working out-of-doors. . . . Writing a poem requires a lot of space, more space for me than writing prose."

"Space from people?" a visitor questions.

"Space—whatever 'space' means. It also involves silence, and more time than I've had available for years." Then, "The solitude of the back field . . . that can be a very inspirational place, the back field, alone seeding in the earth."

While the five-foot-nine poet may run short of time, time reshaped is one of the bonuses the more than 200 harvest-share members receive along with produce. As you head down the sandy path to the little farm stall, your intention is to fill several sacks with vegetables—in August: onions, peppers, red fingerlings, fennel—quickly harvest some jade beans and eggplant from the fields, and dash off. You take only a few steps past the wild blackberry bushes and milkweed when you feel your breath let go as the mystique of the oasis Chaskey has nurtured in the midst of prime Hamptons real estate takes hold.

"When you walk into Quail Hill, you walk out of a nine-to-five business time frame into seasonal time," says Kristi Hood, chef-owner of the nearby Springs General Store. Like many members, she has contributed recipes to two editions of the *Quail Hill Farm Cookbook*. It is a sophisticated primer on preparing the

diverse variety of vegetables a CSA grows. Says Hood, "Scott is very much in sync with the land. He extends his love into the land, his love into what he grows. He is a lovely, spacey, delightful man." You sense this personality in his cookbook introduction.

In 1988, Chaskey was intent on nourishing his beloved soil, not a social community. It quickly became obvious that a very social community was growing alongside the vegetables, and in winter, when land lay silent under ground cover, its friendships deepened.

"The extraordinary thing about this Community Supported Agriculture movement," says Chaskey, "is that it came out of a need that many people had to re-create community. It's reached so many. I never had any calculation in the beginning of trying to create something like this. But it's how it's spun out basically." Twice monthly, Chaskey broadcasts his thoughts on this "broad community—of the soils, of people, of animals" on WLIU, the local NPR station.

Those Scott touches support his community as it interacts with the outside community. There are occasional classes, perhaps on canning or bees. In the apple orchard there is a community pancake breakfast and a gala fund-raising dinner with 150 sitting at a single, long, candlelit, white-clothed table. Top local chefs prepare these meals, clearly volunteering their time with enthusiasm.

Scott is a singular man. There is a palpable chemistry that draws others to him, perhaps because he is so soft-spoken and seems accessible, perhaps because his passions are so visible. That is why he connects as a teacher.

He often arrives in East End classrooms with packets of seeds, soil mix, compost, worm casings. At East Hampton's independent Ross School, students receive a hands-on understanding of the importance of nature's cycles. After meals students walk into a narrow passageway and scrape their plates into compost bins. Twice a week these scraps are carted to Quail Hill's compost heap. "When the Ross kids come out to plant in the spring they see their compost is part of nourishing the soil. Then they help plant the crops that they eat at school. So it's the whole cycle." In addition to farming more than 275 varieties of produce, herbs, and flowers on 6 acres for the CSA, the farm grows crops on another 24 for schools and restaurants, and shepherds 120 more for Quail Hill's Preserve.

Chaskey has inspired many with his local, seasonal message. Joe Realmuto, executive chef at the top

Quail Hill's chalkboard displays a weekly offering.

East Hampton restaurant Nick and Toni's, says, "Fifteen years ago, Scott gave us gardening lessons on what to grow, when to grow. He's an artist so in touch with the earth." On nearby land preserved by the Land Trust, Chaskey set up tents for inner-city children from Camp Erutan (nature spelled backward) to camp overlooking Gardiners Bay and to learn to finger Quail Hill soil. Says Chaskey, "Start-up CSAs come here—one a year for ten years—with their list of questions. They help us seed; we give or sell them the transplants." When Scott arrived he found only one other organic farm, The Green Thumb, on Long Island's South Fork. There are now several dozen on Long Island's East End. Chaskey has mentored most.

"There is something very grounding and centered about Scott's perspective on the world around us," says Fred Lee, a North Fork organic grower and owner of Sang Lee Farms in Peconic. "His poetry dovetails and complements his farming. There are times I think, 'I can't do this.' Seeing how stable and competent Scott seems to be adds to my confidence, [and I realize,] yes, it can be done!"

Scott's influence, passion, and efforts to teach both growers and consumers about saving diverse organic seeds and expanding sustainable agriculture to rebuild soil extend throughout the Northeast. He's been on the NOFA board for ten years, its president for two. Board member Elizabeth Henderson of Peacework Farm speaks of the power of Chaskey's soft-spoken delivery and how he overcame earlier animus. "Under Scott's leadership there's cooperation and negotiation rather than hidden agendas and secret plotting against each other." He's also a board member of Vermont's Center for Whole Communities.

Despite his deep roots in the organic community, Chaskey is a questioning soul. "What is my view of current organic standards?" he asks. "I guess you can tell because we're not certified, although Quail Hill grows organically. We're choosing at Quail Hill not to be certified, even though I'm on the board of NOFA New York, which is a certifier. What I don't support is the attempts at manipulation by big business." What he strongly supports is certification for the many dairy farmers whom NOFA is helping transition to organic operation and teaching consumers about the virtues of organic milk.

For Chaskey, the bottom line for agriculture across the land and in the solitude of the back field is sustainability. "It takes nature 700 years to build one inch of topsoil. The world's six-inch layer of topsoil upon which all agriculture depends is endangered by intensive industrial farming." He hopes to revive an "effective NOFA organic seed program that connected farmers and consumers with the importance of maintaining a viable, diverse organic seed supply."

Tomatoes illustrate what Chaskey means about diversity. He actively disliked tomatoes until the mid-1990s, when a farm member insisted he plant seeds she had saved from an amazing tomato she'd tasted in New Jersey.

"Hated tomatoes. Why? Because I had *never* tasted a tomato," he said. He knew only bland, industrial impersonators.

Scott grew out Terri Stein's seeds, barely believing their flavor. Today, Quail Hill holds a popular community tomato tasting. Some 250 adults and children vote on bite-size samples of the forty-plus varieties Quail Hill now grows—Matt's Wild Cherry, Pruden's Purple, Brandywines, Juane Flamme, Green Zebras. You look down the row of wooden tables and you recognize the man sampling top-ranked Sungolds, the man in the blue-checkered shirt with the contagious smile.

GERALDINE PLUENNEKE *has written for* Newsday, *the* International Herald Tribune, *and other publications, and is writing a book on recovering America's lost flavors and nutrients. She lives in Montauk, New York, and frequents Quail Hill Farm.*

Heroes of the Heirlooms

Antique Apples Make a Commercial Comeback at Red Jacket Orchards

There's a revival of a certain kind happening in the Finger Lakes. This one doesn't involve music, religion, or a theater stage, but it does require earth, air, water, human determination, and curiosity, and plenty of budwood. Near-lost varieties of apples, the fruit America is most famous for, are being given another chance to shine and delight the masses on a large commercial scale. For the flavor-hounds among us, we have Red Jacket Orchards to thank for the pleasure.

In 2006, Red Jacket Orchards, a 600-acre orchard and fruit farm in Geneva, New York, started experimenting with heirloom apples in their already successful retail business of tree-ripened fruit and juices. In 2007, they harvested the first crops from the ten acres of heirloom apples they started, a small yield of several bushels per variety, nothing compared to the usual gold standard of a yield of 1,000 bushels per acre, but the apples come out winners. Indeed, next year's crops look promising enough to ensure that a good many customers will get to taste the difference between an antique apple bred for flavor and versatility and a conventional apple that was bred for travel, size, and beauty.

Red Jacket apple crates stand at attention.

"I love that I can taste history with these heirloom varieties," says Brian Nicholson, president of Red Jacket Orchards, who along with his twin brother, Mark, manages the day-to-day of the business. "Each of these varieties has a story that needs to be told. Everything about the apple is there in the graft, in the cultivar. It doesn't go away. So by using what we've learned from growing other, more usual types of apples, we hope we can grow the heirlooms with equal success and make them more available to customers who want that special experience with more uncommon fruit."

Red Jacket Orchards has an interesting history of its own, as worth telling as that of the fruit they grow. In 1958, the family moved to Geneva from Long Island, where the Nicholsons had been turkey farmers, selling poultry and eggs. With Robert Moses's mega-move to get people out of and into the city via highways, the Nicholsons sold the family business and property to eminent domain and hightailed it out of there. They took the unexpected windfall from the sale and, answering an ad in *The New York Times*, invested it in a 150-acre cherry farm along Route 5-20, which at that

time was a major road that took people all the way to California. Mrs. Nicholson came sight unseen with the children, including son Joe, who would eventually grow up to run the orchard and become known as one of the most innovative and successful growers in the region. Fifty years later the fruit farm is 600 acres and growing, with new varieties of crops and juices being added each year, and Mark and Brian, the third generation, now stepping into management roles for the long haul.

It is that third generation that has brought the Nicholsons back to their family roots, or at least a few hundred miles closer. They started selling product to the New York City greenmarkets back in the 1980s, and Brian remembers that first visit to the city. Brian, Mark, and their older brother, Jay, left Geneva at 4 A.M. with a truck filled with RJO products, driving through the tunnel, blinking at the big city lights, thinking they were going to get killed or at least disappear forever. But they made it safely to Union Square and set up camp. They sold half of what they brought; it was a bit disappointing to return home with a half-full truck, but they were heartened by the comments of the shoppers, such as "We'll see you next week, right? You'll be here with more of the same, yes?" And little by little, as the shoppers came to know them, the RJO guys were more than just encouraged by the savvy New Yorkers; they also learned from them. "We ride subways here, you know," one greenmarket regular told them. "We need our hands free to get through the turnstiles." Brian was confused by this until he realized they were packing their apples in brown grocery bags, just like back in Geneva, where shoppers were getting in their cars, bags safely in the back. So they switched to bags with handles and have kept that ever since. They continue to listen to what their customers want and try to provide them with that unique culinary experience.

Some of the new/old varieties that they are growing for these customers provide challenges, especially for the impatient foodie. "Newtons," Brian claims, "taste much better after they've been stored for a while and the flavors are allowed to develop." The fruit is kept in a cold storage and the starches in them convert to sugar. If eaten straight from the tree, the apple has a texture that is reminiscent of a mildly sweet but raw potato. The return of these long-stored apples, however, is well timed, as North Americans are also returning to the old ways of food preservation. Root cellars are back

in vogue, while canning, curing, smoking, and pickling have become requisites in the curriculum of culinary school programs and professional kitchens. How perfect that the "apple of our eye" wants to spend a season in the cellar, with the rest of the preserved foods, before being chomped on.

All heroes have heroes of their own, and Brian and Mark are eager to nod to Ian Merwin, a Cornell pomology professor, as one of theirs. Ian and his wife, Jackie, operate Black Diamond Farm in Trumansburg, a sixty-four-acre farm where they grow, among many other crops, specialty apples. Ian prefers to try out a large number of the heirloom varieties but on the smaller scale that he and his wife and daughter, who do all the work themselves, can manage. Much of his research at Cornell focuses on the genetic history of these antique apples and also on the variety of flavors produced. During visits to the Cornell Geneva Experiment Station, a depository that houses several thousand types of apple varieties, Ian might sample 100 to 150 different apples before choosing a new one to bring back to the farm.

Here's where budwood comes in. Contrary to Johnny Appleseed's tossing seeds left and right to grow trees, growing heirloom trees is possible only through grafting existing bud branches onto rootstock. The rootstock tells the tree how large to grow, and the budwood determines the fruit. Ian provided the Red Jacket guys with not only most of their graftings for the heirlooms but also the education needed (both Mark and Brian were students of Ian's at Cornell) and experience with each of the varieties that they chose to grow.

"Mark came over in September, a few years ago," says Ian, who is still teaching at Cornell while running the farm, "and we went for a walk through the orchard. He asked a lot of questions about the different apples, looking for the types that would work well on a larger scale."

"It was like walking through a living catalog, with everything I needed to know about the ones that performed well and would be a fit for our customers," says Mark. This was important since many of the other grafts available are grown in regions that differ from the unique climate of the Finger Lakes. "I had a whole selection to choose from that was being grown right here with similar conditions to what we have at Red Jacket, and Ian was incredibly generous to share all of this with us.

"Trial and error can be a costly thing when you are a commercial grower," he continues. "With Ian's help, we could avoid many mistakes." Mark took this back to the Red Jacket family, who weighed the decision carefully and decided to move forward with the experiment.

The RJO gang has ten acres dedicated to heirlooms, a beautiful wide-open field just behind the 5-20 corridor that cuts through Geneva. Behind the gas stations, strip malls, and all that is new and somewhat garish of Geneva are rows and rows of the fruit that fed Benjamin Franklin, Thomas Jefferson, their families, and countless others centuries ago. "I really want to get some signs up here so people know what this is, what we're doing," Brian says.

The ten acres account for about 2 percent of the total acreage RJO has in production. However, once they go into full harvest and are ready for a larger market, Red Jacket will be one of the largest producers of heirloom apples in the Northeast. "I don't know if it makes us the largest, but it definitely puts us on the map," Brian chuckles as he gazes out over the fields of trees no taller than a toddler. If there is such a map, it was created centuries ago by farmers with a vision for well-fed citizens with an eye for apples.

Among the varieties available at Red Jacket are Golden Russets, which have a firm and granular texture with ample tartness; Newton Pippins, which were considered a favorite of Benjamin Franklin; Northern Spy; Lady Apples; the oddly named 20-ouncers; Baldwins; Margills, which are also known as Perfumed Princess because of the lovely smell they send; and Keepsakes, which aren't considered heirloom but are the parent of the Honeycrisp, another unusual variety they grow.

Some small-scale farmers might criticize Red Jacket's interest in growing these specialty fruits for a large production, but there is an opportunity here that has to be acknowledged. Red Jacket is *the* apple producer for New York City. They're at every greenmarket, their juices are on the shelves of many grocers both large and small, and if you want local apples through FreshDirect, the home delivery grocer serving the five boroughs and in the summer, Long Island, Red Jacket is what you'll order. So, if a company that big, with that much of a consumer base, takes a gamble on these heirloom varieties and does well, perhaps these delicious, flavorful, and incredibly nutritious fruits will shove their way into the spaces being taken up by the mass-produced, mealy, bland apples that we've accepted. American farmers are capable of growing incredibly delicious fruits and vegetables, the best the world has to offer, and many are leading us into an agricultural return of growing for flavor, aroma, and culinary bounty. Many farmers are reviving the heirloom varieties, but few of us are actually seeing these goods when they are grown on a small scale in a small town.

Ian Merwin agrees. "The guys at Red Jacket have a real opportunity here. They have a large, sophisticated consumer base, and they're good marketers. People are interested in these antique varieties, and Red Jacket will do a great job bringing them to interested eaters on a large scale."

If the crops grow and sell well, Mark has his eye on a few other possibilities. There's an apple called the Caville Blanc, which was grown by Thomas Jefferson and has as much vitamin C as an orange, that he'd like to add to the list. Also in contention is the Chestnut Crabapple, which is about the size of a tangerine and packs a delicious sweet-tart flavor.

"We're so excited about reviving these classic gems. They're like a piece of living history in the orchards," he says. "It's so rewarding to bring these products to a broader audience. Especially with the chance to tell the history of the apple, since it's also telling the history of our country."

MICHAEL WELCH *is the publisher and editor of* Edible Finger Lakes. *He is a trained professional chef and writes about the people behind the food and farms of Central New York.*

Shelburne Farms

Cultivating a Conservation Ethic

Just before noon on a bright August day in northwestern Vermont, a tractor turns in through the gate of the Farm Barn at Shelburne Farms and disgorges a wagonload of visitors into the courtyard. A few local children dash off to the farmyard corner to say hello to their favorite animals and to check the chicken coop for eggs. Others make a beeline for the cheese room, where they know there will be tasty morsels to sample and cheese makers to watch in action. The wagon driver gives a brief introduction to the Farm Barn for the first-time visitors who remain. As she speaks, youngsters stare in fascination at a chicken taking a dust bath where the stone foundation meets the ground. Adults step back to appreciate the soaring turreted roofline of the 120-year-old building, whose silhouette within the pastoral landscape more readily evokes a fairy-tale castle than the agricultural hub it has always been.

On a similar summer day around 1900, this barn at the heart of the spectacular 3,800-acre model agricultural estate established by Dr. William Seward Webb and Lila Vanderbilt Webb on the shores of Lake Champlain would have buzzed instead with the labors of carpenters, blacksmiths, and wheelwrights. Mule teams would have led wagons full of grain to the Farm Barn over crushed stone roads ribboning through fields and woods according to the plan of legendary landscape architect Frederick Law Olmsted. Flash forward a century, and the Farm Barn still hums as the center of the now 1,400-acre working farm as well as in its newer role as headquarters of the nonprofit environmental education center established by the Webb family in 1972. It is one of a number of impressive Robert H. Robertson–designed buildings on the National Historic Landmark property, but it epitomizes the unique juxtaposition of past and present set within the raw natural beauty of a working landscape.

During the farm's May through October season, the Farm Barn offers a wealth of hands-on experiences that bring to life both the realities of farming and the environmental mission of Shelburne Farms. On a hot and busy summer day, the farm can be a lot to absorb.

So focus on just one sense—say, smell—and starting in the Children's Farmyard, an educational farm within the working farm, breathe in the earthy, funky scent of animals and sweet hay mingled with a whiff of fresh sawdust from the Beeken Parsons Woodshop, an independent furniture-building company specializing in sustainably harvested wood. Move on, walking clockwise, to the sour-sweet dairy aromas of the award-winning farmhouse cheddar operation, which uses only milk from the farm's grass-based dairy herd of 125 purebred, registered Brown Swiss cows. Then catch the smell of warm, naturally leavened bread wafting from the ovens of O-Bread Bakery, another privately owned business on the farm for more than thirty years. Circle back to the Farm Cart, a silver food truck surrounded by wooden trellises wound with climbing squash vines, where a griddle sends out the rich perfume of browned butter from dozens of grilled cheese sandwiches served during a peak-season lunch hour. Order a sandwich and throw down one of the blankets offered for all to share, or sit at a picnic table crafted out of trees from the property. There could be no better way to enjoy all you have seen and smelled.

The Farm Cart is just a few years old, a more recent effort by Shelburne Farms to translate its mission of cultivating a conservation ethic into something that visitors can see, touch, or taste. Melted cheddar between hearty slices of bread dipped into a bowl of fresh tomato or roasted squash soup is not only a thoroughly satisfying meal but also delectable evidence of what the landscape can provide if we care for it. "Our goal is to support healthy communities with access to fresh, healthy food and a healthy environment," explains the nonprofit's longtime vice president and program director, Megan Camp. "We can't just talk about healthy food systems, we have to try to build one here ourselves as well." The Farm Cart's sandwiches, soups, and salads feature Shelburne Farms' cheese and produce from the property's own five-acre Market Garden. Much of it is prepared in the restaurant kitchen of the seasonal Inn at Shelburne Farms, which opened

in 1987 in the renovated original Webb residence known previously as Shelburne House. The restaurant has earned a reputation for creating some of the finest farm-to-table food in the country, with cheese, vegetables, eggs, veal, lamb, and pork from the farm, as well as maple syrup and other wild ingredients foraged from the fields and forests.

From grilled cheese sandwiches at the Farm Cart and house-made lamb ragù served over fresh pasta at the Inn to community offerings like spring foraging walks, backyard farming classes, and seasonal festivals and to a jam-packed education calendar of field trips, family workshops, and multiday courses for teachers and farmers, "all of our programs help kindle human connections to nature and agriculture and build a sense of place and community," says Alec Webb, a great-grandson of Dr. and Mrs. Webb, and president of Shelburne Farms since 1988.

Almost forty years ago when Alec was just eighteen years old and about to head off to Yale, his father gathered the family on the South Porch of a sadly dilapidated Shelburne House. After years of trying to reestablish a viable farm enterprise on the vast estate, Derick Webb had reluctantly concluded that selling most of the property might be the best option. Alec and his five siblings asked for the chance to pursue another avenue. With their father's blessing, they developed a plan for innovative land use and conservation and reinvented the property as an agriculture-based educational and community resource with a working farm at its core. The effort turned into a life mission and career for Alec and his brother Marshall, who now manages the property's woodlands and special projects. Alec never made it to college, but he has no regrets.

"Farming has always been at the heart of Shelburne Farms," Alec recalls. "One of my earliest memories of growing up on Shelburne Farms was the aroma of manure from our dad's overalls hanging in the garage. . . . My father converted a former golf course on the property into pasture for milking cows and built an innovative dairy pole barn in 1952, the year I was born. I remember hot summer days in haylofts, bringing home puffball mushrooms from the fields, or strings of perch caught off Orchard Point, and collecting tubs of shiny brown horse chestnuts in the fall. A great old apple tree near our house must have been there when the Nash family was farming the same plot of land before our great-grandparents came to town."

Vivid memories like these made it impossible for Alec, Marshall, and their siblings to accept that housing developments might replace the fields, the trees, and their favorite fishing spots. Such deeply felt connections inspired them to find a way to preserve Shelburne Farms, and, through its work and powerful presence, they hope to encourage others to become active stewards of whatever place they call home. "Kids will always need meadows to walk through, cows and farm animals to touch, and places to understand the source of our food," says Vermont sugar maker David Marvin, who has served on the Shelburne Farms board for two decades. "We all need special places for time alone and space apart that can help connect body and soul. And we need to respect and enjoy our natural and historic treasures that they may inform and enrich us. Shelburne Farms offers all of this. But, what I find so compelling about this place is that its offerings are only a means to a greater end: to develop a conservation ethic that will ensure this and other special places are available for all children and their children."

At Shelburne Farms, connections happen everywhere. In the farmyard, children learn to make a circle with their fingers and squeeze gently but firmly around the warm teat of a caramel-colored cow with soft, patient, dark eyes. The first squirt of milk never fails to elicit surprise and delight. Sitting in a circle shaking cream into butter is another revelatory experience for all ages. Food "manufacturing" was never so immediate, so personal, and so delicious. On a field trip in the sugar bush, grade-schoolers realize with pride that they can find their way back to a tree to which a partner first led them blindfolded. Without ever having seen it, they retrace their way by listening to the changing sound of their own footsteps, feeling the bark of different trees, and picking up other clues from the forest. During an adult course on traditional survival skills, the group pauses while digging burdock root near Orchard Point to marvel at the unexpected arrival of a shimmering orange veil of monarch butterflies taking a rest in the Vermont woods on their way south.

On a brisk but sunny fall afternoon, Sam Smith, the farmer who runs the Children's Farmyard, is speaking to a group of about twenty farmers about on-farm education. "Many of the most important education experiences are in the unscripted moments," he suggests. As if on cue, a goat wanders through the group and stops to sniff curiously at someone's water bottle, prompting Sam to mention hygiene around animals. A preschooler, oblivious to the adults, follows a chicken into their midst and then stoops to carefully pick it up following the method taught to farmyard visitors. In the spring Sam is responsible for the flock of pregnant ewes. "During a lamb birth," he says, "you get thirty kids around watching, and it's the most amazing thing." On the other end of the cycle, Sam continues, three of his young summer apprentices had recently found a dead chicken while doing their chores. "I was worried about them," he admits, "but they got it. A farm has both life and death." Exposing the real work of farming and helping people to take that learning beyond the perimeters of the farm is critical. "The farm is not a petting zoo, not a museum," emphasizes Megan Camp. "It's not like agriculture in a pickle jar," she continues, meaning that it's not all bottled up in a jar where you can see but not touch. "That is why we try to connect schools with farms in their own communities so that they can experience agriculture as part of the fabric of their communities and not something to just visit."

The farmer education workshop continues the following day in the Market Garden, a patchwork of small fields anchored by a quiet white farmhouse where visitors can see the remains of old brick foundations from the original glass greenhouses in which gardeners tended exotic palms and other delicate plants. Now the focus is on more climate-appropriate ingredients for the Inn and the Farm Cart, from early spring peas to sturdy kale and chard. There's a definite chill in the air as the group, bundled in hats and sweaters, traipses around the gardens. Led by Shelburne Farms educator Erica Curry and assistant market gardener Tasha Brodeur, they are on a treasure hunt for the "fabulous five" of the growing cycle: sun, water, air, space, and soil. The farmers, of course, know about these elements, but they are here to learn how to share this knowledge with visitors at their own farms all over Vermont, as well as in Ontario, New York, Connecticut, New Hampshire, and Delaware. The goal of the two-day course, Erica explains later, is to help farmers "demystify" the language of education and schools and translate what they do on their farms into simple, engaging activities.

Erica pauses to point out a lush green field of rye, and Tasha explains how the farm raised five pigs this year in the Market Garden, feeding them whey from the cheese operation and food scraps from the Inn, supplemented with a little grain. The pigs, in turn, deployed their superior rooting skills to clear and fertilize a promising piece of land that had been covered with brush. "The cooks would bring the compost to the pigs," Tasha says with a grin. "They were so into it and really got to know the meat they would be serving." The pigs provided an education and connection not only for the cooks, Erica elaborates, but for visitors of all ages, illustrating the symbiotic relationships possible in an integrated, sustainable agricultural system. On the nuts-and-bolts side, she adds that it's a good idea to post signs near pigs warning of their very sharp teeth. A few farmers nod knowingly.

The pigs had been sent to slaughter a few weeks previously, and some of that pork was destined for the final Inn dinner of the season. In a celebration that is becoming a tradition, this last meal is dubbed "The Whole Beast," underlining the goal to use as many parts of the pig as possible. By late morning on the day of the dinner, the kitchen at the Inn is thrumming with lard-fueled anticipation as head chef Rick Gencarelli, executive sous-chef Aaron Josinsky, and their crew prepare for a capacity crowd of more than sixty. Rick readily admits that pig is a favorite. "It's the most generous animal," he says as he stands next to a fifty-pound piglet rubbed with salt, cinnamon, crushed red pepper, fennel, and coriander seed. "There isn't any other animal we get so much out of."

In the busy prep kitchen, two cooks are twisting fresh tortellini around a filling made from scraps of house-made mortadella and pancetta. Another has just finished picking the meat from two pig heads for a course of traditional Mexican *pozole*. The ears are sitting on the counter waiting to be deep-fried for a crispy pig salad, which will also include crunchy bites of nose, cheek, and jowl. Among all the porcine pieces, it's almost a relief to see a stack of beautiful Market Garden carrots. "Don't worry, they're getting wrapped in bacon," chuckles a cook.

Aaron is contemplating the possibilities for the mound of creamy white fat rendered from the pig heads. "It'll probably go in the beans," he says before running down into the stone cellar to show off his cured meats like guanciale made from pork jowl, pancetta, and long, slender dried soppresatta sausages wrapped in paper. Upstairs he pulls out the fresh charcuterie: pale boudin blanc, loops of smoked garlic sausage, house-made hot dogs, liver terrine made with a generous ratio of fatback, and a rustic pâté wrapped in pancetta. But he is most excited about his first try at blood sausage, proudly holding up a plump, dark curl of boudin noir flavored with apple, onion, fatback, black pepper, nutmeg, and

One of Shelburne's happy new calves

clove. "It turned out delicious," he says happily, and "it really taught me something."

Apart from their devotion to all things pig, the chefs love this meal because of both the challenge and responsibility it represents. It reflects the approach that Rick, a veteran of the Boston and New York City restaurant scenes, took soon after he arrived to head up the Inn kitchen in 2005. "When I worked in New York," Rick explains, "I would sit down and think about all the things I like to eat, write up a menu, and get on the phone and source it. It was all essentially nameless and faceless. Here at the farm, you go to source it out and *then* write the menu. You know the farmers. You know how they raised their vegetables and their animals. You might even know the animals." That kind of intimate

knowledge of the raw ingredients cannot help but affect how you work with them, Rick says. "It changes how you cook. It makes you a better cook. Every day I am humbled by ingredients."

A few springs ago Rick pulled into the Farm Barn courtyard for a meeting just as Sam Smith emerged from the Children's Farmyard looking for a hand. Rick thought he was just going to help move some animals until Sam told him to suit up in overalls and boots. "At that point," he says, "I figured I was in for more than moving sheep." Rick ended up helping Sam deliver a pair of male lambs. He was at the head of the ewe keeping her still and calm, he notes, while "Sam was at the other end doing the hard part." When Rick tells this story, people often ask if he was uncomfortable when those lambs eventually came to the Inn kitchen. "I felt such a connection to them," he admits, "but not in the way that made me not want to use them. It made me appreciate them even more, deepened the connection. It made me respect the cycle even more."

"When people come to Shelburne Farms, whether they came for a special dinner at the Inn or for a field trip," Megan Camp reflects, "we're always asking ourselves, how do they leave with a better understanding of their role in the world? Have we helped them make a connection between agriculture and the environment?" About 140,000 people visit Shelburne Farms annually and each one has the potential to carry its message away with them. "It's sort of this ripple thing," Megan continues. "We don't ever think that it's Shelburne Farms that's going to change the world. It's through our members and visitors, the educators and the farmers we work with, our partnerships with other organizations. It's all about the multiplier effect." She pauses and smiles. "And we're like the yeast."

MELISSA PASANEN *writes about food for the* Burlington Free Press, *is a staff writer for* Art of Eating, *and is the coauthor of* Cooking with Shelburne Farms: Food and Stories from Vermont.

FISHERMAN ~ *EDIBLE TORONTO* (ONTARIO, CANADA)

From the Fresh Waters

A Glimpse of Life on the Bay

Akiwenzie's Fish & More is our family business, which we started in 2002 out of necessity: to earn more from our commercial fishing company. We have a tradition of fishing in our community, and we are applying our grandfathers' and grandmothers' teachings of using only what we need. Our ancestors would find the best way to use the resources without taking more than they needed to survive.

My family is involved in all aspects of our company. I am the fisherman, and my wife and boys help me on the twenty-three-foot open steel boat when the weather permits. My wife smokes and pin-bones the fresh and smoked fish. Our boys, who are eleven, ten, and eight, help with most aspects of the business and watch my wife and me to learn and be our quality control. They sure do learn fast. The boys have helped us at the markets for the first four years—we've home-schooled them, and they've become our salesmen and barkers. We put our hearts into all we do, and we take care in all we do—as if we were feeding our family. Our fish is yesterday's catch, and our smoked fish is cured with the care of our family values.

I have fished with a number of family members since I was ten years old and fell in love with the waters of Georgian Bay. I fish alone most of the time now, lifting the nets by hand as my family has done for as long as I remember. It is a great feeling being out on the bay and being able to help so many people with great fish. I fish in the same way as our elders have for years and with their long-silent voices still in my heart. Upon occasion I have the great opportunity to feed one of our cultural *dodem*s (clans), the bald eagle.

The water is a precious workplace for me, as I have had many jobs in the past that were not as pristine. I was a high-pressure water blaster in Sarnia for a number of years, working in the "chemical valley" with a surreal environment of dangerous equipment and toxic materials. A few years later, I was in a different type of dangerous and toxic career in nuclear mechanical maintenance at Bruce Nuclear Power Development, but now I find my work environment to be a fragile and unpredictable partner; I now watch more carefully the work area I utilize, for it is our most precious resource.

I am on the water from early spring—about the first week in April—till late January, early February. For the greater part of the year I am pretty much alone on the water except for my fellow fishermen. It isn't till the warm weather sets in that I see the first of the sailboats start to silently sail by while I lift and set my nets. A little later, and the anglers and recreational boaters start to make me feel crowded on our waterway.

I have seen so many wonderful events out on the water it is hard to do justice to Mother Earth in so few words. It's so peaceful to be alone with only your thoughts and nature. I have seen water so still you couldn't tell where the water ends and the sky begins. Some days there are multiple rainbows, fog so thick you can taste it. The sky is a canvas, and the Creator toys with our hearts as He makes one beautiful creation after another. I see the seasons change day by day from the "capsule" of my boat, which insulates me like an ultrahigh-definition television, with all my senses being subjected to almost sensory overload.

I have often hastened up to our house to drag my wife and kids down to witness some spectacular event of nature coming to life up close and personal. Nature in all her glory is wondrous to behold, but she also has an alter ego that can be as dangerous as it is beautiful. In winter I enjoy listening to the large snowflakes landing on the sides of my boat with a whisper. And to the large cumulonimbus clouds that bring the summer lightning shows in the distance—transfixing you as they approach and in awe as they envelop you, and then leaving you feeling insignificant and fragile, all the while exciting all the cells of your being. Making you feel so alive while being so close to demise.

If I had a dream job in mind for everyone to try at least once in their life, it would be my wish that you each could accompany me on my daily commute and toil a hard day's work in my paradise.

. . . .

ANDREW AKIWENZIE *resides on the Chippewas of Nawash First Nation Reserve on the beautiful Bruce Peninsula, near Wiarton, Ontario. He is a commercial fisherman on Georgian Bay, where he catches some of the best whitefish from Ontario's cold, deep waters. He is also continuing a family tradition by respectfully harvesting his daily catch and preserving his cultural traditions. His practices of good living and love for Mother Earth's bounty are setting examples for his three boys by showing them their cultural responsibilities as caretakers and children of the land.*

. . . .

Andrew Akiwenzie and his wife, Natasha, on his fishing boat at the Cape Croker First Nation Reserve

Photo by Lauren Carter

Running the Numbers at New Rivers

A Profile of Bruce Tillinghast

Cooking with fresh fruits and vegetables grown by local farmers all boils down to the math for the owner and head chef of New Rivers, Bruce Tillinghast. Take sixteen dairy farms, then add suburban sprawl, and subtract the sixteen dairy farms. This equation, this disappearance of the farms in Tillinghast's boyhood hometown of Lincoln, Rhode Island, has had a caluculable impact on the venerable Providence chef. His efforts to undo the damage have long shaped the way Tillinghast shops and cooks, both for his restaurant and his home kitchen.

Tillinghast should be the food-shed ambassador for Rhode Island. He speaks with a devotion about local produce and seafood that would sweeten even the sourest cynic. Though humble about the effect his philosophy has had in influencing chefs across the state, Tillinghast will be the first one to tell you that the flavor of food harvested close to home just cannot be beat.

"Just try local, seasonal asparagus. You can get asparagus 365 days a year now, but there is just nothing like asparagus in season . . . nothing like it. The taste is sweet. It is truly wonderful. And though we could get raspberries in February from Guatemala, you really can't beat the berries in season from places like Little Compton," Tillinghast declares.

Aside from fruits and vegetables, Tillinghast is also bullish on shellfish harvested in Rhode Island waters. "Rhode Island has some of the best hard-shell clams around. There is just no comparison. The clams that have lately been flooding the market from South Carolina farms lack the freshness, as well as the flavor, of a locally harvested clam. You can even tell the difference in the color of the shell."

Tillinghast started New Rivers with his wife, Pat, in 1990. In that time he has developed relationships with area farmers that have turned into friendships and working collaborations. When Steve Ramos, of Steve's Organic Produce in Bristol, makes his delivery to the New Rivers kitchen, Tillinghast's grin runs from ear to ear as he pores over the contents of each container, exalting in the beauty and aroma of the fresh greens.

Mâche is one of Tillinghast's favorite greens and can be harder to find than most. Steve Ramos grows mâche, among many other herbs and greens, for New Rivers. Together he and Tillinghast worked on finding a variety of mâche with distinct flavor and, when picked at the proper maturity, is exactly what Tillinghast recalls from market trips in France. Mâche, a small-leaf green sold in little bundles, is a staple in the markets of France during spring and fall, when the temperatures are chilly. In early springtime Tillinghast counts on mâche, sorrel, breakfast radishes, rhubarb, and, of course, asparagus as soon as they become available locally.

In the kitchen it easy to see how Tillinghast, a Rhode Island School of Design–trained graphic designer, turned to food for artful expression. There is inherent creativity yet stylish simplicity in the dishes he develops for New Rivers—all of which illustrate a deeper understanding of the ways an immigrant population has shaped the food culture of Rhode Island.

With ease and comfort that reflect his gentle and affable manner, he settles in behind the stove, but not before he is totally ready to begin.

"In this business we have a term called *mise en place*, which is very important if you are cooking in the home or in the restaurant. It's a matter of having everything in place, all your ingredients prepped as far as you can in order to assemble a dish at the last minute," explains the chef. "In doing so, home cooks will have more time to spend with their guests. In the restaurant, everything is at hand when we need it, especially during the rush."

The littlenecks Tillinghast is preparing have just been delivered by quahogger Dan McGowan. McGowan has been quahogging for thirty years and is an old friend of the chef. The littlenecks were just raked from the bay and their dark, glistening black shells shine in the light over the stove. The shell color lightens with heat from the burner, yet the meat stays plump, as a result of the clams' freshness and the gentle precision with which they are cooked.

Tillinghast working the stove at New Rivers

"One of the important things I learned early on from Madeleine Kamman [whose cooking school Tillinghast attended before opening New Rivers] was learning to deal with fresh ingredients and matching food flavors of the same season and of the same geographic area."

When Chef Tillinghast is too busy at New Rivers, he can count on his *chef de cuisine,* Beau Vestal, to procure the ingredients that his bustling Providence restaurant needs to feed an adoring public. Beau makes weekly rounds to gather produce from area farms and markets in Rhode Island or just over the border in Massachusetts to Four Town Farm. He is also an avid forager, and his finds often make their way onto the evening's menu.

Tillinghast keeps in close contact with his friends at local farms to stay informed about what is available for menu planning. On the bottom of the weekly menu he includes what he calls the "sustainability statement," giving customers the rundown on what local farms have contributed to their meal. "A lot of people comment about it. Many of our customers choose to come here because they have read the list of farms on our Web site or have heard about the fact that we are trying to support sustainable agriculture."

The menu changes about six times a year, but often, when new items come in from a farmer, those items will pop up on the menu that evening. Similarly, when seasons wane, Chef Tillinghast is ready to adapt. Most important, he remains committed to supporting the local farmers and is very encouraged by the support he receives from the community of customers who are aware of his efforts.

"It's very upsetting to me to see how rapidly farmland has disappeared in the state of Rhode Island. Once a farm is lost, it is gone forever. Farming is not a renewable resource in Rhode Island. Cooking this way is important to me because I don't think we can necessarily count on getting our food from far away forever. I would hate to see our farms disappear in the meanwhile."

GENIE MCPHERSON TREVOR *is a writer living in Providence, Rhode Island. She is also the editor of* Edible Rhody.

Photo by Chip Riegel

Massachusetts Avenue Project

Charting a Course for Local Food in an Urban Environment

During Buffalo's era as an industrial powerhouse, the West Side of the city stood proud, flush with European immigrants, tidy homes, family-owned businesses, markets bursting with fresh food, and sidewalks that played host to hopscotch and marble games. Today, the once-thriving West Side—which runs between Buffalo's urban core and the Niagara River—can, like many residential areas in postindustrial cities, be likened to a gap-toothed smile. Vacant lots have replaced modest pre–World War II homes, empty storefronts line the nonresidential streets, and the sidewalks are more often covered with litter than the chalk-line remainders of childhood games. While the West Side is in the beginning stages of a quiet and hopeful resurgence, boasting pockets of bustling businesses and recently restored homes, much of it remains abandoned and disheveled.

When observed from above, one of the brightest specks in this part of the city covers approximately half an acre of residential land. On it stands raised beds rich with well-tended soil and late-summer produce. A straw-bale greenhouse provides the backdrop to the colorful garden, and the recent award of a 1,000-gallon rainwater harvesting system ensures plenty of hydration for this tender spot of land during the dry months. Though any neighborhood block club would be proud to claim this little patch of sustainably farmed urban agriculture as its own, it is instead both the inspiration and the method for the Massachusetts Avenue Project (MAP).

Founded in 1992, MAP initially emerged from the fold of a strong neighborhood block club. By 1997, it had a permanent staff and was functioning as an outreach organization for neighborhood youth. After a time of sorting out both its mission and its structure, in 2000, it officially incorporated, having expanded its horizons even further than its founders could have imagined.

Today MAP encompasses a variety of programs, stemming from both its figurative roots in the neighborhood and its literal roots in the ground. Its overall mission is to "nurture the growth of a diverse and equitable community food system to promote local economic opportunities, access to affordable and nutritious food, and social-change education." But in practice its goals are accomplished through three distinct programs: Growing Green (a multifaceted youth-based program), Food Ventures (a microenterprise development program for adults), and the Mobile Market (a farm stand on wheels).

GROWING (UP) GREEN

At its most basic level, Growing Green is an urban agriculture youth development program, a model that's been found effective in cities across the country. MAP's eight-week summer program, subsidized by the city of Buffalo, employs a diverse group of thirty to thirty-five neighborhood kids who range in age from fourteen to eighteen. These students work the farm, learning about the process of growing and harvesting food using sustainable farming practices and techniques. Germinating seeds, composting, and vermiculture are just a small sample of the hands-on curriculum they experience.

"When our kids first come to us, they don't really know much about where their food comes from or how to grow things. They might not even be interested in any of that," says Diane Picard, Growing Green's program director.

But participating in the process of tending the farm and reaping its crop provides MAP's youth with an opportunity to learn about responsibly raised food, healthy eating, and working hard as a member of a team.

"Eating is so personal. It's about your family, it's about your culture, it's about your daily routine—it's very personal. But it is also this amazing branch which provides kids the chance to start thinking about access and privilege, region and globalization, and all of those types of things," says Erin Sharkey, MAP's creative director and outreach coordinator. "It's a privilege to work with these kids around food. I think it's a clear justice thing, it's clear that people deserve food, that it's about necessity, and that it's empowering to start talking about those things."

In his capacity as Growing Green's education coordinator, Jesse Meeder is both firm and approachable, his ease with words and his serious tone encourage the kids to listen to him, but his beach-bum looks and casual manner make him seem less like an adult and more like one of the kids. Meeder works with the students year-round, developing programming that they as a group can then take on the road. By way of games, skits, and other hands-on activities, MAP's teens teach their peers and younger children about important but simple food-related issues like choosing a healthy snack, making applesauce, or understanding the importance of eating local. "I think that too many times a youth program is a gymnasium where unsupervised kids hang out. I think that what we really want to do is say, 'Hey kids, this is your life, this is your future, this is your city. We're not creating a program to pacify you, we're creating an opportunity for you to step up and grab this life.'"

When asked about what changes can be seen in the teens who work the program, there are endless stories of kids making better choices about their diet, of character development, of the lessons that the opportunity of having expanded experiences can teach almost any teenager about themselves and others. "But we're not the kind of organization that is looking for kids to have a lightning-bolt moment," Meeder says as he tips back in his chair, having almost as much difficulty sitting still as one of his kids might. "It's all about opening a discussion or a perspective that they can explore and develop their own opinions on. So we work on increasing their vocabulary on a subject, their knowledge on a subject, but we're not going to expect kids to drop soda or suddenly love gardening. It's all about that base of knowledge and appreciation for something different."

Growing Green's efforts to provide teens with paying jobs structured around an urban sustainable farm, to teach teens to make educated food choices and then in turn use that information in a community outreach platform, would be accomplishment enough, but these are not Growing Green's only tools for training, education, and development. Regular, well-attended cooperative community dinners help to make good use of excess produce and serve to teach the kids about planning and organizing a meal. An annual food conference for teens is also planned and run by the youth program and staff. With both of these projects kids learn how to use design programs to develop marketing materials and then put those materials to good use.

What is perhaps Growing Green's most publicly recognized project is its youth enterprise program, headed by Zoe Hollomon. This program has developed a line of value-added products that includes Amazing Chili Starter and Super Duper Salsa. These products—soon to be joined by a fruit-based salad dressing—can be found on the shelves of over a dozen specialty stores and supermarkets in the Buffalo area. The line, made from locally grown produce and packed at a copacker not far from the city, provides additional revenue with which to pay teens for their hard labor during the nonsubsidized school year. Additionally, it supplies kids with an opportunity to understand the basics of business.

"I treat them like owners and managers of their own company," says Holloman, a woman with a bright personality and eyes to match. "The youth are involved in every aspect of the business. They go to the farm, meet the farmer, visit the packing facility, make cold calls to potential retailers, learn about inventory, and participate in product demonstrations. After the kids develop these skills—and you basically hand them the responsibility of handling this big thing, this business—they're nervous and hesitant, but after they have the opportunity to do all of these things, they realize that if they can do this, they can do important things."

FOOD (AD)VENTURES

With over ninety jobs created and over forty new businesses under its belt, Food Ventures is an exciting and successful part of the MAP family. This microenterprise offers comprehensive and individualized consulting and resources for adults interested in developing food-based small businesses.

Assistance with product development, understanding food safety and packaging requirements, developing marketing skills, and gaining industry insight are just a few examples of the many services offered to people enrolled in the Food Ventures program. Also important is the ability to "batch-up" new recipes, navigate the sometimes arduous process of adhering to USDA labeling standards, and sourcing the best ingredients at a good price.

This one-on-one counseling and tutelage works hand-in-hand with MAP's commercial community-use kitchen. Together the two have worked to provide the launching pad for some of Buffalo's most well-recognized artisan food lines, food vendors, custom caterers, and niche restaurants. Participants have access

Massachusetts Avenue Project's raised beds of onions and squash

to the fully licensed commercial-grade kitchen, cold and dry storage areas, and restaurant-quality tools like chafing dishes and hotel pans. Unlike any other business model in the Western New York region, Food Ventures nurtures aspiring entrepreneurs, helping them to make the connections required to develop a solid business model and a delicious marketplace-friendly product.

Trudy Stern, owner of Tru-Teas, is just one of the many success stories from Food Ventures. "MAP is part of a long tradition of local, community-minded, progressive foodies who have always been here in various incarnations. We know that beautiful, locally produced, good food is revolutionary," Stern says. "I found Food Ventures when I came back to Buffalo with an idea to make and sell Mad Yak Tibetan Hot Sauce. [They] introduced me to the network of small food processors in New York State and made a commercial kitchen available for my first food venture."

Donnie's Smokehouse, a destination restaurant on Buffalo's East Side that is respected for its standards and quality, is the current incarnation of what began as a Food Ventures project. When owners Racine and Ellis Leverette (husband and wife) found MAP, they felt as if they'd struck gold. "Food Ventures led me to the Small Business Development Center and helped me get my ideas about my business in order," Racine explains. "They were there when no one else was. The kitchen was outfitted with everything I needed to start my catering business. And now, here we are today. If we'd had to do this without them, it would've been a long and difficult road." Donnie's specializes in delectable BBQ and has received high awards in competitions across the country for its secret recipes. "MAP was a big help. They offered a wealth of information I wouldn't have had access to, but they were also an inspiration."

FOOD FOR GROWTH

In 2000, MAP teamed up with Samina Raja, an assistant professor of Urban and Regional Planning at the University of Buffalo. Raja had been interested in community gardening in urban settings and began to think about how cities could be better planned in order to accommodate access to healthy foods in urban areas. MAP was trying to find funding, and Raja seemed like the light at the end of the tunnel. Diane Picard approached her.

"MAP needed statistics and facts to back rhetoric," Raja tells *Edible Buffalo*.

So Raja set about her research, ultimately releasing a well-respected and often-cited report entitled "Food for Growth: A Community Food System Plan for Buffalo's West Side." This report made local headlines, opened eyes, and helped MAP to secure funding and bolster its mission. The report, in essence, asserted that Buffalo's West Side is made up of veritable "food deserts" where there is no access to food at all or access is limited to small corner stores carrying items with long shelf lives—unhealthy foods laden with preservatives, additives, and trans fats.

There's a chill in the air, and kids are running around the parking lot, giggling and squealing. Some have managed to cover almost all of their clothing in brilliant purple paint, the brightest hue in a West Side parking lot on a dreary fall afternoon. Just over a dozen teens are working in coordination with the Growing Green staff to ready their latest project, designed to lessen the plight uncovered by Raja's study. Its body purple and its nose lime green, MAP's new eggplant-inspired Mobile Market is scheduled to hit the road within just a few weeks.

The vintage Winnebago has been gutted, its 1970s-era benches and foldout table/bed replaced with modern wooden shelving and cubbies designed to showcase the lovingly raised produce from MAP's urban farm. The interior, painted out with a soft spring green and a warm peach color, has room for a variety of products and even a cash register. The Mobile Market will travel the streets of its own neighborhood—as well as those of Buffalo's East Side—selling fresh fruit and vegetables to people who lack the necessary transportation required to make a trip to a grocery store. The Growing Green youth and their mentors will staff the "produce department on wheels" in addition to using the opportunity through conversation and skits to demonstrate the importance of eating healthy to Buffalo citizens young and old alike.

Other area farms that use sustainable practices will help to boost supply if demand reaches beyond the capacity of MAP's own garden. This won't be the first time that MAP has reached out into the community to make connections with rural farms. This practice of looking within as well as beyond the city's borders has helped MAP become part of an important and fast-growing network of people and organizations passionate about building a sturdy local food system in Western New York; being an area with thousands of farms and a rich agricultural legacy, Western New York is ripe for change.

NEXT SEASON

Good-natured and articulate, Michael Tritto, MAP's new executive director, is excited about the future and MAP's ability to spread its mission to other urban areas with similar struggles. "We see our role as being rooted in this neighborhood, serving our residents here on the West Side. But we also hope to run our programs as models . . . as learning tools for other groups to come and observe and receive consultation.

"I'd like to see a nonprofit microprogram [that will] spread our expertise and help other organizations do what we've done. How we can leverage this program to have a more significant impact is an issue. But there's also something precious about the organic, familial size of our organization . . . and the culture is something that has to be nurtured. We want to see more happen, but I think what we want to do is help others replicate our success."

In a few short weeks the snow will come. Most likely it will be in fits and starts until after the new year, so with the exception of what Growing Green can bring to life in its organically constructed greenhouse, aspects of the program's work will have to wait until Western New York's growing season begins. Meanwhile, students will venture to conferences and meetings to practice their public speaking skills and teach others about what they've learned and what MAP is all about. Others will work on the launch of the new salad dressing, while some will stay focused on reaching other kids through Growing Green's various education and outreach programs.

"I think the institution of public school does a lot to kids and to their psyches. They're one of many kids in a room, and the schools are focused on the kids passing tests and being quiet," says Holloman. "The kids don't get enough of the types of experiences that develop independent thought, of voicing and challenging the administration, and those are the skills that will make them leaders in the future. I think we help them with those opportunities by providing them with these skills, skills which also build their confidence."

"[Having those skills] builds community amongst other kids who are thinking about their world and about how they have an impact on it," replies Sharkey. "I think that it is powerful that they have each other. To be honest, the hardest part of our job is to stay out of the way. We give the kids the tools, and then we step back and get out of the way."

"If you're looking for heroes here," comments Meeder, "the only ones you'll find are the kids." He pauses. "The kids are the heroes here at MAP, no question."

CHRISTA GLENNIE SEYCHEW *is a former food editor for a popular Buffalo magazine. Currently, she works as a freelance food writer and as cofounder of the nonprofit Field & Fork Network, an organization dedicated to connecting Western New York producers with consumers.*

ORGANIZATION ~ *EDIBLE NUTMEG* (CONNECTICUT)

CitySeed

Satisfying a Community's Taste for Change

When you love food, your cravings can drive you pretty hard. Whether you've found yourself road-tripping across state lines to get to your favorite snack shack, spending a weekend stove-side to re-create your grandmother's secret recipe, or schlepping home your body weight in edible souvenirs, you know that a good meal is a powerful motivator. For Jennifer McTiernan H., Anne Gatling Haynes, Harvey Koizim, and Judy Sheiffele it was the lure of a juicy, ripe, local tomato that led these four New Haven, Connecticut, neighbors to found CitySeed, a nonprofit organization whose innovative programs have made it a force for change and one of *Edible Nutmeg*'s local heroes.

A COMMUNITY CRAVING

New Haven is a diverse city with a dinner menu to match. *Taquerías* and Turkish kebab houses, renowned burger joints and hot-dog stands, and—most famously—red-sauce Italian joints and road-trip-worthy pizza parlors are just a few of the options available to the eager eater. For those wishing to whip up their own home cooking, however, fresh food was not nearly as prevalent. "You just couldn't find a fresh tomato," explains Jennifer, now CitySeed's executive director, "not to mention one that was grown in Connecticut."

In 2004, the four neighbors found a solution to their salad-bowl sorrow—they launched a farmers' market in their own section of town, Wooster Square. The community's response surpassed all expectations—even those of the participating farmers who, on the market's very first day, had to send runners back to the fields for a midday harvest to keep up with the demand of their customers. As farmer Peter Rothenberg of Northfordy Farm in Northford, Connecticut, describes the market, "It just caught on like wildfire. It gives people a sense of community that is so lacking these days. People are happy at the market—they're smiling—it's an event."

A sense of community is a strong bond that many cite when talking about their local market, and you can

Shoppers at the Wooster Square Market

feel it when you visit—among the eaters, the farmers, everyone. "Bringing my product to the market is more than selling. It's an exchange," says Nunzio Corsino of Four Mile River Farm in Old Lyme, Connecticut. "I look forward to seeing my market friends—both my customers and the vendors." Ideas for what to grow and how to grow it flow freely between farmers and eaters alike. Growers share tips for maximizing New England's abbreviated growing season. Eaters pepper them with questions about their methods and their forecast for the harvest. Peter explains, "For these farmers, eaters aren't consumers, they are part of the farming process. Bringing food to the market is another part of the growing cycle of preparing the soil, putting seeds in the ground, and harvesting."

In its second season, CitySeed launched three more markets in three very different New Haven communities: the Fair Haven section of the city (in collaboration with Junta, a Latino-based nonprofit, and GAVA, a local merchants association), Downtown (in collaboration with Town Green, a community-betterment organization), and Edgewood Park (in cooperation with Westville Village Renaissance Alliance). Each market

reflects the personality of the neighborhood. As Benjamin Gardner, CitySeed's program coordinator, notes, "A lot of the people who come are fiercely loyal to their market. It gives them a sense of pride." That's because CitySeed's programming springs directly from the needs and desires of the community. "It's not like CitySeed sat there with a map and a handful of thumbtacks, plotting the next spot for a market. Each of these markets started because the community came to CitySeed and asked us to have one there."

THE ECOSYSTEM OF FRESH FOOD

The markets, however, are just one facet of CitySeed's work. Government policy, community outreach and education, food access and security, farm viability—these may not be the first thoughts that pop into mind when you take a big bite of summer's first juicy, ripe, local tomato, but for CitySeed they are all pieces of the fresh-food puzzle. As Jennifer explains, "Food is everything. It touches everything—the environment, social justice, family connection, community involvement—it puts all of these things together." CitySeed has developed a wide range of programming and partnerships to address the whole ecosystem of community, grower, eater, and public policy that make a healthy food system possible.

Much of CitySeed's energy is devoted to behind-the-scenes policy efforts. In partnership with like-minded organizations they are working to change the rules, such as what defines a farmers' market and how much (or how little) is spent on ingredients for school lunches, that often keep segments of the population, such as seniors and kids, from having better access to fresh food.

CitySeed reaches out to the community with educational tools that appeal to everyone from dedicated locavores to fresh-food newbies. For three seasons their Farmers' Market Recipe Cards, which feature recipes from some of the top chefs in the state, have given eaters all across Connecticut creative ideas for enjoying local ingredients. CitySeed's preschool program, Growing Healthy Eaters and Readers, encourages good eating habits among children and their families through hands-on literacy-based activities and farmers' market field trips. Bilingual materials—such as newsletters that provide market information and tips for working with available produce and a cookbook that features market-goers' favorite recipes—reach into New Haven's Latino community with helpful information and knowledge sharing.

CitySeed has developed innovative programming to clear some of the most challenging hurdles confronting nutritionally at-risk communities. One such program is the Community Sponsored Market, or CSM, which hand-delivers boxes of produce, called shares, fresh from their Fair Haven market each week. A number of the shares are sold at face value to area employees and residents whose schedules preclude them from shopping at the market themselves. The sales from these boxes help to subsidize the market. Bolstered by grants from area organizations, reduced-cost shares for Food Stamp and WIC recipients and community groups that represent those in need are also available. The CSM program made it possible for CitySeed to distribute over 1,100 subsidized shares to New Haven residents in 2008, providing farm-fresh food to those who need it most. The guaranteed income from purchased shares also gives the farmers the working capital they need to be able to support markets such as Fair Haven, where underserved communities need and want better access to fresh food but do not have the economic power to fully support a market. As CSM farmer Peter Rothenberg says, "The CSM program is the quintessential win-win. It takes a lot of energy, but it works."

Of course, you can't have good food without environmentally and economically sustainable farms. CitySeed has organized a number of programs to connect the dots among growers, eaters, and chefs. Through the Buy CT Grown Steering Committee, CitySeed provides area growers with technical marketing assistance—helping them to get their farm message out. In 2008, the group launched www.buyctgrown.com, a searchable database that allows eaters to find local producers, products, and farm-related events in the state. Their Seed to Table program is a budding project that will help smooth the distribution channels between farmers and area chefs.

A BRIGHTER FOOD FUTURE

Too often the local foods movement is labeled as the elitist fancy of gourmands and foodies. A stroll through a CitySeed market proves that most eaters, however, aren't looking for fancy, just fresh. A mother getting fresh carrots for her kid's lunch, a young couple looking for apples for their first pie, a senior gathering some root vegetables for a soup—these are the kind of eaters you can find on any given day at a CitySeed Market and farmers' markets all across the country. To a growing number of eaters fresh, local food isn't a luxury—it's dinner.

Jennifer sums up CitySeed's objectives simply. She hopes that in the future "fresh, nutritious food will be available to everyone, and that farmers will be able to support themselves by providing it." These goals, shared by a growing number of eaters and organizations across the country, sound less like a manifesto for indulgence and more like plain common sense. A fresh tomato on every plate. It's a craving worth satisfying.

SHERRI BROOKS VINTON *is a writer and speaker who enjoys teaching eaters how to support local, sustainable agriculture with their food choices. Her monthly newsletter,* Sustainable Solutions, *can be found at www.sherribrooksvinton.com.*

Photograph courtesy of CitySeed

People, places, things

ALLEGHENY (PENNSYLVANIA)

The Allegheny Mountain Region in western Pennsylvania is rich and alive. Local chefs and farmers are always proclaiming, "Everything grows here!" The residents are lucky to have such a large community—which encompasses rolling fields and farmland or urban metropolitan gardens—dedicated to sustainability.

Maggie's Mercantile A vegan, vegetarian, and raw-foods restaurant utilizing ingredients from Maggie Raphael's organic farm and greenhouse.

Penn's Corner Farm Alliance This is the largest CSA in the region, connecting more than sixteen local growers with home tables and local restaurants.

East End Food Co-Op Pittsburgh's only customer-owned natural foods store.

Milestone Specialty Produce A local greenhouse that provides lettuce and salad mixes to more than ninety-five restaurants and employs adults with psychological and behavioral health problems.

Chef Bill Fuller Corporate chef for the big Burrito restaurant group, which has six unique restaurant concepts in the region, all incorporating local foods on their menus.

www.ediblecommunities.com/allegheny/peopleplacesthings

BOSTON

One of the most exciting aspects of Boston's current food culture derives from very traditional roots: farms surrounding the city providing food to the local communities and the nearby cities. To this day, you can drive within ten miles of downtown and be among strong, thriving family farms. These farms remain integrated in their own communities as well as in Boston proper through farm stands, farmers' markets, CSAs, and directly into the kitchens of the city's most-popular restaurants.

Cider Hill Farm, Amesbury A farm that is aggressively working to incorporate new methods of energy use on their farm and also working to change legislation to make it more attainable for other farms.

Kelley Erwin Kelley is the driving force in the Farm to School program. She works as a liaison between farms and school systems, bringing locally grown food into Massachusetts's public schools.

Taza Chocolates One of the few chocolatiers in the United States that produces chocolate by beginning with grinding cocoa beans sourced from small cooperatives in the Dominican Republic.

Fried Clams, Woodman's of Essex Fried clams were first made on July 3, 1916, in Essex by "Chubby" Woodman as a way to increase the sale of his locally harvested clams.

Peter Davis, Chef, Henrietta's Table, Cambridge Peter was a pioneer in sourcing directly from local farms and food artisans.

www.ediblecommunities.com/boston/peopleplacesthings

BROOKLYN

While Brooklyn is perhaps best known as being a community of nineteenth-century émigrés and twentieth-century blue-collar disco dancers, it has undergone a remarkable renaissance in the last decade. Legendary birthplace of the egg cream and the hot dog, Brooklyn's kitchens are now more likely to offer slow-cooked grass-fed lamb or community garden–grown heirloom melons. As young hipsters have moved in next door to old-timers, this urban oasis in the shadow of Manhattan is a delicious destination in its own right.

Junior's Cheesecake This is one creamy concoction from the borough's coolest diner, a landmark that welcomes visitors with a neon glow from its perch at the base of the Manhattan Bridge.

Tom Mylan Tom was the founding meat man behind the proteins at Marlow & Sons and Diner, later wielding his cleavers at Marlow & Daughters, the borough's newest all-sustainable butcher shop. (He has since decamped to launch his own venture.)

Sixpoint Brownstone Beer Made right in Brooklyn, this American brown ale is named after one of the borough's most beautiful features. (It's awfully tasty, too.)

Red Hook Ball Fields Every weekend all summer long, Latin American vendors set up stands to sell tacos, *huaraches*, *agua frescas*, *pupusas*, and *arepas* while amateur soccer leagues compete in the fields overlooking the Red Hook waterfront.

East New York Farms More than just trees grow in Brooklyn: This lower-income neighborhood boasts a community garden so well managed that they sell at a farmers' market just outside the neatly kempt rows.

www.ediblecommunities.com/brooklyn/peopleplacesthings

BUFFALO

The food culture of Buffalo and its surrounding region is rooted in a long agricultural history and robust ethnic foodways that provide a diverse culinary landscape. Despite the short growing season, the proximity to Lake Erie and Lake Ontario and the nutrient-rich soils allow farmers to grow a wide variety of crops from apples, pears, and corn to the unexpected peaches, kiwi, and artichokes.

Lake Erie Concord Grape Belt New York's first Agricultural Heritage Region is the oldest and largest grape-growing region in the country. Stretching approximately sixty miles along the shores of Lake Erie, it encompasses more than 30,000 acres of vineyards.

Ethnic-Influenced Foods The region has it all, including Polish (pierogi, *golabki*, *chrusciki*, *platskis*, kielbasa), German (Wiener schnitzel, bratwurst, sauerkraut, sauerbraten, Rouladen, roast beef on kimmelweck, liverwurst, beer), and Italian (cannoli, cassata cake, Italian sausage, DiCamillo Bakery).

Maple Syrup Wyoming County is the second-largest maple syrup producer in New York State.

Confections Local goodies include Fowler's Fine Chocolate, sponge candy, and the Charlie Chaplin.

Samina Raja Samina, assistant professor of Urban and Regional Planning at the University at Buffalo, penned the pivotal "Food for Growth" study, which shined a spotlight on food insecurity issues in the city of Buffalo and which was the driving force for food access to be an integral part of urban planning.

www.ediblecommunities.com/buffalo/peopleplacesthings

CAPE COD

Just seventy-five miles from Boston, Cape Cod is a popular vacation destination, offering over 550 miles of spectacular coastline, historic sea captains' homes, and quaint towns. The Cape's rich maritime history and fishing heritage can be traced from the clambakes of early Native Americans to the fish and chips served up at clam shacks across the Cape today. In addition to clams, oysters, lobster, and cod, the Cape is renowned for its cranberry bogs, with about 1,000 acres under cultivation.

Seafood The Cape is justifiably famous for its fin and shellfish, whether it's cod, haddock, halibut, tuna, flounder, striped bass, and pollock, or lobster, clams, and oysters.

Shellfish Promotion and Tasting SPAT is a nonprofit organization with the goal of boosting Wellfleet's shellfishing tradition. They host an annual OysterFest to fund its scholarship program for people pursuing a career in shellfishing.

Cape Cod Commercial Hook Fishermen's Association The association focuses on building sustainable fisheries for the future and representing the traditional communities that rely on this resource.

Cape Cod Cranberry Growers' Association This is one of the oldest farmer organizations in the country, having been established in 1888. Its mission is to support and promote the approximately 330 cranberry growers of Massachusetts.

Cape Land and Sea Harvest CLASH is a three-day celebration of the rich fishing heritage and abundant local foods of Cape Cod.

www.ediblecommunities.com/capecod/peopleplacesthings

EAST END (NEW YORK)

Buffered by the sea, this Long Island farming, fishing, and resort community seventy miles east of New York City enjoys one of the longest growing seasons on the East Coast, and harvests tomatoes and sweet corn well into fall. While some of its soils have been farmed continuously for four centuries, the East End's culinary renaissance includes a burgeoning wine country, edible schoolyards in most districts, and a farm-to-table cuisine encouraged by discriminating locals and cosmopolitan visitors.

Bonac Clam Pie This signature dish is an amalgam of culinary influences from Native Americans and the first British settlers, called Bonackers. The pie contains clams, onions, potatoes, and a long list of other possible ingredients.

Peconic Bay Scallops Sweet, smaller, and more tender than sea scallops, bay scallops are making a comeback since their die-off in the 1980s, which was due to overharvesting.

Peconic Land Trust One of the oldest land trusts in the country, this group has built on Suffolk County's decades-old agricultural reserve laws, to preserve about one-third of the East End's remaining farmland.

Long Island Wine Country The North and South forks are now home to nearly fifty wineries, offering a trail of tasting rooms and winery-hosted food tastings.

Mecox Bay Dairy and Catapano Goat Farm These two East End award-winning farmstead cheese producers (one is on the South Fork and the other is on the North Fork) sell their products at local restaurants, farmers' markets, and gourmet stores.

www.ediblecommunities.com/eastend/peopleplacesthings

FINGER LAKES (NEW YORK)

With two million acres of farmland, over one hundred vineyards, an increasing number of farmers' markets and Community Supported Agriculture programs, and incredible farmer-to-chef collaborations, the Finger Lakes is one of the most exciting culinary hot spots in the country. From roadside organic cider mills to family-run goat farms; from fair trade regional coffee roasters to "u-pick" blueberry spots, there is an abundance of year-round activity in the local foods movement in Central New York.

Elizabeth Henderson Elizabeth is a pioneer in the CSA movement. Her book, *Sharing the Harvest*, coauthored with Robyn Van En, is the go-to guide for starting and running a successful CSA program.

Hermann J. Wiemer Hermann is one of the most successful figures in the Finger Lakes wine industry and is largely responsible for bringing global attention to the area's wines by insisting on quality and traditional wine-making techniques.

The Ithaca Farmers Market One of the top five farmers' markets in the country. Open for business since 1973, this not-for-profit venture has been a fantastic model for others in the region and has given farmers a reliable and successful location to sell their produce.

Lively Run Goat Cheese The Messmer family consistently creates some of the best chèvre on the East Coast, which is widely distributed throughout the region and in New York City.

Farm Winery Act of 1976 This piece of legislation made it possible for farmers in the area to not only grow grapes for wine making but also to sell wine on their premises.

www.ediblecommunities.com/fingerlakes/peopleplacesthings

GREEN MOUNTAINS (VERMONT)

Here's a statistic that underscores the value Vermonters place on knowing where their food is from—Vermont has the nation's highest per capita direct sales of food products from farmers to consumers, at 5.5 times the national average! With a population just north of 650,000, Vermont is also home to more artisan bakers, cheese makers, and farmers per capita than many other locales with larger populations.

Pete's Greens Owner Pete Johnson is an innovative and entrepreneurial farmer with a CSA that delivers to hundreds of members throughout the state.

Mad River Valley Localvores Volunteer-led, -conceived, and -driven by Valley resident Robin McDermott, this is an exceptional initiative that has raised funds and consciousness.

Kildeer Farm This is a dream farm stand that looks as delicious as everything tastes, operated by innovators and leaders in the organic-growing arena for many decades.

Maple Wind Farm The farm provides low-stress and grass-fed rotational grazing of beef, lamb, pork, and poultry, humanely raised and processed. You can taste the difference.

Red Hen Bakery Owner Randy George uses locally sourced flours and grains in many of his artisan breads, which are baked and delivered throughout the state each day.

www.ediblecommunities.com/greenmountains/peopleplacesthings

HUDSON VALLEY (NEW YORK)

The Hudson Valley—the approximately 125 miles of majestic lands between Albany and Manhattan—is home to some of the country's most enduring food traditions. Once known as the nation's "bread basket," it reigns again as a major agricultural producer, with dairy and milk production its largest sector. A back-to-the-land movement throughout the valley and Catskill region is attracting new farmers and a renewed commitment to local, sustainable foods.

Ken Greene Ken is cofounder and owner of Hudson Valley Seed Library in Accord, New York, and is devoted to developing "heirloom seeds with local roots."

Glynwood, Cold Spring A nonprofit group that helps communities preserve farming through outreach, education, and best-practice development.

Stone Barns Center for Food and Agriculture An agricultural learning and development center that also exquisitely links farm to plate in its on-site restaurant, Blue Hill, co-owned by the renowned chef Dan Barber.

Fleisher's Meat Located in Kingston, New York, this is one of the only butcher shops in the nation to sell solely pasture-raised and organic meat. Founded in 2004, this shop is renewing interest in the raising and consumption of quality meat.

Dairy Farms From Ronnybrook in Ancramdale to Hawthorne Valley in Ghent and throughout the region, there is a new commitment to the production of quality milk and dairy products.

www.ediblecommunities.com/hudsonvalley/peopleplacesthings

JERSEY (NEW JERSEY)

If you've ever tasted a Jersey fresh tomato or enjoyed a Delaware Bay oyster (also known as a "Cape May Salt"), you have a sense of the bounty of the Garden State. From preserving open lands to feeding its inner-city children, New Jersey is a microcosm of the issues and opportunities faced nationwide in terms of maintaining access to fresh foods. Today's interest in local foods has resulted in an appreciation of the farmers, fishermen, and producers who sustain the country's most densely populated state.

Cape May Salt/Delaware Bay Oysters Thanks to a half century of dedicated efforts by scientists and activists, this saltwater delicacy has survived the ravages of parasite and pollution and thrives once again.

Rutgers University Agricultural Experiment Station A leader in food and agriculture through its new Food Innovation Center, Rutgers's experiment station oversees asparagus breeding efforts, promoting 4-H or offering Master Gardener classes.

Ramapo Tomato Considered the true Jersey tomato. As higher-yield varieties became popular in the 1960s, the seeds for the Ramapo all but disappeared. Thanks to Rutgers University, these tomatoes are available again.

Honey Brook Organic Farm Honey Brook, one of the oldest operating organic farms in New Jersey, has the largest CSA program in the nation, with over 2,300 memberships.

Valley Shepherd Creamery New Jersey's only commercial sheep dairy. In less than five years, founder Eran Wajswol has single-handedly revived the art of cheese making in the Garden State.

www.ediblecommunities.com/jersey/peopleplacesthings

MANHATTAN

With a reputation as big as the Empire State Building, "Gotham" has long been at the forefront of America's culinary vanguard. From the iconic hot dog and bagel to kebabs and *bi bim bap*, New York City is a melting pot, a wonderland of so-called ethnic eats. It's famously home to the finest of fine dining, too. And it's a city in love with food from the nearby countryside, boasting vibrant community gardens and the largest network of farmers' markets in America.

The "Slice" The Big Apple owns the crispy-crusted wedge of pizza. It's an egalitarian creation, found on every corner. Wall Street bankers, NYU kids, and cabbies all consider it the ultimate easy meal.

Union Square Greenmarket Launched in 1976, the city's biggest farmers' market has grown from a handful of stalls to selling everything from sheep's milk ricotta to fiddlehead ferns, and it is all grown, raised, caught, and baked right in New York City's backyard.

Chinatown Pot Stickers These fatty and fabulous panfried pork dumplings are served up for about a buck and half—and worth the trek downtown.

Danny Meyer The restaurateur behind the Union Square Hospitality Group, Danny is responsible for the city's heaviest dining hitters: Union Square Café, Gramercy Tavern, The Shake Shack, 11 Madison Park, and, last but not least, the Big Apple BBQ Block Party.

The '21' Club Here you can still order steak Diane and a Manhattan—made with rye, of course—and transport yourself to an era when the men always wore neckties, the ladies wore gloves, and the band played all night.

www.ediblecommunities.com/manhattan/peopleplacesthings

NUTMEG (CONNECTICUT)

Connecticut has been losing 8,000 acres of farmland a year, one of the highest rates of farmland loss in America. Fortunately, many small family farms have survived and their number is increasing, as young farmers see opportunities to follow their dream while meeting the ever-growing demand for fresh, local foods. Once rooted in agriculture, Connecticut is primed to extend those roots a little deeper.

Connecticut River Shad Native to the Connecticut River, these shad are the foundation of one of the oldest commercial fisheries in America.

Cato Corner Cheese The mother-and-son team of Elizabeth MacAlister and Mark Gilman hand-make internationally recognized farmstead cheeses with raw milk from the cows on their Colchester farm.

Plow to Plate An initiative of New Milford Hospital, this community coalition made locally grown food standard hospital fare while promoting healthy eating.

Holcomb Farm This nonprofit project of the Hartford Food System provides high-quality free, fresh food to 1,500 local families supported by the project's 500-member CSA.

The Farmer's Cow Seven Connecticut families formed The Farmer's Cow to secure a future for their families, their dairy businesses, and their land.

www.ediblecommunities.com/nutmeg/peopleplacesthings

PHILLY (PHILADELPHIA)

One wonders if William Penn, the English Quaker, had food in mind when he first referred to Philadelphia as "The City of Brotherly Love." Culinary enclaves, such as the 9th Street Italian Market and Chinatown, thrive alongside countless ethnically inspired BYOBs scattered throughout the city, offering a United Nations of flavor. Today, Philly's food scene is enhanced by the dozens of farmers' markets that have sprung up in the city and surrounding region.

Judy Wicks Founder and proprietor of White Dog Cafe, Wicks—a leader in the local living economies movement—is cofounder of the nationwide Business Alliance for Local Living Economies (BALLE), and founder of the Sustainable Business Network of Greater Philadelphia (SBN).

Weavers Way Food Cooperative Farm A grocery store and community outreach program, this urban farm grows and sells over $80,000 worth of produce a year on 1.5 acres.

Common Market Philadelphia A wholesale distributor that is creating a sustainable link between local farms and the urban marketplace.

The Amish While the country moved to an industrialized food culture in the twentieth century, these "plain people" focused on farming as a way of life. Their religiously inspired commitment to a rural environment produces high-quality food infused into the local foods movement.

Philly Cheese Steak The ubiquitous cheese steak may not be fresh or healthy, but it reminds us of the role that personality and tradition play in maintaining a local food culture.

www.ediblecommunities.com/philly/peopleplacesthings

PIONEER VALLEY (MASSACHUSETTS)

Pioneer Valley agriculture combines the pastoral traditions of New England and the progressive ideals of the notorious "Massachusetts liberal." From the winter harvest of maple syrup, all the way until autumn's last pumpkin is plucked from the vine,

Pioneer Valley farms offer CSA shares, stock community food co-ops, and sell bushels of berries and ears of corn from roadside stands along country lanes. Long home to poets, artists, musicians, and academics, the "Happy Valley" is a bastion of forward thinkers and free spirits, and through the cultivation and preparation of local foods, its farmers bring sustainability, accessibility, and community to those who live here.

Community Involved in Sustaining Agriculture The CISA is instrumental in not only promoting but building the infrastructure that has made local foods and the Eat Local ethos a given in the Pioneer Valley.

The Farmstead at Mine Brook Producers of delicious award-winning Goat Rising chèvre and Jersey Maid cheeses, created at a small farm in the hills of Charlemont. Their cheeses are sold and used extensively throughout the Pioneer Valley.

Food Bank Farm/The Food Bank of Western Massachusetts Half of the farm's output provides over six million pounds of food to hungry people in Western Massachusetts through Food Bank's 400 member agencies, with the other half going to their member CSAs.

Nuestras Raices A social justice organization committed to empowering the low-income urban community of Holyoke through the cultivation and production of local foods, at both inner-city community gardens and recently purchased farmland.

Greenfield Free Harvest Supper An annual community meal created with ingredients donated by Greenfield-area farmers and served to over 1,000 people on the Greenfield Town Common.

www.ediblecommunities.com/pioneervalley/peopleplacesthings

QUEENS

The borough of Queens is the second largest in population in New York City, and the tenth most populous county in the United States. It is a patchwork quilt of small neighborhoods, each one presenting an education in traditional foodways. The taverns of Astoria excel in authentic Mediterranean cuisine while the food stalls of Flushing's Chinatown dazzle the taste buds with exotic Asian delicacies. You'll find real Irish bacon, bangers, and farls in Woodside, and you'll swoon at the scents and sights of Jackson Heights's curry houses. Surprisingly, Queens is also home to the only working historical farm in New York City and the longest continuously farmed site in New York State.

Queens County Farm Museum Dating back to 1697, this working farm is the longest, most continuously farmed site in New York State. Recently the farm instituted a sustainable four-season growing program, providing fresh produce to city residents on a year-round basis.

Flushing's Chinatown More than 390,000 Asian-Americans call Flushing home, and Chinatown's legendary food stalls provide ample edible reminders of their ancestral homes.

The Lemon Ice King of Corona The Benfaremo family has been making their signature fruit-laden Italian ices for more than sixty years. This Queens institution can't be missed.

Astoria Cemented in popular culture as the area where Archie Bunker resided, Astoria is home to one of the largest Greek populations outside of Greece and is, quite possibly, the culinary capital of Queens, with delicious souvlaki, fresh grilled fish, roasted potatoes, and more.

Street Food Throughout Queens, you're likely to run into a mobile food truck such as the famous El Rey del Taco Truck or the myriad halal street meat rovers selling grilled-to-order kebabs and more. Have no fear: The food is incredibly fresh, authentic, and satisfying.

www.ediblecommunities.com/queens/peopleplacesthings

RHODY (RHODE ISLAND)

Rhode Island, affectionately known as Lil' Rhody, is home to a rich and varied food shed with its 850 working farms and over 450 miles of New England shoreline. In a state where everyone lives within fifteen minutes of a local farm or farm stand, Rhody's small size is its strength. Between 2002 and 2007, Rhode Island saw a 42 percent increase in the number of working farms. From the quintessential quahog to johnnycake lore, Rhody's dynamic local food scene champions a unique culinary heritage.

Carpenter's Grist Mill The state's only active water-powered grist mill, built in 1703, was restored by Bob and Diane Smith. Using whitecap flint corn from Stuart Sherman's nearby farm, the mill grinds authentic cornmeal for the signature johnnycake.

Farm Fresh Rhode Island A nonprofit organization working to connect farmers with eaters through farmers' markets, restaurants, school delivery programs, and online.

Casey Farm Owned by Historic New England, this historic eighteenth-century farm is managed by farmer Patrick McNiff, who raises a wide variety of organic produce, chickens, pork, beef, and lamb.

Quahogs Rhode Islanders can't get enough of these hard-shell bivalves, whether simmered in chowders, chopped in "stuffies," fried in fritters, served over pasta, on the half shell, or even personified in cartoons.

Johanne Killeen and George Germon Since 1980, the owners of Providence's Al Forno restaurant have seen foodies flocking from across the globe in search of their renowned grilled pizzas, baked pastas, and desserts made from locally sourced ingredients.

www.ediblecommunities.com/rhody/peopleplacesthings

SOUTH SHORE (MASSACHUSETTS)

The South Shore is proud of its rich and diverse agricultural and aquacultural heritage. Small dairy farms, world-class vineyards, and historic orchards dot this community, which is sandwiched between Boston, Providence, and Cape Cod. The finest oysters in the world are harvested from Duxbury Bay, while New Bedford holds the honor of being the nation's top-grossing fishing port. Although rapid growth and suburbanization increasingly challenge the South Shore, many active local organizations are committed to protecting its unique community.

Plimoth Plantation A bicultural museum, which offers an opportunity for personal encounters with history and teaches the traditional ways of the Wampanoag People and the colonial English settlers of the 1600s.

Southeastern Massachusetts Agricultural Partnership SEMAP is a nonprofit organization whose mission is to help agricultural enterprises in southeastern Massachusetts achieve economic success.

Island Creek Oysters, Duxbury A much-beloved co-op growing the world's finest oysters and scallops. Founded in 1992, they sell 100,000 oysters a week.

Cranberries There are 458 growers and more than 12,000 acres of cranberry bogs in the state; approximately 85 percent are in southeastern Massachusetts. In the 1940s, the town of Carver produced more cranberries than any town in the world.

Macomber Turnip This variety originated in Westport and is highly coveted, as the seeds are not readily available through seed companies; you have to know someone who makes his or her own seed.

www.ediblecommunities.com/southshore/peopleplacesthings

TORONTO

Toronto is surrounded by the Golden Horseshoe, so named because it wraps around (in a horseshoe shape) the western end of Lake Ontario. This region, which encompasses the Niagara Escarpment (a UNESCO world biosphere reserve), Ontario's Greenbelt (the world's largest designated greenbelt), large urban areas, and rich, fertile land and lakes, is made truly exceptional by the devoted individuals and organizations who dedicate themselves to ensuring its healthy, safe, and sustainable future.

David Cohlmeyer, Cookstown Greens In 1988, David began supplying restaurants and hotels with specialty organic produce, much of it unusual heirloom varieties, from his farm one hour north of Toronto.

Michael Stadtländer and Jamie Kennedy Two local chefs and restaurateurs who met while working in Switzerland, they were at the forefront in bringing the field-to-fork movement to Ontarians through Knives and Forks, an organization they founded in 1989.

City of Toronto Kudos to the city and its councilors for being world leaders in recycling programs, local food procurement policies, and other initiatives that have, and will continue to have, a profound impact on the citizens' well-being.

Michael Schmidt Michael, a dairy farmer, has been waging a multiyear battle with Ontario authorities to enable Ontarians to purchase raw milk from farmers. For him, it's all about the right to choose.

The Stop and FoodShare Two organizations that go well beyond distributing food to the needy by striving to challenge the larger social and political systems that allow hunger to exist.

www.ediblecommunities.com/toronto/peopleplacesthings

VINEYARD (MARTHA'S VINEYARD)

A 45-minute ferry ride from Woods Hole and you're on the island of Martha's Vineyard—100 square miles, six towns, surf-breaking beaches, and thriving shellfish ponds. The island is home to an estimated 15,000 year-round residents. A long and thriving agricultural and seafaring history, living local on the island today means fresh produce, seafood, and local meats that are distinctive to Island fare.

The Martha's Vineyard's Shellfish Group The group, a non-profit for over thirty years, has a community-based resource management program that seeks to preserve and expand the Island's traditional shellfisheries.

Rick Karney As the founding president of Slow Food Martha's Vineyard, Rick made great strides toward improving the industry's involvement with RAFT (Renewing America's Food Traditions) and thus indirectly effected an increase in the area's bay scallop population.

Allen Healy Allen started a legal raw milk dairy in Chilmark.

Flavio and Marcia Souza As the chief operators of Island Grown Initiative's Mobile Poultry Processing Trailer, they provide safe, clean, humane, on-the-farm slaughter and processing of poultry for Island farmers.

Gina DeBettencourt Involved with food service at Edgartown School, Gina works proactively to get local foods into school lunch menus and to create relationships with farmers.

www.ediblecommunities.com/vineyard/peopleplacesthings

WHITE MOUNTAINS (NEW HAMPSHIRE)

New Hampshire boasts an astonishing bounty of award-winning wineries and cheese artisans, maple syrup from its woodlots, and fields blazing with sun-warmed berries—all of which complement its breathtaking natural resources. The region's world-class chefs love the pace of life here and vie for what local farmers produce. The seacoast may be small, but the fishermen's cooperative sustainably harvests the most succulent lobster and shrimp to celebrate every season.

Boggy Meadow Cheese A dairy farm on the banks of the Connecticut River that makes farmstead cheese from old alpine recipes using natural culture and vegetarian rennet.

Candia Vineyards Wine maker Bob Dabrowski's boutique winery offers wines from the state's first Frontenac, LaCrosse, Noiret, and Diamond grape varietals, which have been hand-picked to thrive in the robust New Hampshire climate.

The Good Loaf Lynda Shortt, the bread lady, had been baking artisan breads out of her garage before opening a retail shop in Milford, on Route 13. Her breads are simple yet sophisticated.

Polly's Pancake Parlor Polly's is housed in an original 1830s carriage shed, where maple sugar boils while you look over your menu. It also has amazing mountain views.

Sustainable Farm Products at Nelson Farms Sarah and Shawn Nelson are two young farmers who began raising certified organic fruits, vegetables, and herbs with literally their hearts and souls. Sustainable Farm Products is unique in that it has extended the growing season by heating greenhouses with recycled vegetable oil.

www.ediblecommunities.com/whitemountains/peopleplacesthings

SOUTHEAST

Southern hospitality is no cliché, and nothing demonstrates how profoundly it is ingrained in the locals' disposition better than the sharing of food. "Haute" is not the first word that springs to mind when considering Southern fare, but for warmth, hospitality, and generosity of spirit, no place can compare with the South.

Whether it's through an invitation extended to the entire neighborhood to come and enjoy a giant pot of stewing crawdads, a mess of catfish at a fish fry, or a whole hog barbecued in a pit (a technique our European forebears learned from the indigenous population), Southerners excel at preparing their bounty skillfully and serving it graciously. In both good times and bad, food plays an important role in life—and in death. In fact, within moments of a death, the bereaved will soon be answering the door to a succession of friends, family, church members, and other sympathizers bearing food—casseroles, roasts, cakes, pies, and maybe even what the neighbors were fixing for supper. And for months afterward, families will puzzle over to whom all those dishes and casserole pans should be returned.

>>>

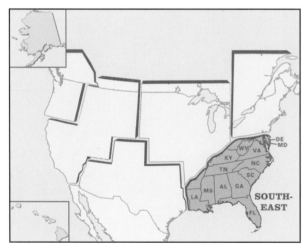

Outsiders often paint the region's food scene with a broad brush. Images fixed in their minds by such references as Granny Clampett serving possum belly with collard greens and cornpone certainly reinforce a stereotype. But, just as many accents and musical styles make up the sound of the South, so do an array of foods and their methods of cooking make up its flavor. Two foods that spring to mind when considering such micro-regional variations are corn bread and barbecue.

Corn bread may be tall and sweet; short, salty, and made with bacon drippings; or filled with canned corn and bits of jalapeño. Essentially, there are as many ways to make corn bread as there are people to make it—and just as many ways to enjoy it. Indeed, a great finish to a long day is a tall glass filled with crumbled corn bread and topped with ice-cold buttermilk, eaten with a teaspoon.

And in the South, "barbecue" doesn't mean a cookout, but rather three distinct things: a method of preparing food, the food prepared in that method, and the event at which that food is consumed. In fact, the more generic use of "barbecue" for "cookout" creates confusion for Southerners when they attend a barbecue in another part of the country and are disappointed to find only burgers and hot dogs being served. One need only attend the world's largest barbecue cooking contest held in Memphis each May to see that this particular food is regarded with a reverence that is rare even by culinary world standards.

Barbecue in the Southeast is almost always pork, but it may be shoulder, ribs, or whole hog; chopped or pulled; dry rub or wet; and it is served with a sauce that may be mustard-, ketchup-, or vinegar-based, thick or thin, and sweet or salty. Allegiance to these variations can be as fierce as that to any college football team, so

as with religion and politics, if expressing a preference for one style of barbecue, it's wise never to disparage another.

Some of the food traditions in the South date back to the colonists and their relationship with the native population, who shared both their foods and their cooking techniques with the newcomers. Local tribes helped the newcomers augment—and eventually supplant—their food supply with beans, squash, wild game, and corn, initially in the form of a mush called "rockahominie" and later shortened to "hominy" by the colonists.

Chesapeake Bay, first home to European settlers in the early 1600s, yielded a wealth of fish and seafood, including blue crabs, oysters, clams, rockfish, perch, and crappie. Bay region residents are currently embroiled in a battle to save these waters and their marine life from the ravages of urban runoff. Efforts to restore health to the bay and educate locals about the significance of its bounty are paying off as new generations of consumers discover aquatic food traditions worth preserving.

Farther from the sea, the citizenry of colonial America found an abundance of wild game. For the competent hunter and trapper, game was easier to put on the table than livestock, with at least one drawback noted. According to the *Virginia Junior League Cookbook*, William Byrd II, the president of the colonial era's Virginia Council of State, wrote that while bear meat contained a "high relish and rested easily on the stomach," it unfortunately "is not a very proper diet for saints. . . . After eating it one is sure to dream of a woman or the devil or both."

So other meats were in order. Thanks to Hernando de Soto, who brought a herd of quite prolific pigs to Florida from Spain in 1539 (several decades before the 1607 English settlement of Jamestown, with its own hog supply), the South found itself with an abundance of pork. With so much on hand, colonists began looking for ways to preserve the easy-spoiling meat, as every day was not a day for barbecuing an entire hog and inviting over all the neighbors. Practices of salt curing and smoking developed, which have been perfected perhaps most famously by producers in Smithfield, Virginia. The swath running from the Carolinas and Virginia through Tennessee and Kentucky and into the Missouri boot heel contains a climate similar to that of those parts of Europe that produce highly prized cured pork. While the humble American country ham has never possessed the same cachet, this

trend appears to be changing. Increasingly, country ham is being shaved thinly and wrapped around melon slices and asparagus spears, treatment once reserved for Spain's jamón, Italy's prosciutto, and Germany's speck. Southern expats living in other parts of the country are known to stuff their luggage with packages of hickory-smoked ham, bacon, and even hog jowls when they return from a visit back home.

South Carolina Lowcountry's shrimp and grits has long been a basic coastal breakfast among shrimpers during the May-to-December shrimping season. In fact, chef and author Nathalie Dupree wrote a cookbook dedicated solely to the shrimp-and-grits combination in both its plain and fancy applications, demonstrating that, as with Florida orange juice, shrimp and grits aren't just for breakfast anymore.

The barrier islands of coastal South Carolina and Georgia are home to African-influenced Gullah cooking, with Frogmore stew, laden with shrimp, smoked sausage, potatoes, and stubby ears of corn, as the prime example of this culture's reliance on one-pot meals and incorporating seafood into its dishes (much like their Cajun brethren do in their own corner of the South). Others include chowders, soups, and bisques made from oysters, crabs, shrimp, and fish caught in hand-woven nets.

This low-lying coastal region was perfect for the cultivation of rice, which arrived from Madagascar in 1685. Rice production eventually spread to the Mississippi Delta country of northern Mississippi, eastern Arkansas, and the Missouri boot heel, where it is a huge part of the economy. In fact, Arkansas is now the largest rice-producing state in the nation. From savory jambalaya to sweet rice pudding, this grain is a versatile staple of the Southern table.

Slavery, too, played its part in augmenting the Southern table, as Africans brought with them okra, black-eyed peas, yams, sesame seeds, and peanuts. It's easy to forget that these foods are transplants, so ingrained in our diet are sweet potato pie, the okra-laden gumbo of New Orleans, the black-eyed peas served not only on New Year's Day but most every day, and even those salty Spanish-roasted peanuts poured into a bottle of Southern-born Coke—or Co-Cola, as many of us still call it.

Deep-frying is an infamously popular method of cooking throughout the region, as is the use of cast iron that is jet black from generations of seasoning. Satis-fying but devoid of nutritional value are green beans tossed into an iron skillet with a spoonful of bacon drippings and a sprinkling of sugar and cooked until the beans are as black as the skillet itself. No Southern kitchen is complete without the ubiquitous coffee can filled with bacon drippings that sits at the ready to serve as both seasoning and cooking fat. While many of us follow somewhat healthier cooking guidelines than our ancestors, it's not unusual to find on the kitchen shelf at least one cherished old book of family "receipts" that instructs us to fry in deep boiling lard and to "prepare brains as usual" before adding them to a cream sauce.

Sweet tea (always iced) is the beverage of choice, while Kentucky bourbon and Tennessee whiskey are a source of pride and craftsmanship. In a tangle of enterprise versus morality, Jack Daniel's is distilled in a dry county. The pungency of sour mash permeates the air, but visitors to the distillery in Lynchburg, Tennessee, must satisfy themselves with the aroma—or head to the next county for a taste.

While the South, like other parts of the country, has suffered from big business taking over the fields, it seems that many of the residents in this historically agrarian society still tend to work their gardens and farms biodynamically. It's more a matter of habit than a conscious effort to be green. Roadside stands laden with fresh produce—with some creatively spelled signage ("cantolep," anyone?)—offer just-picked strawberries, sweet corn, purple-hull peas, and whatever else is in season.

Whether what's on it is identified as home-style cooking or soul food, a table laden with fried chicken; collard greens; black-eyed peas; fried green tomatoes; biscuits and red-eye gravy; sorghum molasses; and pies made of sweet potatoes, pecans, and Georgia peaches evokes a sense of nourishment and well-being. And while these foods have the feel of earthy, basic essentials, the names of some of the region's most famous dishes are evocative of distant places. Burgoo, étouffé, hoppin' John, and purloo—not to mention a minty-fresh julep—bring to mind visions of long, languid afternoons and warm honeysuckle-fragranced evenings spent on the front porch.

With its wealth of native, European, and African ingredients and cooking styles, the South is home to a cuisine that embraces the contradictions of both the traditional and the innovative, the indigenous and the transplanted, giving us the classic American diet.

Master of the Blues

Blueberry Farmer, Organic Trailblazer, Mentor—Meet Mr. Alvin Harris

On his farm in Millington, Tennessee, Alvin Harris grows sun-drenched blueberries, indigo-red Cherokee purple tomatoes, and more. But if you want to taste them, you'll need to make the trip up Highway 51 because he and his wife, Shirley, don't get to the city much. Elusive as the Harrises are, however, their influence in the area is considerable and extends beyond matters of flavor. They are the only Certified Naturally Grown growers in the area and have long been involved in educating others about sustainable agriculture. To me, Harris seems like a Jedi master, passing along lore and experience valued only by a few. To others, Alvin Harris is something more—the keeper of a sacred flame: There are a lot of black farmers, but not a lot of black agricultural leaders. Not that Alvin Harris would describe himself in this way. He's much too focused on what's in front of him to philosophize about his influence.

When my husband and I moved to Memphis from Chicago in 2002, we took regular field trips into the surrounding country, looking for farm stands and anything else that could help us understand our new home. One of the first things I noticed was black farmers, who are just not part of the landscape up north. It's pretty clear that the Great Migration was all about getting away from the farm. In fact, lots of people left. After peaking in 1910, at 16 to 19 million acres, black agricultural land ownership fell by the 1990s to somewhere between 1.5 and 8 million acres. As farmers of all ethnicities all over the United States have left the country behind, blacks have been more likely than whites to move. Alvin Harris doesn't mention it himself, but the Mid-South is losing black landowning farmers at an astronomical rate.

The relationship between Harris and other farmers then becomes a link in a fragile chain threatened by changes in the culture—some of them certainly salutary. There's no glamour in agriculture. Chefs are hot, but for most young people, farming means hardship. It's too tough, and there's no *Iron Farmer* or *Tilling Live* on cable. Furthermore, when farmers' children go to college and later to the cities, they become alienated from the sources of their food. Instead of eating the healthy diet high in seasonal fruits and vegetables that their grandparents relied on, they adopt the contemporary American diet of fast and convenience foods. Ironically, they go to college to learn how to starve. This "starvation," as we know, has real health consequences. But this convenience diet is also starved of flavor.

Of course, they're missing out. I almost missed out on Alvin Harris's blueberries, too. As a Yankee, I'm partial to the tiny huckleberries that grow on rocky slopes in the Appalachians from upstate New York to Maine.

At first, the fat, indolent berries of the South aroused only my contempt. Their flavor lacked focus; their texture was sloppy. I tasted little difference between these berries and the gushy orbs on display year-round in the produce section.

Back in 2003, my compost pile needed a stiff dose of nitrogen, so I Googled "Memphis manure." I never found the dung, but I did unearth information about the Harrises' farm in an article in *Southern Sustainable Farming* by a writer named Keith Richards (no, not the piratical Rolling Stone). In 2003, as far as sustainable agriculture went, Harris looked like the only game in town.

In June of 2006, desperate to take my three-year-old son, Gus, out to pick some fruit, I remembered reading about the Harrises' farm. According to one Web site I found, Harris's farm was already open. Wise and practical people know to call first, but I am neither, so I was genuinely disappointed when Harris, a big guy in suspenders, ambled out through the glade surrounding his house with a regretful look on his face. "I'm not open," he said. We could come back in a couple of weeks. But he saw my toddler and perplexingly changed course. "I can't sell you anything right now, but you can just go and take some berries if you like."

I'll never malign a Tennessee blueberry again. My son, who is almost five now, still remembers that day. We filled a sun hat with hot, winey berries and

tried to make conversation with a giant one-eyed black hog. Later that summer, I returned a couple of times to buy Harris's pungent Cherokee purple tomatoes and looked for him at the Memphis Farmers Market. As he and his wife told me, though, most of their produce stays up in Millington. They freeze or can what they need before selling to anyone else. The one time they sold first, their second crop of lima beans failed. They ended up buying beans to sell from another grower at five dollars a bushel more than they got for their first crop. Because business is brisk up at their farm stand, they need to get down to the Memphis Farmers' Market only in the fat times of midsummer. But they are always connected to their neighbors.

Unlike growers who focus primarily on the health benefits of organic foods, Alvin and Shirley Harris circle back to community. At first, Harris kept gardens so his kids would have a way to make extra money and use their manners. By the late 1970s, however, he started to turn a profit selling produce in church parking lots. He began to envision a new mission. "There were all these small farmers who used to lease their land to big guys and work minimum wage jobs," he told me. Inviting some of these growers in for "Field Days," some sponsored by the Rodale Institute (a nonprofit leader in developing and promoting sustainable agriculture), he showed his neighbors how to make a decent living on their own land without using expensive and harmful chemicals. Meanwhile, he expanded his own holdings, from twelve acres in 1978 to his current twenty-four.

Of course, avoiding chemicals didn't just happen. Harris, who served in the army for twenty years, says that at first he used some insecticides but stopped when he realized he wasn't going to eat what he produced himself. "I was trained in chemical warfare, so I knew what I was using was poison." He didn't have a name for what he was doing at first. He didn't call it organic. He farmed the way he learned growing up. For most of the farmers he knew back then, chemical fertilizers were an added cost they couldn't swing. Instead, they relied on crop rotation, green manures, and the richness of the soil to ensure sustenance for their families. Harris relies on these practices now, but he needed a trip around the world to bring it all back home. Before his service, Harris had raised cotton and corn, but overseas army postings opened his eyes to the many ways food is grown—just as travel had for the pioneers of the organic movement.

Alvin Harris was told on many occasions that organic farming wouldn't work in the South. Undaunted, he finally found a willing extension agent and hooked up with the Rodale Institute. As part of an expanding network of experimental farms, he naturally developed from student to mentor. After all, both he and Shirley, a retired teacher and Tennessee Exemplary Educator, had made education part of their mission for years. Even now, it seems wrong to them that kids don't know where their food comes from and that agriculture is no longer part of the curriculum. According to Mrs. Harris, there is little time for hands-on learning. Sharing their farming experience by inviting student groups and other growers is one way they can work around the limitations of the educational system.

So how does Alvin Harris pass it on? One way is by participating in the Certified Naturally Grown program, a grassroots alternative to USDA Organic certification. CNG bases its standards on the USDA program but reduces costs by relying on peer reviews and mentoring rather than paperwork and bureaucracy. Some participants also say that CNG remains closer to the original spirit of the organic movement, claiming that the USDA regime took away the right to use the organic name and then lowered standards to meet the needs of industrial farmers. Whatever the case, CNG provides a structure within which experienced organic growers can mentor those new to the field. In a time when black farmers are increasingly moving away from growing produce using the old methods, Harris records and archives the old growing culture for future farmers to consult.

There's a reason Alvin Harris is unique. A black farmer who grew crops without chemicals used to be the norm. Now, as black farmers have entered the mainstream of conventional farming, someone like Harris seems out of step. But, of course, in his holistic view of farming he's really several steps ahead, knowing the property, knowing the community—the immediate community. That's part of working the land.

Yoda doesn't do much recruiting in the *Star Wars* movies. His acolytes are either born Jedi or they're out of luck. Maybe it's that way with organic farmers, too—you're either called to it or you ain't. But just as the George Lucas movies of the 1970s and '80s speak to something in the American imagination that craves rebellion in the name of the individual's dream, so does the struggle of the small American farmer to stay true to his or her deepest roots.

In the spring of 2008, **LIZ PHILLIPS** *attended the Symposium for Professional Food Writers at The Greenbrier on an Edible Communities Scholarship. She's still sifting through the enormous pile of inspiration she carried home. Liz writes a family eating column for* Memphis Parent *and blogs about seasonal fruit and Southern food culture (from a Yankee perspective) at Pie for Breakfast (peachesandbuttermilk.blogspot.com).*

Growing Grains of Gold

Carolina Plantation Rice

When you hear that Campbell Coxe of Darlington has reintroduced commercial rice production to South Carolina, you'll likely consider his effort pretty neat. And, true, he has the best rice you'll ever taste; just ask Martha Stewart or Al Roker. But you really have to absorb the bigger picture to appreciate just how special Campbell's historical and cultural contribution really is.

An old adage nails Geechees, or Lowcountry, natives: "This bunch has an awful lot in common with the Chinese. Both groups eat a lot of rice, worship their ancestors, and speak a language nobody else in the world understands." So when the low-carb diet fad hit our region, we dismissed that attempt to rob us of our rice and grits; we didn't need a doctor to tell us that scheme wasn't a healthy idea.

An anecdote about my own grandfather, Ben Walpole, a Johns Island farmer, truly puts in perspective Carolina's reliance on rice. You've heard of the Victory Gardens citizens were encouraged to plant in order to help the World War II effort. Well, Dandy, as we called him, knew that his position on the draft board did not exempt him from wartime rationing, and he soon discovered that his family allotment of rice would not do. So, amid his commercial vegetable operation, Dandy planted a stand of his own rice for practical—and perhaps nostalgic—reasons.

We owe our heritage to Dr. Henry Woodward, arguably our state's most important founding father. The circumstances through which Woodward acquired rice seed must be providential. A ship from Madagascar stopped in Charleston for repairs, the captain gave our Renaissance man some seed, and the rest is history, South Carolina history.

Campbell Coxe is Woodward's cultural heir and a model of a contemporary Southern Renaissance man. Campbell is a fifth-generation farmer, and his family operates several antebellum plantations. In fact, Plumfield, where he grows his famed rice, is our state's oldest colonial plantation still under cultivation.

The Coxe family has just about raised it all. Campbell's grandfather tended cattle before Campbell and his father moved to cotton, soybeans, and wheat. They grow peanuts commercially. All along, the family has cut and sold timber, an operation that continues to thrive. Timber complemented the Roblyn's Neck Trophy Club, which has evolved from a private club to a commercial operation run from the old lumber commissary. Campbell first tried his (green) hand at rice planting in order to attract waterfowl for hunters. He began giving the rice as Christmas gifts, and when people raved over it, he started growing it commercially in 1997.

Harold Kelly is the company's official comptroller, but that title doesn't portray his true job description. "I do everything from cleaning deer and hogs to digging ditches, to giving rice tastings, to handling office accounts and updating Web site capabilities." Harold sums up the mission statement of Campbell Coxe: "That man is all about preserving Southern traditions, especially those of South Carolina."

Like all true Carolinians, Campbell also is a historian. He came to realize something ironic about his state, though. "Plenty of people in South Carolina are making a living talking about rice," and while his preservationist attitude appreciates and, indeed, depends on tourism, Campbell realized somebody in the state needs to be making a living by actually growing rice. After all, why should the western South grow our rice?

Though Harold has known Campbell all his life, he did not adequately appreciate Campbell's sincerity until he started working on the farm. "I ordered some hats with our logo," Harold recalls. Campbell picked up a hat, examined it, and quickly threw it down in anger.

"What in the world is wrong with you?" Harold asked.

"That's no good. That [expletive] hat's not made in the U.S.A., much less South Carolina! I don't want it!"

At that moment Harold realized, "This fella really is serious about what he does!"

Campbell Coxe wading in a sea of Carolina Gold rice

Harold attributes the success of Carolina Plantation Rice to two of Campbell's qualities: his passion for his product and the fact that Coxe is a true farmer. Himself a sportsman, Harold adjusted quickly to his diverse job on the farm, a transition made easier by Campbell's humble leadership. Harold continues, "You don't work for Campbell; you work with him. If Campbell says, 'We're gonna dig a ditch,' he's the first one in the hole with a shovel in his hand."

Once you see Campbell's ruddy complexion and experience his down-to-earth demeanor, you are convinced that Campbell Coxe is not merely performing a job or even living a way of life; you are witnessing a Southern soul who has embraced a spiritual calling. When I toured Plumfield, Campbell exuberantly jumped in the wet rice field to exhibit his product. With muddy shoes and socks, he spoke with pride about the rice. "I just about bored myself to death when I was growing cotton and soybeans," he recalls. "Back then, I never got to see the end consumer. What I love about this is getting to do the marketing and have customers see where the rice comes from. We grow it, harvest it, mill it, process it, market it, and distribute it. The paper trail is all on this farm, and my name's on that bag. Now that's what I call from farm gate to dinner plate!"

Photos courtesy of Carolina Plantation Rice

Heirloom rice awaiting the harvest

Besides ordering directly, you can find Carolina Plantation Rice in Whole Foods Markets throughout the Southeast, in sixty-plus Fresh Markets as far off as Chicago, a number of Viking Culinary stores, Charleston Cooks, and other gourmet shops. If you want your rice prepared, dine at such establishments as Slightly North of Broad and Magnolia's in Charleston, Elizabeth's on 37th in Savannah, and Rosewood Market and Deli in Columbia.

Campbell grows two primary varieties of rice: two hundred acres of basmati aromatic and thirty acres of Carolina Gold. Aromatic has an enticing aroma while cooking and, as Harold says, "You only need rice, water, salt, and pepper." Carolina Gold is the heirloom

rice that made our colony and, later, state so wealthy. It got its name because prior to harvest, the grain had a deep yellow hue, and the rice was said to be worth its weight in gold.

When we head toward the Great Pee Dee River, a steady hum catches our attention. Campbell points to the big diesel pump that keeps river water in the fields. "That's genuine Darlington Tide," he jokes as he gestures toward the pump. Ironically, commercial rice was never grown here; rather, it was grown in coastal areas where tide influenced the freshwater rivers. One of his contract growers plants on the coast, and Campbell yearns for the day when rice makes its tidal comeback. Carolina Plantation Rice is planted in mid-April and harvested around Labor Day. Like cotton, rice doesn't like cold weather, so Campbell welcomes a warm spring. Once rice is planted, water levels must be regulated daily, and diseases and insects are constant concerns. Therefore, Campbell employs a crop rotation of corn to soybeans to rice. This rotation helps control weeds, and soybeans are a legume, which fixes nitrogen into the soil. This practice allows Campbell to reduce his nitrogen (fertilizer) application. A combine with tracks works the soggy field to harvest the rice, and the bottom of the plant is left several months, or double cropped, as a wildlife feast.

But rice production and hunting aren't the only activities going on here. Campbell plants corn that he mills for grits, peanuts, and no-till cowpeas that are seeded in cotton stubble. No-till practices minimize labor and energy costs, prevent erosion, and allow soil to retain moisture. In addition, "the more you till the soil, the more you spread fire ants," Campbell indicates. "No-till is ugly farming, but it's better for the environment." Campbell explains that cover, not food, is essential for bringing back wildlife such as quail. Thus, he allows filter strips 120 feet wide for sanctuary and brood rearing.

"Cowpeas are the true hoppin' John peas, not black-eyed peas," Campbell teaches. Harold points out that besides possessing superior taste, cowpeas have a better structure and don't turn to mush as do black-eyed peas. Cowpeas were brought from Africa to protect the health of slaves by preserving their natural diet. On the plantation, slaves cultivated personal parcels of rice. Campbell grows ironclad peas, a great source of organic matter for the soil. Or, after harvest, the pea vines can be windrowed and baled for hay. Leftover peas are packaged and sold to deer hunters.

"One of our biggest challenges is figuring out ways to utilize by-product," Campbell continues. Cracked rice is used to make rice flour, run through the plantation's grist mill. Campbell considers rice flour superior because it is not "cakey," but rather has a light, thin crust. Rice bran is high in protein, fiber, oil, and vitamins. Once extracted for the production of white rice, the bran is off to the hunting lodge, where it's used to bake pie crusts and cookies.

Rice is packaged in recycled boxes from Bennettsville. The decorative bag is made of cotton because "we're cotton people," Campbell reminds us. His concern for the environment is evidenced in the farm's receipt of the state's first Green-e certification awarded by the EPA to "compan[ies] that purchase at least fifty percent of [their] total energy with renewable energy," according to the Pee Dee Electric Cooperative.

Even the fire-retardant rice husks are recyclable. Some are returned to the fields as organic matter, while recent uses include horse stall bedding and insulation. Additional husks have been converted to rice paper, some of which Campbell displays at the office. "My next venture is making wallpaper out of rice husks," he enthusiastically envisions. "Wouldn't they just love rice wallpaper in Charleston?"

Campbell muses: "I feel like we're functioning in the true manner of a Southern plantation—by the real definition of the word, which is a self-sufficient way of life for a clan community of people in a remote location." In fact, the Coxe family cemetery is in the plantation churchyard. "There's something comforting about knowing that you'll end up right where you started."

This wasn't always Campbell's plan, though. "I was a geography major at Carolina, and I was off to see the world. Well, I'm still here!"

The plantation operation really is a family affair. Campbell explains his introduction to his bride, Meredith. "She came out here for a dove hunt and just about shot every bird in sight. I knew I'd better get to know this little blonde with a ponytail." For their first date, Campbell took Meredith horseback riding. They now have two children, Cam and Hagood. When Cam graduates from college, he plans to return home as a sixth-generation farmer.

Despite this unique plantation lifestyle, Campbell defies stereotypes. While every bit a gentleman, Campbell Coxe is hardly a gentleman planter; he's a country-boy farmer without a glimpse of pretense. "I'll tell you one thing: There aren't any hoop skirts or mint juleps around here," he reminds, still squishing around in wet shoes and socks.

FORD WALPOLE *lives and writes on his native Johns Island, South Carolina. He earned a BA and MA from Clemson University and teaches English at James Island Charter High School. Ford and his wife, English, have two children: English Calhoun and Ned.*

Behind the Bottle

Wines of Garden Gate Vineyards

In the hot North Carolina summers of Bo Whitaker's youth, when the blueberries were ripe and ready for picking, his grandfather would send for raisins. "I could always tell when my grandpa was going to make blueberry wine," Bo remembers. "He'd tell my grandma, 'Go to the store and buy boxes of raisins.' You put raisins in blueberry wine. It's like a starter." Thus was the start of Bo Whitaker's love affair with homemade wine.

For North Carolinians of Bo's generation, this story is not unusual—except for the fact that his grandfather didn't just make wine. Charlie Howard, known to most as Uncle Charlie, was one of the best and most respected bootleggers in Davie County. "They made a lot of money, and they helped a lot of people. It was just a way of life," says Bo. "A lot of people didn't think it was right, but it was a living," he adds. For Uncle Charlie, part of making a living was keeping people happy. For his best customers, he would top off a crate of white liquor with a bottle of some of his homemade blueberry wine.

Bo fell in love with his grandfather's blueberry wine as a teenager, but he didn't fall into the craft of wine making until much later. First, he married his high school sweetheart, Sonya; started a family; and put in thirty-four years as a line superintendent for the local power company, EnergyUnited. When Bo retired in 1999, he took some time to figure out what he would do next. He had always considered making wine but wasn't sure he could make a go of it until one day, when he followed Sonya and a friend to visit a local vineyard. It was close to harvest time, and Bo was inspired by the rows of vines heavy with fruit. "I said right there, 'This is what I want to do,'" Bo recalls.

Bo and Sonya started Garden Gate Vineyards in 2000. They planted blackberries, strawberries, raspberries, and, of course, blueberries. But they also planted grapes. Bo planted his first vines right next to their house, filling an acre with hard-to-find muscadine and scuppernong varieties: Hunts, James, Triumphs, and Magnolias. Part of the reason they chose those grapes was that they didn't just want to make wine; they wanted to be able to sell grapes for people to use to make their own juice, jams, jellies, or to eat whole. But that first year in business, the vines were too young to bear fruit, so folks across Davie County brought their grapes to Garden Gate Vineyards—people who knew Uncle Charlie, people Bo helped get power to their homes when he worked for the electric company, and people who simply had more grapes than they could handle. All told, they were given 6,000 pounds of fruit. "No one would take a penny," remembers Bo. But all of them would receive a case of wine.

Today, thirteen different wines are made from what's grown at Garden Gate Vineyards. And there's no beating around the bush: All of the wines are sweet. "People from the South have a sweet tooth," says Bo. "People come in and say they want some sweet muscadine or sweet scuppernong like their grandparents made." The Whitakers want to create a wine that's of the place, of the people, and, yes, of the soil. "I've heard old people say it better than anything," explains Bo. "The taste comes from the dirt." And there it is: the folklore of *terroir*.

The dirt at Garden Gate Vineyards is farmed by one set of hands: Bo's. It's a tiny operation (there are no paid employees), so Bo tends the vines and Sonya tends the business. But at harvest time, they have some help. Friends and family flock to the vineyard to pitch in. In return, they get a covered-dish dinner—and maybe a glass or two of wine. "It's like years ago when you primed tobacco," says Bo. "You always had plenty of good stuff to eat and plenty of people."

Plenty of people flock to Garden Gate Vineyards. A stone's throw from Interstate 40 and just thirty minutes southwest of Winston-Salem, it's easy enough to get to. It might just be hard to leave. Tucked into a residential neighborhood on the outskirts of Mocksville, the winery sits on the corner of the aptly named Scenic Drive. The Whitakers don't advertise, but word of mouth has brought people to their doorstep from

all over the world. Even if folks don't have a taste for sweet wines or have never even heard of a muscadine, they will be enchanted by Garden Gate. The Whitakers have transformed their home of almost forty years into a beautiful and welcoming oasis. The place is so modest and inviting that you might think to ask to borrow a cup of sugar before you even think about having some wine. But the tasting room does inspire a lingering visit, and part of the draw is the promise of Sonya's home-made bread, which is offered at each tasting.

Another draw is the retail experience. Primarily self-taught, Sonya has filled the tasting room with examples of her pottery, which is all for sale. Figurines, decorative plates, and garden ornaments cover every shelf and surface.

Garden Gate Vineyards is a wonderful stop for agro-tourists traveling through the state, but it's also a hangout for Mocksville locals. Friends and neighbors stop by regularly to crush some of their own grapes, drop off some homemade jam, or share stories of Uncle Charlie. A group of old-timers have a standing date every Monday, when they hold court on the patio, telling tales and talking politics. The sense of community there is strong. So is the sense of history.

"What we're trying to do is make [wine] as close to the way it was made years ago," says Bo. "That's the reason I like to make blueberry wine. It just reminds me of being a teenager at home, when it was being made there." Considering the future, he adds, "Really and truly, I would like some of my kids to do it for the basic fact that [the craft of making alcohol] has been in my family all these years. And now it's legal, and I'd just like to see my kids carry it out. Whether they will or not, I don't know."

AMY EVANS *is the oral historian for the Southern Foodways Alliance. She has stood in pig lots in Cajun Country, behind bars in Louisville (cocktail bars, that is), and on oyster skiffs on the Apalachicola Bay to collect the stories behind the food. Most recently, she's been wandering vineyards, collecting stories about grapes. Amy appreciates a good meringue and can never eat too many oysters. Visit www.southernfoodways.com.*

Photo by Amy Evans

Old-fashioned Charcuterie

Belmont Butchery, Richmond, Virginia

Just ask about exciting career choices for women, and it's a safe bet that becoming a butcher would not head the list. Butchering might not even make it to the top 100. So when *Food & Wine* magazine reports on a small but remarkable career trend—young women wrapping themselves up in butchers' aprons—it's not surprising the magazine calls them "renegades," embracing a career traditionally considered man's work.

One of these renegades is Tanya Cauthen, butcher, chef, and owner of Belmont Butchery in Richmond, Virginia. Her mission: to bring back the "old-fashioned" butcher's shop where customers can count on purchasing top-quality meats—pork, beef, lamb, and poultry—cut to order. And because Belmont Butchery also boasts a high-end charcuterie, customers can dream rich dreams of carrying away pig's liver mousse.

Cauthen grew up living all over the world, learning firsthand about European butchery from shop owners who still fully break down carcasses, something modern American supermarket butchers seldom do. A Swiss-trained chef, Cauthen moved back to Virginia in her early twenties and worked every angle of the food world, from cooking to food writing. Becoming a butcher seemed a natural career progression. "I was frustrated by the lack of good meat. I had to use my restaurant connections to get what I wanted," she says. "I saw there was a need. What I don't know I can learn, I thought, so why not?" A solid business plan got Cauthen the financing she needed, and it took a mere three months to build out and open in the fall of 2006. "It happened so fast, I didn't have time to freak out," she says.

By serendipity Cauthen bumped into young, energetic Chris Mattera just when he was thinking of opening his own butcher shop. While in college, Mattera had been a student at the recreational cooking school Cauthen ran. "Come work for me," she remembers telling him—and he agreed. "Chris is amazing and wise beyond his years," she says. "I feel lucky that we connected and that I found someone with a common purpose. . . . He is an employee but also a kind of business partner."

Mattera, a Cordon Bleu–trained chef, can trace his infatuation with cooking, and especially with charcuterie, back to his childhood, when he started making sausages at the age of ten. "I asked my grandfather for a meat grinder," he says. "My family moved from New Jersey, where good sausages were plentiful, to Virginia, where they were not. So I had to make my own."

As an adult Mattera spent time in Tuscany to sharpen his charcuterie skills. He apprenticed with a traditional Tuscan butcher whose family has been at the trade for at least three generations. "I have a working knowledge of the scientific process of what's going on when you are processing meat," he says. "But that is not the tradition of what is done, the curing of meats over the past thousand years. I wanted a better grasp of the artisanal side of things." For thirty-five days Mattera worked as part of the family team, jumping right in to get the sense of butchering and of how to make salami and sausage.

Bringing those skills back to Belmont Butchery, Mattera is now Cauthen's production manager and charcuterie expert. "We offer two dozen different fresh sausages that we rotate through according to our whim," he says. "I also make the best hot dogs on the planet, and we sell a whole assortment of pâtés and terrines, plus duck confit and our own bacon, including Italian pancetta and lardo."

Not only is Mattera a charcuterie whiz kid, he also has an infatuation with pigs, an animal he describes as "the king of meat. . . . . They are beautiful, intelligent, and delicious," he says. While dreaming of the day when his wife will permit him to own his own pig to devour backyard weeds, Mattera contents himself with working with pigs and pig parts at the shop. After all, he says, pork is six times more delicious than chicken and so versatile that it can be pulled, roasted, stir-fried, fried, smoked, and stewed. "Good pork is like good wine," he adds. "The *terroir* really shines through. You can taste what the animal has eaten. For example, if a pig ate acorns, you can taste the nutty sweetness."

The pair may bring their own slightly different perspectives to the business, but they share both the zeal for and the dedication to sourcing meats from local farmers. They understand that in order to raise quality meats and to have them slaughtered under stringent USDA rules more labor is required, resulting in higher wholesale costs. "We look for animals that are humanely and, ideally, organically raised," says Cauthen. "But if the meat is not good or if it is too expensive, the farmer is priced out of the game."

While gentle and nonpreachy in their educational efforts, Cauthen and Mattera do emphasize the benefits—for people's health, the health of the environment, and the health of the local economy—of consuming hormone- and antibiotic-free, humanely raised local meats. To their mutual satisfaction, Cauthen and Mattera believe that about 10 percent of their customers are finally getting it—the whole concept of buying local, sustainable, and better-quality meats, even if they cost a little more. "I divide the customers into two groups," says Cauthen. "One has discretionary income and can afford the best. The other is of thoughtful eaters who have been reading *Heat* and *Omnivore's Dilemma*. They may not have the disposable income to buy here regularly . . . but they want local, because it is better for them."

Does the success of Belmont Butchery forecast the resurgence of the family butcher? That could well be, the pair agrees. Not only are consumers making the connection between food and health, they also understand the big disconnect between the "big box" markets and the local economy and personal service. "We have people who come in all the time saying, 'I want the regular,'" says Cauthen. "It's about creating a relationship with customers." And that extends to their offering cooking advice, according to Cauthen, who notes they get frantic calls all the time from customers, especially on Saturday afternoons. "We stay on the phone with them. In our society, so much is anonymous, and we have lost a lot of the human touch."

Looking to the future, the pair feels they have found the right formula: good service, quality meats, and exacting techniques. "We are doing it correctly," says Cauthen, a fact confirmed after Mattera spent time in Tuscany. "The nice thing is, Chris could see

Tanya Cauthen and Chris Mattera of Belmont Butchery

the third-generation butchers doing what we are doing. Okay, we are not frauds." That's taking butchering to the next level, a boon to Richmond residents, and an inspiring example for others in the small wave of traditional butcher shops that have opened in Maryland and Virginia in Belmont's wake.

. . . .

Food writer, cookbook author, and restaurant critic **ALEXANDRA GREELEY** *lives in Virginia, where she cooks, eats, dreams about, and experiments with foods from all cultures. As coleader of Washington, D.C.'s Slow Food convivium for more than eight years, she has worked ardently to support local, sustainable farming.*

. . . .

Photo by Aaron Springer

Just Good Food

Hanging Out with Chef Mike Lata

Chef Mike Lata talks about local foods with an almost evangelical fervor. In his opinion, the perfect asparagus just might change a person's life. Perhaps people who claim to not like this quintessential spring vegetable say so because they have eaten only the variety that has spent long days being shipped from California. When you treat them to farm-fresh asparagus, they are introduced to an entirely different vegetable, one they just might love. This is the goal at Lata's downtown Charleston restaurant, FIG, which he co-owns with manager Adam Nemirow. There, Lata brings area products from the farm to the table, a sometimes-daunting task in a busy fine-dining restaurant.

"It's our MO," he says. "When we get it, it's as good as food can be. It defines how food can be."

Such intense passion comes as no surprise once you hear Lata's story. During his childhood in Springfield, Massachusetts, Lata and his siblings spent much time with their maternal and paternal grandparents, all of whom had substantial gardens. "They put us to work," says Lata. "They had to hoe potatoes so we would all hoe potatoes." Lata loved the natural progression of the raw ingredient to the end product, and thus the seed was planted. Yet, Lata did not consider cooking as a career until years later when he heard Julia Child speak. At the time, he was attending college and feeling pretty uninspired by his major in communications. Hearing the grande dame of American cooking awoke a drive in Lata that jump-started his culinary career. He dropped out of school and began cooking seriously. From the Black Dog Tavern on Martha's Vineyard to Bacco in New Orleans, Lata honed his kitchen skills.

However, it was not until moving to Atlanta that Lata truly found his culinary identity. There, he worked in several restaurants over a short period of time and just could not find the right fit. Lata remembers feeling a bit at a loss and even considered leaving the business. That's when he happened upon Ciboulette, a small French restaurant located in a strip mall. The menu caught his eye, and with good reason, as the founder turned out to be acclaimed French chef Jean Banchet. Lata says it was a wake-up call, and he was willing to give 110 percent, meeting chef Tom Coohill (Banchet's protégé) at the restaurant's door every morning. There he learned the foundations of good cuisine, and his work ethic paid off with his promotion to *chef de cuisine* by age twenty-two. During this time, Lata began to consider what would set him apart from other chefs. "When I sat down and thought about it, I got most excited when I got fresh vegetables."

Luckily for Lata, the Georgia Organic Growers Association had just formed, and when he called the president and stated his goal, she took him under her wing. Lata soon established relationships with many area farmers and began to carve out his niche as a local ingredient–driven chef. This very trait attracted the attention of Charleston's Anson Restaurant, which began recruiting him to take over its kitchen. The first step in the courtship was a visit to Celeste Albers's Wadmalaw Island farm, where he viewed firsthand the bounty the Lowcountry could offer. Lata remembers that it was late October and Albers's vegetables impressed him. "She was as good if not better than any [farmer] I had seen," he says. Subsequently, he took the job at Anson and made the move to Charleston in 1998.

At the time, Lata recalls, only one Charleston restaurant saw the relevance of local produce. Lata's devotion to the cause inspired him to spread the word. He continuously praised Albers's product to other local chefs, and soon she delivered all over town. Lata himself received several truckloads a week; Albers remembers delivering him "loads and loads of kale." She also remembers the challenges that Lata met in those early days. "He took some ribbing," she says, recalling that other chefs jokingly called him "veggie boy."

Ultimately, Lata's zeal won out. In 2001, he opened FIG at 232 Meeting Street, a restaurant where he could have a serious platform for his ideals. The full meaning of the restaurant's name is subtle yet imperative to fully understanding the concept. FIG is more than just a summer fruit; it is an acronym for "Food Is Good."

"We loved the name because it embodied our mission," says Lata. "You don't have to build a restaurant with Rosenthal china and Riedel stemware to show your dedication to quality food and service. At the end of the day it's just good food."

Lata backs up such strong statements with a simple restaurant concept. The dining room is comfortable but spare, and the menu reads like a good news story—short and to the point. The lack of wordy descriptions heightens the focus on Lata's raison d'être—the ingredients. The dishes could almost act as a directory of local farms. The Sea Island Deviled Eggs come from Albers; the Caw Caw Creek Country-Style Prosciutto comes from Emile DeFelice; the Roast Suckling Pig comes from Ted Chewning. The menu changes almost daily as the local farmers face the reality of nature. Albers says there's always the chance she might have to call with some unfortunate news like "The deer just ate it!"

Therefore, there must always be a "Plan B"—meaning that Lata does purchase some produce from a conventional purveyor. Usually, he buys certain staple vegetables like fennel, endive, and radicchio from such a purveyor to ensure that he can always provide a full menu. Albers commends Lata's dedication throughout this delicate creative process. "It's not easy to do," she says. "I have a lot of respect for him for sticking with it—using whatever I have."

Lata obviously embraces the challenge of writing a predominately local menu but laments that the real challenge comes from the decline in farmers. "The government needs to help out with more incentives and make it a plausible field to go into," says Lata. "Without tax breaks and ways to help on the real-estate side, it's a mountain to climb."

Thankfully, Lata seems able to deflect such deterrents with the same sharp focus he uses on his dishes. "I plan to stay on track, do what I can to help the farming community, and help further solidify Charleston cuisine."

Lata's reward becomes obvious when he speaks of his favorite preparations of local ingredients: "a simple asparagus soup from Ted's asparagus, Celeste's potatoes roasted in duck fat." His confidence and enthusiasm in such talk makes his way seem the natural choice in restaurant dining.

Mike Lata passionately attending to the food at FIG

SARAH O'KELLEY *is a New Orleans transplant to the Lowcountry and contributes frequently to* Edible Lowcountry *and other publications. She is also a partner in the restaurant* The Glass Onion, *one of the region's most significant supporters of seasonal local foods.*

Dr. Strangeleaf

. . . .

or How I Learned to Stop Complaining and Love the Kudzu

How do you plant kudzu? You throw it down and run.

So goes the joke in the southeastern United States, where the vine grows with the tenacity of a leafy green pit bull. It is estimated that this aggressive foliage grows a foot a day in summer and covers about seven million acres. That's enough to cover the entire state of Massachusetts and overlap its neighbors.

It is hard to deny the beauty of a kudzu land-scape, whether it's blanketing a hillside or taking the shape of a barn or a tree that it has swallowed. In fact,

Kudzu gone wild

those lush, verdant landscapes are as characteristic of the South as all the admonitions to "See Rock City" that call from the rooftops of barns across the region.

Not many people actually consider eating the pesky vine. And why not? Kudzu is plentiful, an understatement if there ever was one. It's free, every part is edible—leaf, blossom, stem, and root—and it's a nutritional powerhouse, high in fiber and loaded with protein, vitamin A, calcium, and potassium. You don't even have to plant it—it's there for the picking. All that's involved is a little ingenuity—and the willingness to look past kudzu's reputation as pigeon in plant form.

While growing up in the rural South, I was taught that kudzu was an evil thing, with an acquisitive, destructive nature. Although I knew it was the enemy, I secretly admired its beauty and wondered if it harbored a good side that I'd never been allowed to glimpse.

Today as a chef, I try to be empirical, the scientist unfazed by any food's bad rap. Thus I began my experimentation with kudzu. I started out simply, eating the leaves raw, then blanching them in a bit of salted water. Unadorned, they taste profoundly green. Then I fried them in a bit of oil, salting them and munching on them like potato chips. Prepared this way they taste decidedly protein-y. If you've ever had pappadum in an Indian restaurant, you know what I mean.

I discovered that the larger the leaf, the tougher it is and the more difficult it is to eat. But the young, tender leaves, which are available in the late spring and early summer, have a soylike flavor and are easy to assimilate into a meal. When you see the re-greening of the kudzu commence after its winter nap, rush out and pick a basketful of brand-new leaves and try your hand at cooking them.

Be sure you know your kudzu's source—you don't want foliage that has been sprayed with pesticides. It may grow conveniently right up to the edge of the road (and could possibly engulf your car should you stop to change a flat or make a cell phone call), but resist the urge to do your harvesting along the beaten path. Be sure to ask permission if you're collecting kudzu on someone else's land. They probably won't mind—have

you ever heard anyone complain, "Somebody stole my kudzu"?—but they'll surely want to know what you're up to. They can also tell you if they've engaged in chemical warfare against your intended dinner.

I'm sure no Southerner would make the mistake of picking poison oak or poison ivy when seeking out kudzu (given the average Southerner's acquaintance with all three), but it bears mentioning that all these plants produce similar three-leaf clusters. I don't think any self-respecting plant would attempt to grow anywhere near kudzu, however, so the chance of confusing it with poisonous vines is slim.

Just what can you do with kudzu?

Use the leaves for most anything you'd do with any other green. Substitute them for grape leaves to make dolmades. Bake a quiche (see Kudzu Quiche in Puff Pastry, page 214). Add the leaves to a salad or cook them up just like you would a pot of spinach, kale, or mustard greens. If you're willing to give kudzu a try but want to ease into it slowly, mix the leaves with other greens and cook them all together. I've found this the best way to make those horsey ol' collards more palatable.

In the late summer, pick the purple, grape-scented flowers to make jelly, candy, or wine. Some people batter and deep-fry them like squash blossoms. Use the sap to make syrup. Cook the roots just like you would any other root vegetable, either alone or in combination with carrots, turnips, parsnips, and rutabagas.

Dried, powdered kudzu root works well as a thickening agent in cooking. It's a traditional staple in Asia, used as a treatment for alcoholism and an array of other ailments, but that's another story.

If you don't want to eat kudzu, you can still feed the nutrition-dense foliage to your livestock. And you can make candles from the blossoms and weave baskets from the roots.

Essentially, kudzu is out there for our use and experimentation. With some seven million acres of it at your disposal, the supply is practically limitless, so if your experiment flops, no worries! There's plenty more kudzu where that came from.

CAROL PENN-ROMINE *is a writer and chef who has contributed to* Gastronomica, *the* Christian Science Monitor, Cornbread Nation IV: The Best of Southern Writing, *and* Food Jobs. *She is past editor of* Edible Los Angeles *and writes for several* Edible *magazines.*

Photo by Carol Penn-Romine

Saving the Southern Soul

The Southern Foodways Alliance

Collard greens cooked in a well-seasoned "pot likker" with a side of cast-iron-skillet corn bread, and, of course, made without sugar, is a microcosm of a place, a culture, a race, and a region. That, simply put, is the Southern Foodways Alliance (SFA). It originated when a small group of champions of Southern-food chefs, writers, and educators huddled in a conference room at *Southern Living* magazine and were challenged by then–graduate student John T. Edge to find the culture of the South in foodways and to preserve those histories of the plate. Since then, Southern Foodways has become an almost magical, as well as a dedicated, intellectual, and far-reaching organization. What's more, SFA gives most of its members the chance to have very personal walks through their ever-changing homeland and the opportunity to advocate local and regional delicacies.

Southern Foodways is a loose federation. Some of the most nationally celebrated Southern chefs sup at the same table with sociologists enjoying local quail in a country ham broth. Food writers swap stories over bourbon and catfish with students of Southern culture. Media giants like *The New York Times* and *Southern Living* are entertained by the South's best professional eaters while debating the fine points of buttermilk, fried chicken, and, of course, barbecue (the noun). They all hug, learn from, and break bread together with folks who enrich the land, keep up the traditions, and envelope the culinary South. SFA is a scholarly search for the South, where instructors with sun-chiseled faces have dirt under their fingernails and bleary-eyed researchers glean from fellowship and a common belief. Southern Foodways Alliance "looks at the evolution of southern food culture over time. It is not an act of preservation but one of documentation, which implies both continuity and change," says now–executive director John T. Edge.

Local foods play a role in SFA because they are the cornerstone of SFA. Each year, Southern Foodways takes an in-depth look at different phenomena, whether they be of the land, ponds, oceans, or stills, and how they have affected the culture and livability of the South. To understand local food is to drive down a highway of cultural differences together—both white and black, Arab and Jew, Hispanic and Asian—for we all have been on this land and supported one another in some fashion and in the creolization of our foods. Local foods become the center of rebuilding communities, and Southern Foodways has been there to rebuild fabled restaurants in Katrina-stricken New Orleans and to provide scholarship opportunities for deeper learning. It has taught its members the reality of local foodways by showcasing the farmer, the seed saver, the dairymen, the pitmaster, the master distiller, the ingredient-driven chef, and the tamale maker with a reverence for them all. As John T. puts it, "This idea of local foods in the South is not pretentious; it is not prissy and it is not something we learned from California."

Southern Foodways changed my life. My parents, both from the Depression-era rural South, transported to city dwelling, at times seemed ashamed of eating out of the garden as they had done growing up. Fatback, collard greens, field peas, and turnips were not the foods for company, but they where the foods we ate and loved as a family. When I worked in New York City for a while, the fancy and the new intrigued me, but the greenmarket system also beckoned me with ramps, and heirloom tomatoes, and baby collards. I took joy in cooking from those markets, and when I was back in North Carolina I sought out farmers' markets to buy from. But it was my first trip to Oxford, Mississippi, and the Southern Foodways annual symposium in 1998 that made me question what was really in my soul as an eater and a person. SFA has given me the road map to my own culture and family. It has given me pride. SFA has taught me how the regional groups of the South relate. It has shown me passion for the people who toil to determine smart growth and land use and to keep traditions alive, people who strive for exceptional flavor and quality in our foods. All come under a large local banner. SFA has put me in my mother's kitchen—this woman who travels three hours to pick her collards from the same farm every

year—to record her secrets and understand her joy of food. The organization has made me obsessive about local and now, through *Edible Piedmont*, about celebrating the faces of local foods in a very public and far-reaching way.

My epiphany is not unique among the membership of Southern Foodways. It's a path that every member has journeyed down in some form or other. Southern Foodways is a community of communities—from the cotton fields of the Delta to the red clay of the Carolinas. SFA not only preaches to the choir, but has taken the gospel of food and community throughout the country (New York City and Denver to name a couple). Through oral history, "Pot Likker" film festivals, field trips and day camps around the South, the Southern Foodways Alliance continues to proliferate the message of understanding through food and celebrates the abundance of locale. But at its core is a membership that practices the Southern Foodways ideals in their "neck of the woods." This group is indeed a national hero.

FRED THOMPSON *is a longtime member of the Southern Foodways Alliance, publisher of* Edible Piedmont, *eight cookbooks including* Grillin' with Gas *and* Barbecue Nation, *and has been published in* Bon Appétit, *the* San Francisco Chronicle, Fine Cooking, Everyday with Rachael Ray, Taste of the South, Wine and Spirits, *and* Better Homes and Gardens. *He's happiest grilling seafood on a Carolina beach and eating heirloom tomato and local mozzarella salad.*

People, places, things

BLUE RIDGE (VIRGINIA)

Central Virginia is a land deeply rich in both early American history and the modern eat-local movement. Divided by the Blue Ridge Mountains, this dynamic food community includes college towns bustling with innovative eateries and the intensely agricultural Shenandoah Valley. Its *terroir*-embracing wineries are gaining a worldwide reputation. Farmers, chefs, vintners, activists, and students are all working together to found truly sustainable food systems.

Feast! Called a "gourmet market," Feast! isn't just an intense foodie destination, it also supports eat-local initiatives and many local producers.

Polyface Farm This pasture-based, beyond-organic farm, and its outspoken "conservative radical" steward Joel Salatin, have become national icons of the eat-local movement.

Revolutionary Soup Want proof that eating local doesn't have to be expensive? Savor this basement soup mecca's creations, with ingredients sourced from a dozen local producers.

Southern Exposure Seed Exchange Based out of a commune, this enterprise began from a love for no-GMO heirloom varieties and seed saving, and now is a favorite of savvy gardeners in the Mid-Atlantic.

Vintage Virginia Apples This family-run orchard grows twelve heirloom varieties previously grown by Thomas Jefferson at Monticello, and has recently become Virginia's second hard-cider producer.

www.ediblecommunities.com/blueridge/peopleplacesthings

CHESAPEAKE

The Chesapeake Bay, by Maryland and Virginia, is known for oysters, rockfish, the legendary blue crab, and the shad that spawn in tributary rivers in spring. But the watershed of North America's largest estuary also supports diverse small-scale agriculture. Tree fruits, corn, tomatoes, and wine grapes thrive. The sandy soils close to the bay yield asparagus, melons, and heirloom sweet potatoes. Poultry and livestock abound, dairies are resurgent, and local honeys sweeten the meal for year-round local eaters.

Blue Crabs The uniqueness and fragility of the Chesapeake Bay are summed up in the blue crab.

Ginger Gold Apples Discovered in a Virginia orchard in the 1960s, yellow Ginger Gold apples are a favorite early-season variety, a creamy sweet apple.

Half-Smokes Spicy coarse-ground sausages that are sold only in the Baltimore–Washington, D.C., area. Once staples of corner stores in African-American communities and pushcarts in the business district downtown, they are now harder to find.

Smith Island 10-Layer Cake Smith Island's isolation in the Chesapeake Bay has resulted in a microculture with a distinctive neo-Elizabethan style of speech and a penchant for multi-skinny-layered yellow cakes mortared together with creamy chocolate icing.

Sweet Melons Summer finds farm stands and farmers' markets across Maryland, Virginia, and Delaware piled high with delicious specialty varieties of melons that rarely, if ever, make it to a grocery store.

www.ediblecommunities.com/chesapeake/peopleplacesthings

LOWCOUNTRY (SOUTH CAROLINA)

Some folks think this swath of land along the coast of South Carolina is paradise. With Charleston as its midpoint, the Lowcountry gleans from inland and ocean to fill its collective plate. Shrimp from the boats at Shem Creek, crabs from every bay and inlet, and the elusive local weakfish are just the most obvious bounty from the region. Blend in Wadmalaw Island, rich with agricultural heritage, and the flatlands of the western fringe, and all in all, you get a unique coterie of farmers, fishermen, and eaters.

The Glass Onion, Charleston Three young chefs with pedigrees from Emeril's to Mike Lata's FIG meet the farmers at the back door each morning and devise a menu from what they have to offer.

FireFly Vodka Sweet tea–infused vodka drips with the flavor of the South. Straight or with lemonade, the stuff's great!

Mount Pleasant Farmers Market Every Tuesday it's time to head down Coleman Boulevard to the middle school and the farmers' market. Nestled under huge hardwoods, the market is the anchor that keeps Mount Pleasant cool.

Anson Mills Glenn Roberts grows, harvests, and mills near-extinct varieties of heirloom corn, rice, and wheat organically, and re-creates ingredients that were in the Southern larder before the Civil War.

Celeste and George Albers The Albers family's claim to fame is its raw milk and fresh-rate eggs, both served in some of the finest eateries in the area.

www.ediblecommunities.com/lowcountry/peopleplacesthings

MEMPHIS

From barbecue to soul food, garden tomatoes to peach pickles, Memphis is rich with food traditions. The tea is sweet; the greens are cooked. It's home to the muscadine and the Lady pea. And it's not uncommon for people to name their favorite tomato variety from here (such as Arkansas Traveler). Memphis is also changing: There is a growing movement focusing on local foods and preserving traditions.

Alvin Harris With high humidity and lots of pests, the Mid-South is thought to be an impossible place to grow anything organically. Yet, Mr. Harris has been farming organically in the Mid-South for more than thirty years and has taught others how to accomplish it.

Neola Farms Black Angus Beef Michael and Charline Lenegar raise their steers with the finest of everything. The pampered steers are fed both hay and corn—grown right there on the property.

GrowMemphis Community Gardens GrowMemphis helps those who want to establish community gardens, mostly in poverty-stricken areas where fresh food is totally unavailable.

Jackson Kramer Born in Memphis and trained in Portland, Oregon, Jackson Kramer, chef of Interim Restaurant, boasts more locally sourced items on his menu than any other chef in the city.

Whitton Flowers and Produce Jill and Keith Forrester are young farmers leading the charge with more diverse crops every year with the first Community Supported Agriculture (CSA) in the area. They tirelessly work to help other farmers, schools implementing gardens, and chefs who want to buy local.

www.ediblecommunities.com/memphis/peopleplacesthings

METRO AND MOUNTAINS (GREATER ATLANTA)

Since the first settlers arrived in Savannah, Georgia has always been known as a farming state. Agriculture remains Georgia's largest industry, contributing billions of dollars annually. Georgia is unique in that it has a variety of soil types from the coast to the mountains that provide a diversity of crops and livestock. The range starts at sea level at the Atlantic coast and tops out at 4,784 feet above sea level at Brasstown Bald. This diversity and the variety of products are what make this region so wonderful and delicious.

Emory University Emory has more square feet of building space certified by the U.S. Green Building Council under its Leadership in Energy and Environmental Design (LEED) program than any other campus in America.

Destiny Produce Located on the State Farmer's Market, outside Atlanta, Destiny Produce is the only certified organic wholesale operation in the state.

White Oak Pastures Will Harris produces prize-winning grass-fed beef at his farm in Bluffton and operates its own on-site slaughterhouse with a Georgia Department of Agriculture/USDA inspector on premises to ensure all the meat products meet federal standards.

Farmer D Organics (Darron Joffe) Farmer D Organics Signature Biodynamic Blend Organic Compost is a Demeter-certified biodynamic compost that is made using the organic spoils from Whole Foods Market.

Nature's Harmony Farm Tim and Liz Young raise Bourbon Red and Standard Bronze turkeys, which are on the Slow Food Ark of Taste, which works to preserve regionally distinct foods from becoming extinct.

www.ediblecommunities.com/metroandmountains/peopleplacesthings

PIEDMONT (NORTH CAROLINA)

The Piedmont is defined as the plateau from the mountain foothills to the coastal plain of North Carolina stretched to the Atlantic shores. North Carolina is blessed with earth and climate that make anything almost possible. The Tobacco Road of just a decade ago has been replaced with stoic believers in good, responsible foodways, from organic to heirloom, wild-caught, and heritage food products. In a land where software giants were once the glory boys of economic impact, the farmers now have a respect that's second to none, driving a renewed land and sea agricultural economic engine.

Bone Suckin' Sauce When you make a barbecue sauce in North Carolina, it had better be exceptional. Bone Suckin' Sauce, part of the Ford's Fancy Foods and Gourmet Foods business in Raleigh, has become one of the most beloved and highest taste-ranked sauces in the world.

Ben and Karen Barker The Barkers have been chef and owners of Magnolia Grill in Durham for over twenty years. Long before it was fashionable, they were sourcing from local farmers and even guarantying crops.

American Livestock Breeds Conservancy In a small office in Pittsboro, a group of dedicated folks are successfully protecting the genetic diversity of American livestock.

Larry's Beans A quirky coffee roaster dedicated to fair trade and obsessed with quality. Its plant leaves a very small carbon footprint through its use of solar energy, recycling rainwater, and the prudent use of building materials from demolished properties.

Alex Hitt, Peregine Farms Alex is like the "granddaddy" of local agriculture. Farming for twenty-eight years, he is considered the best when it comes to small acreage production.

And Never Forget Barbecue!

www.ediblecommunities.com/piedmont/peopleplacesthings

SOUTHWEST

It was not so long ago that we heard there was some puzzlement over where our food comes from. The answer, of course, is that it comes from nature—from the land and seas, and from the people who nurture and gather it in to be sent to our tables.

But in the southwestern portion of the North American continent, where so much of the land is arid or semiarid, it might appear to folks from elsewhere that not much is growing, much less anything good to eat, save a few cattle. We all know that the Southwest is famous for beef and also for chile peppers, tortillas, and beans, among other things. But where is all this food coming from in a land with so much dry sagebrush?

Unfortunately, a little too much of it is imported or grown on large industrial farms that rely heavily on irrigation. But take a few minutes to delve into the region's natural history and you'll start to grasp where the real local foods might be hidden. The answer might be that it's in plain sight.

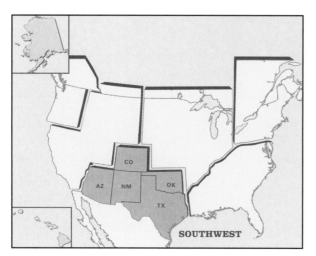

SOUTHWEST

Mesquite, for example, the most common shrub (or small tree) across a huge swath of the Southwest, is not just good for making charcoal to throw on the grill. In fact, that non-necessary usage now threatens this valuable member of the desert ecosystem, which both harbors and feeds a whole host of creatures. The shrub produces protein-rich pods that once were a staple of the native diet and could be an important food once again. People here are harvesting the pods from their own yards and milling them into flour. Home cooks not keen on gathering and milling their own are purchasing mesquite flour from Native Seed/SEARCH or finding it at independent-thinking grocery stores, such as Whole Foods. Local chefs are using mesquite flour to wonderful effect at their restaurants.

A little less surprising as a food source would be the ubiquitous cacti, which might appear (to those same folks from elsewhere) as little more than prickly sculptures decorating the landscape. Several species offer up excellent fruits as well as succulent buds and pads (young branches) used commonly in Mexican and Mexican-influenced cuisines. Likewise, the regal-looking agave, with its impressive rosette of dusky-green spikes, has a core that is very sweet and delicious when roasted. You can buy pieces of agave core on the streets in Mexico, where its most common use is for tequila and mezcal production. Agave nectar is becoming a popular sweetener and is available nearly everywhere in the Southwest—and beyond.

Among the foods for which the Southwest is celebrated, certainly it's the chile pepper that's the best known. Lots of people enjoy New Mexico green chiles, which are canned and widely available, and it's not hard to find a chile aficionado who can reel off local place-

names, such as Hatch or Chimayó, that represent chile *terroir.* Those interested in knowing the wild ancestor of these varieties (and most cultivated peppers, for that matter) have sought out the chiltepín, which, according to the organization known as RAFT (Renewing America's Food Traditions), "grows naturally in canyons and sierras from West Texas through the Sky Islands of southern Arizona, southward into Sonora, Chihuahua, and adjacent states."

Corn, or maize, is another symbolic food of the Southwest, and while substantial harvests of sweet corn do indeed come from the ground in Texas and Colorado, the corn varieties that thrive in the arid regions are those that produce the drier and starchier kernels destined to become hominy, or the masa harina (cornmeal) used in the production of tortillas, tamales, etc. The Hopi people of Arizona, whose corn-growing heritage is part of their ancient, uninterrupted, and deeply spiritual life traditions, plant their corn deep into the ground to access the precious moisture of their desert region.

Tepary beans, also historically grown by the native populations, are making a big impact in the local foods scene, due to their nutritive value, great flavor, and ability to be dry farmed. With greater demand, these plants will be more widely tended, and since they grow here naturally, planting more of them can promote a healthy ecosystem.

Food on the hoof (and paw, and belly), such as bison, deer, elk, rabbit, and, yes, rattlesnake, is not always so easy to spot on a casual stroll through the sagebrush, but most of these creatures are plentiful and very good to eat, if you can catch them! A few ranchers in the Southwest (such as a bison rancher in Texas who you will meet later in this chapter; see page 92) are working to raise some of these animals for sustainable commercial production. Small cattle, sheep, pig, and poultry ranchers as well are learning that there is a big market for pastured hormone-, antibiotic-, and cruelty-free meat, and there is hope that this demand could start to put pressure on standard industrial ranching to shift its practices. Some ranchers are discovering value in helping to save heritage breeds, such as the Spanish goat, Red Wattle pig, Gulf Coast sheep, Criollo Corriente bull, Texas longhorn cattle, and Navajo Churro sheep (a Spanish breed introduced in the sixteenth century and whose wool is integral to the Navajo weaving tradition).

The work going on in the Southwest to save heritage foods and associated food traditions is being aided and abetted by an ardent group of organizations, such as Desert Harvesters, Dine' be' Iiná, Inc. (The Navajo Lifeway), Native Seed/SEARCH, and RAFT, among many others. Also, there is one particular individual, Gary Paul Nabhan, who has been a big instigator in the work to bring native foods back into the public eye.

In speaking of the Southwest region—which, for the purposes of this book, includes Arizona, New Mexico, Texas, and parts of Colorado—we must point out that there are numerous nondesert areas that support full-out production of a wide range of crops. As Marla Camp, publisher of *Edible Austin,* says, farmers in the Lone Star State grow such wonderful Texas-specific items as the Texas Star banana, Texas tart jujube, Lola Queen peach, Texas black persimmon, Texas Shoepeg corn, Texas mission almond, as well as several of the luscious red grapefruit varieties for which the state is famous. She describes Texas as "an ecological, cultural and musical crossroads," where many culinary legacies converge as well. Look at the map created by RAFT of the continent's food "nations" and you can see her point: "The Chile Pepper Nation, the Gumbo Nation, the Bison Nation, and the Cornbread Nation are all part of the food traditions and diet in our region."

Marla's hometown of Austin is in central Texas, where there is a strong tradition of artisan food production. There you can find people crafting excellent cheeses and wines, and brewing beer, root beer, and kombucha squash. Farmers here are growing excellent peaches, pecans, lavender, and mushrooms. And, of course, there's plenty of great barbecue.

Conventional agriculture is strong in Texas as a whole, with the USDA reporting in 2000 that a full 18 percent of the state's land is producing crops. However, the online resource Texas Environmental Profiles warns of soil degradation and erosion in those areas if more sustainable practices are not instituted. Looking over to southern Arizona, we see extensive agriculture (much of

it industrial) in the river valleys, where production of lettuce, citrus, and dates results in significant exports. However, all of that depends on irrigation, which was put in place a century or more ago, well before the explosion in this area's population created a large competing demand on water resources. Water is in high demand all over the desert Southwest due to rampant development, meaning that irrigated agriculture will be in danger for the foreseeable future.

In both Arizona and New Mexico, there is a uniquely interesting story about irrigation, going back to the indigenous peoples, who dug canal networks to get water to their crops. Pamela Hamilton, publisher of *Edible Phoenix,* says that the canals built by the Hohokam people in her area were either replaced or built upon by settlers in the eighteenth and nineteenth centuries, and those are still in use. Something similar occurred over much of New Mexico, where about one thousand canal networks, called acequias, developed during the Spanish period as cooperatively run systems. These were remarkable in the way that they provided a social, cultural, political, and some say even spiritual fabric uniting farmers and villages, and also for the way they mimic and expand upon the riparian habitat, integrating trees and shrubs along the riverbank with crop fields, vineyards, and orchards. This stands in contrast with the high water use of commercial housing development and industrial agriculture.

Kate Manchester, publisher of *Edible Santa Fe*, is both hopeful and cautious about the state of agriculture in her area, saying, "Most every farmer I have ever met in New Mexico is a steward of the land and water—because both are in precious short supply here. New Mexican life was and still is rural agrarian, and there are countless programs at the university, and elsewhere, that teach permaculture and sustainability principles. Because there is no water, we live in the high desert, and the soil is poor, there are many examples of farmers and growers here who place sustainable practices at the forefront of their work—because it's the only way to survive.

Real Pollo

The Red Label Bird with the Gold Medal Flavor

I knew the name pertained to chickens, but what kind of a bird was La Belle Rouge?

I gathered it was a beautiful red chicken, but what else? Curious, I called Don Bixby of the American Livestock Breeds Conservancy, my main information source when it comes to rare breeds. "It's not a breed, it'a protocol," Don explained, leaving me baffled until I discovered that it's not *la belle* but *label*. Label Rouge. Red Label.

Eventually Don confessed that he had experienced the same confusion. But now we know; it's a brand. The name is a sign, like a blue ribbon or gold medal, that suggests one can expect excellence; in this case, a very good chicken. Not merely an advertising gimmick, the quality is real.

And Label Rouge chickens are not something imported from France—they're now here in New Mexico. Thanks to Tom Delehanty and his ranch, Pollo Real, we can now experience what savvy French shoppers have known for the past forty years: that chicken can really taste how chicken should taste, and it's nothing like what usually passes for chicken in this country.

Those who know about Joel Salatin and Polyface Farm's innovative chicken tractors, Pollo Real's chicken yurts, and other systems designed to allow birds to range freely on grass might think that these innovative methods started here. But the whole idea of grazing chickens as a production system actually started in France in the 1960s, when some visionary farmers, frustrated by the poor quality of postwar industrialized chicken and poor economics of farming, put together a pasture-based system that would not only produce better-tasting birds, but would produce better income for farmers and reinvigorate rural communities. The program, called Label Rouge, covers other kinds of fowl as well as meats, but pasture-raised chicken is its leading product. It's been successful in accomplishing its various goals.

The main goal of Label Rouge was, most simply, to produce a superior-tasting bird, a chicken that was reminiscent of the farmyard birds so many people had grown up with. Excellent flavor is a hallmark of the program's success, so much so that regular taste tests are conducted to make sure that any participant's birds are of such high quality that they are, in the program's words, "vividly distinguishable" from conventionally raised chickens. Not just better, but vividly so.

This superior flavor is gained by putting a great number of protocols in place, the most important one having to do with the genetics of the birds. Label Rouge uses slow-growing birds that take three months to reach maturity, in contrast to the six weeks allotted for the industrial Cornish crossbreed. These hybrid birds bred from "rustic" stock are big, hearty chickens that are innately well suited to life outdoors. Tellingly, two of the four breeds used in the Label Rouge program are called "rangers" because they tend to range far and wide for good things to eat. Being older and kept outdoors except at night results in a chicken that has good flavor and a firm, pleasing texture.

Of course, many things must be in place to achieve high quality besides the breed, and that's where a long list of protocols and practices comes into play. For example, the birds are given nonmedicated feed. They're never fed any animal products or given growth stimulants or other inappropriate additives. They are allowed a minimum life span of twelve weeks and cannot be subjected to a journey of more than two hours or sixty-four miles to a processing plant. Their beaks are not removed nor are their toes trimmed. Whether fenced or not, the chickens are raised in open air—truly in the outdoors, not just given a patch of grass to walk onto. One picture I've seen shows the birds ranging in an unfenced forest. The chickens are housed at night, but the buildings are limited as to the number of birds that can inhabit them, and there can be only four buildings per farm. In between flocks the farm area must be rested for at least three weeks, which is good for the health of the farm.

The list of rules goes on in great detail regarding weight, stock density, feed rations, and so forth. Judgment as to how well the standards are met is given by a third party, but, in spite of the strictness of the program's standards, members tend to surpass them, not unlike those organic farmers here who grow to a higher standard than that allowed by the U.S. Department of Agriculture. Label Rouge standards, however, are higher than the USDA's to begin with. Industrial natural and organic chickens are raised pretty much like other factory-farmed birds. The birds are pushed through their life cycle in six short weeks, which is hard on them. They're also debeaked and clipped, they're kept in crowded conditions, and that so-called access to the outdoors happens only in the last week of their lives. By then they have no interest in going out of doors because they don't know what it is.

While it's not so hard for a restaurant to claim that its chicken is organic, if it's industrial organic you may not find it much more appealing than eating a regular, cheaper supermarket chicken.

All of the protocols demanded by the Label Rouge program result in healthy, well-developed, good-tasting birds. As you would expect, they cost more than idustrial birds, but that hasn't kept Label Rouge from being a success for over forty years. Today it commands 30 percent of the poultry market in France, despite that the cost to the customer is considerably higher. The French are, after all, known to value quality and taste more than Americans do, but a lot of us care about these things, too, and are willing to pay the higher price for high quality and simply enjoy it less often.

Delehanty and his wife, Tracey, have been feeding northern New Mexico good organic, truly pastured chicken since 1997. Until now they've been raising the industry's standard bird, the Cornish cross, but that is about to end.

"Increasingly," Delehanty explained recently over lunch, "we've found problems with the birds. The eggs come contaminated with *E. coli* and septicemia, but the company won't tell us that or provide us with a test, so I have to take my chicks in to have them tested for disease and contamination, which is especially important for us since we don't us the antibiotics that are part and parcel of large-scale industrial poultry. This isn't the case in Europe. The French chickens are thoroughly tested by the breeders for all important viruses and diseases, including avian flu, before they're sent out; they're far more rigorous in their standards, so we feel much better about their quality."

Delehanty also points out that compared to the giants of the chicken industry, Pollo Real is far too small

to be heard let alone catered to, so essentially it's not a situation that can improve. While Pollo Real's grazing methods, organic feed, and better care have resulted in excellent chicken, Delehanty, who comes from generations of Wisconsin chicken farmers and has a feel for the old barnyard breeds, has longed to be doing something with more interesting breeds of birds. I wondered if he was interested in raising old American varieties, such as those watched over by the American Livestock Conservancy Board.

"They're great birds," Delehanty says, "but far too slow growing to make sense commercially. They take even longer to mature."

So it turns out that the rustic hybrids in the Label Rouge program fit his needs far better than old breeds. As for their flavor, that was confirmed when the Delehantys traveled to Italy in 2004 to attend Terra Madre, the meeting of 5,000 small-scale food producers from 132 countries put on by Slow Food International. There they were able to taste some Red Label birds that had been brought to the gigantic food fair by some French poultry farmers. "They kept giving us these little pieces," Delehanty recalls, "but even so they tasted like a good yard bird. We really liked it."

Eventually a breeder came to the United States via France, England, and Canada, and started raising the hybrid chickens—Poulet Nu, a reddish-brown bird with a naked neck; the Gourmet Black, "which looks a lot like a Barred Rock," Delehanty says, as well as the Bronze and Gray Rangers, vigorous foragers that like to roam far for their food. The Rangers arrived first at Pollo Real, then the Nus and the Gourmet Blacks. I asked Delehanty what it was like working with new breeds of birds after so many years with the Cornish crosses. "They're beautiful!" he enthused. "Their colors are just gorgeous, and they have these long legs and handsome heads. They stand a lot taller, and they're much more active than the other birds. You'll never see them park themselves by the feed. They go right out into the yard and graze. They need less protein than other birds, but even so, they grow pretty fast, and with those longer legs, you get more muscle." More muscle means better texture.

Despite the speedy maturation of the breed, Delehanty follows the French rules, raising the chickens for twelve weeks, which is partly what gives them better flavor and greater size. A six-pound bird makes a magnificent Sunday dinner. To find out whether there

Tom Delehanty with one of his favorite redheads

really was a difference in taste, I roasted the regular bird and the Label Rouge bird side by side. Using no herbs, I just rubbed them with salt, put them in a searing hot cast-iron skillet, and roasted them at 475 degrees, turning three times in all. I carved each bird and served the pieces to three people who didn't know which was which. While carving, I could hardly stop tasting the Red Label bird; it was so good, and the experience was the same for my tasters. Two of them commented on the utter deliciousness of the French bird—it clearly had better flavor than the cross—and it was also firmer-fleshed. The third taster, my husband, doesn't much like chicken in the first place. Accordingly, he found the French birds too "chickeny." But then, that's just the point—they really are chickens, and they do have their own real flavor. They taste like chicken can and should!

Next week at the Santa Fe Farmers Market I asked other people if they had tried Pollo Real's French chickens. Those who had raved.

"Incredible flavor!" enthused one.

"They were so moist," recalled another.

"Fantastic!" exclaimed a third, while a fourth mentioned that the meat was darker and juicier.

Interestingly, these are pretty much the same kinds of comments that have been made about the heritage turkeys Delehanty raises, which are also rustic breeds: They're juicier, have darker meat, firmer texture, more flavor, and tend to be more elongated and less ball-like in shape.

With so much enthusiasm from Delehanty and the customers for the new birds, I had to ask him what the challenges were for him when it comes to raising them. "There aren't any, really," he said. "In fact, they're a joy. We're creating a culture of food, and by sharing our food and what we know, hopefully we can change the direction of industrial organic to food that comes from the heart and soul. In the end, cheap food is cheap. It devalues everything and makes us, as a people, incredibly unrealistic." The beautiful French chickens aren't cheap, but they have great value. You'll know when you cook one that this is doing chicken right.

DEBORAH MADISON, *cookbook author and founding chef of Greens restaurant, has been connecting the dots between eaters and growers by writing about farmers and food producers for the past ten years. She's especially fond of Tom and his big chickens!*

The Seasonal Muse

Life at Boggy Creek Farm

Winter . . . our favorite culinary season! Even the Boggy Creek chickens cluck in joyous anticipation for the cold-season greens that take over the farm from November to April.

Just after dawn on a December day, the harvest ladies (mother and daughter Marias and Andrea, and I) head out to the field to cut broccoli and cauliflower, pull root crops, and bunch greens. But first we have to pause and admire the beauty before us. In undulating rows stretching over two hundred feet, south to north, various greens, freshly dewed and intensely colored under a leaden sky, paint a vivid canvas: green chards ribbed in red, white, and yellow; broccoli leaves tinted viridian green; the gray-green "bubbled" dinosaur kale against the bright greens of spinach, carrots, snow peas, and arugula; the glossy green romaines, some freckled with burgundy; and the warmer-hued cauliflower and mustard greens. The view is pure ecstasy for greens lovers. We taste all of it with our eyes first.

Now out in the field, bundled against the cold and garbed in canary yellow slickers if it's raining, we bend, constantly, to the task of selecting the best leaves for bunches, then place the individual leaves in one hand while we cut more. Often, for support and to save our backs, we prop on one knee the elbow of the hand that's grasping the growing bunch. Finally, the unwieldy bouquet is corralled with a rubber band, the ends of the stalks trimmed, and then the bunch is placed atop others in the waiting wheelbarrow.

We aim for at least ten or twelve varieties of greens for market, including the leaves of Brussels sprouts, broccoli, and cauliflower. Many years ago, our friend John Welsch suggested (and was enthusiastically supported by our chickens) that these *Brassica* leaves are quite edible. Indeed, there is even more nutrition in the leaves and stalks than in the flower buds.

Unfortunately, through the winter months, the chickens are confined to their large run, which, tragically, has a great view of the fields. If they were to roam free all day, their wise lust for greens would easily demolish the first six feet of every row. However, any visitor walking the farm in winter knows that this is not an ironclad prohibition. Monitored visitation to the bounty is sometimes tolerated, and the little telltale triangular pieces of pecked-out spots on the leaves at hen level are the proof. (Folks not in the know must think we have a real problem growing a complete row of good-looking greens.)

To further compensate for the tantalizing view from the henhouse, I harvest cosmetically imperfect larger leaves and haul armloads of them to the run, where the deliriously happy occupants quickly eat them down to the ribs—pinning the stalks to the ground with their feet for leverage. They would finish off the stalks and ribs, too, if they had teeth—another injustice.

In wheelbarrow after wheelbarrow, the vibrant, official bunches of greens are transported to the "salad shed," where they are rinsed, placed stems down in tubs holding an inch or two of water, then immediately trundled to the walk-in cooler. There they will drink and rest for tomorrow's big performance.

On the market tables the next morning, the stars of winter quickly disappear in the first hour. The harvesters hustle to provide an encore via bunches brought still quivering with life from the field to the waiting receptacles. "It's better than growing it yourself," one customer tells me. "Yes," I concur. "You didn't have to bend over, and you didn't have to share with the chickens."

Indeed, small sacrifices are required from both human and hen in order to offer and enjoy the resplendent edible rainbow of cold-loving greens.

CAROL ANN SAYLE *grows nine acres of organic vegetables with her husband, Larry Butler, on two farms. Market days are Wednesday and Saturday, 9 A.M. to 1 P.M., at their East Austin farm. Visit boggycreekfarm.com for more information.*

TransFARMing Suburbia

One Lawn at a Time

When some folks think about farms, they hold an idyllic vision of red barns, chickens, cows and vast fields of vegetables . . . at least that's what I used to dream of. These days I'm doing my best to add a slightly different option to the palette. You see, along with my partner, Kimberly, I operate Community Roots, Boulder's first urban multiplot farm. In case you're new to the term, an urban multiplot farm is a collection of gardens that are situated right in urban homeowners' front- and backyards. Putting a collection of these plots together makes a farm, and a farm is what we have made.

In the fall of 2005, I came up with this crazy idea of using my neighbors' yards for growing vegetables. My goal was to develop an alternate career that would satisfy my desire to farm without my having to lay out large financial investments in land and machinery. After a winter squirming with excitement, I went to work in the spring of 2006. We built a makeshift hoophouse in our backyard to start seedlings and found a few brave neighbors. At that point, I'd had a few years of experience growing vegetables but was not at all prepared to operate anything on this scale—year one was a real roller-coaster ride!

There were times I almost gave up, discouraged because I wasn't sure if this was really a viable enterprise. I needed support, so I did some online research and found Wally Satzewich, who lives in Saskatoon, Saskatchewan, Canada. He and his wife have been successfully farming multiple urban plots for a number of years *and* were making a decent living. That was all the encouragement I needed to keep trudging ahead. Just as I found out about Wally, he was preparing to release a series of guides that outline what he calls SPIN (Small Plot Intensive) farming. Along with his associate, Roxanne Christensen, from Philadelphia's famed Somerton Tanks farm, Wally is spreading the SPIN phenomenon all over the United States with new farmers springing up every day. I'm fortunate to be one of the first in this country to apply the SPIN model. In 2007, we added additional plots, made our first restaurant sales, began selling at the farmers' market, and initiated my proudest achievement yet: our Community Supported Agriculture (CSA) project. We started our CSA with just four member families, but grew to nine by the end of the year. It was a wonderful experience to know that we were growing food for, and creating relationships with, families who lived just down the street from us.

Now, here we are in 2008, growing in thirteen plots that amount to a half acre of intensively cultivated land. Most of these plots are within a few blocks of our house, and three of them are from our next door (and backyard) neighbors. We are selling at the Boulder Farmers' Market consistently on Saturdays, and our CSA has expanded to twenty-five members, partly due to our new relationship with Frank Hodge at Father Earth Farm in Lafayette, who will be growing some of the more space-dependent crops like tomatoes, winter squash, melons, and corn.

We're not doing this alone. We have opened our operations (and our home) to a whole fleet of motivated volunteers, interns, apprentices, and employees. The year 2008 was an experiment in community, and it's proved to be a huge success. We piloted Community Fruits—homeowners allow our crews to harvest and distribute the unused fruit from their trees. We've also added Community Coops to our repertoire, in partnership with a local project called Urban Hens, which builds chicken coops for homeowners. There's room in the model for backyard honey projects, flowers, herbs, and the list goes on and on.

We have a new addition to the team—Steve Morgan, a committed, adventurous soul who is taking the Community Roots model to northern Boulder's Newlands neighborhood. He's developing gardens, planting vegetables, and building community there as part of his SPIN farming debut. My hope is that as Steve and I and others around the state (SPIN farms are getting started in Denver, Fort Collins, and Steamboat Springs) are creating an economically feasible model of urban agricultural entrepreneurship that will engender more locally grown food, more connected communities, and healthier cities. As energy costs rise, food costs

Kipp Nash tending one of Boulder's urban "farms"

will continue to soar, creating an environment that makes local growing pay off. Small-acreage farmers and multiplot urban farmers are on the cutting edge of a lively and important market, gaining and retaining skills for more security in an uncertain future.

Every day I hear from folks who find inspiration in Community Roots. I think growing food and creating community are things that everyone yearns for. People are latching on to the idea of Community Roots because Community Roots gives us a real outlet right here in our cities to do these things. There are a number of levels one can get involved in. Everyone can grow vegetables. Grow in your backyard, your front yard, or use a community garden plot or a windowsill, if you live in an apartment. If you want to get involved in growing for your community, start a neighborhood garden club. Interested in multiplot farming or small-acreage farming? Look at the SPIN farming Web site (www.spin-farming.com) or hunt down one of the SPIN farmers in Colorado. If you want to sharpen your skills, volunteer at a farm.

It's time that we all find our passion in caring for each other and the planet. The global economy is coming back to the local economy. I'm tickled because I see how "going local" really means coming together as community. Know that with enough elbow grease and determination dreams can become reality . . . even if you have to let go of the romance of the red barn and the fields of grain.

KIPP NASH *is in his fourth year of operating Community Roots from his home in South Boulder's Martin Acres neighborhood. He lives with his partner, Kimberly, and her twelve-year-old son, Kaleb. For more information on their project, visit www.communityrootsboulder.com.*

At Home on the Range

A Profile of Thunder Heart Bison

In the morning, before the heat sets in, Hugh Fitzsimmons drives his truck down rutted wheel tracks, looking for signs of his bison herd. He's in no hurry, though his ranch is vast. "Thirteen thousand acres," he says. "More than I deserve."

Five miles per hour is slow enough to notice the richness in the endless grass, and Hugh likes to point out the details. Whip snake. Roadrunner. Jack rabbit. Mesquite. A 1920s-era windmill, revolving slowly.

Hugh has a copy of this land's original Spanish grant, made to one Juan Francisco Lobrano in 1811. His family has raised cattle here—on more than 40,000 acres now partitioned among the Fitzsimmons siblings—since 1935. It's hard to imagine that it ever looked much different, if you take out the power lines, tire tracks, and a few semimodern houses and outbuildings.

In fact, you could argue that the land's most significant transformation took place long before Señor Lobrano, in 1753, when the last southern bison was sighted in Dimmit County. Its second most important moment occurred in 1995, when Hugh began bringing bison back to the land, a few at a time. Today, his herd is three hundred strong.

"I wanted something that would take care of itself," Hugh remembers. "Not a lot of vet bills. Something indigenous."

Bison fit the bill. For hundreds of years, until being decimated by hunters who killed for tongues and hides but left bodies to rot, bison have been indigenous to huge sections of North America. But by the mid-1800s, American red meat was synonymous with cattle, a relatively new import to the plains. Cattle could be fattened, shipped, butchered, and sold in a way that seems impossible and unsustainable to a few iconoclastic ranchers like Hugh.

"Most cattle end up in feedlots, and we've basically destroyed them with diseases and hormones," Hugh says.

In *The Worst Hard Time,* a brutal account of how the destruction of the prairie created the Dust Bowl, Timothy Egan describes bison as "the finest grass-eating creature on four legs."

Hugh takes it further: "Even the hoof of the buffalo is the shape of a sharp spade," he says. "It flips over the earth, aerates it, and then flips it back." Grassland sustains bison; bison sustain grassland. The trick, Hugh says, is not to interfere.

"Ranching is really simple," a professor once told him. "It's keeping it simple that's hard."

Hugh tries to keep his ranch simply, even as his Thunder Heart Bison becomes an increasingly complex business. Hugh and his wife, Sarah, began by selling bison meat at Austin farmers' markets and quickly expanded. After they won the prestigious international Gallo Family Vineyards Gold Medal Award (in the meat and charcuterie division), high-end chefs developed a taste for Thunder Heart Bison—not just as a cutting-edge ingredient, but as delicious, healthy, grass-fed red meat—lean, high in protein, and every bit as flavorful as the fanciest aged beef.

Beyond meat, Hugh's bison also produce robes (luxurious rugs), decorative skulls, polished horns, and supple, high-rent buffalo-hide bags sophisticated enough to fly off shelves at boutiques in places like Aspen, Colorado.

"I never get over how hard this animal works for us," Hugh says. "In life and in death."

There's no way around the fact that bison have to die to produce bison products, and that's what will happen today—not a slaughter but a harvest. Hugh sent his very first bison to a slaughterhouse but found the adrenaline-soaked meat inedible. After that, he became a "field harvester," shooting a very few four-year-old animals in their natural habitat, pulling the trigger himself, in full view of the rest of the herd.

Hugh knows of only two other bison ranchers who harvest this way, though he's sure there must be a few others.

This is a very strange development—that a killing method Hugh considers by far the most humane isn't more widely used.

At about 10 A.M., ranch foreman Freddie Longoria and USDA inspector Bob Flowers meet Hugh not far from where he hopes to encounter bison. At any given time, his herd ranges over his entire acreage, having separated itself into the social/family groups Hugh calls "pods." Each pod contains both sexes and all generations.

Bison harvest days provide Bob his few chances to do his job outdoors instead of inside a slaughter-house. He's come prepared to do both a premortem—determining whether the animals to be harvested are healthy—and the postmortem—analyzing blood samples for traces of antibiotics, disease, or added hormones. He's never found anything of the sort in a Thunder Heart Bison, but rules are rules. Besides, he and Hugh enjoy their friendly, slightly sarcastic rapport.

The day is fresh and sunny, pleasantly scented with sage. As soon as Hugh's truck appears in the clearing, about twenty-five bison come racing over, massive but surprisingly agile. A few cows with young calves stand farther away; an old bull hangs out by himself; the young males seem to spend all their time chasing each other, sparring, wallowing (another sign of aggressive posturing), and attempting to mount passing cows, who generally ignore them. It's hard not to graft human personalities onto the herd.

"Well, I learned my lesson about that," Hugh recalls. "I had a bull, somewhat domesticated—when I gave him alfalfa cubes, he just walked right up and took them from me. But one day I ran out of cubes. I just held my hands up, and he slammed his head at me. He didn't hit me. He stopped *just* short. Still, I felt all 2,100 pounds of him run through me—it totally electrified my body. Never again will I treat one of these animals like a pet. They're wild animals."

After dispersing alfalfa cubes to lure a few bison away from the coming harvest, Hugh rolls down the driver's side window and spends a long time pinpointing young bulls who can produce the bone-in rib-eye racks to send to the upscale restaurant Daniel in New York City. "These are French chefs," Hugh tells Bob. "They like their fat."

A tractor and a refrigeration truck drive into the clearing. Hugh waits for them to cut their engines. A huge older bull approaches the passenger side of the truck, making a loud, deep, prehistoric sound, like water gurgling down a colossal drain. His giant head looms less than six feet from the car window.

Conversation in Hugh's truck dwindles. At the end of the "alone time" he always takes to prepare himself for the kill, Hugh picks up his rifle and hits the stereo's ON button. The sound of Oscar Peterson's liquid piano riffs floats into the air, blending, in a counterintuitive way, with the general stillness.

Hugh raises his rifle, waits several minutes for a humane shot to present itself, then shoots, hitting one animal just behind the ear, successfully severing its medulla oblongata. The bull drops instantly onto its side.

As soon as they hear the *pop* of Hugh's gun, the cows disappear into the underbrush, chasing their calves ahead of them, but showing none of the terror of a deer running from a man-made noise. They seem only to have decided that a field with a *pop* is no place for a calf.

Meanwhile, the young bulls amble closer, some touching their huge heads to the dying animal.

"It's normal behavior," Bob observes. "They're community creatures, and they sometimes rub up on each other at times like this."

The felled bull's head rises and falls; then it's over. In the next ten minutes, Hugh shoots three more bison, this time while standing a short distance from the truck. The rest of the pod still shows no signs of leaving, so Hugh drives his truck slowly through the clearing, throwing alfalfa cubes to lure them farther from the tractor that has pulled in next to the first dead bull.

In less than half an hour, the tractor has hauled each animal up by one foot to let its blood drain out, then loaded all four into a refrigeration truck for the trip to the processing plant, where they'll be turned into a variety of cuts of meat, including the French racks.

Hugh waves his arms at the remaining bison, perhaps shooing them away or maybe in some kind of salute. Either way, they disappear over a rise, into a less inhabited part of the ranch.

"Every time I pull the trigger, I think this is the worst thing and the best thing," says Hugh, emerging from his centered mood. "You're taking a life and you have to do it correctly, honoring the animal. It's a pretty heavy thing."

"I understand that," Bob agrees. "I have friends who ask me how I can do what I do for a living. I tell them that the T-bone they eat has to come from somewhere."

Nobody on the ranch today was inclined to flinch from the truth. American carnivores have always eaten bison, once so necessary to maintain the grassland that supported so many forms of life. And now, after a long interruption, Hugh's land, his family, and people as far away as the East Coast are being sustained by bison again. "It makes you grateful for every bite you put in your mouth," he says.

ROBIN CHOTZINOFF *is a freelance writer and the author of* People with Dirty Hands: The Passion for Gardening *and the memoir* Holy Unexpected. *She thinks there is no better place to grow and eat food than Austin, Texas.*

Distilling Peak Spirits

Once past the unlocked gate, the short road into the heart of Jack Rabbit Hill mimics a western rendition of a Wyeth painting: rustic grasslands, delicate light, and a familiar sense of place. The house on the hill is home to the Hanson family, Jack Rabbit Hill Estate Winery, and Peak Spirits, a premier biodynamic distiller.

Surrounded by vast, panoramic vistas of the North Fork Gunnison Valley, state-of-the-art equipment on the idyllic ranch generates more than twenty varieties of spirits—eaux-de-vie, grappa, and whimsical aperitifs, along with smooth, full-bodied vodka and gin. While their strengths and flavors vary, the soul of every Peak Spirit is local, organic fruit. The fruit is the

essence of this venture and the force that lured Anna and Lance Hanson to Western Colorado.

In 2001, she was a fourth-grade teacher, he a software executive in Northern California. Family brought them to Hotchkiss that summer, where Lance's parents and his sister, Heidi, shared seventy-two acres on Redlands Mesa. On their way home, somewhere outside of Reno, Nevada, the couple recalls being struck by a radical idea.

"It was really funny," Anna recalls. "We loved California. We weren't looking for a life change or a reason to leave. Yet here we were, on the road, talking about the farm, and felt a pull, a very strong pull." The land

was a magnet, urging them to return, till the soil, and create something new. "Heidi had sprung the concept of putting in a small organic vineyard, and she was a meticulous farmer," Lance continued. "We had no background in farming, organic or otherwise. But suddenly we envisioned something bigger."

The Hansons sold their home in California and were back on Redlands Mesa within two months. They bought Heidi out, moved into a small barn-apartment on the land, designed and built their new home, and opened Jack Rabbit Hill Winery in time to celebrate their first harvest in September 2002. As the first growers to raise grapes on Redlands Mesa, they faced challenges, not the least of which was a 1,400-foot jump in altitude. They mounted wind machines on thirty-foot towers above the vineyards to blow warm air down into the soil's floor and drive away the frost.

Inside, their first Colorado winter spawned notions beyond the vines. The Hansons' first step was to introduce Jack Rabbit Hill wines to the Aspen Saturday Market. The couple recalls selling their first bottle of wine at 9:15 A.M. on July 5, 2003. "That was the moment," Lance vows, "I was sure the new business was going to work."

The Hansons' next move was a broad strategy to create a cooperative, strictly organic enterprise designed to produce an expanding palette of pure, value-added premium spirits. "We decided to hedge our bets and install a distillery so that we were not so single-threaded, not so dependent on our ability to grow the fruit," says Lance. He and Anna won a grant from a regional land trust designed to preserve local agriculture. Their thesis was a gain-share pricing program, like profit sharing, designed to support neighboring farms by paying them an above-market price for their fruit.

Steve Ela, a fifth-generation farmer and one of four local growers who work with Peak Spirits, speaks highly of his partnership with the Hansons. "Since our annual production is relatively small on the national scale, we have to be creative in using our strengths as an industry," he says.

Ela, who is also president of the board of the Organic Farming Research Foundation based in Santa Cruz, California, regards the collaboration as vital to his own business. "We can direct-market our first- and second-grade fruit, but still have 'thirds'—peaches, apples, pears, and cherries just as good as the firsts, but small or dinged, cosmetically challenged. Peak Spirits

provides an outlet for them, capturing their excellence, the flavor and subtle essences that still distinguish them as a premium grade fruit." The venture essentially minimizes Ela's risk by recycling what used to be his waste.

The Hansons used their grant money to hire the consulting services of Jorg Rupf, founder of Hangar One Vodka in California and the first organic microdistiller in the United States. Anna and Lance built the small distillery shed with the help of a local plumber and electrician, assembling a 150-liter, German-made Holstein copper pot still two days before Jorg's arrival. They were giddy with excitement.

"Jorg is the kingpin in the microdistillery business," Lance explained. "The fact that he was willing to come here and assist us validated what we were doing. He taught us within a matter of two or three days what would have taken us twenty years to learn on our own."

The first Peak Spirit scheduled for production was the eau-de-vie (French for "water of life"), a lush fruit brandy, but a tricky proposition given its relative obscurity in the American marketplace. "We began with brandy because every other small distillery began with vodka," says Lance. "We know it's a niche market. Most people can't even pronounce their names (oh-de-vee), but we spent some time in Europe, developed a passion for these spirits, and saw them as a way to prove ourselves. The phenomenal fruit here provided the essential logic: These brandies are all about showcasing the fruit."

Peak Spirits began distilling eaux-de-vie in spring 2005, targeting the savvy international market just outside their gates—tourists and part-time residents in Aspen, Vail, and Telluride. For the lighter-weights, Peak created peach and pear aperitifs, spirits made with less alcohol (18 versus 40 percent) and a savory, natural sweetness from the juice. The Hansons call them "eau-de-vie on training wheels," bearing the distinctive aroma of the original but with a milder bite.

In July 2006, Peak's organic vodka hit the market, followed fifteen months later by their gin—the first USDA-certified organic gin produced in the United States. All Peak Spirits are distilled in small batches, hence the term "microdistilling," an industry growing rapidly in this country, but still limited to about fifty licensed businesses nationwide.

According to Anna, pot stilling produces a "more expressive, more complex spirit," due to the time, labor, and attention invested in the technique.

The Hansons crush their fruit whole, pits included, to create the "mash," which is then fermented in 2,000-liter stainless steel vats (made in Italy) and moved through the distillery on forklifts. The still produces a high-powered brew, between 65 percent alcohol and 200 proof. Some varieties, including the vodka and the grappas, are redistilled to create more neutral spirits. All are ultimately "cut back" to ingestible levels with pure mountain spring water from a private source on CapRock, a scenic lava-rock formation twenty miles above the ranch on Grand Mesa.

Today, Peak Spirits is one of only two biodynamic distilleries in North America. In June 2008, Jack Rabbit Hill and Peak Spirits became Demeter-certified biodynamic, completing a two-year transition from the USDA-certified organic practices. Rudolf Steiner, founder of the holistic system that predated organic farming in 1920s Germany, believed that biodynamics could reinstate agriculture to its vital role in fusing people to the land.

Following the 2008 grape harvest at Jack Rabbit Hill, Hanson released CapRock Biodynamic Vodka, Peak Spirits Biodynamic Estate Grappas, and Jack Rabbit Hill Biodynamic Estate Wines.

Lance and Anna Hanson, along with a growing number of local farmers, all agree that working cooperatively enhances culture and grows community. Together they are restoring natural rhythms to Western Colorado by changing the way we eat, drink, and savor the spirit of life.

KAREN CONNINGTON *is a writer inspired by the arts and sustainable innovations for a small planet. She is the former owner of the Heather Gallery in Aspen and Basalt, Colorado.*

Photo by Michael Brands

ARTISAN ~ *EDIBLE SANTA FE* (NEW MEXICO)

Joe S. Sausage

There is a legend in the making in Albuquerque. For two years in a row now, Joe S. Sausage has taken the first-, second-, and third-place honors in the sausage category of the Scovie Awards. These awards are given out to the top-winning contestants at the National Fiery Foods and Barbecue Show held annually in Albuquerque. Joseph C. Cucunato, Jr., better known as "Joe S. Sausage," is fast becoming mythical. Many foodies throughout the town speak of him with great reverence. "He's a professional who makes an honest product in the tradition of Slow Food," states Carey Smoot, chef and owner of Albuquerque's Downtown Gourmet.

Joe is without a doubt the antihero of sausage making. Often attired in clothes befitting a truck driver rather than an epicurean, Joe looks as if he stepped out of a big rig. Complete with black work boots, a baseball cap, and an oversize chained leather wallet, his style is distinctive. But don't be fooled by his looks. Joe is passionate about his craft. His retail store is just off of Rio Grande Boulevard in a back alley behind Bath, Brush, and Beyond, a dog-grooming salon.

Trained as a microbiologist, Joe spent his days toiling in a lab before moving west in 1997. He left his hometown of Kenosha, literally the heart of Wisconsin sausage country, and laid claim to a new land and a new venture in Albuquerque. With him he carried a deep-rooted cultural sensibility and memory of his family's ancestral roots in Calabria, Italy. Once settled in Albuquerque, Joe began to yearn to better know his heritage. He needed a way to reconnect, and sausage was the definitive remedy. At first it was Italian sausage, which his grandparents had made so often, that sparked his senses. After countless tastes of supermarket sausage and attempts to re-create a memory, Joe realized that "I was out of my element. It was a desolate culinary landscape, and I had had it." Thus began his search for

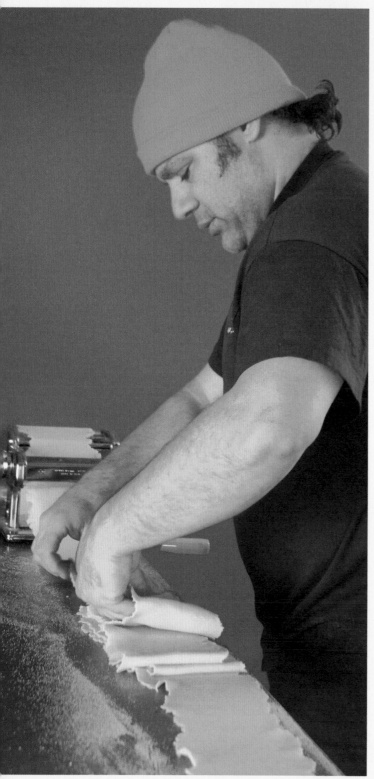

Joseph Cucunato stacks sheets of his handmade pasta.

the right recipe and quality ingredients that would satisfy his taste. After experimenting in earnest, Joe finally made his first Italian sausages.

Today Joe is passionate about quality and freshness and uses only certified organic pork and chicken from Wholesome Harvest in Iowa (www.wholesomeharvest .com). The sausages are made country style, chunkier to the bite than their ordinary supermarket cousins. Joe prefers using as many locally grown spices and herbs as he can, often picking whatever herbs he needs from his own garden. Along the way Joe has found himself also making pasta for his growing customer base. As with his sausage, Joe uses quality ingredients—Italian semolina flour, water, and olive oil for the pasta.

Fillings for his handmade raviolis can include anything from his fresh Italian sausage to fresh mozzarella or feta, Gorgonzola, and kalamata olives. They are simmered for seven and a half minutes in sea-salted water, lightly drizzled with extra virgin olive oil, topped with crushed red pepper, a sprinkling of sea salt, and Pecorino Romano cheese. They have a sexy luster and are perfect "to the teeth," leaving you craving for more.

Joe is a minimalist in many regards. He uses a rolling pin and a stainless steel, hand-cranked pasta machine, and relies on his nose, taste, and sense memory when he creates his handmade sausage. Production is limited, and the sausage line is as eclectic as his clientele. He has a handwritten board with the day's offerings, which can include Sweet and Hot Italian, Polish, Bangers, Jamaican Jerk, Maple Blueberry, New Mexican Roast, Andouille, Chicken Basil, Bacon Sausage, and Sausage Centurion, which is made with bay leaf, cracked pepper, crushed red pepper, roasted piñon, and, of course, pork. He is creative and experimental, and there are new sausages appearing on his board regularly.

As spring neared in Joe's neighborhood, a wafting of something incredible spiced the air. There he was in his shop, making Grilled Paella Under Sausage.

RANDY SHAMLIAN *is a freelance food writer and film producer who has practiced the culinary arts for more than thirty years, winning several contests along the way for his apple pies. He is the author of* A Slice of Apple Pie.

Photo by Jennifer Esperanza

Neighborhood Gathering Place

A Day at the Downtown Phoenix Public Market

It's not yet daylight when the regular crew of four homeless men shows up to help Cindy Gentry, mastermind and executive director of the Downtown Phoenix Public Market, set up before the vendors arrive. It's strangely quiet as the men position the tents, tables, and shade screens, transforming the drab, empty, inner-city parking lot into an inviting space for the 1,500 shoppers who will start arriving in about two hours. They work in unison and without interruption as the sun comes up and begins to warm the air. Rosie, known to the regulars as "the market dog," wanders the market, sniffing for food and greeting the familiar vendors as they begin to arrive.

Nuna Dow arrives early. This is her first day at the market. She's managed to find a parking spot close to her table, but unloading all the food and paraphernalia she has carted to the market to decorate her table is proving more difficult than she had anticipated. Nuna, a former restaurateur, caterer, and food writer, is now a vendor at the market. She's offering Middle Eastern cooked food for carry-out or to eat at the market. It's obvious she's a market novice because she isn't familiar with the routine. But she gets into a groove quickly enough as the shoppers trickle in and her young helper arrives to dish out samples of an intoxicatingly delicious lentil soup. Other vendors come to sample her food. This is a congenial atmosphere, and vendors help each other by sending shoppers to other tables, so it's important for everyone to know who and what's new.

The market opened on a rainy day in February 2005 with just fourteen vendors and has grown to almost sixty. Maya Dailey, a local small farmer, was among the first fourteen. Maya's business is a family affair, with her teenage son and daughter helping out with setup, selling, and teardown. The Market regulars flock to Maya's space for the freshest herbs, vegetables, flowers, and freshly laid eggs. The sweet smell of basil permeates the air around her stall as shoppers crowd around the produce, examining each bunch of radishes while they chat with Maya about the best way to serve the gloriously fresh kale she's brought that day.

The fun of shopping at a farmers' market is that you never know what you're going to find. "It's sort of like a culinary Christmas every week, to see what kind of magic someone has culled from our harsh climate," says Sloane Burwell, a regular who has missed only about three days since the market opened. "I've gotten to try a whole range of things I hadn't had before like Africa Burr gherkins and Armenian cucumbers and Sambuca Blueberry Jam."

One of the newest vendors is a tomato farmer who has brought bushels of beautiful heirloom varieties of all sizes, shapes, and colors. In a month, he'll probably be gone, as the season for tomatoes in the desert comes to a close, but right now his fine-looking crop of colorful fruit is creating a stir as word travels through the market that there are fresh tomatoes for sale.

The mix of vendors makes this market unique. Everything for sale at the market is grown or made by the person selling it. In addition to fresh local produce from Maya or One Windmill Farms or Crooked Sky Farms, there are handmade chocolates by Wei of Chocolate, locally produced olive oils from Queen Creek Olive Mill, freshly made farmer cheese from the women at Rainbow Valley Nursery, and lip-smacking BBQ pulled pork sandwiches from Grady and his wife, Carolyn, not to mention amazingly tasty bean pie from Nubian Queen Universal Catering. Shoppers can buy handmade aprons or expertly crafted wooden jewelry made from fallen Arizona trees directly from the artists themselves. Market goers are serenaded by up-and-coming musicians while they stroll past merchants offering handmade soaps and tie-dyed children's clothes and fused glass wall hangings and handbags made from recycled newspapers. It's a cornucopia of shopping opportunities.

Cindy is the brains and very often the brawn at the market. Her vision of creating a venue that would serve as a neighborhood gathering place as well as an opportunity for commerce is a reality because of her dedication to the project. Through her tireless efforts,

Cindy has managed to convince civic leaders, community organizers, politicians, and just about everyone that a public market serving the downtown community is a necessity. The market exists to bring the community together, to provide an outlet for local foodstuffs, to encourage minority- and women-owned businesses, and to provide shopping for local residents in what is still pretty much a food desert with little access to retail sources of fresh foods.

The neighborhood around the market, like many others in big cities around the country, is in a period of revitalization and gentrification of real estate, with services like food stores and retail lagging behind, so the Market makes an important contribution to the quality of life for the area's residents. The demographics of downtown Phoenix have slowly changed from a business center, bustling during the day but deserted at night, to a vital hub of young families, singles, and retirees who want to be close to the cultural and sports centers in the heart of the city. Arizona State University, with its main campus in Tempe, has recently opened a downtown campus and dormitories, creating an influx of younger people who are looking for places to eat, play, and shop. The Downtown Phoenix Public Market provides not only a place for them to buy food but also to learn and interact with the rest of the local community.

The market's mission to improve the health and welfare of the commuity is evidenced in part by the educational opportunities offered by the Permaculture Guild, a group of enthusiastic environmental proponents. The Guild, a nonprofit education organization with a mission to create green living solutions, offers weekly workshops in landscaping, vegetable gardening, and raising backyard chickens in addition to other classes. The topics focus on how to accomplish gardening in the desert climate in a sustainable and environmentally sound way.

The workshops are held in an indoor space adjacent to the outdoor market. If all fund-raising efforts go as hoped, the indoor space—approximately 3,800 square feet—will be dedicated as a grocery store open six days a week (the outdoor market is now open one day and one evening a week) featuring wares and foods of the market vendors and other regional producers, as well as local wines and beers.

Open-air markets should be a rarity in the desert, with summertime temperatures in Phoenix hovering around 110 degrees many days. Much of what makes the location workable during the heat has been donated. Huge blowers and shade cloth hung from the poles that support the tents over the vendor tables help to keep patrons and merchants from roasting. Market customers are a hearty lot undeterred by the weather, determined to get fresh produce before the summer heat has a chance to wilt both the food and the vendors. Some even linger despite what can be a suffocating heat because this is community at its best. People mill around, tasting, inspecting, and chatting.

Cindy darts from vendor to vendor making certain each one has what she needs to succeed that day. Cindy is a hands-on CEO who doesn't mind getting her hands dirty. She sets up tents, carries water, empties garbage, and soothes frayed nerves, always being available and accessible to everyone. All the neighborhood regulars know Cindy. They expect her to be there, and she never disappoints them. She watches lovingly over the Downtown Phoenix Public Market. At one point, she makes a recommendation to a volunteer in an unusually demanding way that is out of character. In a minute, she returns to apologize for being so pushy. But that's the way mamas are about their kids and the market is most certainly Cindy's baby.

As the market winds down for the day, some shoppers hang around to pick up the last remaining items for sale. The vendors pack up quickly, chattering to one aother about the day's events. The same group of volunteers who came at daybreak to set up is back to dismantle the equipment. Rosie is back, licking up spilled drinks and dropped food. In a short time, the bustling market is a drab parking lot again, waiting for its next transformation into a neighborhood gem.

SHARON SALOMON, *MS, RD, is a registered dietitian, freelance writer, and dedicated eater who hopes to someday meet the challenge of balancing all the calories she consumes in the interest of research with enough exercise to keep her weight stable.*

The Gentle Giant

....

Chef Greg LaPrad of Quiessence

Ah, the glamorous life of a chef—or so it seems on TV. Instead, picture a young man in a blood-spattered white jacket, hunched over the large carcass of a steer, cleaver in hand, ready to dismember the animal. For a chef like Greg LaPrad, however, who is passionate about every aspect of food, this is the life of his dreams.

Greg, a graduate of Johnson & Wales, is the young, energetic, curious, stubborn, disciplined, very serious chef who now heads up the kitchen at Quiessence Restaurant and Wine Bar at the Farm at South Mountain in Phoenix, Arizona. The restaurant, located on a working farm, is reached by driving down a dirt road lined with pecan trees. It is rustic, tranquil, and surely one of the most individual restaurants in Arizona, both for its location and the culinary philosophy of its chef, a gentle giant of a man dedicated to serving the best that Arizona has to offer.

Greg spent his formative years in Massachusetts in an area where farm stands and cornfields were commonplace. His family had a vegetable garden in the yard, and they made their own wine. LaPrad's mother, at least in his early years, was a stay-at-home-mom who took great pride in preparing multicourse elaborate meals for her family even on weekdays. Dinnertime at the LaPrad household was never just a tuna sandwich.

Greg's kitchen initiation came after his parents divorced. His mother spent less time cooking, so Greg took over. As a teen, Greg spent months working on and perfecting his marinara sauce.

After his parents' breakup, Greg spent weekends with his father, also a cooking enthusiast. They shopped for food together on Saturday afternoons and spent the weekend cooking, often using ingredients purchased directly from farmers or grown in their own backyard.

Although Greg expressed an interest in becoming a chef, his parents had other ideas about his future, so he followed their wishes and enrolled at the University of North Dakota, majoring in engineering with the intention of becoming an airline pilot. All the while, LaPrad was reading cookbooks and watching the Food Net-

work, soaking up cooking tips and information from some of the great cooks of our time. Greg was particularly influenced by the writings of Alice Waters, whose passion for seasonal cuisine made a deep impression on him.

On 9/11, fate intervened and changed Greg's college and career plans. The airline industry was laying off pilots after the tragedy, so Greg jumped at the opportunity to switch careers and follow his dreams. He left North Dakota for Rhode Island to attend Johnson & Wales to become a chef.

After graduating from the culinary program at the top of his class, fate intervened again when LaPrad's uncle, an investor in Michael DeMaria's restaurant, Michael's, at the Citadel in Scottsdale, Arizona, arranged an introduction for his nephew. LaPrad knew that DeMaria was a Slow Food member who shared his interest in local sustainable cuisine, so the opportunity to meet the chef appealed to him.

Greg arrived in Arizona never intending to stay. This was to be a stop on the way in his training. He was eager for the opportunity to learn from Chef DeMaria but expected to move on as many young chefs choose to do to further their education. From dishwasher to prep cook to lead line cook, Greg climbed the ladder quickly because of hard work, dedication, and skill. Under DeMaria's tutelage, Greg learned how to run a restaurant kitchen and a business—lessons that would prove invaluable in the near future at Quiessence.

Greg left Michael's for a short stint at a hotel restaurant in Denali National Park in Alaska over the summer. La Prad says, "What I learned there prepared me for a leadership role in the kitchen. We were constantly busy, and I got a very important introduction to a high-volume kitchen."

When LaPrad returned to Arizona at the end of the summer, he was not sure what he wanted to do. He answered a newspaper ad for a job at Quiessence Restaurant and was surprised that he got the job so easily. Pat Cristofolo, the president and CEO of Santa Barbara Catering, the parent company of the restaurant, was impressed with Greg from their first meeting. "I

Chef LaPrad focuses on final touches.

remember telling my executive chef at the catering company, 'This guy is something special. He's got it,'" says Cristofolo.

Cristofolo trusted her instincts and hired the young chef to head up the kitchen at Quiessence. She appreciated his desire to add more locally grown ingredients to the menu. It seemed a natural direction for a restaurant with fresh produce grown outside the front door at Maya Dailey's farm.

While at Michael's, Greg had become good friends with another chef who shared his passion for using local foods, Tony Andiario. Greg brought Tony in as his *chef de cuisine* as soon as he could. They immediately set about to overhaul the menu and the kitchen.

Chef LaPrad had a vision shared by Cristofolo and Tony. But it was challenging at first to get the regular customers to come on board.

"At the beginning, there was turbulence," says LaPrad. "We were transforming the menu almost daily. We spent hours debating about the direction of the restaurant and the structure of the menu. And we did this all in front of the customers. They didn't understand why they couldn't have tomatoes with a salad in January or why so many of the items on the menu shared similar ingredients. Slowly the customers became educated to our point of view."

Cristofolo was supportive throughout the process, allowing her new chef to run with his vision. "Greg has always surpassed my expectation. Some chefs have a talent for food, which Greg does. But he also is brilliant in many areas. He's great with numbers, an organizational genius, and a thoughtful and compassionate man. His drive to succeed is unmatched. I'm grateful that our paths have crossed."

Soon LaPrad was making a name for himself in the community as someone with a passion for using the freshest locally grown ingredients in unique ways. Farmers who were as dedicated as LaPrad to organics and sustainability started showing up at his door with produce and offers to grow hogs, chickens, and steer to his specifications. He now has a network of Arizona farmers producing much of what he needs for the restaurant.

Maya Dailey is still one of his main suppliers. "Greg is a gentle and compassionate soul who walks his talk. His consciousness, creativity, and local purchasing habits can be experienced at every bite. It's a pleasure to share the farm with him," says Dailey. Those sentiments are echoed by all the farmers who work with LaPrad.

The menu at Quiessence is based on what is seasonal but also available in the quantity and quality that Greg demands. Although he tries to use almost exclusively local products, he does source from outside of Arizona when necessary. LaPrad's insistence on quality sometimes means not taking shortcuts. The cooks make their own pasta, kneading by hand.

"I don't care about speed. I care about having the food come out right," says Greg.

LaPrad and Andiario fabricate most of the hogs, steer, lamb, and chicken that are delivered whole to the restaurant. They have spent hours learning to fabricate a whole animal so as not to waste any of the usable flesh and bones. In fact, LaPrad and his staff have learned to cure their own meat, serving probably the most popular charcuterie plate in town.

"When you cook the way we cook, you feel connected to the food. I have an intimate relationship with the food. When I look at a case of one hundred pork tenderloins at the butcher shop, I think 'those came from fifty different animals.' I know all about the animals from which our tenderloins come," the chef proudly proclaims.

Terri Nacke, founder of La Bella Terre in Scottsdale, Arizona, greatly admires Chef LaPrad. "His labor of love is painstaking. He does everything in-house. He butchers his meat, handcrafts all pastas, and creates with the best seasonal ingredients."

Greg says, "I know Tony and I are developing a reputation for being difficult to work with. We're not really difficult. We just strive for perfection in everything we do. We are tough taskmasters. We don't take shortcuts. Maybe I'm even a bit anal. Even the walk-in has to look a certain way."

Andiario is a staunch supporter of his boss. "Chef LaPrad is not the first to embrace a local philosophy, but he is a pioneer in his own right. He is committed to following his beliefs and staying strictly within the boundaries he has created for himself. He is an inspiration to me as well as [to] all of his cooks."

Judging by the positive reviews and the filled tables, the future looks bright for Quiessence. The diners finally understand LaPrad's philosophy and are learning to do without tomatoes on their salads in January. They appreciate the freshness of the ingredients and the creativity that the chef brings to his food. And Greg continues to expand his troupe of farmers and purveyors who fill his kitchens with lovingly grown Arizona products.

Quiessence recently started serving lunch again after many years of being a dinner-only restaurant. Although it means longer hours for Chef LaPrad, this was a change he fought for.

"I wish we didn't have to charge so much for the food we serve," says LaPrad, "but our ingredients and labor costs force us to charge those prices. I wanted more people to be able to eat our food, and that's why I started serving lunch. The prices are lower, and more people can learn about our approach to eating."

Chef Greg LaPrad is a modest, passionate, big bear of a man who puts his heart and soul into the food he serves his guests. He is inspired by nature and firmly committed to the concept of seasonal and local. He describes himself as "not good at schmoozing," preferring to stay in the kitchen. "I want my food to speak for itself." It does—gloriously.

SHARON SALOMON, *MS, RD, is a registered dietitian, freelance writer, and dedicated eater who hopes to someday meet the challenge of balancing all the calories she consumes in the interest of research with enough exercise to keep her weight stable.*

A Champion of Native Foods

Janos Wilder's Quest for Flavor

When Janos Wilder landed in Tucson in the early 1980s, he was fresh from a cooking stint in France with the mission of opening a restaurant in the desert that honored the rural French philosophy of cooking.

He says, "The most important thing I learned was that the heart and soul of French cooking was the relationship between the chef and the gardener." In fact, he searched for gardeners and farmers for his Janos restaurant long before he scoured Tucson for cooks and servers.

In retrospect, Wilder's foraging for ingredients for his Southwestern restaurant helped plant the seeds for Tucson's local foods movement. In a soft, raspy voice, the gregarious, bearded chef laughs at the notion he had grandiose plans to save the planet's food systems. At the time his purpose wasn't politically, economically, or even environmentally based.

"There wasn't a local foods movement back then," he says, "We were just using local foods."

Before Wilder's eye-opening experience of cooking from the land in France, he worked at a historic inn in Boulder, Colorado, where, out of both necessity and convenience, he incorporated local ingredients into the frequently changing menu. It was the late 1970s and the notion of restaurants cooking with local ingredients was still in its infancy. Alice Waters's Chez Panisse had opened only a few years earlier. No one was connecting the geopolitical dots between local farmers and farm-fresh restaurant cuisine, not even Wilder, who is a political science graduate of UC Berkeley.

In the beginning, Wilder says that the driving force behind his desire to feature local ingredients on his menu was purely from a chef's perspective—flavor. It was about getting the best-tasting ingredients available. Ingredients freshly harvested from the surrounding area simply taste better than produce that's traveled across the country, or the globe for that matter.

"I can fly in ingredients from anywhere in the world. The whole world is available to any chef. But I have a focus," he says. "I can really inform the cooking with the foods of the region in a very authentic and soulful way."

Incorporating local, indigenous ingredients certainly forms the basis of his restaurant's culinary identity, but his interest in the foods of the southwestern region seems to go beyond creating a brand. Wilder's cooking is driven by a deep respect for the place where he lives.

In 1983, the same year Wilder opened his eponymous restaurant, Janos, a nonprofit organization called Native Seeds/SEARCH (NS/S) was created to protect and preserve the crop seeds of Native Americans from the Southwest and northern Mexico. Unaware of each other, Wilder and NS/S were nonetheless on parallel paths. Wilder wanted to feature local ingredients on his menu; NS/S wanted to preserve local ingredients by acting as a seed repository for regional crops—and not just *any* local seeds but ancient, indigenous seeds.

Early on, Wilder researched and explored various local ingredients, including beans, corn, squashes, and *verdologas* (purslane), which grows wild in the Tucson arroyos (washes). Although he eventually crossed paths with NS/S, it wasn't until a friend who served on the seed bank's board asked him to host a benefit dinner for NS/S that Wilder discovered the treasure trove he now cherishes. Since 1997, Wilder has hosted the annual Fall Harvest dinner at his restaurant to celebrate and support the seed bank's mission. He joined the board and he uses NS/S ingredients extensively throughout his menu to further spread the gospel of the organization's contribution to the region.

But Wilder doesn't just embrace primordial plants and seeds. He embraces *all* local farmers, backyard gardeners, farmers' markets, and Tucson's Community Supported Agriculture (CSA) options. He keeps in touch with one of his early growers, a woman who supplied the restaurant with fruits and vegetables. He says they bought as much as the restaurant could use and often times more.

"Back then it was hard—it's still hard," he says. "There weren't a lot of outlets for her produce, and in the end, we alone couldn't support her." His voice trails off as he thinks about the loss of this particular farmer's work but perks up again as he talks about the recent

Janos Wilder at the harvest

"Now we have more people who are interested in this [local foods]," he says. "And that helps me as a chef because it provides the farmers with more outlets, more opportunities for them to build sustainable businesses." A healthy farming community is obviously beneficial to a regional cuisine–based restaurant, but in Wilder's view, it's critical to the future of his community.

To help ensure the viability of the farmers who supply his restaurant, Wilder hosts local farm dinners, featuring the produce, meats, and artisan products of his network of growers and land stewards. That's not unusual—lots of restaurants hold farm dinners—but Wilder holds the dinners *in honor* of the farmers. The farmers are guests of honor at his table, and Wilder uses the dinners as a means to introduce his diners to the people behind the plate. The dinners, like the farmers' markets, give consumers the chance to make a personal connection with the farmer.

"We see a lot of food fads and trends come and go. I'm not a guy to jump on those things. Some things are enduring. Good culinary practices, good flavors, and common sense are enduring. Raw food? Not so much. This [local, sustainable food] isn't one we are going to see come and go. It's fundamental. At its core, it's a very egalitarian way of doing things," he says.

With such an intense level of commitment to incorporating local ingredients into his menu, does Wilder have his own garden outside the restaurant door like so many restaurants do these days?

"No, we don't have space with good southern exposure, but we are composting," he says. "Besides, I kill stuff. Best to leave the growing to people who know what they're doing," he says with a laugh.

With his restaurant approaching the thirty-year mark in a few years, it's safe to say that Janos Wilder does know what he's doing—serving Tucson through his community service with Native Seeds/SEARCH, which honors the past by looking to the future, and championing the connection between the chef and the gardener so that both may thrive in this patch of the desert.

signs of a community beginning to recognize the value in eating locally. He points to the establishment of a local CSA in 2004, the increasing foot traffic at area farmers' markets, and the overall awareness among the public about where their food comes from—and why it's important.

GWEN ASHLEY WALTERS *is a restaurant critic, food writer, cookbook author, and regular contributor to* Edible Phoenix. *Just for fun, she dishes about food on her blog at penandfork.com.*

Photo above courtesy of Janos Wilder. Photo at right courtesy of Sustainable Food Center

Sprouting Healthy Kids

The Mission of the Sustainable Food Center's Program

"Betsy is a fat girl's name," chanted Hunter Watson on our bus ride to and from third grade each day. Try as she might to ignore him, Betsy rarely succeeded. She greeted her mother at the bus stop most days with wet eyes.

The cruelty of those words and their implication for Betsy's life pierce me to this day. Our cultural anxiety about weight has reached a fever pitch once reserved only for issues of class and race. Thirty-second ads for diabetes-management products now threaten to outpace soft-drink spots. High blood pressure and cholesterol-reduction drugs are marketed as fervently as French fries. We're at war with our food system, and our children's health is on the front line.

In light of the pandemic, Sustainable Food Center (SFC) seeks to empower children and adults through projects like Sprouting Healthy Kids. Launched in fall 2007, Sprouting Healthy Kids takes some of the best elements of SFC's programs—supporting local farms; spotlighting locally grown, seasonal produce; and teaching healthy food preparation—and sculpts them to blend with a middle-school curriculum. The result

Sprouting Healthy Kids program student visiting Green Gate Farms

is an in-class/after-school project full of fun, hands-on activities, and lessons like "Planting a Recipe" and "Justice, Equality and Food: The United Soil of America."

At the heart of the Sprouting Healthy Kids project is moving locally grown foods into school cafeterias however possible. To help facilitate this, SFC—in conjunction with the Community Food Security Coalition—worked to incorporate a "geographic preference" into the 2007 Farm Bill. As a result, schools may now express a preference for buying and serving locally grown food and gain the opportunity to connect directly with local farmers.

Sprouting Healthy Kids helps create, and works in tandem with, school gardens—instrumental in increasing our children's understanding of, and appreciation for, the food system. Companion elements accompany the project, like a gardening and cooking activity guide for after-school clubs, TEKS (Texas Essential Knowledge and Skills)-aligned healthy food lessons,

and a three-day Sprouting Healthy Kids Education Institute that generates additional lessons for the core curriculum. Participating teachers receive continuing-education credits and a monetary stipend for submitting their farm-, garden-, and cooking-based activities and presentations.

"We made things from the food we grew and learned that not everything you eat needs to have meat in it," says Jailyn Bankston, an eighth-grader and a Sprouting Healthy Kids participant. "I've never had some of the stuff we ate, like dill and pesto."

Improving the variety of fresh foods available, providing comprehensive nutritional information, and encouraging healthful choices offer children solid tools toward good health. More important, Sprouting Healthy Kids plants the seeds for a positive relationship with food that will bloom and grow throughout a lifetime. For some children, it might even include a more peaceful bus ride home.

SUSAN LEIBROCK *is Sustainable Food Center's community relations director in Austin, Texas. A third-generation University of Texas grad, Susan lived in New York City from 2000 to 2007, working in the restaurant industry and the flagship office of J. Walter Thompson (JWT). She can be found at Austin Farmers' Market and at www.cakeaustin.com.*

A Celebration of the Southwest

One Seed at a Time

If no one is concerned about saving seeds, there will be no more plants for tomorrow. If that sounds melodramatic, consider this: Two-thirds of crop species once documented in America have vanished. Gone. That is the assertion from RAFT (Renewing America's Food Traditions—a coalition of seven prominent nonprofit food, agriculture, conservation, and educational organizations)—and why these highly respected groups have aligned their efforts to prevent further declines.

One RAFT partner is Native Seeds/SEARCH, a Tucson-based conservation nonprofit dedicated to the preservation of the plants and seeds of the American

Southwest and northern Mexico. NS/S, formed in 1983, serves as a seed bank, managing a collection of nearly two thousand varieties of the traditional seed crops grown by area Native American tribes. It also operates a farm near Patagonia, Arizona, to perpetuate future seed generations, documents the historical and current uses of the seeds and plants, and, coming full circle, distributes seeds back into Native American communities, returning them to their ancestral homes.

The bulk of the protected seeds are known as the Three Sisters: all manner of beans, corn, and squash. But other seeds, such as cotton, chiles, gourds, and melons, are also preserved. Not all the seeds are indigenous to the area. Some, like watermelon, were brought by European settlers, but adapted well to the desert environment, and thus became part of the cultural history of the region. The seeds managed by NS/S are heirloom, meaning they are passed on from generation to generation. Before commercial seed companies existed, every seed was considered an heirloom.

Just how are the seeds saved? In a freezer; a standard home-type freezer to be exact. The seed bank has five such freezers, holding from just a few teaspoons of very small seeds like amaranth to thousands of seeds of corn and beans.

Seeds are living, breathing organisms, and therefore have a shelf life, according to Dr. Suzanne Nelson, director of conservation for NS/S. Nelson, who holds a master's and a PhD in plant agronomy and genetics from the University of Arizona, has been a part of the organization since 1995, and says, "I have the best job in the place. I oversee all of our programs and efforts that deal with seeds, whether it's conserving them in the seed bank, growing them out on the farm, or getting them back into Native American communities."

NS/S's farm in southern Arizona is critical to the mission of conservation, according to Nelson. Because the seeds are alive, they must be planted at some point to continue their cycle of life. Some of the work might not seem glamorous—winnowing and cleaning seeds from pods in order to preserve them—yet each step, from testing the seed's viability to planting, harvesting, cleaning, and documenting, is crucial to the seeds' long-term survival.

NS/S staff, about seventeen to twenty paid employees at any given time, relies heavily on volunteers to accomplish its goals of protecting the thousands and thousands of seeds. While the organization has a list of two hundred volunteers, according to Julie Evans, director of operations, it is a core group of about thirty-five who contribute time every single week at one of the sites. Nelson says that while they may not have as many active volunteers as they could use, they rely heavily on the ones who do contribute.

One volunteer, Amy Schwemm, moved from the Phoenix area to Tucson in 1998 so that she could volunteer on a regular basis. Schwemm, who was raised by her New Mexican grandfather and Mexican grandmother, grew up with a backyard garden and felt strongly connected to the mission of NS/S. She spent

Christmas lima beans

the first year and a half working in a variety of roles—harvesting plants from the field to cleaning pods to get to the seeds to keeping archives on each seed harvest—and eventually joined the ranks of paid staff.

Schwemm has since left NS/S but she is still intricately connected to the organization. She realized an opportunity to start her own business after the NS/S lost its source for traditional mole powders. "People were asking for the mole powders and we didn't have a source. I grew up eating mole so I decided that I could make them."

After researching the ingredients and tinkering with various combinations of NS/S chiles, seeds, and spices, she launched Mano y Metate (www.manoymetate.com) in 2007. Today, NS/S is Schwemm's biggest customer, and she credits the organization with helping her succeed, supporting her mission just as she supports theirs.

The seed-saving efforts of NS/S generate far more seeds than it needs to conserve and distribute back into the Native American communities, so the rest of the seeds are sold through the NS/S retail store on Fourth Avenue, near the University of Arizona, and online at www.nativeseeds.org and through an annual catalog, mailed to donors, previous buyers, and anyone who requests one. The sales allow the organization to help support itself and spread the message about their conservation efforts.

The organization also supports itself through memberships, donations, a creative adopt-a-crop program, and two annual fund-raisers. The annual Fall Harvest dinner started modestly enough with only twenty to thirty attendees. Chef Janos Wilder of Janos Restaurant cooked for the first dinner in 1997, and has hosted every dinner since. Instead of a few dozen attendees, the dinners now attract a robust one hundred or so, but still offer an intimate opportunity for NS/S supporters to actually taste the reasons why protecting the local ecosystem is so important. Wilder creates multicourse dinners showcasing at least one NS/S product in each course.

Key to Wilder's Fall Harvest menu construction is marrying ancient NS/S products with modern, cutting-edge cooking techniques, and integrating flavor profiles that create harmony between ingredients that normally aren't paired. For example, for one dinner Wilder created a Tohono O'odham yellow watermelon soup and topped it with a contemporary shrimp ceviche and grapefruit granita. An ahi tuna dish was wrapped in thin slices of Tohono O'odham ha:l, seared and served swimming in a broth of prickly pear juice, crowned with caviar. "Ha:l" is O'odham for "squash," and grows during the late-summer monsoon season, making it a perfect seasonal ingredient for Wilder to draw upon.

Then there was the bacon-wrapped quail, stuffed with pork carnitas and pasilla chiles on a johnnycake with caramelized onions, Minnie's Apache Hubbard squash and chiltepín salsa (yes, that's one dish). Minnie's Apache Hubbard squash was discovered by a previous NS/S executive director, Kevin Dahl, in 1998 at a tribal fair near the White Mountains in eastern Arizona. It was literally covered with blue ribbons, having won first place in several categories from the judges.

Dahl spent the next few days tracking down the grower. He found Minnie Nachu, a White Mountain Apache, after trekking around the reservation, knocking on doors and asking if anyone knew of a woman named Minnie who grew squashes. Once he found her, he told her he wanted some seeds from her award-winning squash to add to the NS/S collection. Her daughters translated his request since she didn't speak English, and she just laughed. Surely this man was crazy, she thought. She couldn't imagine anyone wanting her seeds—much less envision the seeds going into a seed bank, whatever that was. But as a result of Dahl's efforts, another heirloom squash was saved for future generations.

NS/S doesn't actively collect seeds anymore, although as they come across seeds that aren't in their collection they certainly incorporate them.

Dr. Nelson says, "It takes an extraordinary amount of work to maintain what we do have. We've really started to focus on bringing [the collection] up to industry standards, identifying what we have, eliminating redundancy, and identifying gaps between what has been collected and where it's been collected. It is a big iterative process that helps inform where we want to focus collection efforts in the future."

The future. That is the bottom line, the purpose of Native Seeds/SEARCH. The work—by the staff, the volunteers, the donors, the Native Americans, and the backyard gardeners planting NS/S seeds—is a celebration of the historical culture of the Southwest. Sharing the traditions of planting, cultivating, and harvesting revered local ingredients is keeping the seeds alive for future generations.

GWEN ASHLEY WALTERS *is a restaurant critic, a food writer, a cookbook author, and a regular contributor to* Edible Phoenix. *Just for fun, she dishes about food on her blog at www.penandfork.com.*

People, places, things

ASPEN

The name Aspen invokes many images—world-class ski resort in Colorado, western heritage, outdoor playground, cultural mecca, and great, fresh, local fare. One of the greenest cities in America, Aspen has overcome the challenges of growing at high altitudes with microclimates and rocky soil and now produces high quality food. Farmers, food artisans, vintners, and spirit makers from four nearby valleys supply restaurants with locally grown food worthy of the Aspen reputation.

Jerome Osentowski, Central Rocky Mountain Permaculture Institute Jerome was the creator of alpine greenhouses capable of extending the growing season in mountain regions.

Mark Fischer Executive chef of Restaurant Six89 and Phat Thai, Mark was one of the first chefs to source from local farmers.

Ryan Hardy Ryan introduced the "farm-to-table" concept in Aspen's most exclusive restaurant, Montagna, and supplies many restaurants with goods from his own farm.

Red McClure Potato The Roaring Fork Valley in Colorado once supplied more potatoes than the entire state of Idaho. The potato was reintroduced in 2009.

Peak Spirits Organic Gin The first USDA-certified organic gin produced in the United States.

Oogie McGuire This sheep owner has the largest flock of Black Mountain Welsh sheep in the United States at Desert Weyr.

www.ediblecommunities.com/aspen/peopleplacesthings

AUSTIN

Central Texas is generous to its local foods eaters, blessed with two long growing seasons producing a wide variety of foods throughout the year, barring severe drought conditions or an unusually frigid winter. One can enjoy citrus, *Brassicas,* leafy greens, nuts, and root vegetables in the late fall and winter and tomatoes, berries, peaches, peppers, melons, eggplants, and squashes in the spring and summer. Driving this bounty are countess farmers and producers who are dedicated to sustainable farming practices, Community Supported Agriculture (CSA) programs, farmers' markets, farm stands, and hardworking nonprofits.

Dai Due Supper Club All locally sourced menu served on farms and homesteads. Chef/owner Jesse Griffiths is one of the area's most ardent champions of local foods.

Urban Roots Urban Roots is a youth development program that uses sustainable agriculture as a means to transform the lives of young people and to increase the access to healthy food in Austin.

Broken Arrow Ranch Owner Chris Hughes is an artisanal purveyor of high-quality, free-range venison, antelope, and wild boar meat from truly wild animals.

Cocoa Puro, Kakawa Cocoa Beans Fresh-roasted whole cocoa beans covered in layers of dark, milk, and white chocolates and velvety cocoa. One of the stellar products created and handmade by Tom Pedersen; his wife, Donna; and their daugher, Anna.

John Dromgoole's The Natural Gardener John is a longtime and beloved crusader and spokesperson for organic gardening in Central Texas.

www.ediblecommunities.com/austin/peopleplacesthings

DALLAS AND FORT WORTH

Texas's Six Flag history produced a food culture as rich and diverse in variety as the communities of Texas. Small family farms and ranches producing fruits, vegetables, and grass-fed meats are coming to the forefront and serving the communities with a host of local products. From hearty steaks and regional offerings such as Tex-Mex, to small artisans carving their niche, Dallas/Fort Worth is an exciting food destination.

Tom Spicer Local purveyor of seasonal produce, Tom is Dallas's own culinary warrior, offering amazing mushrooms, specialty greens, veggies, and fruits.

Lavon Farms Lavon Farms in Dallas is one of the last remnants of Texas's agrarian past in the middle of urban sprawl. Third-generation dairy farmers produce and sell products from their Guernsey and Jersey cows.

Paula Lambert's Mozzarella Company Paula is one of the most famous artisanal cheese makers in the country. Besides Italian cheeses, she also makes goat cheese and Mexican cheese.

Kim Pierce Food writer for the *Dallas Morning News* for over thirty years, Kim currently keeps the area abreast of fresh- and local foods happenings through the eatsblog.guidelive.com.

Rahr & Sons Brewery Located in Fort Worth, Rahr's is a local microbrewery working hard to reduce its carbon footprint; its total electricity use is from renewable sources.

www.ediblecommunities.com/dfw/peopleplacesthings

FRONT RANGE (COLORADO)

Known as Colorado's food shed, the Front Range—including Denver, Boulder, Fort Collins, Colorado Springs, and towns in between—offers beef, buffalo, elk, local pine nuts, chiles, dude ranches, cowboy cooking, Native American cooking, Russian dumplings, quinoa, Hmong farmers, and pockets of Japanese, German, and Italian folks with their food traditions who came here for mining or industry, or because of World War II internment. The Front Range is home to a growing number of dedicated organic farmers, and Boulder is the center of the natural foods industry—the cooking found in homes and restaurants reflects that love of excellent, healthy, and local foods.

Abbondanza Farms Owners Rich Pecoraro and Shanan Olson's vision is to co-create a bioregional food system, which provides local schools and community with farm-fresh, nutrient-dense food year-round.

New Belgium Brewery This is great beer from an employee-owned, green-energy brewery. They prioritize local ingredients with barley from the San Luis Valley, and are supporting research for co-grown hops.

Boulder's Farmers Market One of the most diverse, thriving growers-only farmers' markets in the country, with everything from glistening fresh veggies to grass-fed meats, raw milk cheeses, eggs, flowers, fresh pasta, sprouts, even local crawfish.

Potager Opened in 1997 by Teri Rippeto and her dad, Tom, Potager has been local and organic from day one! Teri shops the farmers' markets with her little red wagon every week and bases her specials on what she finds there.

Chile & Frijoles Festival, Pueblo An awe-inspiring feast of chiles in every incarnation: roasted, fried, planted, raw, and shiny. The farmers are there with their roasting barrels and the whole city smells like, well you guessed it, chiles!

www.ediblecommunities.com/frontrange/peopleplacesthings

PHOENIX

The explosive growth Phoenix has experienced over the past fifty years has fueled opportunity for chefs and food artisans, who are able to draw upon the area's unique local ingredients to build thriving businesses offering gelato, bread, jams, salsas, goat cheeses, and more.

Navajo Churro Lamb is a wonderful, scruffy little breed perfectly adapted to the region's harsh climate and traditionally used on the reservations for both meat and wool.

Indigenous Wild Foods These include prickly pear and saguaro cactus, chiltepíns, mesquite.

Nogales Hot Dog Stand Here, Sonora meets Arizona on a fluffy bun.

Bob McClendon, McClendon's Select Bob is an organic pioneer, a chefs' favorite, and an incredible citrus/vegetable farmer.

Tohono O'odham Community Action TOCA brings back traditional Native American farming such as dry farming of tepary beans.

www.ediblecommunities.com/phoenix/peopleplacesthings

SANTA FE

Originally inhabited by Native Americans and settled by the Spaniards in 1598, the high desert of North Central New Mexico has produced some of the most unique farming and food traditions alive in America today. Dry farming methods proliferate, and the ancient acequia system is still a thriving part of this agrarian landscape. Buffalo, deer, and elk remain part of the diet here, as do corn, beans, and squash—and, of course, the New Mexico chile.

La Montanita Cooperative The Coop carries over 1,100 local products from approximately 400 producers. Local foods purchases account for 20 percent of Coop sales. With 13,000 member households and a staff of 200, they emphasize team management, living wages, and generous employee benefits.

New Mexico Native Chile The chiles, sometimes called the Chimayo, Dixon, or Velarde, are grown in the northern part of New Mexico and have been part of the local diet for centuries. Chiles are eaten fresh, either red or green, and also dried whole or ground into a coarse powder that forms the basis for regional sauces and other dishes.

Fresh Bison Also known as the American Plains Buffalo, they are still raised in New Mexico. They are a delicious source of protein raised without hormones, antibiotics, or growth stimulants, and are low in fat and cholesterol.

New Mexico Farmers Marketing Association The association is committed to supporting the state's farmers and growers by assisting in starting new markets, and growing those already in existence.

New Mexico Acequia Association The mission of the Acequia Association is to sustain New Mexico's way of life by protecting water as a community resource and by strengthening the farming and ranching traditions of its families and communities.

www.ediblecommunities.com/santafe/peopleplacesthings

CALIFORNIA AND THE WEST

Go for a walk in Northern California and within a few steps, you're likely to run into something local and delicious to eat. It could be a rosemary-laced duck confit with a salad of roasted figs, goat cheese, and walnuts served at the neighborhood temple to haute cuisine, or it could be a ripe plum falling from a branch overhanging the sidewalk. Food happens here with great finesse and fanfare . . . and sometimes food just happens.

Mostly, it's a matter of geography. The West Coast enjoys a gloriously mild climate that allows farmers to keep their fields in production year-round. Add to that endless miles of shoreline and rivers famously rich with seafood (though much of that is now imperiled). California, with its long summer drought, has one highly significant and splendid feature that makes food growing possible—the regal Sierra Nevada. This high mountain range traps and stores prodigious amounts of water in the form of snow. That snowmelt, flowing through the fertile soils of California's vast Central Valley, creates the stage for a world-renowned growing region. Almonds, walnuts, tomatoes, rice, tree fruits, olives, and, of course, grapes are grown here in epic quantities.

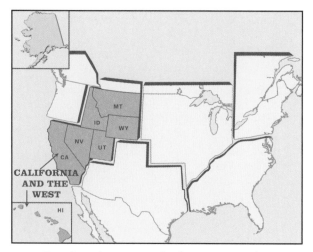

But also, it's a matter of culture. America's western lands have a dramatic modern history that has brought a convergence of cultures—a gathering of cuisines and traditions that have infused and inspired each other. Beginning with the influx of Hispanic peoples in colonial times, through the European and Asian invasions of the gold rush, and in resounding booms ever since, people have come from all corners of the world. Each group has brought its foods, so many of which can be grown here. That diversity has engendered a great curiosity and sophistication of the palate. The produce of the West is truly treasured by the people who live there; it is a fact of the landscape, both rural and urban.

The deep appreciation by our western denizens for their local foods is part and parcel of their reverence for the natural beauty of the landscape—for the places where the foods are grown and also for the places where they are prepared and shared. The kitchen garden, a feature of so many homes and restaurants, sits here within a landscape first noted by the artists rushing in with the gold-era hordes. The nature of marine-influenced light, the grand vistas, and the unique shapes of rocks, plants, and dwellings inspired a new school of art, the natural aesthetic of which can be found on menus and plates, in dining rooms and even in cookbooks. It extends as well into groundbreaking movements in the preservation of public parks and agricultural easements. The beauty of the land drove the Scotsman-turned-Californian John Muir toward the idea of the national park system at Yosemite, and it drove those following in his footsteps to the establishment of a coastal park (Point Reyes National Seashore), designed to encompass and assist the historic dairy farms of western Marin County. Both

are the precedents to a national call to preserve open space that also can preserve agriculture.

While America is spoken of ubiquitously and profusely as the land of plenty, in California, it is most naturally the case that food abounds. The first journals by California settlers reported skies made dark by billions of waterfowl in flight and bears scooping schools of salmon right out of the rivers. For thousands of years before the newcomers arrived, the indigenous peoples had been amply nourished by game and seafood and a cornucopia of native nuts, herbs, seeds, roots, and berries. Increasingly, those native foods are being recognized in the local foods movement, and the rituals of their gathering are being restored by tribal descendants.

The West is facing enormous pressure on its resources by an expanding population as development carves its way deeply into productive farmland. While we are coming to learn of the equal pressure on resources from corporate monoculture farming, we know the struggles of small and midsize farmers to survive. Concern for the health of our local food production industries makes our knowledge of and support for them essential. It is at the heart of this movement to know where our food comes from and to sustain the local sourcing, and it is why we feel compelled to tell stories such as those that follow.

The effort to support local-food production has its roots in the San Francisco Bay Area, epicenter of the Free Speech Movement of the late 1960s, when the call went out to "get back to the land." Many of the small farmers that now supply our burgeoning urban farmers' markets were city kids, who had been drawn to the Bay Area from other parts of the country and who saw the beauty of the surrounding landscape. Land was relatively cheap back then, and so tilling those first acres out in the country required more courage than cash. And since the point was to live close to the land rather than work it for fortune, the principles of organic farming had great appeal. The new farmers clustered into enclaves, and so we find strongholds, such as the Capay Valley, where organic farming is now many decades old. In these places regional branding can lead to an appreciation of the special *terroir* of an area. We know, for instance, that Brentwood produces stellar peaches, figs, and corn; that Capay melons, tomatoes, and eggplants will be superb; and that the milk and cheeses from Sonoma and Marin are some of the world's finest.

Recent concerns about meat, but also the acknowledgment by many health and food professionals of the nutritional value of meat (and the pleasure of eating it) have encouraged a growing number of ranchers to step up to the awesome challenge of production that addresses the health and well-being of the animal, and concurrently the health and conscience of those who eat it. What began in California with a few poultry producers running chickens and turkeys on the range has expanded with the proliferation of grass-fed beef and buffalo (which are lighter on the land), and the pasturing of pork. (The pig turns out to be the paradigm of sustainable husbandry.) Following closely on the hooves of this trend has been a revival of the art of charcuterie. Long-standing local sausage maker Bruce Aidells has now been joined by a battery of chefs curing meats that live up to the standards of European masters of the art.

The emergence of superior produce, meats, and dairy products in the region has been accompanied by a general revival of interest in craft. It began early with the continuation and advancement of the artisanal bread making for which San Francisco is famous, and a renaissance in wine making in the 1970s that showed California wines could rival the best of Europe. But today, we find the interest in old-world food crafting extends into production of artistic local beers, truly great farmstead cheeses, fragrant olive oils, and sumptuous chocolates. Even coffee roasting has become a small-scale craft operation again.

The weak link in the resurgence of a strengthened local food system is one that is seen worldwide as the crisis in our oceans becomes tragically apparent. The emergent problems of taking a diminishing wild resource into domestic production have made vivid the dangers of reengineering nature to meet our desires. Farming the open seas remains beyond our means, and the destruction of riparian habitats for the purposes of building and extracting other resources (water, electricity, minerals) has brought our fisheries to the brink. Local groups are restoring large numbers of creeks, which could perhaps bring steelhead and salmon back inland, but there are larger efforts afoot to reconsider the dams on our rivers that have cut off the salmon from their historic spawning grounds. It would be a great victory in the local foods movement to see the rivers flow freely again.

Foraging is a long-standing tradition in the West, and one that has evaded the kind of regulation that gave domestic food production its homogenizing corporate formulas. Wildcrafters bring mushrooms, seaweeds, seeds, berries, and herbs to our markets and restaurants, allowing us to taste the wild flavors of our locales. Many of us simply go out foraging for ourselves, and when a neighbor finds no need for the citrus, figs, olives, plums, persimmons, pomegranates, prickly pears, walnuts, or almonds raining down on his property, we race the squirrels to haul in the harvest. The fragrant Meyer lemon, too delicate for large food systems to handle, is a prized denizen of nearly every yard or apartment balcony, and anyone without a tree of their own makes friends with someone who has one. Backyard poultry ranching is growing in popularity, and eggs get traded for Meyer lemons, or are just given away whenever a neighbor complains about the clucking.

Distribution of locally produced foods, at a low ebb in the 1960s when the corporate food system was in ascendance, found its local champions in the San Francisco Bay Area with companies like Greenleaf and grocers like Berkeley's Monterey Market. These companies made small farms viable, as have the farmers' markets. Some of the Bay Area's farmers' market associations are now a quarter century old, even though shopping at farmers' markets has only recently come into vogue across the nation. At these markets we can find the local kiwifruits, avocados, and pistachios among the onions, artichokes, and a growing array of crafted food products: jams, pickles, pastries, and all manner of sweet and savory sauces.

California is not unique as a producer of local foods, but it is indeed exemplary and it has projected the image of a new fresh and local lifestyle across the country. Those of us who have been appreciating our local foods feel gratified that as the trend is emulated, each locale is discovering its own *terroir*—the unique tastes of its region.

Moving east and inland from California into the interior West, the picture of local food production turns more black and white, as dry, barren lands of basin and range make the growing of food a test of will for farmers looking to make a living at their efforts. Wild fish and game, mushrooms, and berries can be found almost anywhere that receives enough moisture, so hunting and gathering abounds, and rangelands have supported commercial meat production since the West was first settled.

But people in Montana, Wyoming, Utah, and Nevada want their fresh fruits and veggies, just as Californians do. Fortunately the glowing green spirit that makes a person into a home gardener is irrepressible, no matter where people put down roots, and gardeners do indeed manage to wrestle produce out of the ground. Some areas have been able to support small truck farms producing quantities of seasonal crops, such as melons, tomatoes, peppers, tree fruits, and salad greens, and now, the burgeoning local foods movement is rewarding those small farmers' efforts. Watch what happens as new technologies in sustainable farming emerge. Hopefully, we will see local foods as a viable choice throughout the West.

Hawaiian Islands

Located roughly 2,000 miles southwest of the United States mainland, the Hawaiian Islands represent a distinct bioregion shared only by other equally isolated Pacific Ocean islands of similar tropical latitude. Land-based native foods in this geologically young island archipelago are few; nearly everything here that's good to eat (except seafood) was initially brought by one or another of the islands' immigrant groups.

Waves of settlement by Polynesians, Chinese, Koreans, Japanese, Filipinos, Portuguese, and mainland Americans, along with significant visits by various explorers, traders, and whalers, have created diverse and utterly unique food traditions here, making the Hawaiian Islands a fascinating place to study as a food shed. For instance, at a traditional Hawaiian feast, you would surely eat poi (made from the all-important staple food taro root), as well as dishes composed from sweet potatoes, coconut, breadfruit, plantain, coconuts, sugarcane, pork, chicken, and even dog, plus all manner of seafood. Much of the feast would be cooked in a pit oven known as an *imu*.

Beef, introduced in 1793 by Captain George Vancouver, is important to the Hawaiian food shed, as is coffee, which was first introduced in 1817. But it wasn't until the late nineteenth century that pineapple and sugarcane, grown on plantations owned and run by American settlers, grew into the top sources of revenue for the Hawaiian economy.

For over a century, this island state has regarded itself as an exporter of food, with 85 percent of total production heading to distant markets in 2008. But Hawaiians have watched in dismay recently as the big pineapple and sugar producers have been abandoning the islands in favor of new homes where land, labor, and the logistics of shipping are cheaper and easier. In the face of climate change, diminishing oil reserves, and an unbalanced and faltering world economy, the archipelago's geographic isolation begins to look like a red flag. Hawaiians (including the governing Lingle-Aiona administration) are rethinking the idea of food as dollars and instead considering their food resources as important for feeding themselves. The stories we like to hear from that region are those of Hawaiians producing food for Hawaiians.

Can Good Fruit Survive in the Age of Marketing?

. . . .

Friend's Ranches and the Ojai Pixie Tangerine

Tony Thacher occupies a particular niche in the social ecology of the Southern California community of Ojai Valley. He carries on family traditions of innovative farming and service to the community with a characteristic modesty that would be remarkable most places but which people in Ojai more or less expect of him. He; his wife, Anne Friend Thacher; and their children, Emily Thacher Ayala and George Thacher, farm as Friend's Ranches, growing about seventy-five acres of tangerines, Valencia oranges, other citrus, and avocados. Their stubborn persistence as independent operators is admirable in the face of ever-increasing industrialization and homogenization of agricultural production.

The Thachers are key players in a cooperative endeavor to grow and market a local tangerine, the Ojai Pixie tangerine, where their history and reputation for probity are crucial components of the effort.

The Friend and the Thacher families have resided in Ojai as long as citrus has been grown here: Tony's grandfather and Anne's great-grandmother both arrived in the 1880s.

Anne's father, Elmer Friend, established the business and the principles by which it is still run. Born in Ojai in 1897 when the orange business was very young, he acquired parcels of land over the years. He was a hard worker and a hard taskmaster. He didn't borrow money (except from family) and he didn't believe in the stock market; his success was attributable to habits of independent thinking. In the early years of DDT, according to Anne, Elmer used it for two years running, saw that its effectiveness declined the second year, and stopped using it thereafter. During a prolonged drought in the 1940s, he purchased a parcel of land near a creek for the purpose of digging an adequate well, ran pipe several miles to serve his other properties, and ended up saving other growers' ranches as well. In the 1950s, he was one of the first growers in the Ojai Valley to change from furrow to sprinkler irrigation, a huge savings in time and money. In the 1960s, disgruntled that

Sunkist sent all the highest-quality fruit to export, he opened his own packinghouse to make sure that the general public had an opportunity to buy the best possible fruit. He also established relations with wholesale buyers interested in and willing to pay for high-quality fruit. That the returns from Sunkist were low was an additional incentive—by selling the fruit direct he got to keep more of the money.

Tony's grandfather, Sherman Day Thacher, contributes another aspect of the Friend's Ranches' presence in the Ojai Valley: community service offered with exceptional modesty, honesty, and selflessness. Arriving in the Ojai Valley in 1887 as a drifting young scion out of Yale—Sherman had tried business and the law and been miserably unhappy at both—he intended to stay two weeks and instead ended up staying forty-four years. In addition to starting the Thacher School, which has developed into one of the finest independent schools in the nation, he was one of the most public-spirited citizens in the small community of early Ojai. He once wrote, "I have always felt that the highest duty of a citizen is to do all he can for the community in which he lives, for the public good." It would be a cliché, except that he actually lived what he said. That spirit lives on in the Thacher family and is an important aspect of their role in the community.

Neither Tony nor Anne set out to be farmers. As young adults, Anne had begun a career as a chemist and Tony as a geologist, but in the winter of 1969, an El Niño storm triggered landslides that washed Elmer Friend's brand-new packinghouse into the Ventura River. Tony and Anne answered Elmer's call for help and never went back to their other lives.

Tony and Emily work the orchards and do the farmers' markets with the substantial help of the Estrada family: Felipe (now retired); his brother Reyes; his son, Lupe; Lupe's wife, Angela, and son, Omar. Three generations of Estradas work in the orchards, in

the packinghouse and at the farmers' markets. The only thing they don't do, so far as I know, is inside sales and, as Emily says, "the damn bookkeeping."

A word about the orange business, the tangerine business, and the relationship between the two:

The orange business grew up with California. By the 1920s, it had developed a sophisticated production, marketing, and logistics infrastructure, and it thrived for decades.

However, in the late years of the twentieth century, as orange orchards planted fifty and eighty years earlier grew less productive, as farmers grew old, as farming became less lucrative, and as markets changed, the sophisticated, entrenched infrastructure of the orange business prevented it from adapting to changing economic and social conditions.

Retail outlets consolidated, leaving fewer customers. Those customers decided that the American consumer preferred a seedless navel orange to a seeded Valencia orange. Florida had long ago taken the juice business from California, leaving California growers to sell Valencias to the fresh market. Globalization of commerce and transport meant that counterseasonal navels from the southern hemisphere could come into U.S. markets during what had formerly been the Valencia season, and the market for Valencias shrank. High water and labor costs and the strong dollar threatened exports. The distribution infrastructure—the whole way that oranges were picked, packed, sold, stored, and transported, which had grown up many decades prior—is set up in such a way that the California orange industry was incapable of putting on the super-

market shelf fruit that had the flavor of fresh-picked fruit. Growers would not willingly eat their own fruit if they had to purchase it from a supermarket because it didn't taste good. The orange business declined.

In the early years of the orange business, to enter into the tangerine business was to be a small-timer, a marginal player. You were on your own, and you didn't have the big marketing machine, the national recognition, or the logistical support of the orange business.

But Elmer Friend had a different perspective: If he'd been a stock market kind of guy, he'd have been sure to maintain a diversified portfolio. He sold Valencias through Sunkist, as the Thachers still do, but for decades he packed his own Dancy tangerines, wholesaling them directly to Asian customers in San Francisco for Lunar New Year. Once he had his own packinghouse, he began selling mail order as well. He planted one or two trees of many varieties of citrus, looking for fruit he could sell; he planted a significant number of what were then called "Algerians": a small, seedy variety of clementine. He was always on the lookout for new markets. When a coalition of faith-based antihunger activists persuaded Gov. Jerry Brown in 1979 to allow farmers to sell direct to consumers at what are now called Certified Farmers Markets, Elmer was right there at the first one, in Gardena, a suburb of Los Angeles.

PRODUCE FROM THE FRIEND'S RANCHES

The citrus grown at Friend's Ranches is amazingly varied, and oh so good! Tangerine varieties include: Pixie, Satsuma, Fina Sodea, and Caffin clementines, Lee, Shasta Gold, Tahoe Gold, Yosemite Gold, Gold Nugget, W. Murcott, Robinson-Lee, Page, Seedless Kishu, and Dancy.

Also grown are Moro, Tarocco, Sanguinelli, and Vaniglia Sanguigno blood oranges; Smith Red Valencias; Minneolas; Cara Cara navels; grapefruit; lemons; and avocados. And, of course, Valencia oranges—the fruit on which the Ojai Valley's reputation for excellent citrus was first built.

Elmer Friend's heritage of looking for more fruit to sell and more markets to sell to established the base from which Friend's Ranches has moved into the twenty-first century.

If growing tangerines formerly marked someone as choosing to play outside the big leagues, by the year 2000 orange trees by the thousands of acres were being pushed out, and tangerine orchards were being planted by the hundreds of thousands of trees.

In recent years very big players have started growing tangerines—for example, Sun Pacific and Paramount Citrus have planted hundreds of thousands of trees in the Central Valley. Other big operations have also invested heavily in different varieties of tangerines. These new players have an advantage over orange growers in that they have designed their sales and distribution infrastructure to meet current market conditions. For instance, Sun Pacific and Paramount Citrus have jointly created a brand they call the California Cutie™—it's really just a box into which they plug different varieties of tangerine as the season progresses from November through April, starting with clementines and progressing through W. Murcotts. If it's seedless, it qualifies as a California Cutie.

The California Cutie, which is only one among several such newly created "tangerine products," is a diabolically brilliant idea, the essence of industrialized agriculture: note the ™, denoting intellectual property; since it's a construct, not a piece of fruit, the difference between varieties can be erased in order to optimize marketing. It's not a variety of fruit with individual recognizable characteristics of flavor, texture, etc.; it's a brand with attributes that can be associated with it by spending millions of dollars in marketing.

In Ojai we started selling Ojai Pixie tangerines twenty years before Big Ag decided tangerines were where it's at. In the mid-1990s, without guile but with an appreciation of the fact that we had something special and that we had to sell the specialness, we set about to create our own tiny "brand" for the Ojai Pixie.

Tony Thacher and I planted the first commercial plantings of Ojai Pixies at about the same time, around 1980. When I decided to plant Pixies, I consciously modeled myself on Elmer: I did not want to plant Valencia oranges and sell them to Sunkist; I did want to grow something I could sell myself. I'd say that the main difference between Tony and me in planting Ojai Pixie tangerines was that Tony, who was already selling at farmers' markets, had a sense of where he would sell them, whereas I was just fleeing a disastrous venture in avocados and thought the Ojai Pixie was an astonishing piece of fruit that I'd be able to sell, somehow.

As the '80s went along, the Thachers and my family, the Churchills, began to create a market for Ojai Pixies—Tony through farmers' markets and some of his existing wholesale tangerine customers, the Churchills through direct sales to new wholesale customers. Ojai Pixies were a difficult sale at first. Individual customers have always liked them immediately because they are sweet, seedless, and easy to peel, but retailers initially resisted them because they didn't get ripe during traditional tangerine season, they are often small, and they are not highly colored. Those were still the days when produce retailers acted like everything that could be sold had already been discovered, so getting them to make room for something new was a struggle, but over time we found our market, and it was a good one.

Because the Ojai Valley developed along with the orange business, it is full of no-longer-economic orange orchards ranging in size from tiny to substantial. In the 1980s and '90s as Friend's Ranches and the Churchills developed the market for Ojai Pixies, other growers wondering what to do with their ground decided to gamble on Pixies, so that now, in 2010, there are some thirty-eight growers with upward of 24,000 trees planted. Because there was no one else to market them, and because it seemed far better for us to hang together than separately, we created the Ojai Pixie Growers Association, a loose affiliation of growers who came together to create a market for Pixie tangerines and to develop an association in the marketplace between the Pixie and the Ojai Valley.

That the Ojai Pixie Growers Association exists and functions owes a lot to the Thachers. The "Friend" ideas—growing top-quality, unique fruit and selling it ourselves—are the very basis of the venture. The "Thacher" qualities—that nobody thinks the Thachers are in the game to profit at the expense of the others, that everyone believes that the Thachers have the group's interest at heart—help us to get through each season eager to begin the next one.

Deciding to make a little brand for the Ojai Pixie followed from deciding to sell our own fruit: It just seemed logical that to sell the Ojai Pixie we'd have to point out what was special about it.

Ojai Pixies have grown in wholesale sales from 3,000 or 4,000 pounds in 1988 to 1,400,000 pounds in 2008. In the overall scheme of the produce industry, Ojai Pixies are insignificant: California orange sales for 2008 were 44,000,000 forty-pound cartons, as opposed to our 56,000 twenty-five-pound cartons. However, the Ojai Pixie Growers Association has created a market where there was none, and it has created a brand, however small, re-associating "Ojai" with the idea of "delicious fresh citrus." It is a source of pride and income in the community.

The development of late-season, fully industrialized tangerines-as-commodities threatens the market for Ojai Pixies because the new "tangerine products" are in the market at the same season as the Ojai Pixie, they have a large amount of marketing dollars (there was a $7,000,000 campaign behind them for 2008–2009), and they will cost less than Ojai Pixies on the shelf.

If the Ojai Pixie tangerine is to remain competitive in the marketplace and continue to be a source of pride and income to the community, a number of things will have to happen: Growers of Ojai Pixies will have to agree on a vision for the future; we will have to maintain high postharvest quality of our fruit so that it continues to be the most delectable citrus on the shelf—our only hope in the marketplace is that people will recognize that it tastes better than other similar-appearing but cheaper fruit; we will have to get better at differentiating Ojai Pixies from other "tangerine products" in the face of multimillion-dollar marketing campaigns. If there's a viable movement for food authenticity out there in the United States, the Ojai Pixie will have to latch onto it for dear life in hopes that people will reward us for growing what we say we grow, instead of trying to sell them something unidentifiable.

So what do Ojai Pixies have going for them, in this decidedly lopsided struggle for survival against the tide of industrial agriculture? Among other things, there's the heritage and life experience of the Thacher-Friend family: innovative farming and marketing accompanied by stubbornness, hard work, modesty, honesty, and good humor. Oh, yes, and a really good piece of fruit.

JIM CHURCHILL *grows many varieties of organic citrus and avocados in Ojai. Information about the farm that he and his wife, Lisa Brenneis, own is at www.tangerineman.com. He is a charter member of the Ojai Pixie Growers Association and is on the board of Food for Thought Ojai.*

A Portrait of the Farmer as a Young Man

Memories of Broccoli Handling, San Francisco's Mean Streets,
and the Kindness of Strangers

Fresh broccoli is health food, but it almost killed me.

It was back in the early 1980s, when I worked at Star Route Farm in Bolinas. After a day in the fields, I'd walk downtown, buy a six-pack at the liquor store, and sit on the sea wall at the end of Brighton Street looking out over the ocean. When it wasn't foggy, I could see the San Francisco peninsula off to the southeast across the Gulf of the Farallones. As the evening sky grew dark, the distant city lights would brighten, and soon San Francisco would float free from the hills to which she's moored and sparkle in the night from across the water like a magical ship. If I was going to make the drive south to the city later that night to deliver the farm's harvest, I wouldn't drink. But San Francisco glittered all the same for being so near at hand, yet so far from my world.

Now that the largest organic farms are owned by the largest corporate farms, and most of the little independent-hippie-natural-food stores have been swallowed whole by the big fish, vegetables are displayed for retail like sculptures or jewels. It's funny to think back to those early days of the natural foods movement, when consumers half expected organic vegetables to be beat up, wilted, or dirty compared to "regular store-bought vegetables." Some perverse customers needed organic produce to look battered, as if being unclean or un-cooled was proof that the vegetables had really sprung from the earth.

ONE LONG COLD CHAIN

In the early 1980s, Star Route Farm had thirty acres under cultivation, which made it one of the largest organic farms in California. The vegetables we grew were beautiful in the field. But the industry was young then, and farmers and storekeepers alike lacked the tools—and sometimes the knowledge—to perform the postharvest handling procedures that could help deliver on the whole promise of organic, fresh, and natural.

Take broccoli. Truly fresh broccoli is a revelation. When I worked at Star Route Farm I didn't earn much money, and I saved my wages for important things, like beer and toilet paper. I ate everything I could from the fields. The first time I cut a head of broccoli and steamed it four minutes later, I was amazed at the sweetness. Any dressing or sauce would only have clouded the fresh purity of the flavor.

But delivering some facsimile of that green sweetness to a distant customer is tricky. As broccoli ages, it begins to express the odor and flavor of the mustard oil that characterizes every member of the *Brassica* family, from arugula to broccoli to cabbage to kale. Nowadays, organic growers follow the same postharvest handling practices for broccoli as chemical farms do. These procedures help retain some semblance of freshness in the crop over time and distance. Back then, the economies of scale that make postharvest technology possible were not yet present.

Here's how it works. As soon as commercial broccoli is harvested, it's packed into a waxed cardboard carton and the boxes are stacked on a pallet. The pallet of broccoli is then forklifted into a hydro cooler, where water chilled to 34 degrees is rained down through the boxes, washing away the field heat, until the core temperature of the broccoli drops into the thirties. Then the pallet of chilled broccoli is forked from the hydro cooler into a chamber where each box is pumped full of slush ice so that the broccoli is embedded in a square artificial glacier.

The broccoli is then held in a refrigerated warehouse until it's sold. The ice melts, but it melts slowly, trickling cold water through the broccoli stems. After the sale, the refrigerated truck that comes to carry the broccoli away backs up to the portal of the refrigerated warehouse until the rubber lips of the insulating diaphragm kiss the square mouth of the refrigerator trailer and create a seal. Then the doors are raised and the pallet of broccoli is trundled from the refrigerator warehouse into the refrigerated trailer. The doors are closed, the truck pulls forward, the lips unlock, and the truck drives off across America—eventually depositing it into another refrigerated warehouse at a regional distribution center.

Food scientists will tell you that it is almost as important to the shelf life of green vegetables that their storage temperatures be stable as it is that they be sufficiently cold. Fluctuating temperatures cause tissue breakdown, just as warm temperatures do. At the regional distribution center, pallets of broccoli are broken down into smaller units for delivery in other refrigerated trucks to outlying stores, where the boxes of broccoli will be stored in walk-in coolers. From there, individual bunches of broccoli are lifted from the boxes where they nest and laid out for the consumer to ogle on beds of crushed ice or perhaps stacked in a pyramid beneath florescent lights and treated to an intermittent icy mist.

These are the links in the "cold chain" that makes our "fresh anytime anywhere" produce departments in chain stores possible. Unless or until the frantic increase in the cost of oil one day makes waxed boxes, water chillers, freezers, ice, and trucking too expensive to ignore, it's this cold chain that makes fresh broccoli cheap enough to waste.

IN V.V. VERITAS

But in the early 1980s, the natural foods industry was only just coming to grips with the techniques of postharvest handling or the goal of serving a national market. For Star Route Farm, as for most organic farms in the greater Bay Area, marketing a crop meant harvesting vegetables during the day and hauling them to Veritable Vegetable in San Francisco at night. Veritable Vegetable, or "V.V." to produce insiders, was a feminist organic-produce distributor collective. The women at V.V. delivered to all the little hippie health food stores. Veritable has matured into an institution: Even men work there now. It makes me happy to see V.V.'s trucks on the road today because I know she's a survivor who's managed to evolve in the face of stiff competition.

When the women at V.V. complained to us that our broccoli was turning yellow, we had to listen. They suggested we find some way to ice it down. We didn't have an ice machine on the farm, and we didn't know where to go to buy one that could make the quantities

of the crushed ice slurry we would need, so my boss told me to buy ice in town. There isn't much "town" between Bolinas and San Francisco, especially if you consider that I delivered at night in a big truck that was hard to park. So I'd leave the farm around 9 P.M., late enough to avoid traffic but early enough to get to the liquor store before it closed for the night. I'd drive slowly around the Bolinas lagoon to avoid hitting animals. The eyes of raccoons and possums foraging for food on the tidal flats would flash in the glare of the headlights. Just past Stinson Beach I'd gear down for the slow grind up the grade that hugs the rocky cliffs and I'd stay in low third past Slide Ranch and gear down even lower for the descent to Muir Beach. The swirling fog in the headlights was disorienting, but I'd keep the window cracked open so the fresh air would keep me alert, and I could smell the brine of the ocean and hear the boom of the surf at the bottom of the cliffs. The uphill grade past Green Gulch was steep, and the road downhill into Tam Junction was curvy. I wouldn't pick up speed until I got onto southbound 101.

The streets of San Francisco were jarring after the wilds of West Marin. I'd blink against the brightness and watch for drunks and tourists instead of coons and possums. Veritable Vegetable was located in the warehouse district south of Army Street. I'd stop at a liquor store on Bayshore Boulevard that was nearby and stayed open late. The night clerk got to know me. He couldn't leave the register, but he'd take my money, hand me the keys to the freezer they had out in back, and I'd load all the bags of ice they had in their cooler onto my truck. I'd spread the boxes of broccoli out across the loading dock at V.V. and open them to ice them down. Then I'd rip open the bags of ice, one by one, and pour the ice into the boxes, then close them, restack the pallet, and roll it into Veritable's cooler.

It wasn't cheap, it wasn't efficient, and it probably wasn't even effective, but back then, that was the best we could do.

BRASSICA KNUCKLES

One night when I got to the liquor store, both lanes of Bayshore Boulevard were blocked by a couple of pimps with flashy cars. I don't know for sure they were pimps— they could have been librarians dressed to kill, out for a night on the town in dark glasses and comporting themselves like fighting cocks, so that ignorant country

boys like myself would presume they were successful pimps. The casual manner in which these two men took the whole street for their own was threatening. I parked behind them and stepped into the liquor store.

"Sorry, Boss," the clerk said. "No ice in back, but you can take what we've got in the store." He waved me toward the refrigerator cases full of beer. "It's closing time anyway."

I went down the aisle, past the display racks of potato chips and the shelves of cheap wine. In the back corner there was a freezer locker with some ice—not enough that I'd be able to ice down the broccoli in conformance with optimum postharvest protocol but more than I could haul out to the truck by hand. I went to get my dolly.

The two men were still blocking the street, but out of their cars now, strutting, boasting, and swaggering. They knew each other, but it wasn't clear they liked each other. One of the girlfriends was thirsty. "Come on, baby," she called out over the dissonant blare of music pulsing and clashing from both cars' stereo systems. "Get me a drink."

I pushed my dolly back to the liquor store and proceeded to the rear of the store. I laid the dolly down so I could load it. I was on my knees pulling out ten-pound sacks of ice when I heard the two push their way into the store. *Ding* went the bell. They both wanted liquor—Courvoisier for the one, Johnnie Walker for the other. And they each wanted to be served first. It wasn't going well for the clerk, who had to decide which arrogant prick of a customer to offend. I straightened up to pull my dolly. From where I stood I could see that the clerk had slipped one hand under the register. Just then, another man entered the store: white, bald, and wearing a camouflage army-surplus jacket. He grabbed the first bottle of wine he came to and shoved it onto the counter next to the register.

The pimp/librarians pushed forward to object, and the white guy reached to pull a handgun out of his jacket. If he was intending to rob the store, he'd picked a bad night. Before he had his pistol drawn and leveled, the clerk and both pimp/librarian dudes pulled their guns on him. I dropped down behind the Cheetos and the Ding Dongs. There was a frozen moment while the bald man with the gun decided whether or not he cared if he got shot. The clerk broke the ice.

"No worries, Boss. Just leave."

And he did, moving slowly backward out onto the sidewalk. I peeked around the snack rack. The clerk pushed the two bottles of liquor toward the pimp/librarians.

"Thank you, sirs. On the house. Come back soon. We're closed for tonight."

ANGEL WITH A MUSTACHE

If delivering produce into the city in the middle of the night had its film noir moments, there were things about it to appreciate, too. The night shift always plays by its own rules. Meddlesome middle managers are tucked away in bed. Working nights means you never get enough sleep, but the stress of having your circadian rhythms scrambled is partly compensated by a degree of freedom not often seen during the day. There's a we're-in-this-together feeling that gives you something in common with everyone else you meet, a camaraderie among strangers that's missing in the daylight.

I remember one night run from the farm into the city. It had rained off and on all day, and at dusk the storm intensified. I left the farm at ten in the evening and drove slowly around the Bolinas lagoon. The tide was rising. The incoming wall of seawater acted like a dam at the mouth of the lagoon and blocked the outward flow of rainwater streaming down off the ridges of the Golden Gate National Recreation Area (GGNRA). The lagoon was full to the brim and wavelets already lapped at the pavement.

At Stinson Beach the wind hit the truck's broad side like it was filling a sail. Highway One was closed ahead due to a mudslide, so I turned up the Panoramic

Highway and away from the coast to take a detour over the shoulder of Mount Tam. There was no traffic and no creatures to be seen. All intelligent sentient beings were snug in their nests, tucked under rocks, sheltered in the holes of tree trunks. The road was covered in twigs and fir needles whipped from the trees by the wind. I stared into high beams and navigated around loose rocks in the roadway. When I crossed the Golden Gate Bridge, I felt the full force of the gale, and I held the steering wheel tight in both hands to keep the truck from bucking.

Trucks that cross the Golden Gate always pass through the toll plaza in the far right-hand lane. Since I entered the city on a regular schedule, every Tuesday and Thursday around 11 P.M., I'd gradually come to know by sight the woman who worked for the Bridge Authority in that lane's booth. When her mustache and beard grew out enough to contrast oddly with her eye shadow and rouge, it became obvious, even to me, that she was a he.

When I pulled up to her booth that night, she seemed like she was waiting for me.

"You hauling potatoes, sugar?" she shouted up.

"How'd you know?"

"You're all over the scanner! Northbound C.H.P. turned around to look for you. Your potato box lids have been blowing off all across the span."

"Oh, shit!"

"No shit!" she replied. "He'll ticket you. Littering. Spilling your load. Causing a traffic hazard! Take the Presidio off-ramp. They won't look for you there."

I gave her my money and took her advice, dodging back into the cover of the tall black cypresses in the Presidio. Sure enough, when I got to Veritable Veg-

etable, the top layer of potato boxes, fifty in all, were missing their lids. I hadn't secured the plastic tarp well, and it had blown away, exposing my cargo. The strong winds I encountered on the Golden Gate must have sent the lids flipping and twirling off in the night like bats. The potatoes were wet from the rain and glowed bright red under the florescent lights in the warehouse.

Several years ago in the dead of winter I took my family for a vacation in the City. It rained the entire time, but we had a nice time anyway. Some friends who were off traveling let us house-sit their home in Sutro Heights. Late one afternoon I took my kids, Lena and Graydon, for a walk in a lovely park that perches high on the cliffs above Ocean Beach, and we wandered down the rain-washed city streets to Baker Beach.

The clouds over the sea lifted long enough for me to see the outline of Bolinas Head on the northwestern horizon. So much had changed in twenty-five years. The same rocky Marin Headlands, the same black cypresses in the Presidio, the same gray, choppy water under the Golden Gate Bridge, but I was different. I had my own farm now, south of San Francisco, with a wife, kids, employees, and a sagging body to care for.

My kids got bored as I stood there looking out across the Golden Gate, and they tugged at me to leave. So I left. I knew what had happened to the organic food movement I'd come of age in, and I keep in touch with my friends at Star Route Farm, but I left wondering whatever happened to the clerk, the pimp/librarians, the thief, and my drag-queen toll-taking angel.

So much water under the bridge, but what a beautiful bridge.

ANDY GRIFFIN *of Mariquita Farms cultivates thirty-two acres of vegetables near Hollister. Years of studying philosophy at UC Davis were excellent preparation for twenty-five years of hoeing weeds, driving trucks, managing field crews, and feeding cows. Andy has been to many of Northern California's best restaurants, usually via the backdoor pushing a hand truck. He hopes one day to be as sophisticated and widely traveled as the vegetables he grows. He writes the Ladybug Letter, www.ladybugletter.com.*

Turning Kernels into Gold

It's a hot, dusty September day at Full Belly Farm. Rich Leavey crouches down to examine a few dry-looking ears of corn piled at the foot of the sun-bleached field. One ear of Hopi Blue catches his attention. With kernels alternating red, burgundy, and crimson, the appearance is a warmer, richer texture than he's accustomed to seeing on this variety. After examining it for a few seconds, Leavey surmises that some brightly varied Fiesta corn must have lent its warmer yellows and deeper browns to this plant. "What's really appealing," he says with the measured New England enthusiasm that betrays his Vermont roots, "is getting these unique off-types that you haven't seen before." He then adds, "I'm going to have to save some seed off of this!"

In today's world of genetic engineering, it is refreshing and reaffirming to see such delighted surprise in a marvel that nature offers up all on its own, and on an ear of corn, no less. Of late, corn seems to be the poster child for all that's wrong with the industrial food system, whether it is Monsanto's Bt Corn or end products like high-fructose corn syrup (the alleged culprit in the obesity epidemic) and ethanol (seen by many as our deus ex machina out of the energy crisis). Corn is an ancient food and a basis of the traditional diet and system of agriculture in Mesoamerica. Coevolving with corn were beans and squash. Known as the Three Sisters, this triad provides a full nutritional complement of amino acids, fiber, and a host of vitamins and minerals. The Sisters also work symbiotically in the garden: Corn offers its stalk for the bean to climb, the beans fix nitrogen in the soil to provide fertility, and the squash gives ground cover, helping to retain moisture in the soil and protecting all three from the invasion of weeds.

"Corn is a heavy feeder, needing a lot of nitrogen," says Leavey, explaining that at Full Belly they tried the traditional Three Sisters plan, interspersing beans directly with corn. "It was a nightmare for harvesting," he says, adding that the arrangement is better suited for home gardens. Instead he has planted cranberry beans and the tiny Trail of Tears heirloom beans in large swaths between the corn.

In addition to raising corn that's meant to be eaten fresh, Full Belly Farm produces several varieties that are intentionally allowed to dry: Yellow, a bubblegum pink Strawberry Popcorn, ornamental Fiesta corn, and Hopi Blue. The farm recently added the latter to grind into cornmeal during the slow winter months. "We wanted to start doing more value-added crops," Leavey explains, referring to the practice of increasing return by processing certain crops into products like flour, baked goods, or preserves. He expresses surprise at how popular the cornmeal has turned out to be. "Last year we sold out so fast that we had to start grinding the ornamental corn instead," he says. "For some reason, it really clicked with people."

Despite the heat, high sun, and the abundance of tomatoes, melons, and stone fruit ripening on the farm, Full Belly's two-acre cornfield, crackling in the dry wind, seems to whisper the end of summer. Looking over the drying field, Leavey remarks, "Corn is a great end point to a long succession of crops." Once the corn and beans are sufficiently dry to avoid rot, the farm's new harvester will sweep through the field, depositing the sheared kernels and naked beans into bins, while turning the remaining plant matter back into the field. It will rest beneath a cover crop until spring, when a new round of crops will be planted. In 2010, the corn will find itself somewhere else on the 200-acre farm, continuing on a complex rotation that keeps Full Belly's soil, livestock, and produce healthy.

WINTER'S WORK

In early February, the farm is quiet. Goats and sheep, heavy in pregnancy, graze fields thick in vetch and clover, and through the damp, dark earth, shoots of tender grass poke up to color the farm's pathways. Meanwhile, cold-weather crops like broccoli, kohlrabi, and braising greens thrive amid the bare limbs of fruit trees and grapevines.

Just before lunch, Joaquina Jacobo, dressed in rubber work boots, a full-length apron, and a hooded

sweatshirt, fires up the four-foot-high stone grinder. Her job this morning is to grind cornmeal and wheat for this week's CSA boxes. Surrounded by five-gallon buckets of wheat berries, and Hopi Blue corn kernels resembling a wealth of garnets, Jacobo feeds the rumbling grinder. As it gives her violet-colored cornmeal in return, she quietly tells us that her daughter just recently learned how to make corn bread at her local grade school in Guinda.

Jacobo is one of Full Belly's forty year-round employees. For some long-term employees, the farm offers health benefits, something only 19 percent of California's organic farms do, according to a 2005 study at UC Davis. "Providing year-round work is something we are very committed to," explains Judith Redmond, who along with Andrew Brait, Paul Muller, and Dru Rivers, founded the farm in 1985. She is standing inside the open barn, keeping warm in a wool sweater. Around her are neatly packed bags of wheat berries, whole wheat

flour, multicolored popcorn, blue cornmeal, sun-dried tomatoes, and other dried fruit, waiting to be packed into CSA boxes or to be sold at farmers' markets. "We decided to grow grains in part because it was something that could be processed during the off months, providing additional work," she says.

At the height of summer's busy season, the farm employs as many as sixty people, most of whom are Mexican immigrants who work by the hour. Full Belly is known for its generous wages and for having helped some workers buy houses in the community. In a 2004 article for the Rodale Institute, Full Belly farmer Paul Muller mused, "Wouldn't it be nice if in the future we judged organic farmers by how well they are taking care of all parts of the agriculture system, making sure farm labor is as healthy and cared for as any aspect of the farm?"

At Full Belly Farm, corn, one of our greatest American treasures, is one means to this end.

. . . .

ELIZABETH LINHART MONEY *is a freelance food and travel writer who has written about sustainable food systems from Alaska to the Bay Area. Based in San Francisco, she fantasizes about amber waves of grain returning to California's farms.*

. . . .

Photo by Cheryl Koehler

Growing Interest Keeps Tradition Alive

East Bay Charcuterie

Look around a neighborhood grocery store, or even a national supermarket chain, and you could believe that the business of curing meat is alive and well. Salami and ham are easy to find in the lunch-meat section or behind the sandwich counter.

But these commercial forms are almost always made with inferior meat and chemical additives that speed up the curing process. The traditional forms of cured meat—Italy's *salumi,* France's *charcuterie,* hams from America's South—are dying out. Industrial production has pushed the ancient practices out of the market, and the generation that might have kept them alive often chooses a life away from hard physical labor, grinders, fat, and big slabs of meat. Who can blame them?

Flavor has suffered because of it. Compare commercial pepperoni ("sausage soaked in kerosene," says a friend of mine) to the handcrafted version from Christopher Lee, chef and co-owner of Berkeley's Eccolo restaurant. Lee's rendition has a subtle flavor and succulent meatiness. His other cured meats—from salami to prosciutto—offer similar epiphanies.

Lee is one of a few East Bay chefs reviving traditional European charcuterie in the Bay Area, half a world away from its origins. It's a risky move for a restaurateur. When Lee buys meat by the pound for these products, he knows that he'll lose roughly 20 to 30 percent of that weight to evaporation. Add to that the value of time. Even a small salami hangs for three weeks in the restaurant's walk-in before it can make any money. A prosciutto ham hangs for fifteen months. Most restaurants understandably buy the charcuterie from someone else rather than make that investment.

But Lee, who worked at Chez Panisse for seventeen years before starting Eccolo, has a passion for cured meats and the complex flavors found in the traditional forms. It began in 1984, when he met salumi producers as he traveled through Tuscany. At the time, Lee didn't know much about the topic: The techniques are usually passed from father to son, and little information was available to Lee in books he read here in the United States. When renowned salumi maker Dario Cecchini invited Lee to work with him, Lee jumped at the chance. "At first, I was really interested in prosciutto," says Lee in his quiet voice. "There are only three ingredients to worry about: pork, salt, and time." But because you have to wait so long to see the results, it can be time-consuming to master the proportions and techniques. Lee says it took him three or four years to perfect his prosciutto, and now he considers it one of his specialties.

Even a straightforward salami benefits from Lee's expertise. "The aging and spicing is fundamentally different among the salumi," he says as we look at the meats hanging in his walk-in. "You don't want to spice the larger salami too much. They develop complex flavors and you don't want to overpower them." Lee talks about the walk-in's microclimate that he's carefully established. Since he doesn't use any additives, he needed an active population of the beneficial mold that ferments the meat as it cures. "We used to scrape the mold off of old salami to seed the population, but now we don't have to," says Lee, pointing out that the environment has become self-sustaining with a unique culture that adds its own character to his hams and salumi in the same way that different populations of yeast contribute subtle flavors to sourdough.

Lee's long experience with cured meat has made him more a mentor than a student, and he teaches and advises the next generation of chefs. He trained his sous chef, Lori Podraza, when she took an interest in the process, and now she does the bulk of the cured meats for the restaurant.

Chef Taylor Boetticher from Berkeley's Café Rouge came to ask for Lee's advice about salumi, and Lee suggested Boetticher study with Cecchini in Tuscany. After Boetticher returned from his Italian apprenticeship, he and his wife, Toponia, started a charcuterie business in the East Bay called Fatted Calf. Their wares quickly gained a cultlike following among the area's gourmet cognoscenti, their farmers' market stalls clean out early, and Fatted Calf products appear on the menus of many Bay Area restaurants.

While Eccolo focuses on Italian salumi, Fatted Calf's wares seem to be all over the map. "Mostly what we do is French and Italian," says the busy chef as we talk. But then he mentions that Fatted Calf is known for its *merguez*, a traditional Moroccan sausage. At a farmer's market on a recent Saturday, the stall was selling spicy Mexican-style chorizo as well as the drier Spanish form. The Boettichers also sell confits, rillettes (meat cooked slowly in fat and then shredded), terrines, and *crepinettes* (sausages wrapped in caul fat).

One might wonder if the diversity points to a lack of focus, but the array of possibilities clearly excites Boetticher. "One of the things that really fascinates me," he says of charcuterie, "is it's inherent in every culture of the world. There is an infinite number of flavor and texture combinations. It keeps inquisitive minds rolling." Certainly it keeps Boetticher's mind in motion. "I read a lot," he says in a hurried tone, "and every time I go somewhere, I'll check out charcuterie in the area to increase my knowledge." It's clear that Fatted Calf is the product of a deep passion.

Lee and Boetticher timed their ventures well: Consumer interest in traditional charcuterie seems to be growing. "When we first started," says Lee, "it was hard to get people interested in our meat and cheese plate." Now Eccolo sees thirty to forty orders a day for the antipasto platter that showcases the handcrafted products, and the staff makes 100 to 150 pounds of salami every few weeks. Boetticher recently added a farmers' market stall at San Francisco's Ferry Plaza to the one he maintains at the Berkeley Farmers' Market, and he's considering a third. Meanwhile, more restaurants continue to place orders for Fatted Calf charcuterie.

Though Lee suggests that some of this renewed interest might come from the recent infatuation with low-carb diets, he also notes that in the Bay Area, "people are just more into food, and they're more interested in traditional ingredients."

Christopher Lee carefully preps ingredients.

I jokingly suggest to Lee that one day Italians might come here to learn their ancient craft. He smiles, but there's a tinge of sadness in his expression. He sees the decline in traditional salami production in Italy, and it clearly upsets him. "There's a reason these practices have persisted," he says, "and I think it's worth preserving."

DERRICK SCHNEIDER *is a freelance food and wine writer based in the San Francisco Bay Area. In addition to writing for* Edible East Bay, *he has written for* The Art of Eating, *the* San Francisco Chronicle, *and* The Wine News. *He teaches wine appreciation classes at UC Berkeley Extension and maintains a popular food and wine blog at www.obsessionwithfood.com.*

Photo by Melissa Schneider

A Toast to the Future of Water

. . . .

Hawaii's Ocean Vodka

Each year millions of people escape to Hawaii, leaving behind jobs and responsibility in favor of stretches of warm sand, tropical fish, exotic flowers, and a license to drink regardless of the time of day. Amid this sun-drenched bacchanalia, beside countless swimming pools and man-made lagoons, it is easy to forget the reality of how fragile the island ecosystem is.

Withered, yellowing taro leaves cast shadows over a spider web of parched earth that had only a few months before been bathed with the cool runoff from a volcanic stream. The emaciated field stands in stark contrast to the tropical oasis of palm fronds, bananas, and ti leaves that festoon the crevices of a now-seasonal stream bed. A few hundred feet up the slope a deep mossy trench diverts water to the sugarcane fields in the valley and to resorts on the arid western shore of the island, leaving a muddy trickle as its only homage to generations of farmers who worked the land. Maui is constantly entwined in a feud over where water goes, to whom it belongs, and how it is used. The vast Pacific stretches out as a constant reminder of how close, yet far away this resource often is.

Ocean Vodka was likely in part inspired by the eastern shore of Maui. Shay Smith, the founder and CEO of the family-based company, was born on the Keanae Peninsula, one of the last remaining communities that continue to practice the ancient art of Hawaiian agriculture. These early years helped shape his current beliefs and ignited his passion for preserving the island's fragile natural resources. His experiences taught him to respect family, revere the ocean, and to be resourceful with what the island provides.

In 2004, already well established in the construction industry, the Smiths had been thinking about new business opportunities that they could pursue together as a family. One afternoon, while enjoying an afternoon cocktail, Shay noticed an ad for Mahalo Deep Sea Water. This innovative entry into the ever-popular bottled-water market relied on a $100 million desalinization facility built by Koyo USA on the Big Island of Hawaii. Not only was the water from the ocean, it was drawn from 3,000 feet below the surface with pumps developed by NELHA—The National Energy Lab of Hawaii Authority. Each day the lab pumped 2,000-year-old water near the floor of the ocean to the surface in an effort to create electricity. This century-old concept is often referred to simply as OTEC—Ocean Thermal Energy Conversion. Unfortunately, due to the low thermal efficiency of the process, the laboratory was never successful in creating enough energy to be financially viable. It turns out their greatest asset was the seawater the system produced.

Today, NELHA is home to a diverse collection of aquatic-based businesses, ranging from aquaculture to endangered sea horse preservation and bottled water. The mineral-rich ocean water, alleged to be far more pure than surface water, is highly sought after in Japan, where it is believed to help the body absorb vitamins. This demand explains why Koyo has quickly become Hawaii's largest exporter.

As Smith looked down at his vodka cranberry, something clicked. The vodka he was drinking was 80 proof, or 40 percent alcohol by volume. Would it be possible to create a vodka using desalinated ocean water as a base? He eagerly called a consulting firm that specialized in distilled beverages. After a brief conversation, things did not look good. The high-end vodka market was oversaturated, and the consultants warned him to be cautious. Despite this disheartening first opinion, Shay was confident there would be a market for vodka produced in Hawaii. He contracted a distillery in Idaho to create an extremely concentrated alcohol using organic corn and rye. This base was then shipped to Kahului, Maui, where the family added the remaining 60 percent of deep-sea water before bottling.

There are several advantages to this method. From an environmental perspective, it requires less fuel to transport an alcoholic base to Hawaii than to transport finished bottles of vodka. The flavor of the finished product is also unique because the mineral-rich ocean water is blended directly into the finished spirit, leaving it higher in essential nutrients than many other brands. Finally, completing the bottling process on Maui helps contribute to the local economy and provides jobs for Maui residents.

Shay's speculation was well founded. Today, four years after production started, over one million bottles of Ocean Vodka have been sold. The product has also received such accolades as being named the official vodka of Hawaiian Airlines, as well as being included at the Sundance Film Festival and the VMA awards—not bad for a company that self-admittedly relies on "The Coconut Wireless" (Hawaiian word of mouth) for the majority of its publicity. "In Hawaii good things are spread by coconut wireless; but who knew it worked on a global scale," said Shay, after listing off Japan, Guam, Fiji, and Europe as emerging markets.

Recently the family has been working on prototype batches using organic sugarcane pulp from Maui as a spirit base. Ideally they would like to support Hawaii as much as possible, and are looking at new recipes and products to help build their line. In their spare time they have even helped the Maui Pineapple Company promote their products in Japan, a testament to their dedication to preserving local agriculture. The Smiths also contribute a portion of the proceeds to help preserve Hawaii's ocean, in hopes that their children will be able to enjoy it just as they have.

Shay doesn't have much interest in flavored products. "The best flavors to mix with our vodka grow in our backyards," he exclaims, citing upcountry lavender, *lilikoi* (passion fruit), mango, and pineapple. "Sure, we could make a flavored vodka, but we would rather see people supporting local farms and experiencing truly fresh products."

As with all good ideas, people have taken notice of all the buzz surrounding Ocean Vodka. In 2009, a new entry into the arena of high-end local vodka promised to create competition at hotels and restaurants across the state. Pau Maui Vodka, distilled from pineapple pulp, could be a serious contender with its designer packaging and limited-production allure.

Because of environmentally conscience businesses like Ocean Vodka, Hawaii is taking great strides toward a greener future. There are hopes that through the use of composite components OTEC might one day be a viable source for clean energy. For now we will have to be content knowing that our vodka cocktail helps contribute not only to the advancement of clean energy but also the preservation of our oceans.

JOHN COX *is a strong advocate for local foods and supports local farms and ranches as executive chef at El Monte Sagrado and director of the Culinary Think Tank. When he is not in the kitchen, he enjoys traveling, food writing, and taking photos for several* Edible Communities *magazines.*

The Baker's Nose Knows

Le Petit Outre, Missoula, Montana

The temperature inside the brick oven at Le Petit Outre bakery has stayed at a constant 450 degrees for nearly ten years—twenty-four hours a day, seven days a week. Thermal stability, says Leif Bjelland, Le Petit's owner and founder, is indispensable to good baking.

During these ten years of thermal stability, Le Petit Outre has applied old-world craft to new-world ingredients and grown into a load-bearing, quality-of-life-boosting pillar of this small town in western Montana.

Missoula has fallen in step with the rhythm of the oven that never sleeps. The daily bread, pastry, and espresso drink specials are embedded in the calendars of its patrons, and woe to him who forgets to pick up his baguette for a dollar on Wednesday. The no-frill counter service is walk-in, walk-out only, with no bathroom and just a few unattended tables on the street corner during the warm months. The décor is spare and elegant. The croissants, when you bite into them, explode into a thousand crumbs.

An array of fine olive oils from Europe and California lines the shelves, along with a small assortment of aged and artisan vinegars. Occasional olive oil tastings allow Missoulans to compare the cultivated and crafted *terroirs* of the world's best olive-growing regions, brushed on a slice of Parisienne baguette. There is a sense of unwavering quality in every corner of the operation, from the olive oils for sale to the espresso drink lineup, to its top-notch artisan baked goods made with a short list of ingredients—many of which, including the wheat, are locally sourced—and there are no additives or preservatives.

If the baked goods are Le Petit Outre's backbone, then the brain stem of Missoula's town hearth is the playful, experimental spirit that Le Petit cultures—a reflection of Missoula's funky, eclectic personality. Le Petit has integrated itself into the soul of Missoula by applying tested, old-world techniques to local, high-quality ingredients in a postmodern context that's in tune with the currents of this whimsical community.

One prominent agent of this integration is the bicycle that handles deliveries of baked goods within a short radius of the bakery (a van carries the larger and long-haul loads). Bjelland, an avid cyclist and former competitive racer who admits to being a dreamer, credits much of the bakery's staying power to the workplace culture. "It's all about fun—a guerilla theater of sorts—seeing what you can get away with, changing perspectives and challenging conventional systems. I always had an image in my head of bread in bikes."

As a venue to test new products, the farmers' market has been the perfect place; each year it offers a lineup of goodies available only at the Saturday-morning market affair. Bjelland's experimental spirit has resulted in products such as a loaf made from spent grain, a by-product of the brewery next door, and a savory morel mushroom Danish—available in late spring when the morels are sprouting from the ashes of last year's forest fires. Another seasonal item worthy of note is a Christmas fruit bread that will actually get hungrily devoured—out of pleasure, not guilt. Others, like the cranberry Struan rolls (a bag of which, for me, is required on any hunting trip), along with Le Petit's new label "Alfredo," which offers sourdough pizza dough and a line of beet, spinach, and saffron pastas, are available only at the bakery and at select retail outlets around town.

Bjelland claims that "a perfect combination of ignorance, arrogance, and calculation" is responsible for his bakery's ten years of steady growth. This complex brew of ingredients is evident in his approach to baking as a combination of science and art.

"Leif is a chemist," says Brock Gnose, a longtime employee. "He smells the dough and figures out what it needs."

"Breathing and smelling what you are tasting is much overlooked when enjoying good food," Bjelland says. "When I see a bread from someplace foreign, I often smell it, while my wife sits at the opposite side of the table wondering about her husband, the guy who smells his bread before he eats it."

What, exactly, is the baker smelling for?

"One of the impurities of yeast is lactic bacteria," he explains. "They occur at a rate of about five parts per million. When we use a pre-ferment that has yeast, we are giving those lactic bacteria more time to build its army of flavor builders—lactic acid equals creamy flavor."

Thus, by monitoring climactic variables like ambient temperature and humidity, smelling the dough, and controlling the time the dough proofs (proofing occurs when the yeast begin consuming sugars in the wheat, causing the bread to rise), Bjelland multiplies the lactic-acid bacteria content in his dough, creating breads with a distinct rich, creamy flavor.

While understanding the science is key, Bjelland believes that making craft bread is more like alchemy than chemistry, a combination of hands, heart, eye, and—yes—we can't forget the nose. His passion and skill have found an eager audience among the ranks of his bakers, who are well cared for, loyal, and committed to the art of artisan bread.

"A few days ago someone mixed what they thought was the best dough," Bjelland says. "The dough was divided, formed, let rest for the final proof, cut, and placed in the oven. It came out of the oven looking like hell. Hell is an overstatement, but that's how the person felt. That is how I have felt, and I truly believe if you cannot connect like this, you are not an artisan, you are not a baker."

Soulful, alchemical talents notwithstanding, Bjelland gives full credit for the quality of his product to his 22,000-pound oven, every brick of which was imported from France along with a Frenchman named Claude, who put it back together again on this side of the pond. Claude told Bjelland that the oven "is from a village that's still in the Dark Ages."

"The oven's design has been common in European villages for centuries," Bjelland explains. "The city center would have an oven similar to ours that people could bring their dough to and bake it on a daily basis. It has no moving parts, three decks, and can hold one hundred loaves at a constant temperature."

Meanwhile, the bread's perfect golden crust, he explains, is due to high water content in the dough. When the dough hits the stone decks of the brick oven, "you get a tremendous kick from the bottom of the bread." The water vaporizes, creating a steamy environment in the oven that caramelizes the loaves' exterior and creates what Bjelland calls "an interesting crumb." Thermal stability, he says, is also a hallmark of a quality espresso machine, and Le Petit's espresso surely belongs on the short list of any Missoulan espressophile.

Le Petit Outre is like an Americanized immigrant that is fully devoted to its roots, even if it's here to stay. It's a little corner of Europe in the mountains of Montana—but unmistakably here and not there.

In 2006, Le Petit acquired a 12,000-square-foot warehouse on the edge of town to create an expanded retail space for specialty foods and to satisfy Missoula's insatiable demand for Le Petit Outre's baked goods. True to form, one of the first things Bjelland did after closing on the new space was to bring Claude the oven builder back to Missoula, along with another load of bricks and hardware, to create another town hearth. With the new space . . . new possibilities.

"Now that we have offices with doors, desks, and phones we will begin working on the 'Birdman' project," he says. "We hope to find bakeries similar to ours in other demographics that can bake and distribute 'Birdman Bread' in their markets."

A mixed-grain bread with lots of polenta, Birdman is, along with the Parisienne baguettes, Le Petit's most popular item. The polenta helps make it a perfect toaster, and Missoula has become addicted to Birdman sandwiches in its lunch boxes, on its breakfast tables, and for midnight snacks.

Le Petit have begin making and distributing Mexitana tortillas in the new space, which will be shared with Big Dipper ice cream, another homegrown Missoula institution. There will also be expanded retail space and hot-food options like pizza. The details, though, have yet to fall into place. One thing that will be there for sure, he promises, is "magic."

ARI LEVAUX *writes "Flash in the Pan," a nationally syndicated weekly food column for locavores.*

From Whisk to Microphone

The Evolving World of Evan Kleiman

Some people are so well known that they're readily identifiable by a single name. On the Los Angeles food scene, one of those names is Evan.

In the twenty-five years since she opened Angeli Caffé, Evan Kleiman's Thursday-night family-style meals have become legend. First there is the feast, which centers on a theme, perhaps a seasonal item like tomatoes, or a calendar event like Thanksgiving or Passover. Then there is Evan herself, the executive chef who slips out of the kitchen to schmooze with diners, discuss the evening's themed meal, and greet those eager to meet the voice of *Good Food*, which broadcasts across the country each week on KCRW Radio. In fact, we once brought friends visiting from Chicago to Angeli for one of Evan's Thursday-night meals. They were thrilled to meet the woman whose radio show they listened to faithfully.

When Evan wearies of chat, be it at the restaurant or on the radio, she can always retreat to the kitchen, to her garden, or to her computer, where she has produced four cookbooks. But then the urge to explore food, ideas, geography, history, and culture strikes again, and she's off to Italy with a group of culinary travelers in tow. If she elects instead to do her exploring at home, she has an entire radio audience to listen to her adventures as she interviews guests from across the spectrum.

Because of all these hats she wears, Evan increasingly is coming to identify herself as a culinary voyeur, a title she says has described her since childhood. Growing up as the only child of a single mother, she spent a lot of time by herself, reading and dreaming of large families and of other cities and other countries, and what it would be like to have different lives in different places.

"Reading defines me about as much as cooking does," she says. Some food books are not just collections of recipes but narratives that reveal a lot about the cultures from which they come. "I'd read about Viennese food, the grand black-and-white balls, pre–World War I life. Food was like theater for me. I still love vintage books."

Could you also name her passion "culinary anthropology"? Quite possibly. Naomi Duguid and Paula Wolfert are certainly food anthropologists, and it is writers like these whose work intrigues and inspires Evan. Anyone listening to *Good Food* for the first time might wonder why she interviews so many people whose business is not specifically some aspect of food production. But what these people have to say reveals how food is central to our lives on many levels, from the cultural to the religious, from the political to the sociological.

"People reveal a lot about themselves when they talk about food, and sometimes they even give you a twist on your own life," she says. "Often it can be through something as simple as a family recipe."

In addition to her work at the restaurant, Evan interviews anywhere from four to ten people each week for her radio program, including artists, writers, scientists, and doctors—people whose connection with food may be tangential, but whose opinions on food are no less important than those of chefs or food producers.

"This is what makes me different from other food people," she explains. "It's not just about what's on the plate, but how food conveys the totality of society and culture that fascinates me."

Food politics is of especial interest to her, so she not only reads the works of writers like Raj Patel, author of *Stuffed and Starved: The Hidden Battle for the World Food System*, and Michael Pollan, author of *The Omnivore's Dilemma*, but she invites them onto her program to discuss those crucial connections between the science of our food and the living of our lives.

It's much more than an idle, pedestrian interest that drives Evan to learn about other cultures through food.

"When you know what your 'enemy' cooks and eats and you envision him sitting down to a meal with his family, you're more inclined to see him as a human being, not as some evil person to be fought," she explains.

It is apparent that being a culinary voyeur involves considerable breadth and depth of reading and research, all of which Evan loves. At some point, however, equilibrium must be maintained.

"When I get too much in my head, I go cook," she says.

But whether she's in the kitchen or at the farmers' market, Evan's thoughts never stray far from the sociology of food. In fact, she recounts the wake-up call that the events of September 11, 2001, sounded for her personally: "9/11 happened on a Tuesday, and the next day was market day. I had to shop for the restaurant, but I didn't want to go out. I went, though, and it was the best thing I could have done. Everyone was subdued, but they were making eye contact. I think we all realized that it was important to make a connection with others. What a life-affirming place to do that! The farmers are feeding us, and we're buying their food and supporting them. I remember weeping, feeling touched by this sense of community around me there at the farmers' market. I didn't want to take it for granted anymore."

And she doesn't. While, sadly, many people have no clue where their food comes from, few remain oblivious when Evan is around.

"Several years ago when I was first beginning to get involved with Slow Food, I spent a lot of time visiting farms and talking to farmers. One day I was at a farm with a kid who worked for me, and he asked me, 'What do they do to this food to make it edible?' I asked him what he meant. He said, 'It comes out of the dirt, right? What do they do to it? Do they nuke it or what?' I had to explain to him that dirt isn't actually *dirty*."

As for the realities of a harsh economic climate, Evan sees a silver lining in people developing a closer link with their food supply.

"I hope more people are encouraged to plant a garden at home," she says. "Growing your own food completely alters the way you think about food and feeding your family. It really changes you." She notes that charitable agencies that assemble groceries for the poor are realizing the value of including fresh produce whenever possible. For a long time food pantries accepted only sealed boxes and cans of nonperishable food. Evan takes it as a great sign that they now welcome fresh produce and meat, too, and sees it as a great opportunity for more people to become educated about good food. WIC (Women, Infants, and Children) vouchers now make up a significant amount of the currency used at the Hollywood Farmers' Market, and she feels this is

Evan shows off one of her delicious creations.

a good indication that the message is getting out there about the value of incorporating fresh fruit and vegetables into the diet.

"The name 'Hollywood' evokes a world of glitz and glamour, but the reality is that a lot of the people who live there are the working poor," she explains. Evan finds this kind of turnout at the farmers' market encouraging. So are the increased opportunities for farmers to visit children in the classroom and to invite them on, quite literally, *field trips*, to see what the farmers are doing and how it affects them. This is an important step in helping children connect the dots between the farm and their own plates.

While Evan owns up to enjoying a favorite (but unnamed!) junk food now and then, she emphasizes that it's only an occasional digression. For those who are interested in weaning themselves off of a steady diet of mass-produced and overprocessed foods, baby steps are typically what's needed to set them on a successful path toward better nutrition.

She identifies this progression: A guy may start out microwaving a frozen hamburger in a bun from the store. This encourages him to try something else, something a little more challenging, and he continues until he sees that cooking for himself is not arcane or difficult. In fact, it can be downright enjoyable.

Regardless of what they decide to call it, she hopes home economics will soon stage a comeback. The Food Network is helping make the business of cooking more visible and acceptable, especially among men. Evan says she's amazed—and amused—by how men are attracted to making salad dressing in particular.

"What is it that draws them to it?" she asks. "Is it the whisk!"

While Los Angeles can certainly be a scene defined by trends, Evan feels that "trend" doesn't apply in the same way to this city's awareness of sustainability and eating in season. She explains:

"The thing about Los Angeles and California is that we're way ahead of the curve when it comes to health. Local cookbooks from the early part of the twentieth century show a preoccupation with fresh fruit and vegetables. I think the idea of seasonality and freshness was already there, although perhaps dormant in the minds of Californians. Now that the light bulb has gone on, people are flocking to the farmers' markets.

"Appearance and health concerns are not a trend out here, because so many people in L.A. earn a living with their faces and bodies. There's a recognition that fresh, seasonal food is necessary for maintaining their health and good looks. It has made a deep impression on these people."

Evan is encouraged by the younger generation's attitude toward food, noting that the children who come to Angeli tend to have sophisticated palates and know what they want to eat.

"It's like it skipped a generation," she says. "In the fifties women stayed home and kept house and cooked. In the sixties the thing that suffered was the family table, as more women entered the workforce—not that I'm at all against women working. For a while, gourmet food became a way of expressing status in society, but it was disconnected from daily life. That's gone now, and the younger generation is cooking—it's just a natural part of how they express themselves. And the family table is becoming important again.

"Younger food professionals take for granted the world of food diversity now. They support the players in this effort. I came to organic and farm-fresh late, not until I was in my forties. They're in their twenties, and they get it already. So I don't think it's a trend—it's an actual turning of the page."

And Evan Kleiman most definitely has had a hand in turning the page for Los Angeles.

Angeli Caffé sits in a stretch of Melrose Avenue that's dominated by the edgy and the hip. In fact, the front of Angeli wraps around the entrance to a body piercing and tattoo parlor, which can be a little disorienting for first-time visitors to the restaurant. But there's great symbolism in this, as the restaurant began a quarter century ago as a super-trendy place to eat. Over the years the edges have smoothed, and it has become what she describes as a more egalitarian, family-friendly place, while never letting go of its appreciation of a good time.

"We've established a tradition here," Evan explains. "When children come, they get dough to play with while they wait for their meal, and we bake it." For many of these kids, it's their first time to handle food in its unfinished, potential-food form, and it makes a deep impression on them and on their parents as well.

"It's important to have a good food experience, not something that's intellectually taxing," she says. "Angeli is unfussy. We serve simple food that's to be enjoyed. At the end of the day it's about an inviting place and a good meal."

While Evan loves her restaurant and cooking, she finds that she doesn't identify as completely with her role as chef as she once did. "What I do is a combination of cooking in the restaurant, which I've done for twenty-five years, and then having the radio show for ten years now. It's interesting to see how full circle I've come."

As she has moved beyond feeding individuals to informing entire communities through her weekly broadcasts, Evan has begun making plans to venture beyond cookbook writing to narrative writing. Even fiction is on her mind for future projects. She notes that blogging has been a valuable entrée into this new phase of writing and credits it with helping her experiment with different styles so that she can find the right voice through which to explore the world by way of its food and food traditions.

Evan notes that a lot of people who don't deal with food daily have no idea how deeply it runs through everything. In response to this, she says her life goal is to be the culinary love child of Charlie Rose and Jon Stewart, "to understand the reality of food in its many facets while seeing how silly it all can be."

Balancing depth of knowledge with a light touch is what she hopes to achieve, and listening to *Good Food* reveals that Evan Kleiman is already succeeding at this goal.

CAROL PENN-ROMINE *is a writer and chef who has contributed to* Gastronomica, *the* Christian Science Monitor, Cornbread Nation IV: The Best of Southern Writing, *and* Food Jobs. *She is past editor of* Edible Los Angeles *and writes for several* Edible *magazines.*

Photo by Carol Penn-Romine

ORGANIZATION ~ *EDIBLE OJAI* (CALIFORNIA)

Helping to Sprout a Movement

Food for Thought Ojai

The lunch recess bell rang, putting an abrupt end to the din of yelling, laughing, running kids on the playground. I waved to my twin daughters as they trudged back to their third-grade classrooms, wondering how they were adjusting to their new school in Ojai after our move from Oakland. As I walked across the now-deserted lunch area, a slight gust blew an empty potato-chip bag around my ankles. I headed for the nearest trash can. Peering in, I surveyed the aftermath of school lunch: piles of Styrofoam trays laden with chicken nuggets and mashed potatoes, unopened bags of baby carrots, dozens of half-full cartons of chocolate milk, Lunchables trays, apples with a single bite taken out of them, chip bags, plastic water bottles, paper napkins, candy wrappers, plastic sporks, soda cans, and other fast-food refuse. I continued walking past the chain-link fence surrounding the school garden. It was clear that at some point, the little garden had been loved and nurtured, but faded signs sitting askew in beds filled with weeds and crabgrass attested to recent neglect.

Over the next couple of weeks my daughters and I grew comfortable with our new school—there were, after all, wonderful teachers, a caring principal, great kids, and stimulating programs. But, like persistent gnats, thoughts of overflowing trash cans, weed-filled garden beds, and bad food going into little bellies kept buzzing around in my head. How could it be that in the midst of all the fresh fruits and vegetables I saw growing all around me in this agricultural county, kids in school were eating so much highly processed, artificial food? And was it necessary to generate so much trash at lunchtime? Why was the garden abandoned?

It is true that five years of living in the Bay Area, a "blue-green" island of liberal foodies and environmentalists, had colored my thinking, almost as much as my twenty-odd years of working on national and international conservation and environmental issues. My daughters, too, had become fully indoctrinated in the ways of good, healthy food: At the tender age of seven they had once admonished their friend's mom for pulling into a McDonald's for a quick meal during a long car trip. But my thoughts also wandered beyond food and gardens to the larger world and the distressing disparity between this careless waste and the poverty I'd seen in the developing countries where I had lived and worked for over a decade. What were we teaching our kids? How could I call myself an environmentalist and not try to raise awareness with my kids and their peers in the next generation who would inherit this earth? And how could lessons in healthy living and good food be translated from the frenetic, cosmopolitan Bay Area to bucolic, eclectic little Ojai, a town of about 8,000 nestled against the Los Padres foothills?

I found myself thinking out loud about these things in the checkout line of our local health food store one day. The friendly checker said, "You should talk to that woman over there—she's writing articles about healthy food and local farmers. Maybe she's someone you should talk to?" I approached the woman and introduced myself. "That woman" turned out to be Tracey Ryder, and the articles she was working on were for her new publication, *Edible Ojai*. Tracey told me that the person I really needed to talk to was a tangerine grower named Jim Churchill, who was doing something with schools and farms in Ventura. I then contacted Jim, who in turn connected me with a woman named Pat McCart Malloy, a genial powerhouse of a parent who had managed to institute a "farm-fresh" daily salad bar at her children's public school in Ventura. This, I soon learned, was an endeavor at the forefront of a new farm-to-school movement, inspired by Alice Waters and her Edible Schoolyard ideals, hatched and realized in California by a handful of school districts in Los Angeles, Davis, and Ventura.

Pat invited me to sample the school salad bar lunch. Over crunchy carrots and celery, ripe red tomatoes, and an abundant plate of salad greens, Pat told me that she was working not only with Jim Churchill but also with a fellow named Steve Fields, who, as part of his Master Gardeners certification, was helping her install some classroom garden boxes. Steve and Jim, it turned out, lived in Ojai. I called them both and asked to meet them to see if we could get something going for Ojai's schools. I recall asking Jim why he was helping schools in Ventura when he lived in Ojai. "Ah," he said. "I was waiting for you," meaning he needed a parent to start planting the seeds of change. So with that first meeting of the minds in the fall of 2002, a triumvirate—a parent, a farmer, and a gardener-businessman—was formed that would kick-start Food for Thought Ojai, California's fourth farm-to-school program and part of what would soon be a nationwide movement of thousands of similar programs that are attempting to connect local farms to schools in a potentially win-win effort to get more fresh, locally grown healthy fruits and vegetables into school meals while supporting local farmers.

Our first order of business was to meet with the Ojai Unified School District's superintendent and get his blessing to work with school food service staff to start a school lunch salad bar that featured fresh, seasonal, and local produce. He gave us the green light, and off we went, purchasing a salad bar unit for our first pilot school and sourcing and procuring organic fruits and vegetables from local farms. Flyers were sent home in backpacks announcing our new Friday salad bar that would commence September 5, 2003, featuring sweet cherry tomatoes from Tutti Fruiti Farms, crunchy cucumbers from Fairview Gardens, petite carrots and yellow seedless watermelon from Underwood Farms, mixed baby greens from McGrath Farms, and end-of-the-season juicy peaches from Scattaglia Ranch, all grown within a hundred-mile radius of Ojai.

I had to go to work the day the salad bar would be launched, but Jim and Steve were going to help out. I called Jim just after I knew the lunch bell would ring, anxious to know how it was going. "Can't talk! Line goes out the door! There are parents and teachers, too!" he said in staccato notes. I bit my nails and called back about twenty minutes later. "We ran out of watermelon and tomatoes! Steve has to go to the grocery store right now to get more!" In the succeeding weeks, there were many laudatory remarks from teachers and parents. Things became a bit less chaotic, the lines remained long, and teachers became regulars on salad bar Fridays. Fall melons and apples shifted to winter offerings of tangerines and persimmons (or "permissions" as some of the kindergartners called them), while we began planning a roll-out salad bar lunch to two more elementary schools in the Ojai school district. We all patted ourselves on the back and felt we were on to something but dreaded the logistics of delivering enough local produce out of the backs of our cars to schools to feed almost a thousand kids.

Realizing we needed more hands on deck, we invited community members and formed a steering committee that met regularly around my dinner table. Our combined expertise now included a chef, a graphic designer, a couple of farmers, a registered dietician, an environmentalist, a retired principal, and a retired teacher. We expanded our horizons, feeling that we needed to offer kids a chance to really understand where their food came from and just what went into growing it. We won small grants that enabled us to take students on field trips to local farms and introduce them to the farmers growing items featured on the salad bar. Many of them had never been to a farm or had the experience of pulling up a carrot or picking a red ripe strawberry, still warm from the sun. Very few carrots or strawberries made it back to the bus, consumed on the spot with exclamations of "the ones in the store sure don't taste sweet like that!"

Flush with these little successes, we staged our first fund-raiser featuring a movie star (Tony Shalhoub, star of a film called *Big Night* about an Italian chef trying in vain to educate the American pizza palate), a movie (*Made-Up*, a film starring Mr. Shalhoub's wife, Brooke Adams, and his directorial debut), a sell-out crowd, and a delectable VIP dinner prepared by local chefs using local produce. The proceeds, combined with a few more small grants, enabled us to tackle the Topa Topa Elementary School garden. With years of neglect, the clay soil had become as hard as cement, so, armed with pickaxes and shovels, a small army of parent volunteers and their kids tackled the renovation. We toiled an entire weekend, rebuilding broken garden boxes and irrigation hoses, pulling up weeds, replacing tired dirt with rich, dark topsoil, laying down weed cloth and mulch on pathways, fixing class signs for each garden box. The garden gate was framed by an old trellis arch that stubbornly leaned to the left, supporting some withered climbing white roses. I tried to straighten the trellis, then mulched, fertilized, and watered the roses. Our dirty, tired but happy crew admired our work— the clean new garden beds, the graceful pathways— then said our good-byes and headed home.

Almost six years later, Food for Thought Ojai's Healthy Schools Program is healthier than ever, clearly fulfilling a need in our community and schools, a pioneer among the thousands of farm-to-school programs that have since sprung up across the country, working to address the epidemic of childhood obesity while supporting local farms. Food for Thought Ojai has matured to become a comprehensive program that teaches our children to make healthy choices lasting their lifetime and strives to increase levels of agricultural and environmental literacy. Our program includes nutrition education classes, farm field trips, and garden-based lessons. We have added a new component called "Up and Down the Wastestream," which teaches kids about consumption, waste, and that when something gets thrown away, there really is no "away." Students conduct waste audits, strategize about how to reduce waste, maintain worm bins, and collect food waste for garden composting. We are embarking on new efforts to help the school district minimize all waste—paper, energy, water—and switch to green cleaning agents and paints and become a model "green school" district. We've fostered garden clubs at all the elementary schools, where kids pour into the garden during their recess times to work with our garden coordinators to weed, mulch, and harvest. Then, at school-parking-lot farmers' markets, the little farmers proudly ply their beets, lavender, Brussels sprouts, beans, squash, mint tea, and sweet peas to parents and teachers.

All of these elements are integrated to complete the cyclical lesson of producing, consuming, and discarding while learning to tread as lightly as possible on the earth. We hear plenty of anecdotes of students "teaching up" to their parents, asking where the apples in the fruit basket came from, why the strawberries from the supermarket don't smell or taste like the ones from the farm they visited, and can they please purchase reusable water bottles. Our volunteers revel in the feeling that they are planting the seeds of change in young hearts and minds. In many ways there is evidence that the adult community has caught up to our children in learning the lessons that reconnect them to the earth that sustains us all.

It hasn't all gone smoothly. We've battled food service directors, tried to win over resentful lunch ladies, fought to change school policies to support healthier school food, worked hard to raise money and

Meihers Oaks students harvesting peas

to pass resolutions to green our public schools. We are still working to overcome a centralized food distribution and conventional agricultural system that values efficiency and long shelf life over the freshness, taste, and better nutrition offered by produce from small local farms. We even went to Washington, D.C., to lobby for changes in the Farm Bill that would give priority to local farms for school food procurement. And as we've grown we've added wonderful part-time staff but have to constantly chase funds to keep our little machine humming. We've been lucky in that regard with generous supporters who believe in our mission. We naively asked a rising rock-star friend and some of his surfing legend buddies to headline a fund-raising concert called "Locally Grown." The stars lined up in our favor, and Jack Johnson and the Malloy brothers agreed to do the event. Our plan was to sell tickets at the Sunday Farmers Market for a few weeks. As we arrived to set up our little table and cash box, we were astonished to see a several-blocks-long line of young and old (some had even spent the night on the side of the road to hold their place in line). We were sold out within hours. Locally Grown has since become a much-anticipated biannual event showcasing rising talent and extolling the environmental and health virtues of eating locally grown food.

Food for Thought Ojai has matured into a registered nonprofit, and most of the old guard on the Steering Committee have been replaced by an energetic young board that includes doctors, a nutritionist, a banker, educators, farmers, chefs, and, for good measure, a lawyer. They have together crafted a clear-eyed vision and a mission statement, and are ready to take it to the next level, broadening our sphere of influence into the community with a Films for Thought series, "Plant to Plate" cooking sessions, and trading lessons and experiences with a sister organization in Hawaii and other farm-to-school programs around the country.

My twin daughters are in high school now. They still prefer to eat dinner at home rather than at the fast-food joints that ring their school, preying on teenagers. They both earn spending money working at the Sunday Farmers Market, selling fish or berry pies and Churchill Orchard's eclectic citrus and avocado varieties when those are in season. And the garden trellis that frames the gate at their elementary alma mater still leans to the left.

MARTY FUJITA, *PhD, was formally trained in evolutionary ecology and has twenty years of experience working for the environment at home and abroad. She is a member of Ventura Ag Futures Alliance and is the founder and president of Food for Thought—Ojai Healthy Schools Program.*

Photo by Timothy Teague

People, places, things

BOZEMAN (MONTANA)

Nestled in the high mountain valleys of southwestern Montana you'll find renowned cattle country, where locally raised, grass-fed cattle and bison are prospering as well as growing in popularity. The well-watered valleys (just north of Yellowstone Park and 45 degrees latitude), with long, sunny summer days are excellent for short-season and cool-climate vegetables, with peas a traditional favorite, and seed potatoes a growing cash crop.

Jenny Sabo Jenny and her family are extreme locavores, purchasing only 5 percent of their food commercially. A good portion of Jenny's time is spent teaching others to eat locally.

Community Food Co-op Since 1979, the Community Food Co-op has consistently grown its business model in accordance with the increasing demand for fresh, local, and organic food.

Western Sustainability Exchange A nonprofit that for fifteen years has helped ranchers convert to sustainable practices and form partnerships between local producers and buyers.

Jessica Wilcox As the dietician for Livingston HealthCare, Jessica has turned the traditional institutional food model on its head by introducing local foods into the system versus traditional packaged food.

Gallatin Valley Botanical A family-owned farm, they provide local and organic food to 120 CSA members, 15 restaurants, and local farmers' markets, paving the way for other small local growers in the valley.

www.ediblecommunities.com/bozeman/peopleplacesthings

EAST BAY (CALIFORNIA)

East of the San Francisco Bay lies a community with a brief (California gold rush to World War II) but rich history as a food-producing region followed by an era of cultural blossoming (epicenter, Alice Waters and Chez Panisse) that helped launch the local foods movement (the word "locavore" was minted here). Producers of artisanal food products abound and a new urban farming movement is growing by leaps and bounds.

Chez Panisse Since Alice Waters founded her legendary restaurant in 1971, it has been the central inspiration for the movement to bring local, seasonal products to the table.

City Slicker Farms A grass-roots organization that advocates for food justice and works to increase food self-sufficiency in the African-American community of West Oakland.

Bryant Terry This chef/food justice activist is the author, with Anna Lappé, of *Vegan Soul Kitchen: Fresh, Healthy, and Creative African-American Cuisine* and *Grub: Ideas for an Urban Organic Kitchen.*

The Ecology Center in Berkeley The center has been running certified organic farmers' markets since 1987. They also run Berkeley's recycling program and maintain an education center.

Rick and Kristie Knoll of Knoll Farms These farmers supply area restaurants with produce from their ten-acre piece of land in Brentwood, where urban sprawl has threatened a historic growing region.

www.ediblecommunities.com/eastbay/peopleplacesthings

HAWAIIAN ISLANDS

The Hawaiian Islands: Images of beauty immediately come to mind—a paradise in the middle of the Pacific. In the past, these islands were all about local. Each island has so much to offer: the chefs, the farmers, and the community. "Talk Story" is the Hawaiian term for sharing information: We Talk Story about old traditions, as well as promote the importance of supporting local. The Hawaiian Islands are unique in that they are surrounded by the Pacific Ocean; therefore they must be independent in terms of food source. Sustainability is a must.

Nancy Redfeather Nancy is committed to teaching organic agriculture to the Big Island youth through her current project, Hawaii Island School Gardens Network (HISGN), which is sponsored by the Kohala Center.

Ken Love Ken, executive director at Hawaii Tropical Fruit Growers, is a specialist in tropical fruit horticulture, working on local sustainability issues for Hawaiian farmers, value-added product development, and farmer-chef relations.

Alan Wong This chef and restaurateur is known as one of the cofounders of Hawaii Regional Cuisine. In addition to Alan's restaurants, he created the Farmers Series Dinner—"Taste Hawaii."

Hawaii 2050 Sustainability Task Force This group has developed a blueprint for Hawaii's preferred future. It reflects the hopes and aspirations of Hawaii's people.

Exotic Fruits and Vegetables The Hawaiian Islands are blessed with exotic fruits and vegetables, most of which are available only through local farmers, including poi, dragon fruit, cacao, ginger, pohole (fern shoots), ulu (breadfruit), Star apple, Mountain apple, and lilikoi (passion fruit).

www.ediblecommunities.com/hawaiianislands/peopleplacesthings

LOS ANGELES

Los Angeles has a food community as rich and layered as its 200-year history would suggest. Not confined to the glamour and hype of its Hollywood eateries or famous chefs, the real L.A., as its residents know well, plays host to one of the most diverse collections of Latin American and Asian cuisines there is. Underlying it all: its wealth of farmers' markets and its growing movement toward sustainable living.

Community Services Unlimited Neelam Sharma's programs teach inner-city youth to garden, cook what they've grown, and understand their culture through their food.

The Green Truck Hungry Angelenos are no longer stuck with the quasifood options at their corner quick-stop market. These shops-on-wheels provide healthy, organic eats and are powered by vegetable oil, of course.

Grand Central Market This 1917 downtown landmark caters to both the Hispanic population and to those who work downtown, selling fresh produce and a variety of authentic Mexican foods, including a dazzling array of prepared moles.

La Brea Bakery For the past two decades, Chef Nancy Silverton has raised the bar for a good loaf of bread in Los Angeles and has offered her artisan bread nationwide.

Little India This part of town distinguishes itself as the go-to place for an authentic Indian meal—or for everything you need to make one yourself.

www.ediblecommunities.com/losangeles/peopleplacesthings

MARIN AND WINE COUNTRY

As you cross over the Golden Gate Bridge heading north out of San Francisco, you enter Marin and the wine country. From the rugged Pacific coastline and sheltered bays where oysters and other shellfish are being farmed, to rich farm and ranch lands, to world-class wine-growing areas, this region is an extraordinary cornucopia of locally produced foods and wines. Literally minutes from major metropolitan population centers, you can tour one of the many certified organic farms in the region and dine on the foods and wines—many of which are now being produced using sustainable, organic, and biodynamic methods—produced on these farms.

The Paris Wine Tasting of 1976 This contest is said to have put California wines "on the map" and caused a great uproar in the wine world, which had long held that France was the foremost producer of the world's best wines.

Star Route Farms, Bolinas The oldest continuously certified organic farm in California was founded by Warren Weber in 1974 on five acres—using horse-drawn sulky plows and cultivators, and a lot of "long-haired ambition."

The Gravenstein Apple A native of Denmark and one of the best all-around apple varietals. Sebastopol in Sonoma County is known for its production of these apples and hosts an annual Gravenstein Apple Fair.

Straus Dairy and Straus Family Creamery Family-owned Straus Dairy became the first certified organic dairy west of the

Mississippi River in 1994 and is the only California milk producer that runs both an organic dairy and an organic creamery.

Laura Chenel America's first commercial producer of goat cheese. In 1979, Laura began producing chèvre in Sonoma County, after a fact-finding trip to visit goat-cheese producers in France—and because she loved goats.

www.ediblecommunities.com/marinandwinecountry/peopleplacesthings

MISSOULA (MONTANA)

Missoula, nicknamed the "Garden City," has a rich, varied, and vibrant food scene. This western Montana community boasts many thriving farmers' markets, Community Supported Agriculture (CSAs), and natural food grocers, as well as local artisans producing award-winning breads, chocolates, and libations. The Farm-to-School and Farm-to-College programs, a Buy Fresh Buy Local–Farm to Restaurant Collaborative, and the Western Montana Growers Cooperative actively connect its many farmers and producers to the marketplace.

Garden City Harvest This collaborative organization believes in the need to revive Montana's regional tradition of producing one's own food for one's community, including the 20 percent of Missoulians who live in poverty.

Bob Marshall, Biga Pizza Bob has a philosophy that supporting the local community and economy is just as important as making sensational food and is part of what makes a restaurant good. He uses local, organic ingredients sourced directly from producers in the state.

Le Petit Outre This operation follows the time-honored bread-baking traditions of Europe. The breads are handcrafted using traditional methods and four basic ingredients: Montana wheat flour, water, sea salt, and yeast.

Kettlehouse A neighborhood brewery and taproom, Kettlehouse is known as "the little brewery that cans." Using local and regional grains and hops, they are the world's earth-friendliest brewery.

Hmong Farming Community Since their arrival in the Missoula area in the late 1970s, members of the community now play a large role in the Missoula Farmers' Market, and they make up about 40 percent of all vendors.

www.ediblecommunities.com/missoula/peopleplacesthings

OJAI (CALIFORNIA)

Agriculture in Ventura County provides the cultural heartbeat of this fertile area. The Ojai Valley, in particular, has many unique microclimates, so farmers can grow a wide variety of fruits and vegetables year-round. Integral to the rich history and culture of the area is the Latino community; and the idea that the land is sacred and worthy of protecting is part of the legacy of the area's indigenous people, the Chumash Indians. Local farmers, the vanguard of the sustainable movement, have become tireless activists in their efforts to preserve that legacy so that the land and the rest of us will thrive.

The Pixie Tangerine This petite Mandarin hybrid is totally seedless, intensely flavored, and oh-so-easy to peel. Today more than 25,000 Ojai Pixie trees grace the Ojai Valley, thanks to two dozen farming families.

Marty Fujita, PhD Marty is the founder and president of Food for Thought. FFT, in partnership with the Ojai Unified School District, has developed several programs including Up and Down the Waste Stream, which teaches students the five R's: reduce, reuse, recycle, rot, and rethink.

The Ojai Vineyard Considered one of the top visionary wine makers in the country, Adam Tolmach produces handcrafted wines that include Rhone varietals, Chardonnay, Riesling, and a knock-your-socks-off Pinot Noir.

Aromatherapy Throw away all those scented candles and head to the fields of Oxnard in peak strawberry season to smell the real thing. From April to June, up to 10 million pints of strawberries are picked, packed, and shipped daily.

Food Share In 1978, Jewel Pedi and six friends began offering food to the homeless under a bridge near the riverbed in Ventura. Today, Food Share and its partners provide meals for more than 40,000 hungry people each month.

www.ediblecommunities.com/ojai/peopleplacesthings

SACRAMENTO

California's agriculture industry is number one in the nation and number one in the world, and at the heart of it is the Sacramento Valley, with crops ranging from wine grapes to poultry to vegetables and everything in between. California family farms provide jobs, create habitat, and grow the fruits, vegetables, meat, and grain products that feed families throughout our nation.

Community Alliance with Family Farmers CAFF's mission is to build a movement of rural and urban people to foster family-scale agriculture that cares for the land, sustains local economies, and promotes social justice. It has been in existence for more than thirty years.

Davis Joint Unified School District's Farm-to-School Connection This program opened its first salad bar in 2001 at Pioneer Elementary. Now the program has expanded, offering locally procured, seasonal produce two days a week to all eight elementary schools in the school district.

Capay Valley Grown Capay Valley Vision and the valley's growers created the Capay Valley Grown logo, a place-based identity and brand for this unique valley that encompasses more than 150 agricultural producers.

UC Davis Good Life Garden The Good Life Garden contains an ever-changing edible landscape, which features organic and sustainably grown vegetables, herbs, and flowers, accompanied by compelling food and health educational signage for the benefit of faculty, students, staff, and visitors.

PlacerGROWN This is a nonprofit membership organization formed to assist local agricultural producers market their produce and agricultural products and to enhance the viability of agriculture in Placer County.

www.ediblecommunities.com/sacramento/peopleplacesthings

SAN DIEGO

More than 6,000 farmers in the San Diego area have developed a reputation for quality, high-value crops. San Diego has the twelfth-largest farm economy among California's more than 3,000 counties and has more small farms than any other county. With its mild Mediterranean climate, San Diego is the number-one producer of avocados. It also has the greatest number of part-time farmers and is number two in farms with women as principal operators. San Diego epitomizes small-town community in a very large metropolitan area.

Jay Porter Jay is the proprietor of The Linkery, a neighborhood restaurant where they know where their customers and all their food come from.

Jeff Jackson Jeff, executive chef at The Lodge at Torrey Pines, was a chef delegate to the 2006 Terra Madre. His own trademark culinary style strongly adheres to using fresh ingredients and seasonal products from local organic purveyors.

Stone Brewing Legendary among craft beer lovers, Stone Brewing is best known for their Arrogant Bastard Ale and their commitment to sustainable, eco-friendly business practices.

Peterson Specialty Produce All the produce is grown organically on Blue Heron Farm, featuring over twenty varieties of fresh, certified organic baby lettuce; wild honey; and other seasonal fruits, including passion fruit, raspberries, strawberries, mangoes, and pomegranates.

American Tuna American Tuna is comprised of six fishing families from San Diego. These families represent generations of fishing for albacore with the "pole and line" method.

www.ediblecommunities.com/sandiego/peopleplacesthings

SAN FRANCISCO

You may leave your heart in San Francisco, but you won't go away hungry. The city is populated with chefs and food artisans devoted to showcasing Northern California's sustainable cuisine. With a year-round growing season, an ocean full of seafood, and an infamous wine country nearby, eating local is a mantra easily practiced in the San Francisco Bay Area.

Bi-Rite Market With a new farm in Sonoma, Sam Mogannam closes the loop between the soil and the grocery shelf. His Bi-Rite Market celebrated its tenth anniversary in 2007 of providing the neighborhood with organically and sustainably raised meats, poultry, and produce.

Let's Be Frank Made from 100 percent grass-fed beef, and blessed with more than twice the omega-3 fatty acids of feedlot grain–finished beef, Let's Be Frank hot dogs are good for the rancher, the cattle, the land, and the consumer.

Tataki Sushi Raymond Ho and Ken Lui run one of the only restaurants in the country with a menu devoted exclusively to seafood that is sustainably farmed or fished.

Cowgirl Creamery Since 1997 Cowgirl Creamery has been producing organic cheese in Point Reyes Station, California, and promoting artisan cheese makers throughout the United States and Europe.

Magnolia Brewpub Any visit to San Francisco's Haight-Ashbury district demands a refresher stop at Magnolia. Enjoy artisan beers and a brewpub menu featuring locally sourced ingredients.

www.ediblecommunities.com/sanfrancisco/peopleplacesthings

SAN LUIS OBISPO

Residents of San Luis Obispo often feel they live in paradise. However, there is concern that most of their locally grown food gets shipped away. Among the farmers (young and old), the blossoming CSAs, the bustling farmers' markets, and the locavores, there is a growing movement to strengthen the return of the local foods system.

'Ncredible Edibles These folks are on fire, transforming abandoned backyards or grass front lawns into food forests.

American Flatbread Pizza Clark Staub and his team are making delicious natural pizzas baked in a primitive wood-fired earthen oven.

Nature's Touch Nursery and Harvest Melanie Blankenship, the owner of this specialty plant nursery and grocery store, is a genius networker for local farmers and artisan food creators.

Clark Valley CSA Eric Michielssen is a weekend farmer who has a flourishing CSA, speaks at various events, and is a fun, generous, and passionate farmer who loves to share his wisdom.

Central Coast Brewing This is a local brewery known far and wide for its variety of handcrafted, one-of-a-kind microbrews and signature ales.

www.ediblecommunities.com/sanluisobispo/peopleplacesthings

SANTA BARBARA

With a unique topography of coastal mountains and valleys along with a mild Mediterranean climate, Santa Barbara produces everything from world-class wine to year-round delectable produce, locally caught seafood, and regional specialty foods. The rich culinary landscape includes Latin-influenced food from the days of the Spanish missionaries, the Santa Maria–style Barbeque, which makes the marinated beef tri-tip famous, and Santa Barbara's own wine-country cuisine that focuses on seasonality and complements the local wines of the region.

Oscar Carmona, Healing Grounds Organic Nursery Oscar offers a Horticulture Therapy Program, in which adults with mental illness participate in growing high-quality organic vegetable and herb seedlings that are sold to local retail stores.

Fairview Gardens One of the oldest organic farms in California, run by the Center for Urban Agriculture, Fairview Gardens is an internationally respected model for small-scale

urban food production, agricultural preservation, farm-based education, and CSAs.

La Nogalera Walnut Oil This is the product of the combined efforts of three walnut growers in Santa Barbara County.

Santa Barbara Mariculture This company is pioneering new eco-friendly methods in aquaculture to grow oysters, mussels, clams, and scallops.

s'COOL FOOD Initiative This initiative promotes sustainable, "cook from scratch" school food-service systems throughout Santa Barbara County and focuses on procuring local foods for the area's schools.

www.ediblecommunities.com/santabarbara/peopleplacesthings

SHASTA-BUTTE (CALIFORNIA)

Nuts, stone fruits, olives and their juice, rice, grazing, microbreweries—the northernmost part of central California is known for all. Now, wineries and farmstead cheeses win prestigious national awards. Millers grind wheat and produce bread from brick ovens, families sell artisan chocolates and cow shares, new farmers' markets get planned in low-income areas and accept Electronic Benefit Transfer (EBT), and nutritionists bring Farmers of the Month into local schools. A small population spread across a vast area, people come together around food.

The Healthy Lunch and Lifestyle Program A nonprofit in Redding, organized by Bridgette Bricks-Wells, this program provides schoolkids with boxed organic lunches at competitive costs, sourcing from local farmers whenever possible.

Craig Thomas Craig, chef at Red Tavern Restaurant in Chico, began welcoming local farmers and home gardeners with their produce at the door of the restaurant's kitchen decades before it was fashionable.

Growing Resourcefully, Uniting Bellies GRUB is a collective of young people that offers a CSA, teaches young kids to garden at schools, collects kitchen scraps from local restaurants to compost, and maintains a list of Chico's fruit trees from which to glean.

Alger Vineyards John and Linda Alger employ organic and biodynamic practices to grow grapes for their wines. The vines are irrigated with water drawn from the bottom of a trout pond on the property.

North Valley Farms Chèvre A farmstead goat cheese produced in Cottonwood by Deneane and Mark Ashcraft. North Valley Farms is the first goat dairy farm in the nation to win the Animal Welfare Approved Seal.

www.ediblecommunities.com/shastabutte/peopleplacesthings

PACIFIC NORTHWEST

People living in the Pacific Northwest are passionate about their food. They are equally passionate about the rugged land, the bountiful waters that surround it, and all of the beauty and riches that nature offers them, which are many. They understand that every-thing in our ecosystem is interconnected and interdependent, and that those connections extend out and around the planet. That's just how people in the Pacific Northwest tend to look at things.

Perhaps that vision comes from observing the salmon, which, it could be said, is the most important natural food resource of this region. Salmon are as beautiful to watch in nature as they are delicious to eat, whether they are prepared as sushi, roasted on a cedar plank, or smoked and dried—the way the ancient people of the Pacific Northwest did in order to have high-quality protein available to eat whenever they needed it.

Salmon are hard-wired to travel from the mountain streams where they are born, out to the sea, and then back to the place of their birth, where they procreate and die. Before the historically recent interruptions to that cycle, wrought by obstruction of the waterways

>>>

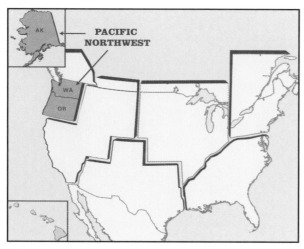

and the practice of aquaculture (which also precludes the natural cycle), the salmon runs were prodigious, and salmon served as an abundant food source not just for man, but for the whole ecosystem—even the plants. To learn more about how that works, go to the Web site for Salmon Nation, www.salmonnation.com. There you will also find a map that shows the vast habitat of the Pacific salmon, which includes the coastal regions of Oregon, Washington, and British Columbia, south to Baja, north to Alaska, west to Russia and Japan, and inland as far as these brave fish have been able to swim.

The indigenous peoples of the Pacific Northwest found many other sources of nourishment in the natural environment besides the salmon. They looked to the waters for shellfish, finfish (including the precious, oil-laden smelt), water mammals, and seaweeds. They looked to the forests for edible roots, game, huckleberries, blackberries, and chokecherries. A very significant food resource was the trees of the forest themselves, from which they harvested pine needles and shoots (a rich source of vitamin C, essential in preventing scurvy), pine nuts, and cedar to make planks for roasting salmon.

The region remained only lightly populated until the second half of the nineteenth century, when westward-wending pioneers began arriving. Groups following the Oregon Trail more often than not were headed to one specific spot—Oregon's Willamette Valley, now a celebrated agricultural region sometimes hailed as one of the most fertile on earth. At first the valley yielded timber, and as the clearings expanded, there was good grazing land for dairy cattle. When the California gold rush began, the wood and dairy products (butter and cheese), along with smoked dried

salmon, were in great demand as exports to San Francisco and the mining regions.

Today that same valley, now largely denuded of its trees, produces a wide range of crops, including some with ancestry in native plant stocks, such as berries and hazelnuts, as well as high-quality pastured meats and dairy products, and the incredibly successful wines and beers made from local grapes and hops. The present-day food culture in this valley, whose focal point is Portland, rivals anything going on in California, and, in fact, it could be said that much of the food scene in the Willamette Valley is a direct result of so many people bailing out on the high cost of living and cramped spaces in California.

Anyone who joins the annual revelries at the forty-year-old Oregon County Fair near Eugene, Oregon, might detect that the San Francisco counterculture of the late 1960s and 1970s is alive and well in the Willamette Valley, even if the "get-back-to-the-land" clarion call and interest in "health foods" have now morphed into more complex ideas about sustainability. Here you can also visit the Springfield Creamery, where in the '70s Chuck Kesey (brother of Merry Prankster Ken Kesey) and his then-bookkeeper Nancy Hamren produced the first commercially available live-culture yogurt in the United States. To this day, Nancy's yogurt remains connected in many minds with granola, steamed veggies served over Lundberg's California-grown brown rice, and concerts by the Grateful Dead.

No single location among the Pacific Northwest's many agricultural regions rivals the Willamette Valley for its lively scene, but agriculture thrives throughout much of the Northwest region. Mild climate and ample rainfall make for good crops of berries, tree fruits, wine grapes, wild mushrooms, and dairy products all along the coastal areas west of the Cascade Range and up into the fertile Fraser River Valley of British Columbia, providing plenty of local foods to nearby urban markets. However, the breadbasket of the Northwest lies in the rain shadow region east of the Cascades, predominantly on the Columbia Plateau. There, land is plentiful for large-scale farming, but it requires irrigation. Harvests of grains, legumes, potatoes, and onions (such as the sweet Walla Wallas) from the Columbia Plateau are so large that they result in substantial exports. But these crops also amplify the bounty for those who want to eat from the Northwest bioregion.

The gem of the plateau's agricultural sub-zones is Washington's Yakima Valley, where the suitability of the ground to support row crops and orchards was discovered around 1850 when Chief Kamiakin, leader of the Yakama, Palouse, and Klickitat peoples, learned about irrigation from the missionaries working to convert his people. Since that time, this corner of the Great American Desert has become a garden oasis with orchards yielding so many tons of apples, cherries, pears, peaches, nectarines, plums, and apricots that it has earned the title "Fruit Bowl of the Nation." The valley also supports many vineyards and vast fields of mint, asparagus, alfalfa, sugar beets, and potatoes.

The Yakima Valley is an important source for hops, which are in ever-growing demand as the interest in craft brewing has skyrocketed. Oregon, in particular, has been at the forefront of this craze since it began in the 1980s, when blue laws were changed to permit public houses to serve their own house-made beers. Portland boasts more breweries than any city in the world.

Beer is not, however, the only beverage that has made the Northwest famous. Seattle, Washington, an important entry point for coffee beans, has led North America down the road to a full-scale revolution in its coffee culture. What began in the San Francisco Bay Area in 1966, when Dutchman Alfred Peet refused to put up with poor coffee and started roasting his own,

was brought to the world in the name of Starbucks, the humble beginnings of which occurred at Seattle's Pike Place Market in 1971. Now there's no going back.

But it doesn't stop with beer and coffee. Wines of the Northwest have kept a remarkable pace behind California's in gaining recognition for excellence. Willamette Valley's Pinot Noirs sometimes reach beyond California's in the race to rival the classic Burgundies of France. Washington State wines are highly regarded as well, and have been for decades, and there are a surprising number of winemakers in British Columbia who are making notable products. Some, like David and Liesbeth Avery in the Fraser Valley, whom you will meet in this chapter (see page 166), are nearly delirious with the excitement of experimentation in sustainable production.

While this kind of care is admirable in production of artisanal foods and beverages, it's almost unheard of in the fast-food industry. For this reason, the chain called Burgerville bears mention. Its thirty-nine restaurants, all located in Oregon or Washington, are powered by wind energy. The trans fat–free canola oil used for frying the locally grown potatoes is sent off to be transformed into biodiesel, and composting is reaching 85 percent of the waste produced as the chain serves up burgers, fries, sandwiches, salads, and shakes made from locally sourced ingredients. You can order a salad with smoked salmon and Oregon hazelnuts at Burgerville and wash it down with a milk shake flavored with local pumpkins, hazelnuts, or berries (depending on what's in season).

The sustainability ethic is certainly afoot in Northwestern haute cuisine too. People are saying that today's chefs here are first and foremost interested in the use of local, seasonal ingredients, and creating dishes with a full expression of place or *terroir,* rather than trying just to be creative. They have more than a little precedent in this approach, however, since the Northwest was the home of the great chef James Beard, who reveled in a love affair with local, seasonal ingredients well before anyone was talking much about them. Perhaps among chefs working in the Northwest today there is one like Beard, or better yet, many, who will begin to effectively raise awareness of sustainable choices in seafood. For a region where the rivers and seas have provided so generously to the local-foods economy for generations, it would be one of the best ways to thank nature for her bounty.

Meet the New American (Zen) Farmers

Michael and Jill Paine of Gaining Ground Farm

In Michael and Jill Paine's modern split-level farmhouse nestled in the rolling hills of the Chehalem Valley, there's a picture window with a breathtaking view of the ADEA Vineyard and the wooded hills beyond. Next to this bucolic view hangs a framed piece of calligraphy that reads:

Until enlightenment: chop wood, carry water. After enlightenment: chop wood, carry water.

I read the phrase and looked with bewilderment at my host for an explanation. "It's a birthday present I got a few years ago," Michael says with his characteristic wide smile, "to remind me of the Zen of being a farmer."

It's suddenly obvious that I'm not chatting with the average American farmer. At a time when small family farms are disappearing and the average age of farmers is fifty-five, this thirty-something couple is an anomaly. Led by their passion for working the land, a love of food, and a need to prove the loan officers and big-business agriculture wrong, Michael and Jill Paine have done something very risky: They've gone into farming.

Michael's interest in farming began with a stint as a Peace Corps volunteer in Lesotho, the landlocked nation surrounded by South Africa. Working alongside farmers in hardscrabble conditions to create community gardens in poverty-stricken villages, Michael fell in love with farming. Though gratifying, it was also an eye-opener.

"Agriculture is a cornerstone of development in the Third World, but as aid poured into the country, I was amazed at how many big ag decisions were being made by people who didn't know anything at all about farming. Most of those projects failed. That's when I realized I wanted to get involved in the policy aspect of agriculture."

After a year abroad on a farm in Costa Rica, the couple moved to California so Michael could pursue a master's degree in international agricultural development at UC, Davis. The academic training, combined with

introductions to the farming community and working the land at the university, provided Michael with some valuable lessons. "I learned the vocabulary and academics of both organic and conventional farming, but I also learned that farmers only listen to other farmers. If I wanted to make a dent on any policy level, I would have to start farming on my own."

After Michael completed his master's, the Paines came to Oregon, attracted by what Michael calls the "goodness" of Portland's food culture. Jill found a position at Nike, and the couple began to look for a farm of their own. Like many other young farmers, they faced an uphill battle: "Nobody would lend to us. We had a business plan, good credit, the down payment, and credentials," Michael says, throwing up his sturdy work-worn hands in frustration. "One loan officer looked us straight in the face and said, 'This is a great business plan, but there's no way this bank is going to give a loan to start up a farm.'"

Jill nods sadly. "We couldn't believe it! We're not talking about making meaningless widgets here; we're talking about growing food. We desperately need more farmers, not hurdles like an interest rate of six over prime for them to jump over."

Through some creative maneuvering, the Paines managed to secure a loan at a decent interest rate and were able to buy a sloping seventy-six-acre farm an hour west of Portland. Michael and Jill made a conscious decision to sell directly to consumers through the farmers' market and a subscription model known as Community Supported Agriculture (CSA). "Being at the CSA drop and connecting with the people, and knowing their names and their kids' names, and talking with them about what they did with the produce we brought them the week before—that's the best part for us," Jill says enthusiastically.

The Paines are continuing to gain ground. Jill still holds down her day job in addition to being a part-time farmhand, business manager, and full-time mother to their young son, Ely. Michael, with the help of summer interns, has created a successful stall at the Portland State University (PSU) farmers' market and a

The Paines' Berkshire pigs enjoying a meal of local apples

CSA service with sixty subscribing families, including a "Feed-a-Family" program that raises donations so that 10 percent of the farm's total shares are given to food-insecure families in the Portland area.

As for policy making, Michael may not be changing policy on an international level, but he's effecting change locally. He's a volunteer member of the Portland-Multnomah Food Policy Council, an advisory board that helps local government make informed food and farming policy decisions. He's also an active member in the Portland-area CSA Coalition (PACSAC), a CSA farmer-support network. Through the lens of this community service, Michael sees a bright future for Portland's small farms and the consumers they serve. "As gas prices continue to climb, produce from Chile becomes less viable, and locally grown food becomes more important. I think that as our food savvy and local-foods economy develop, a climate is being created where a young family can look at farming as a financial possibility again."

After the Paines finish giving me a tour of the farm—including greenhouses, two irrigation ponds, Berkshire pigs, free-range chickens, and numerous goats—we sit down at the long dining table to a casserole of green chile enchiladas. Michael pauses before digging in and looks at the phrase hanging on the wall behind him. "You'd have to be in some kind of Zen mind-set to do this kind of toil," he laughs, "but, at the end of the day, I feel exceptionally lucky to be able to make a living growing good food for people I know."

Sounds like enlightenment to me.

IVY MANNING *is a cooking instructor and freelance writer. Her work has appeared in* Cooking Light, Sunset Magazine, *and* Food & Wine. *Her cookbook,* Farm to Table: The Art of Eating Locally *(Sasquatch, 2008), explores the edible joy of CSA membership and farmers' markets.*

Photo by N. Scott Trimble

The Biodynamic Woman

....

A Profile of Mary Forstbauer

If you tell me that Mary Forstbauer has ever sprawled on the sofa with a box of bonbons in one hand and a remote in the other, I will have to call you a liar. I don't—and won't—believe that she has idled away so much as one afternoon in a hammock with a well-thumbed paperback and a fruity cocktail. And even if Mary herself confessed to playing Tetris for hours on end, I would have to suspect her of misrepresenting the facts to make the rest of us feel better.

She simply can't have had the time. It isn't just that she's been farming—organically—for thirty years. It isn't just that she takes care of 110 acres of biodynamic soil, producing potatoes, carrots, strawberries, blueberries, eggs, and grass-fed beef the old-fashioned, labor-intensive way. It isn't even that she's the president of the British Columbia Association of Farmers' Markets, on the board of the Bio-Dynamic Agriculture Society of BC, and a founder of both the Certified Organic Association of BC and BC Regenerative Agriculture.

It's all that and quite a lot more.

Mary and her husband, Hans, also have twelve children. No, that wasn't a typo. I mean twelve: two more than ten, born between 1971 and 1992. Forgive me for belaboring the point, but that's like having three kids, and then another three, plus another three, and finally three more for good measure.

"One of my friends, another farmer, gave me this bumper sticker," says Mary. "'Organic farmers are more fertile.' I thought that was kind of cute."

Now, I don't have even one child myself, but I've met a few. To me, one child seems like quite a lot of work. For most mortals, raising two children appears to be exhausting. (One of my friends has two little ones under the age of three, and she can barely tie her shoes. Hell, she can barely remember to put her shoes on.) Three kids can drive some people to distraction. And once you get up to more than three, we're talking about superhuman heroic efforts. We're talking about the same stamina, leadership abilities, and organization skills required by the CEO of a multinational corporation, but without the same support staff.

Of course there was a time—even post-Dickens—when children were viewed as small units of labor, and there's no denying that when you're running a farm it does help to have a few extra pairs of hands. The Forstbauer kids do help out on the farm, but they haven't been kept out of school to do agricultural work. Nope. They've played on sports teams, taken music lessons, and enrolled in French immersion, just like other kids of their generation.

"When I was expecting my twelfth child, people warned me: With so many kids I should be prepared for one of them not to do well." Mary lifts her chin and flashes her vivid blue eyes. "I said, 'I expect them to do well, and they will.'"

She expected them to do well, but she didn't expect them all to be excellent students. Yet every one of them—Natalie, Anthony, Annamarie, Rosanna, Amanda, Niklaus, Timothy, Denis, Travis, Katrina, Vanessa, and Elyas—was an honors student. Beyond academic smarts, many of them excel in sports and music. Mary shakes her head slowly, amazement evident in her expression. "Normally, you'd expect a bell curve. You know, 10 percent would do very well, 10 percent would fail, and the rest would be average. But 100 percent of my kids were A students."

It might have something to do with the food. The Forstbauers grow healthy food in healthy soil, and they start off every day with a bowl of oatmeal. Or it might have something to do with the demanding work of the farm. As children, everyone helped out with weeding or harvest or whatever needed to be done.

Mary tells me about the time one of her neighbors phoned. "Come over right away. Hurry."

Mildy alarmed, Mary grabbed the baby and knocked on her neighbor's door. "Come in. Don't take your shoes off. Just come quickly."

With growing apprehension, Mary followed her to a window that looked on to one of her own fields, where her children were weeding and picking beans.

"Listen to them," said the neighbor, incredulous and pointing. "They're singing." As Mary listened, she

Mary Forstbauer on her farm

heard her kids singing "I'm So Happy," a song she'd taught them when they were little.

In an era of adolescent ennui, Internet addiction, reality TV, and mall culture, it was understandably perplexing to witness a field of children laboring and singing like Snow White's happy little dwarves. It was a strong clue that there was something remarkable about this family.

So the satisfaction of doing good, honest work might have contributed to the Forstbauer kids' suc-

cess, but Mary thinks it's something else. One of her friends, a teacher who had had lots of Forstbauers in his classroom, asked, "Mary, why are your children so wonderful?"

"I told him it's because I empower them without controlling them," said Mary. "I let them make decisions from a young age. They have responsibilities, they make choices, and they live with the consequences. If they're comfortable with their own choices, they're comfortable with their own lives."

As teenagers and young adults now, several of the Forstbauer kids still work the farm together. They share the chores through some mysterious and diplomatic job allocation, rarely arguing about whose turn it is to wash potatoes or weed the Swiss chard. It seems that they have a genuine love of the land and a love of farming. Regular customers who visit the Forstbauers at the farmers' markets say that they can feel the love of the farm as soon as they walk into the stall. It's a powerful thing, that love. I think I've tasted it in their sweet, fat carrots, their enormous beets, and their Northland blueberries.

Mary and Hans started growing organic blueberries in 1977. At the time they had just 7 acres, but as interest in organic food grew, so did demand for their produce. They leased another 20 acres from neighbors before moving to a new farm in 1989. That new farm had 110 acres of lifeless soil. There were no worms, so they began the work of rebuilding the soil. Hans had grown up on a biodynamic farm—they weren't certified in those days, but his father had taken biodynamic training in Germany. When the biodynamic society came to British Columbia, it made sense for Mary to get involved and stay involved. She and Hans began farming biodynamically and are now Demeter-certified. Today there is no shortage of worms or other healthy-soil critters at the Forstbauer Farm.

Now, I know only a little about biodynamic farming, but most of what I've heard makes sense to me. I understand that the farm is a sustainable ecosystem in its own right. Crops are rotated, the cow and chicken manure becomes compost, and homeopathic preparations are used to maximize the soil's health. In a closed-loop system, what's created on the farm is generally used to nourish the land.

The practice of paying attention to planetary movements when planting and harvesting seems a little more esoteric, and I ask Mary about that. She nods thoughtfully, understanding my reason for asking. "I don't know why it works," she says, "but I can tell you that it does. If I plant lettuce on a leaf-planting day and beets on a root-planting day those crops just do better."

As I listen to her, I'm watching two of her daughters in the fields. Beyond being pleasant young people and great students, her offspring are all good-looking. I can't help thinking about the superstar caliber of these kids—all twelve. Suddenly I realize that they must have been conceived on great-kid planting days. There is definitely something to this biodynamic method.

Of course, Mary is busy as I scribble notes in my book. It's late summer, and she and her family are getting ready for market day. A tall young man comes out of the house and ambles sleepily over to the strawberry patch where he reaches down to pick a handful of breakfast. Mary's youngest. A light cloud passes over Mary's face, and she looks serious as she recalls a few years back when she was presenting at an organic growers' conference in California. She happened to mention having twelve children, and someone in the audience took exception. "How can you call yourself a sustainable farmer when you have twelve children? Tell me how that's sustainable."

Mary began to defend herself. She grew all their food. They wore hand-me-downs. But another voice from the crowd immediately jumped in. "I haven't had any kids. She can have my share." And then another defender piped up. "I've only had one. Mary can have one for me." Others joined in, and the offers continued until the group had given Mary permission to have an additional four kids.

Mary can have my share, too. I'd be especially proud to somehow lay claim to her young farmers. Of that brood of twelve, three already have organic farms of their own, and another three are working the Forstbauer family farm with Mary and Hans. That's exactly half of them continuing to farm for a living. One is a teacher, two are carpenters, and one is earning a masters in environmental studies. The younger ones are still exploring their options.

When I look at Mary, I see a practical, powerful, and capable woman. I see someone whose resources seem infinite, but there's still something I don't understand. Twelve kids. Twenty-two grandchildren. A hundred ten acres of farming. President of this, founder of that, on the board of a number of agricultural organizations. Last time I counted, there were still only twenty-four hours in a day. So I have to ask her, "Mary, how do you find the time?"

That clear blue gaze looks up at me. "Those things are all important. And when something's that important, you just make the time."

DEBBRA MIKAELSEN *is a freelance writer and the editor of* Edible Vancouver. *She's growing peas, garlic, spinach, and enormous earthworms in her organic community garden and is trying to perfect the art of pizza making.*

More Waiting

. . . .

Lummi Island Wild Preserves Excellence in Wild Salmon

Off Lummi Island at the northeast edge of the San Juan Archipelago, a half dozen small boats lie at anchor in a row across Legoe Bay. On board, eight chefs wait for their next meal. Any moment now, a school of salmon will swim through artificial reefs leading to nets strung between paired boats, where the chefs must scoop the fish from the water before the school flashes over the waiting mesh.

Men have fished these waters in this way for thousands of years. Until a few decades ago, the boats were dugout cedar canoes manned by the Lummi, Samish, Songhees, Semiahmoo, and other Northern Straits Salish people who developed the method, called reefnetting. Today, aluminum barges support tall lifeguard-like towers from which fishers, mostly men, most of them white, look out for the ripple of salmon.

Chef Seth Caswell, president of Seattle's Chefs Collaborative and chef-owner of the Stumbling Goat Bistro, spent a couple of hours as a spotter atop one of the towers as part of a "Chefs in Raingear" adventure, in which a handful of chefs act as deckhands for a day, experiencing reefnet fishing, a sustainable fishery that harvests exceptionally tasty salmon.

The chefs set out by skiff with their host, Riley Starks, reefnetter and owner of Nettles Farm and Willows Inn. They ride out to one of three "gears"—pairs of boats with a shared reef and net—that make up Lummi Island Wild, a cooperative organized by Starks and his partners to bring their reefnet-caught salmon to market. On the brief ride from shore to gear, the skiff burns the fishery's only fossil fuel. The gears themselves remain in their position an entire season, waiting for fish, not chasing them. It's a quiet operation. Once the noise of the skiff's motor dies, hours may pass with no sound but a gentle wash of waves and rhythmic metallic clanking.

Caswell's turn on the tower falls in one of these quiet spells. He hopes to spot sockeye swimming with the incoming tide toward his boat. Watching the water for fish, Caswell wears polarized sunglasses, a recent addition to reefnetting, to minimize glare. "Polarizing

lenses make a big difference," he says, "because otherwise you're just looking at a reflection of the sky." After seeing nothing but water for nearly two hours, Caswell gives up his position to Joe McGarry, of Bon Appétit Management Company. Shortly after the switch, eager shouts, cranking pulleys, and frantic fin-flapping break the lull.

A school has crossed the net's headrope, having swum through a passage made of widely spaced ropes (tied with plastic ribbons to resemble eelgrass-lined reefs), which narrows and becomes shallower to guide the fish toward the net. Once the school crosses the headrope, the reefnetters have mere seconds to raise the net before the fish escape. The spotter's warning is critical.

After the spotter shouts, deckhands on each of the two boats below activate winches to lift the net. Powered by batteries that were once hauled back and forth to shore for charging but are now charged by solar panels out on the gears, the winches hoist the net by taking up its ropes—first the headrope, farthest from the boats; then the edges, or rimlines, so the fish can't swim out the sides; and finally the midline, restricting the fish to a smaller, more manageable section at the net's back, or "bunt."

The crew on one of the two boats quickly gathers the net by hand to bring the fish to a point at the edge of the boat. The men barely raise the fish from the water as they spill them splashing and plopping into the live well, between the pontoons in the center of the boat. From spotting to spilling, the haul takes only a minute. And then more waiting.

Aboard the Lummi Island Wild gears, the chefs and reefnetters fill part of the wait by sorting and bleeding their catch. They handle each fish individually and return any protected or unwanted species to open water, resulting in almost zero bycatch. Reefnetting is the most selective commercial fishery in existence. The reefnetters return any Chinook to the water, since the catch is severely restricted in Washington after a sudden, drastic decline of returning fish), but depend-

The "Chefs in Raingear" crew hauling in a net full of pink salmon

ing upon season, they will keep sockeye, pink, Coho, or chum salmon.

Lifting one fish at a time, Caswell and his mates hold a wanted fish "like a bowling ball," thumb and fingers on either side of the head. In one quick movement, they expose gills and detach them, then place the fish back in the center of the boat to swim to its death, rather than flopping in asphyxiation on deck.

"It's not a natural death, obviously," acknowledges Caswell, "because you're ripping the gills out. But as you're assisting in the end of the life of this wonderful little fish, it's nice to know that of all the alternatives, it's one of the better ways to go."

It also makes for a better-flavored fish. As Starks points out, "Blood is the first thing to go rancid," so bleeding the fish prevents its having any "off, metallic, fishy flavor." The cooperative's reefnetters take pride in preserving the excellence of these salmon, which, like those from the Copper River, are prized for their flavor.

These salmon are on their way toward British Columbia's Fraser River. Once they reach the river, they stop feeding. The fish need energy for their long freshwater journey, and as they round the southern edge of Vancouver Island, traveling through the San Juans and north past Point Roberts, that stored energy, in the form of fat, is at its peak. Salmon's fat contributes to its texture, flavor, and nutritional value. Tests show that

Fraser River sockeye have a slightly higher proportion of fat than Copper River sockeye—approximately 14 percent to Copper River's 12 percent.

Lummi Island Wild emphasizes the characteristics of these fish, caught at this place, in this way. Starks hopes the cooperative will attract the rest of the world's reefnetters, which number only eleven—all of them in the San Juan region, eight of them off Lummi. Most of those reefnetters currently focus on fishing and leave processing and marketing their catch to Trident Seafoods, which handles multiple species caught in the North Pacific without sorting based on the place or method of harvest. The cooperative, on the other hand, capitalizes on the particular elements of reefnetting that distinguish it for sustainability and quality, from solar power to selective harvest to careful handling.

After participating in the sustainable catch, Caswell and the rest of the chefs return to Lummi to appreciate the quality of that catch. Packing the fish into a slush of ice and seawater, which the cooperative's reefnetters use to avoid the bruising and deterioration caused by layering fish in crushed ice, the chefs carry a selection of their catch to Willows Inn. They prepare a communal meal with ingredients harvested that day by the farmer from Starks's Nettles Farm and by their own hands from Legoe Bay. "Being eight chefs," Caswell says, "we cooked a fantastic meal."

JENNI PERTUSET *writes about reading, parenting, and farming at www.pertuset.net/openbook, and Washington farms at www.ethicurean.com. She's working on a book about young farmers and scheming to join the burgeoning agrarian revival. Jenni lives with her husband and daughter in Seattle.*

Photo by Rod del Pozo

Vintage Memories

∙∙∙

Susan Sokol Blosser Reflects on a Lifetime of Wine Making

Susan Sokol Blosser will tell you she's a farmer who is passionate about the land and growing grapes. She'll tell you she's passionate about her family and the business she's worked hard to bring to the forefront of Oregon wines. But she'll also tell you that after thirty-six years of living those passions, she's looking forward to discovering new opportunities for her considerable energy as she transitions from president of Sokol Blosser Winery, a position she has held since 1991, to the honorary position of founder. She has a bit of time to ponder her options, as she intends to slowly phase herself out of day-to-day operations while she turns more of the details over to two of her three children, Alex and Alison.

Back when her love affair with land began, she was a city girl, a former debutante who had been raised by well-to-do parents on the east side of Milwaukee, Wisconsin.

"It was a real surprise to me how much I love the vineyards. I could have lived my whole life in the city and never discovered that."

That discovery process began when Susan and her husband, Bill Blosser, decided on a whim to grow grapes on a hillside in Dundee back in 1970. There wasn't an Oregon wine industry then, and only a few other people in the state had planted vineyards. But she and Bill were fresh out of graduate school and expecting their first child. Their future was wide open, and they were willing to take risks to pursue their passions.

Their son Nik and the vineyard both arrived in the waning weeks of 1970, motherhood and farming merging for Susan in the beginning years of her adulthood. She carried Nik in a backpack while she ran the tractor to help plant Sokol Blosser's first five acres of grapevines. With the arrival in later years of son Alex and daughter Alison, the vineyard truly became a family affair.

In those days, she says, "we were totally focused on the vineyard and the winery, and we included the kids as much as we could. Despite all the struggle and hard work, I have such good feelings about the time when the kids were little. Those were good years."

Work in the vineyard was never-ending, especially after Susan began managing the land in 1980, the same year Bill became president of the winery. Growing up in an urban environment did nothing to prepare her for that. She celebrated small victories like learning to oil the field equipment and became proficient at operating the vineyard's tractor. Susan was also very willing to take advice. Wine writer and longtime friend Heidi Yorkshire believes that trait has contributed greatly to her success.

"Every stage of her life Susan has always been open to learning from others with more experience. She is utterly unafraid of learning new things. She's also very persistent. She doesn't expect instant results, but she does expect results eventually. It's part of what makes her a marvelous person to be around."

Persistence kept her going through the lean years in Oregon's wine industry. Sokol Blosser produced its first wines under its own label in 1977 and opened a tasting room the year after that. By 1980 there were thirty-four wineries cultivating over 1,200 acres of vineyards, and the Oregon Winegrowers Association had been established to represent the interests of the industry. But the big breakthrough didn't occur until 1985, when Oregon Pinot Noir came out on top of a blind head-to-head tasting with French Burgundy at the International Wine Center in New York.

"The tasting in New York City in 1985 was a real turning point for the industry. It woke up the country and put Oregon Pinot Noir on the front burner. But it took another twenty years for that to turn into a demand that we can't keep up with."

The years of struggle took their toll on Susan's marriage to Bill, and in 1998 the couple separated.

"We had been so focused on building the business, but our relationship suffered. Still, we have a shared history that keeps us close today. Together, we built, helped start an industry, and raised three children."

Susan Sokol Blosser with children Alex and Alison

Sokol Blosser's underground barrel cellar, completed in 2002, was the first winery building to earn U.S. Green Building Council LEED (Leadership in Energy and Environmental Design) certification. In 2007, Oregon Tilth bestowed USDA organic certification on the Sokol Blosser vineyards, making it one of a handful of Oregon's winegrowers to receive that designation.

"We were always environmentalists, but in the beginning we looked down on organic. We thought of organic as 'wormy.' Then we started to understand how everything is connected, and the concept of sustainability became more prominent. Our goal now is sustainability across the entire operation. I believe it's better for the earth, better for the vineyards, better for our employees, and better for our customers."

She hopes also that this philosophy will guide the next generation as it continues the family business and its influence on the industry she helped found.

"Transitioning out as president has been a big emotional challenge for me because the winery is so much a part of me. I don't think I'll ever leave the winery, but I'll be in more of an external role."

Indeed, with a new home on vineyard grounds next door to Alex and his family, Susan has solidified plans to stay physically close. Still, she has complete confidence in her children's ability to take over the reins.

Alex and Alison "are both so capable that one does not stand out from the other. Together they're bigger than either would be alone, and I think they recognize that."

They also recognize the benefits of having their mom's input on the business. Alison says of Susan, "She's not just my mom, she's my mentor, too." Alex describes her as "easily the best boss I've ever had."

Where will Susan Sokol Blosser's passions take her next? After having promoted her book, *At Home in the Vineyard,* published in 2006 by the University of California Press (which she describes as a wine book, a business book, and a memoir), she says, "I look forward to learning how to play."

After that?

"I'm also very passionate about helping people learn about sustainability."

Susan is also quick to credit Bill's work as critical to Oregon's wine industry in its early days, especially his influence on land-use regulations to preserve hillsides in Yamhill County for agriculture at a time when only valley floors were being recognized for their agricultural potential. Bill's interest in the environment was also influential in the couple's eventual commitment toward creating an environmentally sustainable operation, a commitment that earned Sokol Blosser several firsts on the path to sustainability.

In 1997, Sokol Blosser was the first vineyard to be certified as "Salmon Safe" by the Pacific Rivers Council.

CINDY HUDSON *is a freelance writer who publishes the Web site www.motherdaughterbookclub.com. She lives in Portland, Oregon, with her husband and two daughters.*

Photo courtesy of Sokol Blosser Winery

Lotusland Vineyards

. . . .

Experimenting in Sustainable Production

The Fraser Valley, located east of Vancouver, lies between the natural backdrop of the Coast and Cascade mountains. The Fraser River flows through this broad, fertile floodplain and contributes to what is considered some of the most productive agricultural land in Canada, if not the world. The communities of the Fraser Valley showcase fruit and berry crops, eggs, poultry, vegetables, hops, mushrooms, and dairy products. With the abundance of fresh produce, a mild climate, and a West Coast spirit, the region, along with Greater Vancouver, has garnered the nickname Lotus Land.

It was here, in Lotus Land, that David and Liesbeth (Liz) Avery bought a reclaimed gravel pit in 1995. At the time, a sea of hay dominated the ten-acre property, and while the couple waited for a neighboring farmer to cut it for them, they took a walk, hand in hand, through the field. Liz, a gardener with two green thumbs, turned to David and said, "We have to do something with this land. We need to utilize it." David, an amateur winemaker, didn't hesitant in offering his thoughts: "I wonder if grapes will grow here."

After nine months of research, they jumped into their new venture. From the beginning, it was a given for David and Liz that they would farm with environmental responsibility. Liz had always gardened without the use of pesticides, herbicides, or chemical fertilizers, and David, the eldest of seven children, was raised in Mississauga by parents who adhered to the "reduce, reuse, recycle" motto long before "sustainable" and "organic" were buzzwords. David's parents lived off the land chemical and pesticide free and were responsible for introducing a recycling program in Mississauga in the 1970s—the first in Canada.

At first, David and Liz planted grape varieties they liked to drink, but that proved futile. They realized they needed to plant for the climate. More research led to the unique varieties of Switzerland's grape breeder Valentin Blattner. Blattner crosses vinifera varieties with other subspecies "the old-fashioned way" and creates designer grapes. The process of crossing pollen from one variety or species with another resulted in disease-resistant, cold-hardy varieties that thrive in the cold, damp weather of Lotus Land. David obtained the rights to propagate Blattner's varieties and produced his first vintage in 2000, and by 2003 the grapes spoke for themselves through the wine. His 2003 Signature Zweigelt won gold for best alternative red wine in the Northwest Wine Summit "beauty contest," as David calls the competitions. The fact that the rich, fruit-forward, no-tannin wine was organic wasn't even mentioned.

Today, Lotusland Vineyards produces twelve varieties of organic grapes. The vines all have propagation numbers, such as 73-12-64. David's job is to give names to the numbers—Enigma for the red blend; Prism for the dry white. They produced a Gewürztraminer, a name many people have difficulty pronouncing. Instead of trying to pronounce it, customers would ask for the G wine. Liz would say, "Just think: Girls are meaner." When they had a 70 percent Gewürztraminer blended with five other varieties, David asked Liz if he could call it "Girlsrmeaner." "Are you crazy?" Liz responded. But he went ahead and had the labels made for the off-dry wine, and within a week on the shelf, it was the hottest-selling wine they carried.

David, a master vintner, still utilizes his fifteen years of experience in sales and marketing, but he's now a farmer first and foremost. He's creative, mechanically inclined, and hands-on. Dressed in a uniform that usually consists of a brown gingham shirt with khaki-colored pants, he sports a moustache and a couple days of beard growth. His brown hair, peppered with gray, hasn't been cut in a while, a testament to the fact that he's in the midst of harvest and crushing. He rarely has time to talk to visitors anymore and leaves that to his knowledgeable stepdaughter, Rosalie.

A rustic country tasting room greets visitors at the King Road property. From there, vines slopes to the valley below, where more rows spread to the west and the east. Besides housing the wine-making equipment, the winery acts as a laboratory and warehouse. Designed by David, the rectangular concrete and steel building boasts R40 insulation in the ceiling and R20 in the two-by-six-foot walls. The seventeen-foot ceiling allows

David Avery holding a bottle of his organic wine

tection from the elements and allows much of the work to be done outdoors. The building, according to David, may not be decorative, but it's functional.

Inside the winery, a row of stainless steel tanks holds the promise of future wine. These tanks are new, but the steel-caged totes are reused and 90 percent of the barrels are one-use barrels from Napa Valley, originating in France, Hungary, Russia, and the United States. David also found two old milk tanks (stainless steel interior with one-inch-thick insulation of cork) in Saskatchewan and shipped them to Lotusland, where he converted them as necessary for wine.

He tries to be efficient in every way with "back-to-the-future" farming practices, including the salvage of rainwater. Specially constructed and installed gutters around the house and the winery divert water into rain barrels and then through a series of stages (much like the board game Mouse Trap) into one of five storage tanks. David can collect two tons of water in total, which he uses to irrigate the greenhouse and, instead of aquifer water, stores as fire protection. He has also cut his water irrigation consumption by 60 percent because the manner in which he applies compost to the base of his vines prevents wasted runoff.

The farm equipment, including the Bob-Cat and tractors, are used. The driveways are made entirely with reclaimed gravel and asphalt, and the new roof on the house will sport a vegetated green eco-roof on the north side and solar panels on the south side. The winery's vehicles run on biodiesel, which David purchases at the moment, but he is in the process of forming the Lotusland Biodiesel Co-op. In the vineyard, David uses steel for the purposes of organic farming. The end posts are reused drill pipe from Alberta oil drills. Any of the new materials are made from recycled steel. As he says, he's an organic farmer to the "nth degree."

David also involves himself in the community as a volunteer member on the egg board, economic board, and aquifer board, and his commitment to environmental sustainability isn't limited to his own property. He's now responsible for reclaiming six gravel pits and converting them into vineyards, thereby maintaining the land's Agricultural Land Reserve status (the ALR was created in the 1970s to protect land for agricultural production) and saving the land from housing developments and highways. For this, he has won three international reclamation awards. For his organic viticulture techniques, he's considered one of the top five greenest families in Greater Vancouver.

use of all three dimensions of the building. One side is built eleven feet into the sloping ground, and because most of the structure is underground, there's no need to heat or cool the space. The temperature stays relatively steady. The grid of concrete floor is sectioned by troughs designed and built by David. In the laboratory area, he installed energy-efficient radiant hot-water heat, and the only appliance that runs on electricity twenty-four hours a day is the fan (to eliminate a buildup of carbon dioxide). Instead of turning on the lights, David opens the overhead door. Outside, a large overhang offers pro-

In 2004, David surveyed half of the farmland in the Fraser Valley in search of land that was suitable for a use other than growing grass. The thought of using gas to power a lawnmower on large parcels of land spurred him into sending letters to landowners asking permission to use their land for agricultural purposes. The phone started ringing immediately, and David now has sixteen vineyards beyond his own, all small acreages from one and a half to twelve acres. He designs them, installs vines, irrigates, maintains, nets, harvests, and then writes the landowner a check. The owners can simply admire the symmetry and beauty that comes with a vineyard. There have been some compromises. One landowner requested that the posts be color-coordinated with his green tractor. David obliged. Life, he says, is full of compromise. The landowners own everything except the vines, but they have them for as long as they produce fruit. For David the venture means producing the best fruit, and if he's not happy with the fruit, he can blame only himself or, perhaps, Mother Nature, who has in the past used a snowstorm to ravage the structures.

When it comes to planning and planting, David doesn't adhere to the traditional ways. He plants his rows farther apart than normally done. One post supports two vines, which are grown in reused tubing. This means he uses half as many posts. He grows his vines up through the tubing, where they then secure themselves to the wire and send out shoots that create an umbrella that stands five feet, ten and a half inches tall, with the fruit growing at the top of the vine. Traditional vintners would say he's wrong, but he knows he's right. The traditional system—the old system— has the vines grow to two feet tall before they adhere to the wire. The shoots then flop over before reaching the wire and have to be repositioned and clipped in place. As the vine seeks the sun, it has to be topped. The vine reacts and, in an attempt to save itself, sends out suckers, so the sides of the vine have to be trimmed, and that in turn promotes more top growth, again and again. The fruit grows at the bottom of the vine, in the shadows, and the leaves have to be manually removed to allow access to the light. The traditional system is labor intensive. Using the top-growth method, the fruit is more exposed to the light. There's also less maintenance involved. David mows between the rows from time to time, applies compost at the base (which deters weed growth), puts up the netting, and later removes it before harvesting.

David has even found an efficient way to apply sulfur for controlling the growth of mildew. Instead of using the traditional method of spraying, David instead blows powdered organic sulfur on the vines in the early morning while the dew still lingers on the leaves. As the dew evaporates, the sulfur remains on the leaves and begins to off-gas, working effectively for up to three weeks. By using this method, David has to apply the sulfur only three times a year instead of twelve, and he uses only one pound of sulfur per acre instead of ten.

In constant search of the hardiest, most disease-resistant, best-tasting fruit, David has what he calls his "million-dollar row." The vines, the only varieties in the world, are grown close together to create the worst possible conditions, allowing David to see what will happen. If they get powdery mildew, they're fired. If the fruit shows promise, he takes a cutting, grows it, and makes a barrel of wine. If the wine is good, then the variety stays in the program. If not, it's history. It's all about process and patience, not one of David's strongest traits, although he's learning.

David and Liz are hands-on proprietors involved in all stages of production, and in the beginning they thought they could do all the work themselves. Today, they employ a minimum of five staff, maximum of twenty, with even more during harvest season. They also offer a program for international visitors, a venture that provides additional labor for the winery. Lotusland hosts up to five WWOOFers (World-Wide Opportunities on Organic Farms) at a time and offers them the opportunity to learn about the all-natural approach to wine making. These travelers—some engineers, others grad students—come from countries such as Japan, Switzerland, and Germany to gain rural life experience and enjoy the places, people, and things of Lotus Land that David and Liz so appreciate. David even found a way to share what they love about the region with those who drink their wine. The Lotusland wine labels feature photos of Greater Vancouver's favorite places such as Granville Island Market, Stanley Park, Chinatown, and revered things like totem poles, salmon, sailboats, and even local celebrities.

There's another way that David makes his mark. After he read *Liquid Gold*, he started collecting his urine. Author Carol Steinfeld, a writer, researcher, and resource-recycling specialist, explains in her book about the benefits of using urine as a fertilizer. Once David discovered that urine has the correct formula (5-2-3) for growing grapes, he placed two-gallon plastic containers beside each toilet for urine contributions. To date, he's the only contributor. The WWOOFers won't do it. The kids won't do it. Even Liz won't do it. For two years, David has diluted his urine with six to eight parts water to cut the acidity and uses the fertilizer on his nursery stock. These have proven to be the strongest plants yet.

What the kids didn't know was that David took out the toilets one by one and replaced them with urine-diverting waterless toilets from Sweden. He was able to cut domestic water usage by 70 to 80 percent and eliminated blackwater as all the solid waste collected and dried and became ready for composting. Their collected urine continues to fertilize the nursery stock.

Despite hard work and good reviews, farming is expensive, and the Averys don't have deep pockets. But they have conviction. At the end of the day, over a bottle or two of wine, David can't help but remember the answer Robert Mondavi gave when asked how to make a small fortune in the wine industry: Start with a large fortune. Still, the Averys affectionately call their ten acres "buried treasure vineyard." Several times they have witnessed a rainbow touching the vineyard. And they believe.

British Columbia–based **ARLENE KROEKER** writes about food and culture. When she's not hunting down the freshest ingredients, she can be found playing in the dirt with the children of Richmond's Terranova Schoolyard Project.

Market Wonder

Peter de Garmo's and Don Oman's role in Portland's food revolution is clear.

"When I moved to Portland in 1977, Southeast Hawthorne was dead," recalls Peter de Garmo. Sure, there were some notable exceptions, like a model toy store, a Cuban market, and Nick's Famous Coney Island, but what mostly stays with de Garmo from those days is that there were "lots of boarded-up places, a large Latino nightclub, and at least one porno shop."

That's why his decision, in 1983, to choose Southeast Hawthorne as the place to open Pastaworks—a new food emporium featuring fresh pasta, Mediterranean delights, and ripe tomatoes at a time when a garden-fresh tomato was hard to come by in any Portland store—was a risky one. Yet, twenty-five years later de Garmo's move seems downright visionary: Within a year of the shop's opening, three other stores—Murder by the Book, a gelato shop, and Bread & Ink Café— came to life, revitalizing Hawthorne Boulevard. Moreover, with Pastaworks, de Garmo helped spark the food renaissance that Portland is now famous for.

Before becoming a shopkeeper, de Garmo was a professor of Spanish history, first at Boston College and later at Colegio Cesar Chavez in Mount Angel, Oregon, where he met his future business partner, Don Oman, at a protest. When the college folded a few years later, de Garmo and Oman found themselves as unemployed househusbands—cooking family meals, drinking good wines, and discussing neighborhood politics.

On a trip to Boston, de Garmo wandered into a shop that sold fresh pasta. The proprietor told him that the secret to her pasta was the water. "I'd lived in Boston long enough to know that it couldn't be just the water," he recalls. "I thought to myself: If she can make pasta, I bet I can."

When he got home, he pitched the idea to Oman. "Don told me I was crazy. But a month later, he came back wanting to sell pasta." Eventually they got in sync and took the plunge. "The rent was cheap," de Garmo recalls. "We had an old commercial stove that Don had bought for 450 dollars. I found some pasta machines and an old fridge we named Ruth that we still use. We borrowed money from Don's in-laws. We had no business plan. The only budget I have from that time is written in my wife's hand—not Don's or mine."

Peter de Garmo at Pastaworks

Organization and financing were not their strengths. "At first we lost money on the cheese," he confesses, "because you have to turn it. And on wine—because we drank it." But little by little they sold more and more pasta—literally tons of it.

"Don and I were active in neighborhood politics. We knew everybody," de Garmo explains. "Our neighbors became our first customers. Don always said that it helped that my name ended with a vowel so people thought I was Italian." Older members of the city's Italian community eventually found the shop, too. Frank Nudo of Nick's Famous Coney Island would march his customers outside and point them across the street. Many became regulars—always paying in cash, sometimes wearing slippers. "We had the luck of location, timing, and hiring incredible employees," de Garmo insists. "We did it all by the seat of our pants."

While Pastaworks has been at the center of Portland's flourishing food scene, de Garmo is quick to note that he and Oman truly were two of the unlikeliest guys to lead such a charge. Growing up in Los Angeles and later in Northern California, de Garmo had gone to plenty of small ethnic markets, delis, and butchers, yet none of these inspired his idea for Pastaworks, and there is little in his family's culinary history that would have led him to a food career. Of the two, Oman, a construction millwright from Scappoose, was the one who had at least visited Italy once before, but he is Norwegian-American, "where white is the predominant food color," de Garmo jokes.

"We had no idea what we were doing," says de Garmo. "There were two Italian old-timers who traveled up and down the West Coast working for food distributors. Once they had us taste extra virgin olive oil from Tuscany. After we swallowed, we got this flash of peppery intensity. We thought: This stuff sucks. But they kept coming back and having us try new things. Slowly they educated us."

Fortunately for the partners, there was one part of their inventory that didn't depend on education: wine. "What I loved about Italian wine was the flavor and that it was considered a food product," de Garmo explains. "Its purpose is to complement—not displace—food." Their buying principle for wine (as well as the rest of the products they carried on their shelves) was simple: When de Garmo found something he liked, he carried it. And over the past twenty-five years, his palate has created one of the broadest and finest selections of Italian wines in the city and, at one time, in the country. (Don Oman left Pastaworks in 1997 and opened Casa Bruno, a wine importing business, the following year.)

Although pasta is still the shop's number-one seller, it is not de Garmo's passion. What excites him today is the sense of place that defines the local foods scene, its incredible growth and potential, and the young people involved. He sees parallels between our region and what has occurred in Italy in the past two decades: "The most striking thing is the number of young Italians reviving the food and wine traditions of their parents' generation. What all of them have in common is a profound sense of place."

That's what draws de Garmo to Piedmont's food, wine, and culture as well. "I think the reason I have always loved the Basques—going so far as to once convince a wine writer that I actually was Basque—is for the same reason my friends in the Piedmont are so involved in their food traditions," he admits. "It's wanting and nurturing a sense of place." Despite having lived all over the country, his place is Portland.

What de Garmo sees in this new generation of artisan food producers and farmers in the Portland region is a varied group that's firmly rooted to the soil and seasons. "They aren't wide-eyed, but pragmatic," he notes. "They want to succeed. They aren't blinded and burdened by the history. They're not reinventing the past; but using old methods for a different reason—the future."

De Garmo and his son Kevin, who manages Pastaworks at City Market on Northwest 21st, opened a new store on North Mississippi in March of 2009, which Peter calls going "back to the future—a larger and better version of the Hawthorne store when we opened in 1983. Our focus is to do what we do best—cheese, groceries, and pasta."

"We can't and don't offer all things to all people" is how de Garmo explains the narrow focus of goods available at Pastaworks. "We constantly debate what we put on our shelves. That discussion is framed by quality considerations, as in 'absolute' quality, as well as value for quality. Our shelf set is not determined or influenced by vendors. Simply put, we care about the foods that we place on the shelves. And yes, it's nice—

and sustainable—to be able to make a profit from those foods."

The only potential downside to a business model like Pastaworks's is that the shop isn't big enough to corner the market on a particular product. So as supermarkets further expand into specialty food, it's up to the Pastaworks staff to search for new producers and sources. It is a skill this team has always excelled at—Catalonian Siruana extra virgin olive oil, prosciutto di Parma, and jamón serrano are just a few of the products first introduced to Portland by the store over its twenty-five years. And since the shop prides itself on providing the best for its customers and its size enables it to eschew layers of management and large warehouses, the folks at Pastaworks will always welcome that kind of challenge.

MEGAN HOLDEN *is a writer living in Portland, Oregon.*

THE CONNECTION TO SLOW FOOD

In 1989, Carlo Petrini founded Slow Food International in Bra, Italy. Visit slowfood.com.

In 1991, Peter de Garmo's former partner, Don Oman, started the first local Slow Food chapter in the United States in Portland. "All we did was recognize what had been overlooked," de Garmo says. "We realized it was silly to be living in this incredibly verdant valley with the last great salmon run in the world at our feet." Slow Food, with its emphasis on quality and taste, suggested a way to highlight this lush and local edible landscape. Today, Slow Food Portland, one of the largest of the two hundred local chapters, carries out the Slow Food mission on a local level by supporting projects such as Abernethy Elementary School's Garden of Wonders and Growing Gardens' Youth Grow. Visit slowfoodportland.com.

In 1999, the office of Slow Food USA was established in New York City. Its mission is to support and celebrate the food traditions of North America and a food system based on good, clean, and fair food. Visit slowfoodusa.org.

In 2003, de Garmo joined the board of directors of Slow Food USA. In 2008, San Francisco hosted Slow Food Nation on Labor Day weekend—a celebration of American food. The event included an urban garden, a farmers' market, and an outdoor food bazaar, and a speaker series featuring leading thinkers, community organizers, and journalists discussing current food issues, from policy and planning to education and climate change. Visit slowfoodnation.org.

A Force for All Seasons

Tilth's Maria Hines Does the Right Thing

Maria Hines is deep in preparations for the day at Tilth, her acclaimed Seattle restaurant. Her kitchen crew towers above her, but it's clear that she is in charge, managing the whirlwind of movement in her self-described "goat rodeo." Staff members carrying bowls of lemons and trays of onions narrowly avoid collision, shouting warnings of "Corner!" and "Door!"

None of this fazes Hines. While she's petite (and so is Tilth's kitchen), her unassailable spirit is quite the opposite, as is the meat cleaver in her hand.

Hines answers questions while hacking up whole chickens faster than most people tie their shoes. The chickens are Washington-grown Rosies—organic, of course, like almost all of the ingredients she uses.

Tilth, one of only two Oregon Tilth USDA organic-certified restaurants in North America, takes the seasonal, local trend to its natural conclusion. But for Hines, it isn't about the show. It's simply about doing the right thing for the environment, for her suppliers, and for her diners.

From her as-organic-as-possible menu to numerous appearances at local markets, to speaking on sustainability issues throughout the Seattle area, Hines is as no nonsense when it comes to food politics as she is with a cleaver.

There's a personal element among the political, however.

"I don't want to have to make the same damn dishes forever," she says as she nonchalantly sears the chicken breasts she's been preparing. The chicken pops away in the pan, developing a perfectly lovely char. Local and seasonal means changing the menu all the time. It's a tribute to Hines's homey yet adventurous arrangements that diners pour in year-round for dishes like an autumn ratatouille of pepper and eggplant; a white corn terrine loaded with summer chanterelles and sweet onions; or spring pea and Parmesan risotto.

Hines is quick to credit her Puget Sound–area suppliers for much of her success. She's built deep relationships with farms like Skagit Valley's Skagit River Ranch and King's Garden in Tonasket; she talks about

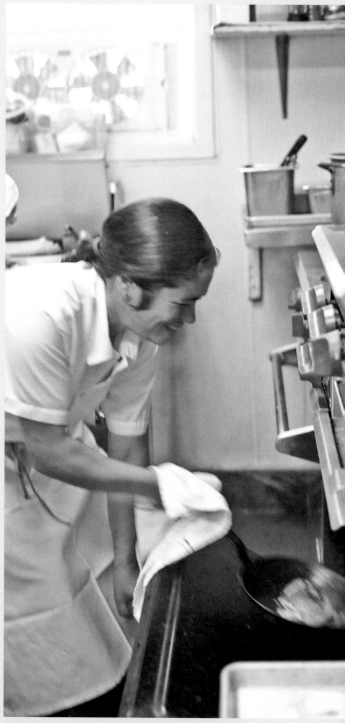

Maria Hines pulls lemony chicken from the oven at Tilth.

them like old friends. Without these suppliers, she says, she couldn't do the work she does.

She's gone so far as to salute the farms and ranches that bring Tilth its goods with Homage to Local Producers, a series of four-course fixed menus showcasing her suppliers one by one.

Hines is set on keeping Tilth a great locals' spot, the kind of place to drop in to after work when cooking at home isn't in the cards. You aren't likely to find lobster or prime rib on the menu. Instead, she makes the most of lesser-used cuts and fresh produce, resulting in down-to-earth dishes that make regulars out of many diners.

One of the most popular items, mini duck burgers, piles generous, juicy three-inch rounds of duck confit onto little brioche buns with house-made ketchup and fig puree. It's the one thing that's been on the menu since Tilth opened in its Wallingford bungalow back in September 2006; like much of Hines's food, it bridges the gap between creativity and comfort.

Back in the kitchen, Maria plates medallions of chicken with an artful turret of her autumn ratatouille and a painted swirl of niçoise tapenade, crowning it with microgreens. The chicken is juicy and tender, the ratatouille pungent and bright. It's unfussy and elegant, just like everything that comes from her kitchen.

LARA FERRONI *is a Seattle-based food stylist, photographer, and recipe writer. More of her words and images can be found at her popular food blog www.cookandeat.com.*

Photo by Lara Ferroni

ORGANIZATION ~ *EDIBLE PORTLAND* (OREGON)

One Handshake at a Time

The Best Way to Build a Regional Food Network

Imagine a world where good food is seen not just as good business but also as a basic human right.

That is the world Ecotrust imagines and helps to create every day.

Ecotrust was founded on a simple notion: There is an intimate relationship between the human condition and the health of all living systems, and by bringing business, society, and nature closer together, the world will change for the better.

If that seems like some pie-in-the-sky vision, perhaps it is, but Ecotrust has spent nearly twenty years turning that vision into reality by, for example, building direct connections between food producers and eaters of all ages.

Why is food so important to Ecotrust? Because where agriculture thrives, so do communities.

As one of four major program areas at Ecotrust, the Food & Farms program is dedicated to creating a vibrant regional food system where sustainability is the underlying value of the mainstream food system—the norm rather than the exception. (The other three areas of Ecotrust work are fisheries, forests, and native programs.) That regional food system is now held up as a national model for what's possible.

Admittedly, Ecotrust's hometown of Portland, Oregon, had a head start on a few fronts. The city is known for its progressive culture, focus on all things local, and a climate that produces an abundance of great food and wine. The regional food network would not have thrived, however, without organization, trust, and partnership between many organizations, public and private.

In part, Ecotrust Food & Farms helps keep this network vibrant and growing by brokering relationships between food producers and food buyers and publishing materials that increase knowledge about food and food-related matters. Chef Dave Barber, owner of Three Square Grill in Portland, credits Ecotrust's efforts for helping to establish many of his relationships with farmers, ranchers, fishers, distributors, other restaurant chefs, and many other regional food buyers. The connections have brought Barber and his customers into direct relationship with the ingredients he puts on his menu and have shortened the distance between the farm and the plate.

Barber says that it's important for him to source good ingredients at his small neighborhood restaurant, and it's important to feature his producers on the menu "so that people who come in for a burger can feel like they are getting a quality product, handmade, and something we really care about."

Ecotrust's publication of *Edible Portland* plays an important part in educating the local community about people like Barber. The award-winning magazine—part mouthpiece, part soapbox, and all celebration of the local, seasonal foods that abound in the region—has gained a broad readership into the thousands. Other publications, such as Ecotrust's *Building Local Food Networks: A Toolkit for Organizers,* help others around the country jump-start their own regional food networks.

"Ecotrust's tool kit was the spark that ignited the farm-to-fork revolution in New Orleans," said Mischa Byruck, who organized the city's first meet-up, where farmers and chefs get directly connected to one another.

THE NEXT GENERATION OF EATERS AND FOOD PRODUCERS

As the regional food network around Portland continues to grow, Ecotrust has expanded its focus to include the world's most vulnerable demographic: children.

When the national school meal program was first created in 1947, cafeteria workers prepared meals from scratch on site. The smell of freshly made bread signaled lunchtime. Today schools are often built without functional kitchens and the production of school food is outsourced to manufacturing facilities on the other side of the country. The irony is particularly bitter when you consider that Oregon's Willamette Valley is one of the most abundant growing regions in the world. Yet, the food served in Oregon's public schools currently comes from all over the United States, regardless of whether the crop is available from Oregon farmers.

Over time the lunchroom has become the most neglected classroom in the school. To address this issue, Ecotrust, in close collaboration with a diverse coalition of project partners, works to promote the long-term health of children by making changes in the school lunchroom that will lead to lifelong healthful eating habits.

Ecotrust's school initiatives include promoting school-based gardens, nutrition, and environmental education; building connections between local foods producers and school cafeterias; as well as field trips and experiential learning opportunities that reinforce healthful options in the cafeteria. It is well established that the child who has planted, tended, harvested, and tasted fresh kale from the school garden will be much more likely to eat kale that shows up in the lunch line.

In 2007, Ecotrust mobilized a statewide coalition and engaged eighty-three government, nonprofit, and for-profit organizations (representing tens of thousands of constituents) to advocate for school food change. What was a loose network during the 2007 legislative season is now a formal entity, the Oregon Farm-to-School and School Garden Network.

Ecotrust also works with select school districts on specific programs such as Harvest of the Month, where one locally grown fruit or vegetable is featured twice a month, and Local Lunch, which helps Portland public schools roll out new main-meal offerings that use regionally grown and minimally processed foods.

Thanks in large part to this work, Oregon is the first state in the nation to institutionalize the notion of good food and healthy kids with full-time positions in both its agriculture and education departments dedicated to getting more locally grown food into school cafeterias.

A FUTURE FULL OF LOCAL FOODS

Perhaps farmer and visionary Wendell Berry had it right when he said, "The present practice of handing down from on high policies and technologies developed without consideration of nature and the long-term need of the land and the people has not worked, and it cannot work."

Students enjoy fresh local food at school.

Regional food networks do not hand out policies from on high; they build them from the ground up, one handshake at a time. Ecotrust believes that regional food economies are the way back to healthier people and a healthier planet. The work Ecotrust does each day—to make connections, to increase food literacy, to improve food for children—demonstrates how to build a regional food economy. These steps are not a panacea but, rather, Ecotrust believes, a step in the right direction.

If there's one thing that history has taught the world, it's that societies do what societies think. So,

what if there was a broadly held belief that regional food economies are one way back to healthier planet?

The Slow Food movement was born from a simple and clear belief—that people can eat better. What if there was a regional food movement, one where tens of thousands of farmers, eaters, and organizations came together, region by region, in an effort to know one another better and work together? Just imagine the power in that: fresh food and inspiration—for young and old.

. . . .

SETH WALKER *is director of marketing and communications at Ecotrust.*

. . . .

Photo by N. Scott Trimble

People, places, things

PORTLAND

Portland's community of farmers, chefs, and eaters has intrepidness that allows them to challenge routine expectations. Maybe it is its lingering pioneer spirit. Maybe looking out on striking mountains reminds those who live there to be determined and farsighted. People move to the Pacific Northwest specifically to entangle themselves in this forward-thinking culture, and so it grows abundantly.

Marionberry Invented at Oregon State University in the 1950s, this cross between the Chehalem and Olallie caneberries is large, juicy, and dark purple. It shines in pies, ice creams, jams, and all by its tart, sweet self.

Chinook Salmon Lewis and Clark raved about their first tastes of this fish, which once swam abundantly in the Columbia and Willamette rivers traversing Portland. The Chinook salmon has deep spiritual, cultural, gastronomic, and economic value for the Native American tribes of the Northwest.

Filberts Oregonians use the word "filbert" to identify the hazelnut, the state's most important nut crop, with over three million trees. It has become essential to Northwest cuisine in all its crunchy, robust richness.

Widmer Brothers Brewery Widmer Brothers was one of the pioneering microbreweries to bring Portland to the forefront of craft beer distillation.

Portland Farmers Market Begun in 1992, the market now stretches to five locations, with more than two hundred vendors sharing the delicious abundance of Oregon agriculture with anywhere from 10,000 to 12,000 local eaters each week.

www.ediblecommunities.com/portland/peopleplacesthings

SEATTLE

A possible new nickname for Washington would be the Picnic State. Driving around Puget Sound, you'll discover more than one hundred farmers' markets, with most of them near a river, a beach, or a park. Load up a bag with award-winning goat cheese, Elberta peaches or Liberty apples, smoked Keta salmon, and some tart huckleberry cider and taste what Washington is all about. Then ask the locals about their favorite coffee roaster—they've kept the best ones to themselves!

Food Lifeline This group develops innovative programs that connect fresh local foods with neighborhood food banks and shelters.

Cheryl Ouellette Cheryl is president of Puget Sound Meat Producers Cooperative, working to provide local ranchers with sustainable processing.

Ozette Potatoes This rich fingerling variety, included as an ingredient in the local Slow Food Ark of Taste, was grown by the Makah tribe as early as 1791.

Jon Rowley For thirty years, Jon has brought outstanding quality, and sustainable practices, to the Northwest. He has been called the "Disciple of Flavor."

Razor Clams These mollusks have two short seasons and a highly devoted following. Careful population management means a total of just fifteen to thirty-five days of digging per year.

www.ediblecommunities.com/seattle/peopleplacesthings

VANCOUVER (CANADA)

It's difficult to say what makes the strongest contribution to Vancouver's delightful edibility—its ideal location on the Pacific Coast and the Fraser River, or the extreme ethnic diversity of its largely immigrant population. Geography and demography merge in a rich culinary scene focused on fresh seafood; fruits and vegetables that spring from the river delta's dark, fertile soil; exotic fungi that thrive in the rain forests; and cooking traditions from Europe, Asia, and Latin America.

Harold Steves The Steves family has farmed the area since 1877, and the fishing village of Steveston bears its name. Harold is an activist for the cause of keeping farmland for farming.

Granville Island This is the go-to place for any gourmet ingredient you might need. Local charcuterie, farm-fresh produce, wild chanterelles, and artisan sake are just the beginning.

Spot Prawns and Side Stripe Shrimp The vast majority of these sustainably harvested local delicacies go to Japan; however, the growing interest in local eating means that increasing numbers of these are staying at home.

Bremner's Juice The Bremner family has been farming blueberries in Delta since 1980. Their juices are made with only premium-grade berries and zero additives

Salmon Candy Imagine smoked salmon marinated in maple syrup and smoked again. A traditional Native Canadian treat, the combination of salty, sweet, and smoky flavors is both memorable and habit forming.

www.ediblecommunities.com/vancouver/peopleplacesthings

MIDWEST

At Edible Communities, we love to broadcast the gospel of local, seasonal foods and to report on the growing awareness in the public at large that it really does matter what we eat and how our food is produced. But so often in everyday conversations we hear, "Sure, but that's only going on in a few places on the coasts, not in the heartland."

We beg to differ. In the Midwest, a stronghold of industrial agriculture and a place where the diet has adhered to a standard of "meat and potatoes" for far too long, there is a growing and deeply passionate movement to bring variety, sustainability, and localism to the forefront of food production and enjoyment.

One piece of evidence that the revolution is in effect is the increasing visibility of certain Midwest organizations and food producers working to counteract the effects of corporate "ownership" of certain key food crops by promoting efforts to revive heritage varieties. For instance, Decorah, Iowa, is the home of Seed Savers Exchange, a seed bank that boasts of over 25,000 seed varieties. The organization is widely recognized for its efforts to empower the small farmers and backyard gardeners who have been saving heirloom

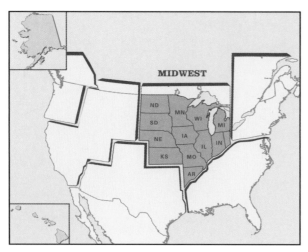
MIDWEST

seeds for generations. Also in the Midwest and Great Plains there are many small ranchers raising heritage breeds of stock animals, including some who are raising buffalo (or, more properly, bison), which are implicitly suited to their native environment. Midwest hogs are getting a makeover as premium, small-production pork products from Iowa, such as La Quercia prosciutto and Vande Rose hams, and are showing up on high-end menus from coast to coast.

The growing regions of the Midwest are vast and variegated. Much to some people's surprise, there is a whole lot more than just the famed corn belt, where this traditional crop has become astonishingly industrialized at a cost to heirloom varieties. If you travel north into the areas bordering the Great Lakes, you'll be in a traditional stronghold of dairy farming, and if you paddle around the glacier-riven Uplands of Minnesota, you'll be among wild-rice harvesters still at work using the traditional (and required) techniques of the Ojibwa, where the stalks are bent over the canoe and the ripened grain is brushed free using "knockers." Wild rice has been named the official grain of Minnesota in honor of that heritage.

Go west and you will be in the Great Plains, which stretch southward from the Canadian border into Texas. This is the home of the buffalo, whose great numbers once made the ground shake. Those high, dry plains were known, early on, as the "Great American Desert" and were imagined to be a wasteland. John Deere's self-scouring plow, however, made it possible to break up the ground, while the bountiful Ogallala Aquifer provided water for irrigation. As a result, the plains came to produce near-endless quantities of wheat, particularly along the 100th meridian. Cattle have also found a home on the range. Once upon a time, they

were driven up from Texas and Oklahoma to railroad towns such as Omaha, Abilene, Topeka, and Kansas City, for rapid transport to the great slaughterhouses of Chicago; now ranches spread out across the region.

When the earliest Euro-American settlers came here through passes in the Appalachian Mountains and along the waterways of the Great Lakes, they transformed the landscape by introducing old-world grains such as wheat, oats, and barley; fruits such as apples and grapes; as well as cattle (both dairy and beef), chickens, domesticated hogs, and horses. Subsequent immigrations of Scandinavians and Germans peaked in the 1880s, with ethnic Scandinavians clustering in and around Minnesota, and Germans spreading throughout the region. Immigration from Central and Eastern Europe and Italy reached a maximum level in the early 1900s; now many of their descendants are to be found in urban enclaves. More recent immigrants have come from Latin America and Asia and have also settled primarily in major cities.

Each of these ethnic populations has brought its own distinctive foodways to the Midwest, expanding and enriching the region's cuisine. Cuisine of German-Americans is so common today that it scarcely seems "ethnic": frankfurters, hamburgers, brats, meat loaf, potato salad, sauerkraut, and mustard, along with schnitzel dishes of beef, pork, or chicken. Specialty sausages are crafted by artisanal producers throughout the region, while small-batch breweries craft their beers using local barley and hops.

Central and Eastern European immigrants introduced goulash, a stew or a soup most often made of beef, red onions, vegetables, spices, and paprika powder, as well as pierogi, boiled dumplings of unleavened bread that are often stuffed with farmer's cheese, onions, and potato. Italian cuisine has become almost ubiquitous throughout the nation, but one of the unique contributions of the Midwest is certainly the deep-dish pizza of Chicago. Mexican food and Asian cuisines are now standbys in Midwestern cities.

Higher-end restaurants are beginning to showcase the regional bounty. In Chicago, Bistro Campagne is a country-style French bistro that offers a seasonally changing menu with locally grown ingredients, while Drew's Eatery serves up a variety of organic hot dogs. In Iowa City, Devotay highlights hot and cold tapas that make use of local, seasonal products, while the Motley Cow Café presents pizza and a wide range of full dinners that make extensive use of local vegetables and

meats. In Milwaukee, Meritage offers a wide-ranging menu that includes various bison-meat entrées, while in suburban Brookfield, Café Manna specializes in vegetarian dishes. Finally, in St. Paul, award-winning Heartlands features an ever-changing menu built around whatever fresh foods happen to be available that day; recent entrées included pan-roasted elk or goat chops. This list of restaurants could go on and on, but the evidence is plain: A revolution in dining has arrived in the Midwest, but it's a revolution that harkens back to, and takes advantage of, the essential foods of the region.

Survival of the Milkman

The Story of Calder Dairy

Nostalgia is a provocative concept—the taking of our memories, both good and bad, and unconsciously polishing away the rough edges until they are shiny, valuable, and worth passing on to our children in the form of whimsical stories. It's important for self-preservation as well, tying us to our roots, family, and communities. Calder Dairy, with its heavy glass bottles and home delivery trucks winding through the neighborhoods of Southeast Michigan, represents the best kind of nostalgia, one that offers self-preservation—no polishing required.

A visit to the farm itself, which rests in the bucolic countryside of northern Monroe County, is the perfect way to begin to understand why Calder milk is so exceptional; the farm is, after all, where the milk gets its own beginning. After peeling off of the interstate south of Ann Arbor, the scenery opens up, giving way to other small family farms studded with red barns made dusty with the remnants of the fall harvest. While the landscape appears to be entering the dormancy of winter, Calder Dairy Farm is still humming with activity, and that's exactly how the Calder family likes it.

"It used to be that everybody could claim a farmer in their background somewhere, but these days that's happening less and less," says farm manager Nicole Noble. So the Calders (who have owned and operated the farm for three generations) opened their farm to the public as a way to narrow that gap in relationship between producer and consumer. Visitors are encouraged to help bottle-feed the young calves each afternoon—a perfect opportunity for children to get hands-on time with an animal that contributes so directly to their daily meals. The calves are soft, charming, and *eager*, often bestowing an unexpected "kiss" after taking their bottles. Visitors can also watch the cows being milked daily in the farm's milking parlor.

While the calves are adorable, Calder Farm is no petting zoo. All the milk that goes into Calder Dairy products is gathered here at the farm. Approximately one hundred cows (both Brown Swiss and Holstein) get milked twice a day, and gathering "milk of a better kind," as the folks at Calder like to say, takes hard work and a commitment to quality.

The philosophy of delivering a product of a better kind starts with caring about the cows themselves. With thoughtful monikers like Violet, Butters, Einstein, and Salami, the cows aren't just numbers. Each one is cared for and fed according to its individual growth needs. "For example," explains Noble, "just like you wouldn't feed a toddler the same as you'd feed a teenager, we feed our lactating moms differently than we feed the moms-to-be." A nutritionist helps formulate the proper ration for the cows, balancing the amounts of protein, fat, vitamins, and minerals found in the various types of feed and silage mixed for the animals. It is through provision of a balanced, tailor-made diet (and *without* the use of artificial hormones) that Calder is able to maximize milk production among their cows.

"For me, and for my father before me, this has always been more of a way of life than a business," says owner John Calder. "Maximizing quantity costs less and is more attractive for supermarkets, but in that pursuit I believe that quality gets left by the wayside somewhere." By staying small, Calder explains, they can maintain high quality from start to finish. The farm grows nearly all the feed for the cows themselves, and cows spend portions of each day grazing during the spring and summer months. "We also choose to pasteurize in small batches, at the lowest temperature required by law, much lower than most commercial milk producers," says Calder. In this way, both flavor and beneficial nutrients remain intact.

In addition to milk, Calder Dairy offers over a dozen other products, from richly flavored buttermilk to drinking yogurt, cream, and butter. They also produce over thirty flavors of ice cream and the *perfect* holiday eggnog, based on an old family recipe. All of these products can be found in wholesale markets throughout Southeast Michigan, but most people needn't look any farther than their front porches. Calder's home delivery

Happy cows at Calder Dairy

service has been providing loyal customers with fresh dairy products since 1956, via their trademark Holstein-printed refrigerated trucks. Who else but your neighborhood milkman can deliver such nostalgia with a smile?

Calder maintains that the home delivery service has been crucial in maintaining a loyal customer base, even through major shifts in the local foods economy. "My father's business had its heyday in the late 1960s and early '70s. That's when everybody got their milk routinely delivered fresh to them. The major shift occurred when supermarkets entered the picture, slowly dismantling the home delivery business," he explains. "When my father started in 1946, there were roughly six hundred dairies in Michigan. Today there's only about fourteen left."

Calder Dairy remained persistent in its desire to keep the milk coming directly to the consumer. Even after John Calder took over the business from his father, the decision was made to stick with glass bottles, keep their delivery service going, and stay small. Fortunately, the last five to eight years have seen yet another shift in the local foods economy and a resurgence in the desire to eat food that has more to offer than a hefty dose of antibiotics, hormones, and a four-week shelf life. Customers are invited to see exactly where their milk comes from, from a "girl" named Butters on the farm, and to the bottling plant a few miles away. For Calder, this is a point of pride.

Today, he sees the lasting success of Calder Dairy as a testimony to his father's vision. "For me, this has been a way for me to honor my parents' hard work," says Calder. "I've taken their dream, added to it, and it has become a dream of my own." Like nostalgia, Calder Dairy has a sense of place, with roots in family, tradition, and community. Each bottle of milk has a story, and everyone is invited to share in it.

ALEX HARRISON *is a writer and expert nosher who finds endless pleasures in stinky cheese, crusty bread, and cold beer.*

Liquidity: The Dream Lives On

A Profile of Boskydel Vineyard

On the cobweb-covered, dingy white wall of the Bos-kydel Vineyard tasting room on the Leelanau Penin-sula, amid the flotsam and jetsam of thirty-two years' worth of bartered art, newspaper clippings, old photos, and pithy sayings, is a discreet sign that says it all: "We don't manage by managing. We manage by being here all the time."

At 81 years of age, the owner gets up every morn-ing at 5 A.M. and is in bed by 9 P.M. When he's not in the vineyard, he's in the winery, 7 days a week from 1 to 5 P.M., 362 days a year. For Bernard C. Rink, aka "Bernie" or "The Wine Nazi," the dream lives on.

The wine industry in this neck of the woods has changed dramatically over the last three decades, but Bernie has not; he is as predictable and pertinacious as orange construction barrels in summer.

Despite his apparently obstinate ways, Bernie is always pondering, always experimenting. "What new grapes should I plant?" "Can I grow Chinese chestnuts and sell them in the tasting room?" "Can I grow Christ-mas trees that are resistant to crown gall?" "Will kes-trels reduce my crop loss from birds?" "Is seaweed spray a good idea for grapevines?" It was this kind of thinking that led to my unusual upbringing.

GOOD TIMES

Bernie C. Rink is my father. I first realized that he was serious about growing grapes when he announced his intention to raze our modest but popular baseball dia-mond in favor of a grape nursery. My brothers and I created that ballpark, hacking it out from a fallow field with a regular push-type lawnmower. We even built a substantial chicken-wire backstop to halt the progress of an errant pitch.

In a rude reversal of the magical *Field of Dreams* scenario, Bernie told us the diamond would have to go, replaced by a crop that no one in those parts had ever heard of: wine grapes. Little did we know that *his* field of dreams would lay the groundwork for the establish-ment of the commercial wine industry in Northern Michigan.

It began in 1965, when my dad got hold of Phil Wagner's book *American Wines and Winemaking* (published today as *Grapes into Wine*). As the library director of Northwestern Michigan College in Tra-verse City, he had access to a lot of books. He also had access to land, having bought sixteen rolling acres in the middle of Leelanau County, the state's "little fin-ger," jutting out into northern Lake Michigan. Sitting on the 45th parallel, the peninsula is on a latitudinal par with wine-growing regions in southern France and northern Italy.

In an effort to turn his five sons into "economic assets," Bernie decided to plant a one-acre test plot of several French-American hybrid grape varieties and a few of the less hardy *Vitis vinifera*: Chardonnay, Johan-nisberg Riesling, and Gewürztraminer. The hybrids were all numbered—Seibel 5279 (Aurore), Seibel 7053 (Chancellor), Seibel 9549 (de Chaunac), Seibel 10878 (Chelois), and Seibel 13053 (Cascade). Seibel, needless to say, had a lot of time on his hands.

As economic assets, we were expected to chop weeds in the sweltering heat of midsummer and pick grapes in the stinging sleet of late fall, not to mention pruning in knee-deep snow in the winter and sorting out the good wood, which would be plunged into our nursery in the spring to repeat the endless, monoto-nous cycle. But it was fun. We used to make up lively little songs about the vineyard to the tune of "Ta-ra-ra Boom-de-ay":

We work at Boskydel,
the closest thing to hell.
We're never treated well,
at slave camp Boskydel.

Working closely with Bernie in the early days was retired Michigan State University chemistry pro-fessor Bob Herbst, who established an experimental vineyard of his own in 1971 on the cooler east shore of Lake Michigan. Due to the difference in microclimate between the two sites, Herbst's hybrids would often ripen a week later.

In the ensuing years, Bernie and Bob played host to numerous would-be winemakers, entrepreneurs, members of the media, and the just plain curious. Many of the individuals who would one day open their own wineries in the region began by talking to these two trailblazers. Both men began their avocations strictly in the amateur sense. But then, with Bernie, something went horribly wrong. The vision of five sons—all that free labor—proved to be irresistible, instilling a larger, grander desire.

THE TRAILBLAZERS

In 1975, construction began on Boskydel Vineyard, the first bonded wine cellar on the Leelanau Peninsula. Bernie owns fifty-six acres of land, twenty-five acres planted in hybrid grapes. A year earlier, on nearby Old Mission Peninsula, business entrepreneur Ed O'Keefe founded Chateau Grand Traverse, a state-of-the-art winery and vineyard operation with an emphasis on world-class European vinifera wines.

In addition to European vinifera, Chateau Grand Traverse produces a unique product line, which blends locally grown fruit with the aforementioned varietals: It includes Cherry Wine, Cherry Riesling, Spiced Cherry Wine, Cherry Wine Sangría, Cherry Ginseng, and Cranberry Riesling.

Boskydel's varietals—Aurore, Vignoles, Soleil Blanc, Seyval Blanc, de Chaunac, and Rose de Chaunac—are decidedly French in character. They are crisp, clear wines with a touch of oak and plenty of time in the bottle. The winery bottles approximately 6,500 gallons per year. Emphasis is placed on intensive viticulture. "If you grow good grapes, the wine will make itself," Bernie says.

In 1977, Leelanau Wine Cellars, Ltd., debuted. Begun by local cherry grower Chuck Kalchik and his partner, attorney Mike Jacobson, the winery is the largest on the Leelanau Peninsula. Nate Stackhouse, their first winemaker, was a congenial, outgoing individual. He and Bernie shared many an afternoon comparing notes and vintages. Nate once helped us out

Bernie at work in the tasting room

people are frequently discouraged. Boskydel is not so easy to find, either. Bernie often asks customers if they are lost. This adds to the mystery and allure of shopping for wine on the Leelanau Peninsula.

Last, but not least, of the early pioneers is Bruce Simpson, proprietor of Good Harbor Vineyards. Opened in 1980, the winery was equipped with 30,000 gallons of stainless steel cooperage and 2,500 French oak barrels. The Simpson family has been in the fruit business on the Leelanau Peninsula since the mid-1950s. Bruce studied enology at the University of California, Davis, until 1978, when he began planting wine grapes, courtesy of our baseball field, uh, I mean, grape nursery. Good Harbor is most famous for its delightful blend Trillium. The label was a marketing masterpiece. Based on a popular Michigan wildflower, the design was widely acclaimed and resulted in increased wine sales.

I would be remiss not to mention Dr. G. Stanley Howell and his colleagues at Michigan State University for their important contributions to the state's wine industry. For a while, Bernie collaborated with "Stan" to provide field research opportunities and copious amounts of wine for sampling.

In 1985, in recognition of the growing importance of wine growing to the state, Gov. James Blanchard formed the Michigan Grape and Wine Industry Council (MGWIC), of which Bernie was a founding member.

ON THE MAP

Driving around Leelanau County, one is struck by the number of vineyards inhabiting fields once delegated strictly to cherry orchards. This is, perhaps, the most telling sign that a once-fledgling industry has put down deep roots. According to the MGWIC, wineries in Michigan now attract nearly one million visitors annually—that's the same as the Sleeping Bear Dunes National Lakeshore and the Detroit Zoo. In the last ten years alone, vineyard plantings have increased more than 60 percent.

with a mysterious pectin haze that developed in one of our reds.

In 1978, Larry Mawby unveiled the third Leelanau Peninsula winery: L. Mawby Vineyards. Called "the best of a new breed of Michigan winemakers" by *Detroit Free Press* writer James Ricci, Mawby began his career producing traditional, estate-bottled, French-style table wines of the highest quality. Now, he makes entirely *methode champenoise* and *cuve close* method sparkling wines. His current annual production is fewer than 8,000 cases. This modest volume allows Mawby the pleasure of wine making in the style he enjoys—small lots made with minimal handling. In a bold marketing move, he named one of his sparklers "Sex." Needless to say, many a customer now enters his tasting room asking for Sex. (Note: Not to be outdone by Mawby's salacious designs, winegrower Silvio T. Ciccone ensconced his superstar daughter Madonna on several labels. So now, you can drive to Leelanau Peninsula and have Madonna and Sex.)

To the uninitiated, Mawby's winery is difficult to locate. Visits by groups numbering more than twenty

From a small handful of Michigan wineries in the mid-1970s, the industry has grown to fifty-six wineries—twenty-eight of which are in the Leelanau Peninsula and Old Mission Peninsula appellations. In the last few years, a *USA Today* article profiled the Leelanau Peninsula as one of four "up-and-coming" wine regions in the United States and Canada. Due to the region's northern latitude, says the article, the Leelanau Peninsula is now poised to take advantage of the recent popularity of Riesling-style wines by becoming a regional champion of this cool-climate grape. Other predominant grape varieties grown in the area include Chardonnay, Pinot Noir, Merlot, Cabernet Franc, Pinot Gris, and Pinot Blanc.

Michigan wines have grown not only in quantity but in quality as well. According to the MGWIC: "To meet changing consumer preferences, today's vintners concentrate on finding the best varieties and locations and utilize the latest technological advances in viticulture and enology. With an impressive dedication to quality, they produce excellent everyday wines as well as an increasing number of world-class wines." As concrete evidence of this quest for quality, Michigan wines received 800 medals at national and international competitions in 2007.

THE MORE THINGS CHANGE

Hunkered down behind a laminated counter supported by old whiskey barrels, Bernie Rink prepares for the daily "onslaught" of customers, who come to see him as much as they come to buy wine. True to his "Wine Nazi" reputation, customers who exceed the eight-person capacity limit are asked to wait outside (there is a sign by the driveway reinforcing this rule). For a long time he closed the facilities at 6 P.M., but now he closes at five. Too many customers were making Boskydel their last pit stop after a full day of tasting. Bernie refers to these valued customers as "teat-squeezers," based on their habit of tasting every wine for free but buying very little.

In an age of instant gratification and planned obsolescence, Bernie is like a small but sharp stone in your shoe, challenging long-held beliefs about wine and life in general. Longtime patrons get it—look forward to it—and flock to his sanctuary every year. "Is Bernie here?" they ask. They quickly scan the tasting room for recognizable and reassuring landmarks: the aptly named Ridgid Tool calendar; the print of Ronald Reagan as court jester; the photo of Bernie and his brother Ted that appeared in *National Geographic Traveler*; the photo of Al Bungart standing next to a freshly dressed pig; the 143-year-old grape-picking basket from Cochem, Germany; the austere orange ceiling fan that has been spinning nonstop with a slight squeak since the winery opened; the national debt calculator; a postcard that reads: "Being of sound mind and body, I spent every last cent."

It's not hard to understand Bernie. He uses words sparingly but well. He doesn't like to be the center of attention ("What kills the skunk is the publicity he gives himself"). He is not self-centered ("There comes a time when all our mirrors must turn into windows"). And he believes in making a good wine at a fair price that everyone can afford.

Bernie's five sons are all grown now, each with his own career, family, and other worldly pursuits. The youngest brother, Andy, lives in Traverse City and makes frequent trips to "the farm." All of them agree that "Boskydel Basic Training" added value to their lives, not to mention a strong work ethic.

A Bernie tradition that endures today: giving a free bottle of wine to newlyweds. It comes with a toast: "Here's to the wings of love, may they never molt a feather, as her little boat and your little boat sail down the river of life together." He also has other, not-so-ready-for-prime-time toasts.

Last year, after fifty-one years of marriage, Bernie and Suzanne's little boats parted company, so Bernie sails on alone. He has his own epitaph ready, courtesy of Suzanne: "He ran out of things to plant, so he planted himself."

JIM RINK *is Bernie Rink's eldest son and lives in Royal Oak, Michigan. In addition to his "regular" job as a public relations consultant for AAA Michigan, he serves as editor of the* American Wine Society Journal. *He has a daughter, Katie; a dog, Holly; a brown belt in aikido; and enjoys directing plays at the community theater level. Whenever possible, he enjoys lava lamps, candles that flicker, long hot showers, and free wine from Boskydel.*

Tradition Meets Technology

. . . .

Herb and Kathy Eckhouse's La Quercia Prosciutto Americano

"La Quercia" means "the oak," and it is the symbol of the region of Parma in Italy, a reference to the majestic oaks whose acorns once fed the pigs of Parma. It is also Iowa's state tree—sufficient serendipity to name an Iowa-based prosciutto company after it.

La Quercia was founded in 2000 by Herb and Kathy Eckhouse, who had lived for four years in Parma and learned to appreciate its artisanal prosciutto. The Eckhouses' dream was to make a prosciutto of their own, but in the meantime they began by importing from one of the best prosciutto makers in Parma. This helped them learn some of the ropes, build a distribution network, and work on the financing of their new plant in Norwalk, just south of Des Moines. They also began experimenting with homemade hams. Using techniques they had learned in Parma and making adjustments for the meat that was raised close to home, they zeroed in on the perfect combination of meat, salt, air, and time (the only ingredients in good prosciutto).

Making prosciutto is a slow process. It is not, as some major American cold-cut producers would have us believe, simply adding extra salt and pressing a cheap traditional American ham. There are no nitrates or nitrites to preserve it. The methods used in Parma, and now in Norwalk, have been refined over centuries. For most of human existence we have had to preserve our meat through myriad curing, drying, and smoking techniques. The cultures around the Mediterranean were the best at it; from the cured Italian fatback known as *lardo* to the Spanish *bacalao*, or salt cod, there are thousands of them, and prosciutto could well be considered the king.

The prosciutto curing process begins with the carefully trimmed ham, or hind leg, of the pig and echoes the seasonal cycle (winter, spring, and summer) followed for generations. The ham is salted and allowed to rest on one side in a cool place. After weeks in the cold (winter), the salt is rinsed off and the ham is hung to dry and develop its flavor in very specific climatic conditions for months.

You'll notice that a lot was left out of that process. Trimmed how? What kind of salt? Cured for how long? What temperatures? What specific climatic conditions? Well, if you can get that kind of information out of a prosciutto maker, then you are surprisingly more persuasive than I. Techniques are zealously guarded from family to family. I can tell you a couple of the differences between the prosciutto di Parma and those of San Danielle and Tuscany. In San Danielle, ham is pressed under a weight to extract more liquid, which leads to an exceedingly sweet ham. In Tuscany, there is extra salt in the curing of the prosciutto, which I have always thought of as a compensation for the lack of salt in their bread. The Eckhouses took what they had learned in Italy and combined it with some modern sanitation and refrigeration techniques. Herb would not tell me the precise times and temperatures, but I can tell you that the equipment used to accomplish his aims is state of the art.

La Quercia's "green label" organic prosciutto made its world premiere in September 2005 at the Slow Food Iowa Harvest Dinner, a part of the Field to Family local foods celebration held in Iowa City each year. Besides serving the ham *naturale*, simply sliced paper thin, guest chef Odessa Piper created three dishes featuring the marvelous new delicacy. First it was served in puff pastry with sage and Northern Prairie "Parmesan" goat cheese (from Woodward, Iowa). Next she served it fried atop a chilled melon bisque, and finally, as part of a prosciutto-walnut compound butter on a pan-roasted Wholesome Harvest chicken breast.

Part of the beauty of prosciutto is that like the slow ideals themselves, it can appeal to nearly everyone, across any taste or socioeconomic scale. Contrary to common misconception, prosciutto is not fancy food, and these ideals are not about food snobbery. Prosciutto is peasant food, a way to preserve and make delicious the otherwise lesser cuts of pork (because historically the chops and loins went to the nobles). Herb and Kathy have transported this classic fare from its origins in the Italian countryside to the heartland prairie, where it has found a new home among America's modern farmers. Its introduction in turn provides an additional market for the sustainable pork producers who supply La Quercia as well as a local source for an imported delicacy.

KURT FRIESE *is publisher of* Edible Iowa River Valley.

Chicago Green City Market

The Legacy of Its Founder, Abby Mandel

SUMMER, 1997

It is a view like no other in the city of Chicago, and only invited guests are allowed in the lush gardens atop City Hall. It's known as "The Mayor's Rooftop Garden," the pride of Mayor Richard M. Daley. On this day, Abby Mandel, her dear friend Alice Waters, and Alderman Vi Daley (no relation to the mayor) were getting a private tour from Mayor Daley.

Her mind churning with possibilities, Abby Mandel was planting a seed for the future, making local, quality, sustainable foods more accessible to Chicagoans. It was the first of many meetings Abby would have with the powerful mayor of the country's third-largest city, and the alderman watched the woman who would become her mentor work City Hall.

"When I first met Abby," the alderman recalls, "she told me she wanted to meet the mayor right away, to make connections. She said to me, 'I want to meet everybody in City Hall that can help me.' And that was my job: Set this up, set that up."

Abby Mandel's vision was to grow a sustainable farmers' market in Chicago, but it was not just about offering fresh sweet corn or juicy peaches; her vision included educating the public about eating healthfully and connecting people with farmers, farmers with chefs, and proving that a sustainable market could be accessible and profitable. In 1999, the Chicago Green City Market (GCM) started small, with just a handful of vendors, but it had big ideas. Originally located on Benton Court, an alley in a downtown Chicago area known as the Loop, it eventually moved north to Lincoln Park, Alderman Vi Daley's neighborhood.

"I thought, 'You need to help her because her goals are great goals and we need to be thinking about healthy eating.' And I knew it was good for our neighborhood," the alderman recalls.

It all started with a vision. In the 1970s, Abby began visiting markets while on vacation in France. "Not the fancy ones but the places the locals and the local chefs went," recalls daughter Holly Sherr. For Chicago, Abby envisioned a marketplace where local products would be all that was sold. In 1979, she created the "Best of the Midwest" show; its goal was to introduce people to regional products. Every year interest in it grew. While neither organic in nature nor sustainable, it was local, and Abby hit the road to find the farmers to participate in the market. Even though it was only once a year, it was, Holly says, the catalyst for Green City Market.

Known to many Chicagoans through her weekly cooking column in the *Chicago Tribune*, which was syndicated in newspapers nationwide, and in the publishing world as a cookbook author, contributor to *Bon Appétit*, and James Beard Award winner, she was a teacher at the grassroots level with a drive to build a market that served the farmers as well as the community. It was a grand vision layered with fund-raising, politicking, recruiting, and team-building. Abby would appear in jeans, Merrill shoes, and a sweater in the morning and buzz from stand to stand on market days. Evenings might find her at a museum benefit dressed to the nines or entertaining friends in her North Shore home, sharing her passion and love for food with her tremendous culinary concoctions. As her friends and family recall, she was always two steps ahead of everyone else, because her mind was constantly spinning with new ideas for

the market. Even in the middle of a conversation she could listen and create a plan in her head at the same time. Rita Gutekanst, board member of Green City Market, saw Abby as someone who could get anyone to do anything, always for the benefit of growing the market. "You just found yourself jumping to meet anything Abby Mandel requested," said Rita, who worked closely with Abby years earlier, when she was a caterer. Legendary as a perfectionist, Abby demanded the highest level of performance from everyone on her team, often intimidating even those who knew her style. "It took a while to 'get her' and understand her," Rita says, "because she moved at lightning speed. She would ask you to do something, and by the time you could do it she had already moved on to the next thing."

Tireless, Abby was known for her extreme work ethic and her unfailing 4:30 A.M. appearance on market days, greeting farmers to be sure they had everything they needed and to help with setup. Jim Law, who worked with Abby when he ran the Mayor's Office of Special Events, notes that not even bad weather would deter her. "I remember walking through the Loop, and I'd see her under an umbrella on a rainy day overseeing a few small tents of exquisite cheese, bread, fruits, and veggies, and she'd be there whether or not the weather was good." Even on days when business was slow, she personally made sure they would succeed. In her mind it had to be a worthwhile experience for the farmers in order to serve the market in the long term. "The first year the market was open, she would buy up everything from the farmers that was left so they would be encouraged to come back the next week," says her daughter. She nurtured the relationships with the farmers because she understood the obstacles they faced coming to market, making sure that the trip into the city was an easy one, that parking was available, and acknowledging that a day at the market meant a lost day of work in the fields.

"My mom always wanted to own a farm or a restaurant, or both," Holly says. "And that's where she felt common ground with the farmers at the market. She appreciated the hours they toiled in the field from before the sun came up until after it set and how the weather could affect not just crops, but sales at the stand."

A unique aspect of Green City Market in Chicago is that Abby handpicked the purveyors for the market, choosing farmers who cared for the land and did not simply use it. While many markets *encourage* sustainable farming, Abby *required* it. Anyone who applies to

become a vendor must write their own sustainability statement and, upon acceptance, post it at their stand. It was a high standard, but the farmers knew her commitment ran deep and her mission of "Know Your Food, Know Your Farmer" was sound. David Cleverdon of Kinnikinnick recalls the day he was approached by Abby. "I learned how real that mission was the Saturday I looked up from my stand at the Evanston Market and saw Abby, with Chef Sarah Stegner, glaring at me in the background, saying, as she pointed at our Kinnikinnick produce, 'When am I going to see this produce in my market?' How could I resist, particularly after I realized the degree to which she actually cared about farmers?"

The determined, compassionate woman forged relationships and developed partnerships with each vendor and supported the farms in many ways. Beth and Brent Eccles of Green Acres Farm felt the genuine connection. "She introduced us to friends, chefs, and colleagues and came to our booth weekly to ask our thoughts about the market that day. She called, e-mailed, shopped, cooked, always with the market on her mind and in her heart," Beth says.

The drive to connect farmers to market reached a new level (unthinkable just a few years ago) when, in 2005, Abby created a special job on the City of Chicago's payroll: Farm Forager. As a way to connect more farmers with outlets for sales and a way to serve the growing need of chefs for local, fresh, sustainable food, Abby convinced City Hall to cofund (along with GCM) a position with an interesting job description: discover and recruit farmers throughout the state to participate in Chicago's marketplace. Professional farm forager Mari Coyne's job is to travel the back roads of Illinois and surrounding states in search of local farmers to participate in a network of agrarians that supplies customers from small markets to large commercial kitchens, including hospitals and schools, to create a local foods economy for the benefit of Chicagoans.

In order to keep the regional agricultural economy growing, Abby required that any product sold at GCM had to be sourced locally. In other words, Bleeding Heart Bakery, a vendor, can't sell anything with chocolate as an ingredient because the cocoa beans cannot be sourced locally. The same goes for no dates, no figs, and no raisins. But in season, at the bakery stands, there are rhubarb tarts, cranberry scones, and tomato flat bread, all made with local or regional ingredients. And nobody seems to feel slighted.

Early on market days, there are chefs loading up their bags with the fruits and vegetables, which were harvested a few hours earlier, only to be appearing on menus and plates the very same day, offering diners truly fresh food with a distinctive taste. Frontera Grill's Rick Bayless sources 85 percent of his ingredients locally at the peak of the growing season and is part of the team of local chefs who followed Abby's lead years ago: At the end of the market day, the chefs offer to buy whatever is left over, ensuring a prosperous relationship between them and the farmers.

"Healthy eating was important to her long before anyone really knew what organic meant," recalls Holly. She was driven to reach as many people as she possibly could, spreading the gospel of healthy food options, centered at the farmers' market.

"Abby believed strongly that our children are the future of sustainability," says Jeanne Pinsof, who worked with Abby to create The Edible Gardens, located in Lincoln Park Zoo's Farm-in-the-Zoo and presented by John Deere. GCM employs a part-time organic vegetable gardener to supervise, plant, and maintain the 5,000-square-foot edible gardens. Its purpose is to fulfill the educational goals set by the GCM board of directors. Geared toward children, especially students on field trips, it offers opportunities for anyone to visit and learn about growing, weeding, composting, harvesting, and cooking vegetables. Children delight in the chance to play with dirt and to learn where food comes from. Because of this partnership with GCM and the zoo, the children learn a lesson to nourish them their entire lives. Teachable moments can also be found in the Sprouts Program, where children absorb the lessons of sustainability while munching on greens, sampling a tart, crunching a cranberry, or concentrating on a cooking lesson. Reaching this generation grows the possibility of future sustainability.

"Breakfast Club," with guest speakers hosting discussions, espouses what Abby was passionate about, that there is a link between good nutrition and well-being and that people need to become educated about this. Authors and chefs also make special appearances on market days. Abby wanted food available at the market so "people could taste the fruits and vegetables, have the fresh foods right there." Alderman Daley remembers the early days. It all started with a pan, a flame, batter, and all fresh ingredients within reach . . . a chef's dream. Abby created a crêpe stand and cooked right in front of market goers. "Abby did it herself, cooking crêpes because she wasn't sure it would be successful, so she did the work." It was a way for people to taste the market in every sense of the word. Just as she did in her syndicated column, Abby taught people how easy it was to eat fresh, healthful, and, now, local foods. Ten years later, the crêpes are still a must-have, but because they are so popular the wait for one can be as long as twenty minutes, teasing the senses of those who wait for their number to be called, and making it impossible to resist watching the people in the front of the line bite into their sumptuous, market-fresh fare.

"The neighborhood loves it," declares Alderman Daley. The market draws families and is a regular weekend destination. "To me, [Abby] developed more than just customers," Jim Law says. "They became patrons, they appreciated that lifestyle, they appreciated the work of the farmers and what they were doing to provide great, healthy, fresh alternatives people would just come back—it was like going to church."

Abby Mandel's ultimate mission was to provide a year-round sustainable farmers' market in the city of Chicago. Sadly, Abby passed away before she could realize that dream, but her legacy will fulfill her wish. Shortly before she passed away she established the Abby Mandel Charity Foundation to help create a market that would operate for the full year in a permanent space in the city of Chicago. Her daughter, Holly Sherr, runs the foundation, and, with her mother's spirit guiding her, she joined the board of Chicago Green City Market, which has been called by Alice Waters one of the ten best farmers' markets in the country.

Twelve years ago and eleven stories above the streets of Chicago, standing in and overlooking the City Hall rooftop garden, Mayor Daley and Abby Mandel shared not only a view of the city but also a vision. As they looked out over the city and beyond, the mayor realized that Abby Mandel's goal was not only impressive, but achievable. As Chicago's Green City Market plans for a year-round market, one remarkable woman's foresight is becoming a reality for the benefit of hundreds of farmers and thousands of patrons. Abby Mandel's dreams have come true.

R. J. LISCUM *is publisher of* Edible Chicago.

Abby Mandel, the highly esteemed founder of Chicago's Green City Market, beamed a broad smile as Mayor Richard M. Daley and his wife, Maggie, exuberantly proclaimed it "Green City Market Day" in Chicago, celebrating the endless passion of the woman Chef Carrie Nahabedian calls the "heart and soul" of the only all-organic and sustainable agriculture market in the city. It is the tenth annual celebration of the Lincoln Park market, and nobody in attendance doubts Abby Mandel will not rest until her vision—making the Green City Market the best in the country— is reached.

Part of that goal includes expanding the offerings year-round with a permanent home for the venue, an idea Mandel hopes to convince the mayor to bring to fruition. In an interview with *Edible Chicago*, Ms. Mandel tells us, "I think the city would benefit because [people] would develop an understanding that there is more agriculture possible, new initiatives that are available, like hoop houses and greenhouses, and all kinds of different growing methods that really can produce throughout the year. It's not going to be [just] strawberries and tomatoes, but it's going to be a lot of really great food."

Mandel says it is an infinite effort to educate the community about sustainable agriculture. "If we don't support and give these farmers money for them to invest in their practices, a farmer's life will be over. There's just a big message there. It's not just about food that tastes good."

RETAILER ~ *EDIBLE TWIN CITIES* (MINNESOTA)

Laurie McCann Crowell

The Personal Story of a Local Foods Activist

Laurie McCann Crowell is a storyteller. She bubbles over with enthusiasm as she tells her stories, which she illustrates with tall bottles of golden honey produced by Don Johnston, a cardiac surgeon at the Mayo Clinic with a passion for bees. Or she takes a wedge of creamy cheese studded with hickory nuts out of the refrigerator at her store and tells of the Wisconsin cheese makers who hand-harvest the hickory nuts. A mother herself, she seems to find inspiration from the jar of Talmadge Farms spicy Russian dill pickles made in Duluth by a mom who raised her kids and put them through school by making and selling seasonal goods.

As the proprietor of Golden Fig Fine Foods in St. Paul, Minnesota, Laurie is the keeper of many stories of the producers whose items she carries in her store. The food items she features are locally produced, made with care, and presented artfully. She might be called the community organizer of local foods for all the effort she puts into seeking fine products and spreading the word about their flavors and quality. The stories she tells, full of admiration for the people who make these fine foods, also speak to her own path as a food artisan who has come to appreciate the craft so much that she wants to share all of these stories with others. Her own

Laurie McCann Crowell at Golden Fig Fine Foods

beginning as a food artisan perhaps makes her uniquely qualified to describe the time and effort that have gone into the work of others.

For twelve years Golden Fig was associated with Laurie's own products—flavored vinegars and hand-blended spice mixes—which she sold at the St. Paul Farmers' Market. She took the name Golden Fig because of the beauty of that image and was inspired by the name of a shop—The Golden Pear—near where she once worked in East Hampton, New York. The place she was working (having responded to a Help Wanted sign in a window during summer break from college) was the Barefoot Contessa. At the time Ina Garten's specialty foods store was a thriving business and gave Laurie her first taste of introducing culinary delights to the public. She was hooked. Instead of going back to college, where she was studying interior design, she stayed on at the Barefoot Contessa for two years.

That was the start of Laurie's career in specialty foods, which eventually took her back to Wisconsin, where she grew up, and then to the Twin Cities, both times lured by jobs managing bakeries. On a whim, she took a class about making vinegars and was inspired again. She began making flavored vinegars for Turtle Bakery, where she was working at the time, and progressed to the spices. Golden Fig was born.

Flavor is something Laurie knows well. She remembers visiting a maple syrup farm as a six- or seven-year-old girl in Wisconsin. "I tasted the sap right from the tree—and wow!—I will always remember the intensity of that flavor," she says. She seems to have a knack for combining ingredients in ways that awaken the taste buds. "I have been making apple spice vinegar now because chestnut apples are in season," she explains on an October day. "And the basil limeade has been selling well. I can't keep it on the shelves."

Her best-selling item ("Out of eighty products, for twelve years in a row," she exclaims) is the Sel de Cuisine, a blend of sea salt, rosemary, tarragon, garlic, white pepper, green peppercorns, chile peppers, and a touch of cinnamon. It seems to hold magic powers, making everything from grilled vegetables to a steak to sliced tomatoes jump with flavor.

Laurie's passion for locally produced foods is intertwined with her love of high-quality artisan products. "Ina Garten always carried local, fresh, seasonal products at the Barefoot Contessa," she recalls. If Garten could champion local products in New York, the same could surely be done in Minnesota. McCann Crowell opened Golden Fig Fine Foods in 2006 with the intention of making artisan foods like hers and the many other local products she was discovering more readily available to the public.

"I had a hard time with the name when I decided to open my store in St. Paul. My focus is on local foods, and figs aren't local at all! But my customers who had been buying my vinegars and spices had come to know the name, so I kept it," says Laurie.

And her customers did, in fact, visit her shop, perhaps drawn by the familiar name, or by the old-fashioned feel of her storefront on Grand Avenue, or by the displays and signs telling of the quality and freshness of the foods she features. They have been treated to an ever-growing, but carefully selected, variety of products. Laurie tells of a woman who exclaimed as she was making her purchase, "I just supported thirteen different businesses with one purchase!"

Laurie has fully embraced the role of linking local foods producers to customers. She seems at ease in her store, greeting customers and offering them samples of pickles or jam. She will gladly tell a customer how to use a spice ("Here, try this squash roasted with curry powder") or one of her flavored sugars ("Sprinkle this on sugar cookies instead of frosting—so much easier"). And with gentle encouragement she shares ideas for a simple, home-cooked meal ("My kids love this dinner," she declares) that is ready in fewer than thirty minutes.

"It makes me feel good when something I have shared or encouraged helps someone, even if it inspires them to make one good meal," Laurie says.

Similarly, she relishes being able to tell a food producer that their product is selling well and to share the comments from customers. She understands the commitment of time and energy, and the loving hands, that have all worked together to bring the neatly arranged items to her store shelves. And she feels the connection to the producers strongly when she tells customers the stories of what they are eating.

Laurie and her husband have two preschool-age boys, and being a parent seems to have intensified her approach to food. Her family makes dinner and eats at home nearly every night. "But most of our meals can be made quickly," she says. "We use just a few fresh ingredients, maybe a key spice or two, and we all sit down to a good meal. And," she adds proudly, "I don't even have a microwave."

She believes fiercely in giving children access to a variety of foods and flavors so that they can know the intensity of taste the way she did when she sampled the maple sap as a first-grader. "We sell kids short when we give them overprocessed foods," she says. "But if we expose them to good foods, and if they know where their food comes from, they will have that for the rest of their lives."

At a recent Minnesota State Fair she and her mother volunteered to work at a booth where children could win prizes for answering food questions correctly. When she held up a carrot—a regular carrot, with its green top intact—70 percent of the kids between four and ten did not know what it was. "They were so used to those prepackaged shaved mini versions that they couldn't recognize the real thing," Laurie says, bewildered.

Like others who work directly with food, who work with the producers of food and know the stories behind what they eat and offer to others, Laurie bemoans the way "nonsustainable, nonorganic agriculture is wrecking the environment." But if anyone is going to help change how we approach food production, in a way that is joyful and appreciative of the goodness of local foods, it is Laurie McCann Crowell. Halloween has not even passed and she is talking about Christmas. "I love the holidays. I just bought a Christmas CD yesterday," she says. But rather than the stress and expense of shopping, Laurie is thinking about the food and the gatherings. "I get so excited about that—helping people bring their families and friends together around food. It's a lot of work, and it's a challenge for us to keep up at the store. But," she says, brimming with contagious zeal, "I love the holidays."

VINA KAY *is a writer in Minneapolis. She is completing a memoir that centers on a family trip to Thailand, a journey that her immigrant parents, both in declining health, believed would be their last trip back to their homeland. She writes regularly for the magazine* Edible Twin Cities *and is a grant writer for Ascension Place, a transitional housing program for homeless women.*

Photo by Michelle Huesen

A Deep Love for the Minnesotan Land

A Profile of Lucia Watson

Imagine always knowing just what you wanted to do and doing it. And what if you just kept on doing it because the work still made you happy? This is how Lucia Watson describes her life, in simple, matter-of-fact language. The story she tells has few frills or flourishes but sounds clean and uncomplicated, like a fresh, crisp apple, or the distinct, earthy flavors of roasted root vegetables.

Watson opened Lucia's Restaurant in the Uptown neighborhood of Minneapolis in 1985. Her vision was, and remains, to offer "a seasonal menu, ingredient-driven, that changes every week." From the beginning, Watson was committed to locally grown food, finding the inspiration for her weekly menu from what the farmers who have long been her suppliers had to offer. "I find the highest-quality, freshest produce, meats, and grains that are available," said Watson, "and those are products that happen to be nearby."

Lucia's Restaurant quickly became popular with the people who live in the Uptown neighborhood but was also a draw for others. Watson describes her customers as eclectic: "young and old, people who come every week, even every day, and people who come in for a special occasion." Two years after it opened the restaurant doubled in size, and four years after that Watson opened a wine bar next to the restaurant. In 2004, she added Lucia's To Go, serving house-baked pastries and breads and a menu of homey dishes, including salads, sandwiches, and entrées. Though the menu is billed as takeout, the space has tables that are almost always busy with people meeting for coffee and pastries or a casual lunch. With its blue awnings and outdoor seating in front of the Wine Bar and Lucia's To Go, Lucia's has become a firmly planted favorite on the corner of 31st Street and Hennepin Avenue.

Watson has a way of making the path to where she is now sound easy, though she acknowledges the hard work of the restaurant business. Her love of what she is doing, which she describes as working with beautiful food, working with the producers of that food, and serving people, permeates her description of every aspect of her work. Watson's roots run deep in Minnesota, so her love of the land and what comes from it is tied up in her sense of place and home. A third-generation Minnesotan, she remembers spending summers at her family's remote cabin across the border in Canada. A vivid memory for her comes to life as she shares it: picking blueberries in the woods around the cabin. "We picked them every summer," she explains, "but it was only at a certain time that they were available. And then my grandmother would make all kinds of good things, muffins and pancakes and jams." Again and again, Watson speaks of food in this way, with reverence, describing foods as "precious" when they are found—like the blueberries—or grown locally. And the narrow window of time when things are available, especially in the quickly changing seasons of the upper Midwest, only add to the sense of preciousness, from Watson's point of view.

"A locally produced winter meal is not only possible but wonderful," says Watson. "We need to remember that locally produced foods are not only fresh produce. Here, in Minnesota, we have an abundance of meats, grains, and root vegetables to draw from. And what we crave is usually exactly what is available."

As she described a possible winter menu—"How about a braised lamb shank, roasted root vegetables, an apple tart?"—it was easy to see what she meant, and to know the longing for slow-cooked comfort foods on a cold day.

It is the people who work the land and tend the animals that are Watson's greatest influence as she plans Lucia's changing menu with her lead cooks. They work with producers to project what meats will be available several weeks ahead of time. Then they build around that with the seasonal vegetables that are available. Just four entrées are on the dinner menu each week. One is always vegetarian (one October week it was squash spaetzle with local cauliflower, broccoli, braising greens, poblanos, sage butter, and hazelnuts). Then there is a chicken dish, and another featuring a meat, such as pork or beef. She also offers up a fish dish each

Lucia Watson at Lucia's Restaurant

Three-Citrus Chiffon Cake or Old-Fashioned Lemon Curd. Interspersed throughout the book are stories and old photos about the people and food of the Northern Heartland: the Ojibwe tradition of harvesting wild rice or the flour milling industry of Minneapolis or the 1926 Minnesota State Fair prize-winning hog. The home cook gathers from this cookbook a sense of tradition that is deep and varied but that continues to grow as the traditions and people of the upper Midwest grow.

Even in her busy life of running a restaurant, wine bar, and bakery, Watson makes time to share her skills with the community around her. For twelve years she served on the board of the Youth Farm and Market Project, an organization that helps urban youth engage in gardening right in their city. Through the project, young people learn about growing produce but also develop an understanding of nutrition and the business skills of selling their fresh-grown vegetables in their community. More recently she has joined the board of the Institute for Agriculture and Trade Policy, which advocates globally for sustainable farming practices and fair trade policies. Both organizations, says Watson, have helped her connect more fully with her own mission of promoting high-quality food and stewardship of the earth.

With all the buzz about local foods, terms like "locavore," and now "Local Food Hero" being used to describe people like Watson, she remains as steady and true to her mission as ever. "These accolades are something new," says Watson, "but local foods is nothing new. This is the way people have been eating for a long time. We got off that path only in the last fifty years. But now we are getting back on track again as a society." Asked what she might tell a skeptic, one who might not see the value of spending more time and money on food, she paused for a moment or two. "I guess I wouldn't talk to skeptics; I would just feed them."

Watson has been relying heavily on the local ingredients she knows as long as she can remember, since the days of picking blueberries and cooking with her grandmother. So the attention that others are giving to local foods now is no fad to her. "It's the real deal. It's what has lasted," she claims.

week. Sometimes it is a local trout, but other times the fish is Arctic char or salmon. Watson is not a purist when it comes to local foods. "I respect that about other chefs, but I could never give up olive oil or some kinds of fish. I am grateful for the bounty available, and I think people want that, too."

The 1994 cookbook Watson authored with Minneapolis food writer and teacher Beth Dooley reflects the same kind of respect for local roots that Lucia's Restaurant embraces. *Savoring the Seasons of the Northern Heartland* is full of the recipes generations of families of the upper Midwest hold dear, like roast chicken or turkey and sturgeon, walleye, and trout. Also featured, however, is a recipe for Hmong Market Soup from a more recent immigrant group to the area. And plenty of recipes call on the once-exotic ingredients that Midwesterners have come to love, like the bright flavors of

VINA KAY *is a writer in Minneapolis. She is completing a memoir that centers on a family trip to Thailand, a journey that her immigrant parents, both in declining health, believed would be their last trip back to their homeland. She writes regularly for the magazine* Edible Twin Cities *and is a grant writer for Ascension Place, a transitional housing program for homeless women.*

Photo by Michelle Huesen

In the Kitchen

Paradise Found at Eve's Table

To be in the presence of a real *balabuste*—Yiddish for "the lady of the house"—is to be in the presence of abundance: of love, strength, generosity, and, of course, plenty of wonderful food. One meal at the restaurant named simply "eve" is all it takes to know that this restaurant operates at the hands of such a woman.

Chef Eve Aronoff opened eve in a cozy corner of Ann Arbor's historic Kerrytown district in 2002, bringing an original and deeply personal perspective to the city's culinary scene. For her the restaurant is a lifelong dream come to fruition, one whose humble beginnings took root when Aronoff was in junior high cooking elaborate eight-course meals for her parents and their friends in East Lansing, where she grew up.

"I would do all this research for the menu and take notes working from my mom's copy of *Craig Claiborne's New York Times International Cookbook* and making dishes like French baked rice and Peruvian avocado soup!" she says, laughing.

Aronoff credits her style not to any one influence but to a variety of experiences gathered over years. When she was growing up, her family traveled regularly to Israel, where she was exposed to Jerusalem's Old City markets—windy paths lined with barrels of aromatic spices and nuts drew her in toward assertive, intricate flavors. Back at home in Michigan, she recalls being surrounded by a feeling of abundance. "Not necessarily in terms of money," she says, "but in terms of warm family gatherings, tables spread with bagels and lox or beefsteak tomatoes and raspberries off the family bushes."

Even her degree in comparative literature colored her philosophy of food as Aronoff found herself captured by the way in which food within the context of a story could be so evocative of emotion and culture. Years later, her formal culinary training at Le Cordon Bleu in Paris helped to knit together her passion for complex, global flavors with traditional French method.

All of these factors converge within eve's menu, which manages to be both masterful and deeply personal. Complex spice blends are contrasted by bright, simpler flavors that make for dishes in balance. The Moroccan-inspired Lamb in Brik, for example, is an entrée of sweet and spicy ground lamb with pine nuts and golden raisins enveloped in flaky *brik* pastry. Served in a covering of vibrant baby spinach and fresh mint with lemon–brown sugar vinaigrette, the spice of the lamb is complemented by mellow sweetness and just the right acidity to keep your mouth watering for more. The Seafood Lasagna with Crisped Prosciutto di Parma is a purely luxurious experience—tender scallops, shrimp, and creamy mussels tucked between layers of pasta and tomato cream, brightened by tangy crumbles of local goat cheese and fresh baby spinach. It is a dish that Eve herself is drawn to when she craves a rich, comforting meal. Even a traditional Amish chicken soup takes on new life with its rich and comforting stock studded with fresh corn, tomato, and farmers' market greens.

Aronoff also embraces the tenets of the Slow Food movement, which include the use of local ingredients as well as the specialties of local culinary artisans. Items like smoked salmon and duck breast prosciutto from nearby Durham's Tracklements are featured regularly on eve's menu, as is coffee from Ann Arbor roaster John Roos, to name but a few local contributors. For Aronoff, it comes down to flavor and feeling. "Getting ingredients trucked in from across the country feels completely different from walking into T. R. Durham's shop next door and just using the key he gave me to pick up more smoked meat for the restaurant," she says. "Just like buying vegetables and fruits that are local and in season, it just feels like the natural thing to do. And so naturally, the food is just going to taste better."

In keeping with the spirit of plenty and hospitality, Aronoff works in collaboration with local individuals—culinary laypeople—who are passionate about food, bringing their talents and tastes into production under Eve's roof.

and coffee and vanilla bean with rum are among the intriguing offerings.

Aronoff's mother makes all of the restaurant's jams, which find their way into anything from weekend brunch dishes to the whimsical Jamtini (Michigan plum jam stirred into chilled Grey Goose vodka). The restaurant also makes seasonal sorbets and house-cured charcuterie in similar collaborative efforts.

That welcoming spirit of creativity earned Aronoff a coveted invitation to cook a meal at the acclaimed James Beard House in New York City. In August 2008, Aronoff and her staff traveled to the house in Greenwich Village, bringing the spirit and the flavor of eve to the James Beard Foundation, whose mission is to preserve, celebrate, and nurture American culinary tradition. It was not only a dream realized for Aronoff herself, but also national testimony to the fact that there is much more to Michigan than a rusty auto industry—there's also a vibrant culinary community.

Truly, Aronoff is no closed book. "The more people care about food, the better," she says. In the spirit of inspiring joie de vivre, as she likes to say—and without fear of competition from other restaurants—in 2006, she authored her own cookbook featuring many of eve's trademark dishes. *Eve: Contemporary Cuisine—Méthode Traditionnelle* celebrates local producers and encourages home cooks to try their menu favorites and then improvise according to season and whim.

In her book, Aronoff conveys her philosophy of hospitality in her restaurant: "You know how in the Torah it says Abraham's tent was open on all four sides . . . well, that is what I want for the restaurant—anybody who comes here should feel welcomed and taken care of."

Guests at eve are handed that philosophy with every plate, from appetizers and drinks to the dish of crisp sugared mint leaves that concludes the meal. "I'm always amazed at how people will choose this restaurant for their celebrations," she says. "People have their first dates here, get engaged here, and even have their wedding reception here. Their memories are made here. I just love that, and I can't think of anything I'd rather be doing."

Spoken like a true *balabuste*.

"Our musician traveled all over the world and talked about the homemade distilled spirits he would see lining the shelves of local bars," says Aronoff. "His wife is French and had been making flavored spirits at home for years. So they began working with us to make seasonal, infused spirits for the restaurant." The result is a small but significant collection of bottles that now line eve's bar: tart and sweet cherries with vodka

ALEX HARRISON *is a writer and expert nosher who finds endless pleasures in stinky cheese, crusty bread, and cold beer.*

Diversity as Dominant Paradigm

The Seed Savers Exchange

About thirty-two years ago, Diane Ott Whealy was given a gift by her terminally ill grandfather. It was a gift handed down to him by his parents, who had brought it to their New World home of St. Lucas, Iowa, from Bavaria in the 1870s. Now he, in his last days, was continuing a tradition that goes back millennia—literally to the dawn of civilization—handing down the heritage that was Diane's birthright.

The gift was seeds. One was a variety of tomato known as the German Pink, and the other was a flower, Grandpa Ott's Morning Glory. A simple gift, but one that would grow into something truly special just as surely as the seeds themselves held glorious bounty within their tiny shells. For Diane's grandfather had not simply planted a seed, he had planted an idea that would save the world.

Diane and her then-husband Kent created the Seed Savers Exchange (SSE) in 1975 from those two original seed varieties. Through a network of thousands of members around the world, Seed Savers "is saving the world's diverse, but endangered, garden heritage for future generations by building a network of people committed to collecting, conserving and sharing heirloom seeds and plants," it says on their Web site, all "while educating people about the value of genetic and cultural diversity. Few gardeners comprehend the true scope of their garden heritage or how much is in immediate danger of being lost forever."

It has since grown into one of the world's largest guardians of heirloom seed diversity. Heirloom seeds are simply those that have been passed down through generations, like heirloom jewelry. They have not been genetically manipulated in any way. With the cooperation of more than eight thousand members worldwide, SSE is dedicated to saving these varieties because the world's botanical diversity is under constant assault from all quarters. Genetically modified crops are spreading worldwide; pests and diseases are evolving rapidly to attack dwindling varieties of plants; and multinational corporations are moving to claim utility patents on particular varieties, meaning they own the seed *and* all its progeny.

The United States Supreme Court declared in December 2001 that it is legal to claim utility patents on plants, making it potentially illegal not just to propagate and sell that seed but even to save seeds of patented plants from the previous season to plant next season. I like to look at it this way: If you are what you eat, then who owns your food owns you.

Combine these alarming trends with the fact that, as was stated at the Terra Madre World Gathering of Food Communities in 2004, "Today, thirty plant varieties feed 95 percent of the world's population. In the past century, 250,000 plant varieties have gone extinct, and another plant variety disappears every six hours. Since the beginning of the twentieth century, Europe has lost more than 75 percent of its agricultural biodiversity, whereas the United States have lost 93 percent. . . . One-third of native cow, sheep, and pig breeds has gone extinct or is on the road to extinction."

The world's ecosystem is based on diversity and cannot function without it. As a part of that ecosystem, agriculture cannot function without diversity either. If you doubt that, study just a little about the Irish potato famine to learn what happens if there is only one variety of a plant.

SSE's approach has been to build a network of concerned gardeners and farmers around the world, set some guidelines for the proper preservation of seeds with their genetic makeup intact, and then carefully catalog, store, and distribute these seeds. They are careful never to use all of any particular seed, always saving some in order to make more.

Anyone can buy seeds from SSE, through their print catalog or through their Web site, but if you become a member of the Exchange, you receive access to twice as many varieties of seeds, some 24,000 in all. Many other benefits of joining SSE's eight thousand members are detailed at the Web site.

If you are ever in the area, I highly recommend a visit to the Heritage Farm in Decorah. SSE operates this small farm that includes the gardens, a historic orchard, and a herd of Ancient White Park cattle. These cattle roamed the British Isles before the time of Christ and are described exactly in ancient Celtic lore. Only about eight hundred are left in the world, and eighty of those are at the Heritage Farm. Visit in July or August to see the gardens in full splendor or to see the three hundred varieties of garlic hanging to dry. In September or October stop in to see and taste the best of the orchard's seven hundred nineteenth-century apple varieties. That is a lot, but, sadly, it is only a fraction of the some eight thousand varieties that were on record in 1899.

By protecting nature's diversity from industrial standardization, Seed Savers Exchange is protecting our heritage and our health. Heirloom seeds carry with them real and vital information about our past, a history that is rich with the wisdom of countless generations. It is no wonder they are recipients of a MacArthur Fellowship or that fellow MacArthur recipient and author Gary Paul Nabhan referred to Seed Savers as "very possibly the most biodiverse place on the planet."

....

KURT FRIESE *is publisher of* Edible Iowa River Valley.

....

ORGANIZATION ~ *EDIBLE IOWA RIVER VALLEY (IOWA)*

Food within Reach

....

Laura Dowd and Local Foods Connection

In 1995, Laura Dowd was at a crossroads. She wanted to provide organic vegetables for her husband as part of his cancer recovery plan, but money was tight. She decided to pay for the vegetables through farm work, so she volunteered with Susan Jutz and Simone Delaty of Local Harvest, a Community Supported Agriculture system in Johnson County.

A CSA is a little like a magazine subscription for farm-fresh food. Participants buy a "share" in the early spring, paying up front for food they will receive throughout the season. In this perfect win-win scenario, the farmers get the cash they need to get the season started well, and the families who join get a box of fresh, seasonal produce each week, all season long. Here in Iowa, that is around twenty weeks of radishes, greens, sweet peas, zucchini, potatoes, tomatoes, squash, and much more. Local Harvest also offers hearth-baked bread, fresh-cut flowers, lamb, pork, and eggs. Everything they offer is organic.

Soon Dowd, Jutz, and Delaty were discussing the challenges involved in putting local, organic food within reach of single-parent households and other economically disadvantaged members of the community. From these discussions, Local Foods Connection was born in 1999. Originally called Adopt-a-Family, the

idea was to solicit donations from CSA members and the general public; then this money would be used to buy CSA shares for qualifying families. Families and farmers both get the support they need; it's a win-win, like the CSAs themselves.

Though by no means easy, the work has paid off for LFC and for the people Dowd affectionately calls her families. Today LFC is a lot more than a charity that raises money and hands out food. Its more than 50 office volunteers do clerical and educational work, and 225 more work with five different area farms. Rather than paying these hardworking helpers (including several from the University of Iowa service fraternity Alpha Kappa Psi), CSAs provide charity credit toward food purchases, which LFC distributes to its clients, and that is only the beginning. LFC educates families about cooking, nutrition, and the advantages of buying locally.

In 2005, when the New Pioneer Co-op in Iowa City sent dividend checks to its members, they included a letter with each check requesting that the members sign these checks over to LFC. The response was so overwhelming that an extremely grateful Ms. Dowd said, "It will change the charity." In 2006, when the Co-op's dividend program was repeated, donations more than tripled.

Laura Dowd (left) with organic farmer Susan Jutz

One of her families (who asked to remain anonymous) emigrated from the West African country of Burkina Faso in 2000. With one parent in graduate school at the University of Iowa and three boys to feed, the other parent's hard work as a nursing assistant wasn't enough. With the help of Dayna Ballantyne, director of the Johnson County Crisis Center Food Bank, they met Dowd and learned of the Local Foods Connection program.

The family loved the food and appreciated help with the unfamiliar vegetables (they liked the zucchini but not the beets, both of which were new to them). They also particularly enjoyed visiting Susan Jutz's pastoral ZJ Farm in Solon. These visits are required of all participating families, and Dowd says that it is sometimes difficult to get the families to go to the farms, but once they are there, it is even tougher to get them to leave. This family enjoyed the visit so much they returned twice with friends, even held a cookout there, and say they look forward to returning soon.

Working with LFC has taught all the families the importance of buying locally. Many now shop the Iowa City Farmers' Market regularly. They've learned that buying locally can be far less expensive (in real terms—when you account for the impact of "cheap" food) and far more nutritious than buying the heavily shipped and fertilized food in the grocery stores. LFC educates its families, volunteers, and donors that the shelf price of food should not be a primary factor in deciding whether or not to purchase it.

The families and the farmers have formed a bond, and Dowd feels it is important to emphasize the knowledge of the hard work that creates this food. This bond between the farmer and the urban dweller also helps slow urban sprawl because people become aware: No farmers, no food.

From its humble beginnings as a dream shared by Dowd, Jutz, and Delaty, LFC grew to include eighteen families and ten farms in 2006, including not just Local Harvest CSA but also Choice Earth, Gooseberry Hill, Oak Hill Acres, Scattergood Farms, Friendly Farms, and Fae Ridge Farms. Calvin and Judy Yoder of Echo Dell in Kalona supply chickens, and each family receives a Slow Food Ark USA–registered heritage turkey for Thanksgiving from Henry and Ila Miller, also of Kalona. A four-person board of directors makes sure everything runs smoothly.

Most of the families are single-parent and are directed to the charity by the Crisis Center, the Shelter House, Goodwill, United Action for Youth, Big Brothers/Big Sisters, and the Women's Resource and Action Center, all amazing and hardworking charities in their own right.

Dowd looks forward to being able to help even more families discover the value and nutrition of fresh, local foods.

KURT FRIESE *is publisher of* Edible Iowa River Valley.

Photo by Kurt Friese

People, places, things

CHICAGO

Chicago is the third-largest city in the United States, set on the shores of Lake Michigan, and vibrant with ethnic neighborhoods and unique culinary traditions. The roots of its multicultural heritage thrive within community gardens and farmers' markets flourishing in the shadow of its glorious skyline. Chefs and residents in Chicago have access to fresh, local produce from an abundant patchwork of family farms from Illinois, Wisconsin, Indiana, and Michigan, which supply the numerous neighborhood markets.

Rooftop Gardens Mayor Richard M. Daley's commitment to make Chicago one of the greenest cities in the nation showcases over 200 rooftop gardens, the most famous of which is atop his office building.

Green City Market This is a year-round, not-for-profit market that brings in farmers from four surrounding states and offers educational programs and chef demonstrations.

The Resource Center City Farm Grows organic produce for some of Chicago's most notable restaurants and provides fresh products to underserved communities.

Uncommon Ground Farm and Restaurant The country's first certified organic rooftop farm, which also serves as a community hub by offering green educational programs and local, seasonal foods in its restaurant.

Goose Island Brewery The father-son team of John and Greg Hall brews a selection of over fifty craft beers at two brewpubs in the city.

Green Grocer Chicago Cassie Green's storefront is a local foods hot spot that supports produce from regional farms and offers workshops on greener lifestyles.

www.ediblecommunities.com/chicago/peopleplacesthings

GRAND TRAVERSE (MICHIGAN)

Northwest Lower Michigan's features stand out to visitors: majestic pines and hardwoods on sandy hills with beaches and fresh water all around. The region's soils, terrain, and weather form an ideal fruit- and wine grape–growing region. This rural beauty makes it a "must come back" for any nature, food, and wine lover—there is a burgeoning sustainable small-farming community here, and each year more superb restaurants open as a stream of leading chefs flows into the area.

Riesling Wines A number of award-winning Rieslings are produced by vineyards on the Old Mission or Leelanau peninsulas, exemplified most recently by Robert Parker's praise of Left Foot Charley Winery.

Dried Tart Cherries Culinary staples in the Northern Michigan pantry. Available along with tart cherry concentrate in most grocery stores and farm markets.

Cheeses A wedge of aged raclette cheese from the Leelanau Cheese Company, made with local milk and each batch handcrafted with great care, received Best of Show at the 2007 American Cheese Society competition.

Fish Lake Michigan whitefish or lake perch fillets from Fish Lake are served broiled at any good local restaurant.

Black Sweet Cherries Locally grown, these cherries are freshly picked and washed and can be found at road stands and farms in July.

www.ediblecommunities.com/grandetraverse/peopleplacesthings

IOWA RIVER VALLEY (IOWA)

The Iowa River Valley is actually comprised of three rivers and dozens of tributaries. The Iowa, Cedar, and Des Moines rivers cut a swath across the rolling prairie of Eastern and Central Iowa on their way to the Mississippi. Along the way they pass the farms, vineyards, woodlands, and communities that make Iowa's food shed unique. From the native Meskwaki nation to the Northern European settlers to newly arrived immigrants from Mexico to Bosnia to Laos, Iowans enjoy rich culinary traditions.

Devotay, Iowa City A leader in the local and sustainable foods movement in the area, Devotay is the restaurant owned by *Edible Iowa River Valley* publishers Kurt and Kim Friese.

Practical Farmers of Iowa With a strong organization, more than two decades of work, and the ability to bridge philosophical gaps in the farming community, PFI's Field Days are educational seminars second to none.

The Leopold Center for Sustainable Agriculture, Iowa State University Created by the state legislature in response to the farm crisis of the 1980s, the Leopold Center upholds the tradition of its namesake, Aldo Leopold, providing some of the most authoritative research available to the sustainable food community.

Seed Savers Exchange An idea that literally began with two seeds, Seed Savers Exchange is now what acclaimed ethnobotanist Gary Paul Nabhan called "very possibly the most biodiverse place on the planet."

The Muscatine Melon The unique *terroir* of the sandy basin where the Iowa River meets the Mississippi makes this luscious, orange-fleshed melon a local delicacy.

www.ediblecommunities.com/iowarivervalley/peopleplacesthings

TWIN CITIES (MINNESOTA)

Typically thought of as "Flyover Land" by residents of the coasts, to those who live here, there's no place they'd rather be. The change of seasons (they have all four!) makes residents appreciate each one all the more. With numerous farms, markets, and food artisans, as well as new immigrant cultures adding to an already-rich heritage, enjoying the abundance, quality, and variety of locally produced foods is easy and delicious.

Native Harvest Wild Rice Native Harvest is run by the Ojibwe community as part of the White Earth Land Recovery Project. They produce true lake-grown, hand-harvested, and wood-parched wild rice.

Trotter's Café and Bakery Trotter's is a wonderful St. Paul café that has been supporting local, sustainably raised food for twenty years.

Mill City Museum This is an interactive museum dedicated to telling the story of the milling industry that fueled the growth of Minneapolis.

Land Stewardship Project An organization that promotes sustainable agriculture, both in policy and in action, their Farm Beginnings program educates new and transitioning farmers on whole-farm planning.

Honeycrisp Apples The state fruit of Minnesota, this tasty sweet-tart apple was developed by the Horticultural Research Center at the University of Minnesota.

www.ediblecommunities.com/twincities/peopleplacesthings

WOW (SOUTHEASTERN MICHIGAN)

Michigan's agricultural history began with the founding of Fort Detroit by Cadillac in the early 1700s. Long before the automobile was even thought of, Southeastern Michigan was known nationwide for the fertile soil, temperate climate, and lake-effect weather that made it a leader in the production of many fruits, vegetables, and grains. With one-fifth of the world's supply of freshwater, the Great Lakes State was and will be again an agricultural force to recognize.

Eastern Market The largest historic public market in the United States. Opened in 1891, this forty-three-acre market is known as Detroit's epicenter for all things fresh—fruits, vegetables, flowers, and otherwise.

Zingerman's Through the years, the Zingerman name has grown beyond the deli to envelope a community of businesses: The Bakehouse, Creamery, Roadhouse restaurant, Coffee Company, BAKE! Classes, mail order, and ZingTrain (a series of seminars designed for business owners of all kinds).

Michigan Apples Between the climate of the Great Lakes and the fertile soil of the region, Southeastern Michigan offers excellent sites for growing some of the finest apples in the world. The Honeycrisp is a favorite, with a crisp, juicy bite and a sweet flavor.

Food System Economic Partnership FSEP was officially launched in 2005 to identify economic opportunities and to implement creative solutions to chronic issues relevant to the food system in Southeastern Michigan.

Franklin Cider Mill In 1837, the year Michigan became a state, this mill was completed, after having been under construction for about three years.

www.ediblecommunities.com/wow/peopleplacesthings

EDIBLE RECIPES

The distinct culinary character of each region in North America is shaped by its seasonal specialties—maple syrup and lobster in the Northeast, chile peppers and squash in the Southwest, and so on. The *edible* magazines publish recipes that showcase the best of what each season and region has to offer, featuring the freshest ingredients at their peak of ripeness; the recipes included in this section are some of the best we have collected.

The recipes are organized seasonally and by course to make them easier to fit into the way you cook. Although some recipes may call for an ingredient not available locally to you, perhaps you'll still be inspired and can enjoy the style of a dish but feature berries instead of peaches or scallops instead of clams. These local specialties may also tempt you to visit some of our wonderful food communities and share the recipes with people you know who live where the ingredients are a highlight.

There's also a list at the end of the book with the recipes organized by region, in case you want to cook according to what's especially bountiful in your community.

We hope that when you make these dishes for family and friends, they not only evoke the place where you live but also become some of your most satisfying and memorable favorites.

SOME TIPS FOR AN *EDIBLE* KITCHEN

Keep things simple. A couple of sharp knives, a sturdy cutting board, one or two heavy-bottomed pans, and a few tools—a wooden spoon, a slotted spoon, a vegetable peeler, and a spatula—are the basics you need.

A well-stocked pantry lasts a long time and goes a long way: Be sure to keep on hand staples such as pasta, rice, dried beans, olive oil, and two or three different vinegars—you'll be a more resourceful cook for doing so.

Cook what's in season at the peak of ripeness and flavor.

Shop at more farm stands and farmers' markets than supermarkets and be patient—wait for peas and asparagus in spring, tomatoes and peaches in summer, and squash in fall. You won't regret not eating a supermarket strawberry in December.

Be thrifty and flexible—ingredients at the height of their season and bought close to the source are abundant and therefore usually more inexpensive. Feel free to substitute fruits or vegetables in a recipe according to season.

As you cook, remove more ingredients from recipes than you add. If you don't have an ingredient, don't let it put you off; try to find a substitute or leave it out and see what happens. You may have created a wonderful dish.

Keep around lots of clean dish towels, which can be washed and reused; banish paper towels from your kitchen.

Experiment and have fun!

FIRST COURSES

Strawberry Arugula Spring Salad   209

Poke   210

Vermont Cheddar Ale Soup   211

A Spring Pan Roast of Oysters   212

MAIN COURSES

Aspen Tri-Tip Roast   213

Glazed Lamb Chops   214

Broiled Shad Roe with Pancetta   216

Linguine with Clams   217

Wild Onion and Spinach Tart   218

Kudzu Quiche in Puff Pastry   219

Sullivan's Island Shrimp Bog   220

Egg Noodles with Fresh Spring Vegetables   223

Wild Salmon with Fava Bean Puree   224

Herb-Roasted Duck Breast with Carrot-
Potato Mash and Chive Butter   226

SIDE DISHES

Collard Tops with Parmigiano   227

Asparagus with Morels and Tarragon   228

DESSERTS

Rhubarb Bread Pudding with Whiskey Sauce   229

The Best Strawberry Shortcakes   230

spring

First Courses

Strawberry Arugula Spring Salad

COURTESY OF *EDIBLE CAPE COD* (MASSACHUSETTS)
MAKES 4 SERVINGS

This is a lovely, simple celebration of spring. The combination of ingredients may seem unusual, but the sweetness of the fruit beautifully balances the peppery bite of the arugula. For the brightest flavors, make sure you buy freshly picked arugula and strawberries at your local farmers' market or farm stand. Serve with a loaf of good crusty bread. If you don't have grapeseed oil, use another neutral-flavored oil.

In a small skillet, toast the pecans, if using, over medium heat, tossing frequently until fragrant, about 2 minutes. Place the pecans into a small dish; set aside.

In a large salad bowl, add the arugula, strawberries, and sliced onion. In a blender, combine the oil, vinegar, sugar, sesame seeds, chopped onion, Worcestershire sauce, paprika, and salt. Blend until the ingredients are pureed. Taste and adjust seasoning as needed.

Toss the blended vinaigrette into the salad bowl ingredients. Garnish with the pecans and goat cheese, if using, before serving.

½ cup pecan halves, optional
6 cups (about 5 ounces) loosely
　packed baby arugula
1 pint (2 cups) strawberries, hulled
　and thinly sliced
1 small sweet onion, thinly sliced
3 tablespoons grapeseed oil
2 tablespoons white wine vinegar,
　rice wine vinegar, or white vinegar
2 tablespoons granulated sugar
1 tablespoon sesame seeds
1 tablespoon chopped onion
½ teaspoon Worcestershire sauce
¼ teaspoon smoked paprika
¼ teaspoon kosher salt
½ cup goat cheese, crumbled,
　optional

Poke

COURTESY OF *EDIBLE HAWAIIAN ISLANDS* (HAWAII)
AHI-ONO-AVOCADO POKE MAKES 2 POKES; SESAME-AHI POKE WITH MAUI ONIONS MAKES 6 POKES

Ahi-Ono-Avocado Poke

¾ pound very fresh boneless, skinless ahi (yellowfin tuna), cut into ¾-inch cubes

¾ pound very fresh boneless, skinless ono (wahoo), cut into ¾-inch cubes

1½ teaspoons finely ground alaea salt (Hawaiian red salt) or sea salt, plus more if needed

1 tablespoon toasted sesame oil, plus more if needed

¼ cup finely chopped scallion

¾ cup red ogo seaweed, rinsed and chopped (see note)

½ large ripe avocado, peeled and cut into cubes

1 teaspoon sesame seeds

½ cup soy sauce

1 tablespoon plus 1 teaspoon hot prepared mustard (such as Colman's) or prepared wasabi, plus more if needed

Sesame-Ahi Poke with Maui Onions

1½ pounds very fresh boneless, skinless ahi (yellowfin tuna), cut into ¾-inch cubes

1½ teaspoons finely ground alaea salt (Hawaiian red salt) or sea salt, plus more if needed

1 tablespoon toasted sesame oil, plus more if needed

¼ cup finely chopped scallion

¼ cup thinly sliced sweet Maui onion or other sweet onion

¼ cup red ogo seaweed, rinsed and chopped (see note)

1 teaspoon sesame seeds

½ cup soy sauce

1 tablespoon plus 1 teaspoon hot prepared mustard (such as Colman's) or prepared wasabi, plus more if needed

Poke (pronounced PO-kee) is a raw fish salad with Hawaiian salt and chopped seaweed—and from there the variations begin. It's considered the casual version of elegant, perfectly cut sashimi. Most people think of poke as a traditional Hawaiian way of eating raw fish—the word "poke" in Hawaiian means a cut piece or small piece. Poke, however, is a melding of the Hawaiian tradition of eating raw fish with the Asian-influenced contribution of soy sauce. Since the 1970s, poke is the thing to have after work with a cold beer, or as a popular pupu at parties.

If you are lucky enough to live on the north shore of Kauai, you know where to go for poke: Kilauea Fish Market, owned by Coriena MacNeil and Steve Knox. There you can sit outside, bring your own wine or beer, and enjoy. Here are two of their favorite recipes.

AHI-ONO-AVOCADO POKE

Place the cubed fish into a large bowl. Sprinkle the salt over the fish and toss to coat. Add the sesame oil, scallions, seaweed, avocado, and sesame seeds. Toss gently. Taste and adjust seasoning as needed.

In a small bowl, whisk together the soy sauce and mustard. Taste and adjust seasoning as needed. Serve with the poke.

SESAME-AHI POKE WITH MAUI ONIONS

Place the cubed fish into a large bowl. Sprinkle the salt over the fish and stir gently with a spatula or fork to coat. Add the sesame oil, green onion, onion, seaweed, and sesame seeds. Toss gently. Taste and adjust seasoning as needed.

In a small bowl, whisk together the soy sauce and mustard. Taste and adjust seasoning as needed. Serve with the poke.

NOTE ~ Red ogo is a type of "limu" (LEE-moo), which is the Hawaiian word for seaweed. Unfortunately, outside of Hawaii, red ogo may be difficult to find, but there are many kinds of edible limu available in gourmet shops or the Asian food area of supermarkets, and they are all great additions to poke, salads, sandwiches, and stews. They are an important source of minerals and vitamins, including vitamins A, C, B12, and riboflavin.

Vermont Cheddar Ale Soup

COURTESY OF COURTNEY CONTOS, INN AT ESSEX AT ESSEX, VERMONT/*EDIBLE GREEN MOUNTAINS* (VERMONT)
MAKES 6 SERVINGS

Skiing, sledding, sugaring—Vermont's cold-weather activities, enjoyed even through the cool spring months—leave you exhilarated. And hungry! A bowl of this soup featuring Vermont sharp cheddar and Long Trail Ale will keep you warm as you cozy up to the fire. Although the recipe is not complicated, there are some tricks when cooking with cheese: Remember not to boil the soup once the cheese has been added; keep it at a low simmer, and stir until all the cheese has been blended into the soup.

In a large saucepan or Dutch oven, melt the butter over medium heat. Add the onion, carrot, celery, garlic, and bay leaves and cook, stirring occasionally, until the vegetables begin to soften, about 5 minutes. Decrease the heat to medium-low and sprinkle the flour over the vegetables. Cook, stirring occasionally, for 3 minutes.

Slowly whisk in the milk, broth, and ale in a steady stream. Cook, whisking occasionally, for 5 minutes. Stir in the Worcestershire sauce, mustard, salt, and pepper. Bring to a boil.

Decrease the heat to low. Discard the bay leaves. Add the cheese by handfuls, stirring constantly, and cook until the cheese is melted, 3 to 4 minutes (do not boil). Serve hot, sprinkled with bacon and drizzled with Sweet Heat, if using.

- 2 tablespoons unsalted butter or extra virgin olive oil
- 1 large onion, finely chopped
- 1 medium carrot, cut into ¼-inch dice
- 1 stalk celery, cut into ¼-inch dice
- 2 cloves garlic, very finely chopped
- 2 bay leaves
- ⅓ cup all-purpose flour
- 2 cups whole milk
- 1¾ cups chicken broth
- 1 bottle (12 ounces) ale, such as Long Trail
- 1 tablespoon Worcestershire sauce
- 1 teaspoon dry mustard
- 1 teaspoon kosher salt
- ¼ teaspoon freshly ground black pepper
- 1 pound extra-sharp cheddar, preferably aged Grafton or aged Cabot (rind removed, if necessary), grated
- 4 slices bacon, cooked and crumbled, optional
- ¼ cup Sweet Heat (jalapeño-infused maple syrup available through gourmet stores and websites specializing in hot sauces, such as Greene's Gourmet of Vermont [www.greenesgourmet.com]) or pure maple syrup, optional

A Spring Pan Roast of Oysters

COURTESY OF FRED THOMPSON/*EDIBLE PIEDMONT* (NORTH CAROLINA)
MAKES 10 TO 12 FIRST-COURSE OR 6 MAIN-COURSE SERVINGS

2 cups heavy cream

1 sprig fresh thyme

2 leeks, white part only, cleaned well and halved lengthwise

2 tablespoons unsalted butter

2 tablespoons dry white wine

½ pound fresh shiitake mushrooms, stems removed, cut into ¼-inch slices

3 pints (3 pounds) shucked oysters with their liquor

½ teaspoon kosher salt, plus more if needed

¼ teaspoon freshly ground black pepper, plus more if needed

20 flat-leaf spinach leaves, cleaned, dried, and cut into chiffonade (see note)

Oysters are a joy to most folks up and down the North and South Carolina coasts, and with the nights still cool in the spring this pan roast of oysters is a soul-warming delight. The natural richness of small-batch heavy cream, when reduced, creates a velvety base to carry the oysters. It is also highlighted with fresh shiitake mushrooms and finished with a topping of tender spring spinach cut into chiffonade (thin ribbons). The mushrooms deepen the broth and add an earthiness to the dish, while the spinach adds another texture and a balancing bitterness.

In a large saucepan, add the cream and thyme. Bring the cream to a gentle simmer over medium heat and cook, reducing the heat as necessary to prevent boilovers and using a ladle to stir the cream if it begins to foam, until the cream is reduced by half, 30 to 45 minutes. In a fine-mesh strainer set in a small bowl, strain the cream; set aside. (Note: The cream can be prepared up to 4 hours in advance and stored in a thermos or double boiler, off heat, until needed.)

Have a medium bowl of ice water ready. In a medium pot of boiling salted water, blanch the leeks for about 60 seconds. Using tongs, remove the leeks from the boiling water and immediately plunge them into the ice water. Remove the leeks from the ice water when cool and shake off any excess water. Cut each leek half crosswise into ¼-inch-wide slices; set aside.

In a large sauté pan, heat the butter with the wine over medium-high heat until frothy. Add the mushrooms and cook, stirring occasionally, until beginning to turn golden, about 2 minutes. Reduce the heat to medium. Stir in the leeks, oysters with their liquor, salt, and pepper and cook, stirring occasionally, until the oysters just begin to curl, 4 to 6 minutes. Stir in the cream and cook until it is just warmed through, no more than 1 or 2 minutes. Taste and adjust seasoning if needed.

Divide the pan roast of oysters into warmed shallow soup bowls. Top each bowl with an equal portion of the spinach chiffonade. Serve immediately.

NOTE ~ To chiffonade spinach, or any other leafy vegetable or herb, such as basil, stack together 5 to 10 leaves and roll them into a cigar shape. Using a sharp knife, slice the roll crosswise as thinly as desired. Toss the cut leaves to separate the strands and use as a garnish.

Main Courses

Aspen Tri-Tip Roast

COURTESY OF *EDIBLE ASPEN* (COLORADO)

MAKES 4 SERVINGS

Located at the bottom of the sirloin, the tri-tip (or triangle) roast is an inexpensive option for local, grass-fed beef. It has great flavor when cooked to medium-rare and, thinly sliced, is as tender as a New York strip. This tri-tip roast is also fabulous cooked on the grill from spring through fall. Serve the sliced beef with cabbage slaw, fresh pico de gallo, and, in late summer, corn on the cob.

The Aspen Dry Rub recipe combines spicy, salty, savory, and sweet notes and works well on grilled or roasted meats and poultry. If you don't have all of these spices on hand, omit those that you don't have or aren't fond of, and add others that you prefer. Be creative, and be sure to write down the ingredients for that special blend that was conjured up on the spot out of necessity or whim; they're easily forgotten when you want to duplicate it.

MAKE THE ASPEN DRY RUB: In a medium bowl, combine all the ingredients. Whisk well. Makes a little less than 1½ cups (about 23 tablespoons). Store in a small glass jar with a lid. The dry rub will keep for a month in the refrigerator with the lid closed tightly.

MAKE THE TRI-TIP ROAST: In a large bowl, rub the dry rub mixture evenly over all surfaces of the roast. Cover the bowl and allow the roast to stand at room temperature for up to 1 hour, or up to 12 hours in the refrigerator.

Preheat the oven to 450°F. Place the meat fat-side up on a rack in a shallow roasting pan. Roast to medium-rare, 10 to 12 minutes per pound or until a meat thermometer inserted into the center of the thickest part of the roast reads 120°F. Remove the roast from the oven and allow the meat to rest for about 15 minutes. To serve, slice the roast thinly, across the grain.

Aspen Dry Rub

3 tablespoons kosher salt

3 tablespoons sweet paprika

3 tablespoons brown sugar or Sucanat

2 tablespoons ancho chili powder

1 tablespoon cumin seed

1 tablespoon fennel seed

1 tablespoon ground coriander

1 tablespoon dried oregano

1 tablespoon sweet smoked paprika

2 teaspoons mustard seed

2 teaspoons freshly ground black pepper

1 teaspoon ground cayenne

1 teaspoon dried rosemary

1 teaspoon dried thyme

Tri-Tip Roast

2 tablespoons Aspen Dry Rub (above)

1 tri-tip roast (2 to 2½ pounds)

Glazed Lamb Chops

COURTESY OF *EDIBLE HAWAIIAN ISLANDS* (HAWAII)
MAKES 4 SERVINGS

¼ cup unsweetened coconut milk

¼ cup pure maple syrup

2 cloves garlic, finely chopped

2 teaspoons mint tea leaves

2 teaspoons dried rosemary, crushed, or dried thyme

2 teaspoons freshly ground black pepper

1½ teaspoons kosher salt

2 racks of lamb, frenched (with meat removed off the bone), each rack cut into single chops (8 or 9 chops per rack)

When these lamb chops come off the grill, you might just be tempted to call them "lollichops"—they smell and look so tempting, you'll want to eat them out of hand right off the bone. During grilling, the marinade creates a slightly crusty, mildly sweet, and incredibly delicious coating that will entice everyone—even people who think they don't like lamb. If you prefer to keep the lamb racks whole, to be cut into chops after grilling, just increase the cooking time accordingly.

In a small bowl, whisk together the coconut milk, maple syrup, garlic, tea leaves, rosemary, pepper, and salt.

In a 9- by 13-inch baking pan, spread the mixture evenly. Add the lamb chops in a single layer, rubbing the surfaces of each chop with the marinade. Cover the pan with foil or plastic wrap and marinate at room temperature for up to 1 hour, or refrigerate for up to 24 hours.

When ready to cook, preheat the grill on high for 15 minutes. Lightly oil the grill racks and reduce the heat to medium-high. Cook the lamb chops for 5 minutes. Turn the lamb chops over and cook until the desired doneness is reached, 2 to 3 minutes for medium-rare. Let rest for 5 minutes before serving. (This recipe also works well using a stove-top grill pan.)

Broiled Shad Roe with Pancetta

COURTESY OF JOHN SHIELDS/*EDIBLE CHESAPEAKE* (MARYLAND/DC)
MAKES 2 SERVINGS

1 large pair shad roe

4 slices pancetta (Italian bacon) or thinly sliced bacon

2 tablespoons extra virgin olive oil

½ teaspoon kosher salt, plus more if needed

¼ teaspoon freshly ground black pepper, plus more if needed

2 tablespoons raspberry vinegar, red wine vinegar, or balsamic vinegar, plus more for garnish

¼ cup fish stock

4 tablespoons unsalted butter, room temperature

For spring to come to the Mid-Atlantic and Northeast, shad—and especially shad roe—must grace our tables. In North Carolina, this native fish gets royal treatment in the small riverside town of Grifton with its Shad Festival. Shad planking (cooking shad on hickory planks) has become legend around coastal Virginia. The fish itself is incredible when simply broiled, and shad fillets are very economical. Shad roe has the essence of the fish—not strong like so many roes—but slightly salty, with an intriguing yet pleasant texture. Chefs from the Carolinas to New York have adopted the practice of wrapping the roe in some type of bacon or ham, thereby adding another local element.

Remember that a splash of vinegar is traditional, and an absolute must, when serving shad roe. This dish can be served immediately with roasted red potatoes or garlic mashed potatoes, and sautéed spinach or baby greens.

Place an oven rack about 8 inches from the broiler. Preheat the broiler. Lightly grease a metal baking pan. Carefully clean the residual membrane from the roe and separate the sacs. Carefully wrap 2 slices of pancetta around each sac. On a large plate, gently roll the pancetta-wrapped roe sacs in the oil, taking care not to break the sacs. Sprinkle all over with the salt and pepper. Place the roe onto the baking pan. Broil the roe for 5 minutes. Turn over the sacs. Broil until done, 4 to 5 minutes. Remove the roe from the pan onto a plate; set aside.

In a small saucepan, add the drippings from the pan. Heat the drippings over medium-high heat until gently bubbling. Stir in the vinegar and cook, stirring, for 1 minute. Stir in the fish stock and cook, stirring occasionally, until reduced by half. Lower the heat to low and whisk in the softened butter, a little at a time, until all of it is incorporated. Remove the saucepan from the heat. Taste and adjust seasoning as needed.

To serve, spoon the sauce onto 2 plates and set 1 roe sac over the sauce on each plate. Add a splash of vinegar over each roe sac. Serve hot.

Linguine with Clams

COURTESY OF *EDIBLE SEATTLE* (WASHINGTON)
MAKES 4 SERVINGS

Fresh clams are always best when cooked briefly in their shells. Teamed here with lots of garlic and a few spices and aromatics, they create the perfect accompaniment to pasta. *Linguine alla vongole* is an Italian classic that's sure to become a favorite in your home. Serve along with a simple green salad tossed with extra virgin olive oil and red wine vinegar and some rustic Italian bread. *Buon appetito!*

Bring to a boil a large pot of salted water. In a large saucepan or a stockpot, heat the oil and butter over medium heat until the butter is melted. Add the onion and cook, stirring occasionally, until softened, about 5 minutes. Add the garlic, oregano, pepper, and chile flakes and cook, stirring frequently, for 1 minute. Add the wine, increase the heat to medium-high, and cook, stirring occasionally, until the wine is reduced by about half, 2 to 3 minutes. Stir in the clam juice and adjust the heat to keep the liquid at a simmer.

Add the linguine to the boiling salted water and cook until barely tender but not yet al dente. Reserve ½ cup of the pasta cooking water; set aside. Drain the linguine into a large colander.

While the pasta is cooking, stir the clams and parsley into the simmering sauce. Cover the pan with the lid and cook until the clams have opened, 5 to 6 minutes. Discard any unopened clams. Add the drained linguine to the sauce and clams simmering in the pan. Increase the heat to medium-high and cook, tossing the pasta with the sauce and clams, until the linguine is cooked to al dente and has absorbed most of the sauce, about 2 minutes, adding some of the pasta cooking water if the linguine is too dry. Taste and adjust seasoning, adding salt as needed. Serve immediately.

2 tablespoons extra virgin olive oil
2 tablespoons unsalted butter
1 medium onion, very finely chopped
5 cloves garlic, very finely chopped
1 teaspoon dried oregano
¼ teaspoon freshly ground black pepper, plus more if needed
¼ teaspoon crushed red chile flakes, plus more if needed
1 cup dry white wine
½ cup bottled clam juice
1 pound linguine
2 pounds littleneck clams or cockles
½ cup finely chopped flat-leaf parsley leaves
Kosher salt, if needed

Wild Onion and Spinach Tart

COURTESY OF AMY CROWELL/*EDIBLE AUSTIN* (TEXAS)
MAKES 4 TO 6 SERVINGS

Crust

1¼ cups all-purpose flour

3 tablespoons finely grated Parmigiano-Reggiano

¼ teaspoon kosher salt

¼ teaspoon freshly ground black pepper

½ cup (1 stick) cold unsalted butter, cubed

2 to 4 tablespoons ice water

Filling

2 tablespoons extra virgin olive oil

½ cup wild onions (bulbs and/or leaves), finely chopped, or 1 leek, white and light green parts only, halved lengthwise and thinly sliced crosswise

1 teaspoon kosher salt

2 cups firmly packed spinach or other tender greens

4 large eggs

½ cup half-and-half or whole milk

⅓ cup jalapeño- or salsa-flavored cream cheese spread, such as Full Quiver Farms Jalapeño Cheese Spread, room temperature

½ cup shredded mozzarella

¼ cup finely crumbled feta, optional

4 small tomatoes, thinly sliced

This is one of the best quiches you're ever likely to make—or eat! The crust is flaky, delicious, and incredibly easy to make and, best of all, requires no rolling. The filling is light and luscious and packed with a wonderful mélange of flavors.

Preheat the oven to 350°F.

MAKE THE CRUST: In the work bowl of a food processor, add the flour, Parmigiano, salt, and pepper. Pulse to combine. Add in the butter using a few short pulses until the mixture contains pea-sized lumps. Add 2 tablespoons of the ice water and pulse, adding more water gradually by tablespoons if needed, just until the dough is moist enough to clump together in a ball.

Hand press the dough gently and evenly into the bottom and up the sides of a 10-inch-diameter tart pan.

MAKE THE FILLING: In a medium skillet, heat the oil over medium heat. Add the onions and ½ teaspoon of the salt and cook, stirring occasionally, until the onions begin to turn golden, 2 to 3 minutes. Add the spinach and cook, stirring frequently, just until wilted, about 2 minutes. Into a fine-mesh sieve or strainer set over a medium bowl, transfer the mixture and, using a wooden spoon, gently squeeze out most of the excess moisture; set aside.

In a medium bowl, whisk together the eggs, half-and-half, and the remaining ½ teaspoon of salt; set aside.

To assemble the tart, spread the cream cheese spread evenly over the bottom of the tart shell. Sprinkle the mozzarella and the feta, if using, evenly on top. Spread the onion-and-spinach mixture evenly over the cheese. Pour the egg mixture evenly over the spinach mixture. Arrange the sliced tomatoes on top.

Bake the tart until the center is puffed up and lightly browned and no longer wet to the touch, 35 to 45 minutes. Allow the tart to rest for 20 to 30 minutes before serving. Serve warm or at room temperature.

Kudzu Quiche in Puff Pastry

COURTESY OF MELISSA PETERSEN/*EDIBLE MEMPHIS* (TENNESSEE)
MAKES 4 SERVINGS

While kudzu is regarded as an uber-invasive weed, its prevalence in the southern United States begs the question—can it be put to a useful purpose? Yes, on the menu. Young, tender kudzu leaves are similar to spinach in flavor. And while spinach is a good substitute in this simple recipe, why not put some of those acres and acres of kudzu to good use?

Preheat the oven to 375°F. In a small skillet, heat the oil over medium heat. Add the shallots and bell pepper and cook, stirring occasionally, until softened, 2 to 3 minutes; set aside.

In a medium bowl, whisk together the eggs, half-and-half, salt, black pepper, and hot sauce, if using. Fold in the Gruyère, Parmigiano-Reggiano, and the cooked shallot mixture. Work in the cream cheese (small lumps are fine). Stir in the kudzu leaves.

On a lightly floured surface, gently roll the puff pastry dough into an 11-inch square. Transfer the dough to a 9-inch-diameter glass pie plate. Trim the excess and crimp the edges. Pour the quiche mixture evenly into the crust, making sure all of the kudzu leaves are submerged in the liquid.

Bake the quiche until the crust is golden brown and the filling is set, 25 to 30 minutes. Allow the quiche to rest for 10 to 15 minutes before serving. Serve warm or at room temperature.

2 teaspoons extra virgin olive oil or grapeseed oil
2 shallots, very finely chopped
¼ cup very finely chopped red bell pepper
4 large eggs
½ cup half-and-half
½ teaspoon kosher salt
¼ teaspoon freshly ground black pepper
½ teaspoon hot sauce, optional
1 cup finely shredded Gruyère (about ¼ pound)
¼ cup freshly grated Parmigiano-Reggiano
⅓ cup cream cheese, room temperature
1 cup loosely packed fresh young kudzu (tiny leaves) or young spinach leaves, roughly chopped
1 portion/sheet frozen puff pastry dough, thawed

Sullivan's Island Shrimp Bog

COURTESY OF FRED THOMPSON/*EDIBLE PIEDMONT* (NORTH CAROLINA)
MAKES 6 SERVINGS

1½ cups long-grain white rice

½ pound sliced bacon, finely chopped

2 medium onions, finely chopped

1 teaspoon kosher salt, plus more if needed

¾ teaspoon freshly grated nutmeg

¼ teaspoon freshly ground black pepper, plus more if needed

¼ teaspoon ground cayenne, plus more if needed

2¼ cups chicken broth, plus more if needed

1 can (14.5 ounces) diced tomatoes

2 teaspoons freshly squeezed lemon juice

1½ teaspoons Worcestershire sauce

2 pounds medium shrimp (40 count), shelled and deveined

¼ cup very finely chopped flat-leaf parsley leaves

1 lemon, cut into 6 wedges

A bog is a close cousin to pilau (pronounced pih-LOW)—a rice dish that usually contains smoked sausage, chicken, and tomatoes. The bog's birth was probably in the Charleston, South Carolina, area during the 1700s, when rice was king. Most likely, it was a slave food and called a bog because rice grew in bogs and, some say, because the slaves were "bogged down" in rice. A chicken bog is more a sibling than a cousin to a shrimp bog. Chicken is a popular protein, especially up-country near the Pee Dee River, but along the coast, shrimp has been much more accessible to rich and poor alike. Over time, bogs spread both north and south from Charleston. In the Wilmington, North Carolina, area shrimp bogs are served as part of a breakfast buffet or for wedding meals and even for political rallies. Shrimp bogs can be huge affairs, much like "pig pickings" inland.

Making a shrimp bog is simple. In fact, you probably have every ingredient in this dish in your pantry, except for the shrimp, which you'll want to get fresh. You'll need thirty to forty minutes tops to make the dish and have it on the table. Applewood or double-smoked bacon lends a rich flavor to the rice and shrimp, but regular bacon also works fine.

In a fine-mesh strainer, rinse the rice well under cold running water. Drain well; set aside.

In a large heavy Dutch oven or stockpot, cook the bacon over medium heat until golden, about 5 minutes. Using a slotted spoon, transfer the bacon to a paper towel–lined dish; set aside. Pour off and discard all but 3 tablespoons of the bacon fat remaining in the pot. Add the onions to the pot and cook over medium heat, stirring occasionally, for 3 minutes. Add the drained rice, salt, nutmeg, black pepper, and cayenne and stir for 1 minute.

Stir in the broth, tomatoes with liquid, lemon juice, and Worcestershire sauce. Bring to a boil, cover the pot, reduce the heat, and simmer gently for 20 minutes. Stir in the cooked bacon and the shrimp and cook uncovered, stirring occasionally, until the shrimp is cooked through, adding more broth if the rice seems to be drying out, about 10 minutes. Stir the bog with a fork. Taste and adjust seasoning as needed. Sprinkle with parsley, garnish with lemon wedges, and serve immediately.

Egg Noodles with Fresh Spring Vegetables

COURTESY OF SHELDON MARCUVITZ AND CAROLE LAITY, YOUR KITCHEN GARDEN AT CANBY,
OREGON/*EDIBLE PORTLAND* (OREGON)

MAKES 4 SERVINGS

It's incredible that so few ingredients can provide so much intense flavor in every bite. The fabulous meaty texture and mild nuttiness of the mushrooms combined with the creaminess of the fava beans and sauce create a winning dish that's sure to create requests for repeat performances.

Cut each leek in half lengthwise. On a cutting board, place 1 leek half cut-side down, then slice it lengthwise into very thin julienne strips. Repeat with the other leek halves. Set aside.

In a large pot of boiling salted water, add the fresh (or frozen) shelled fava beans. Cook for 1 minute (or 2 minutes if frozen). Using a large slotted spoon, quickly remove the beans to a colander set over a large bowl. (The bean-blanching water will be used to cook the noodles, so keep the water at a simmer.) Rinse the beans under cold running water until cool. Using your fingers or a paring knife, carefully tear open the outer hull of each bean. Gently squeeze the fava beans into a small bowl; set aside. Discard the hulls.

In a large sauté pan, melt the butter over medium heat. Add the leeks, toss to coat with the butter, and cook, stirring occasionally, until the leeks are wilted and tender, 2 to 3 minutes. Add the morels, increase the heat to medium-high, and cook, stirring occasionally, until the liquid released from the mushrooms has been reabsorbed, 3 to 4 minutes. Reduce the heat to medium, add the fava beans, cream, salt, and pepper and cook, stirring occasionally, until the sauce has thickened slightly, 3 to 4 minutes. Turn off the heat. Taste and adjust seasoning as needed.

Return the bean-blanching water to a boil. Add the tagliatelle, stir well, and cook, stirring occasionally, until the noodles are slightly undercooked. Using a ladle, remove ¼ cup of the pasta-cooking water to a small bowl. In a large colander, quickly drain the noodles, then add them into the sauté pan with the sauce. Turn the heat to medium-high and gently toss the noodles with the sauce until they are cooked to al dente, about 1 minute, adding some of the pasta-cooking water if the sauce becomes too thick. Garnish with the scallions, if using, before serving.

4 small leeks, white and light green parts only

1½ pounds fresh fava beans (also known as broad beans), shelled if still in pods, or 1½ cups shelled fresh or frozen fava beans (do not thaw if frozen), inner hull still on

4 tablespoons unsalted butter

½ pound morels or other mushrooms, thinly sliced

1½ cups heavy cream

1 teaspoon kosher salt, plus more if needed

¼ teaspoon freshly ground black pepper, plus more if needed

1 pound fresh tagliatelle or fettuccine, preferably egg based

¼ cup thinly sliced scallions, optional

Wild Salmon with Fava Bean Puree

COURTESY OF JOHN EISENHART, PAZZO RISTORANTE/*EDIBLE PORTLAND* (OREGON)
MAKES 4 SERVINGS

Endive Garnish

1 large head Belgian endive
2 tablespoons freshly squeezed
  lemon juice
1 tablespoon extra virgin olive oil
¼ teaspoon kosher salt

Fava Bean Puree

2 pounds fresh fava beans, shelled
  if still in pods, or 2 cups shelled
  fresh or frozen fava beans (do not
  thaw if frozen), inner hull still on
½ cup extra virgin olive oil
¼ cup water
1 teaspoon fresh thyme leaves
½ teaspoon kosher salt, plus more if
  needed
1 teaspoon freshly squeezed lemon
  juice, plus more if needed

Salmon

4 wild Oregon salmon fillets (6 to 7
  ounces each) or other wild Pacific
  salmon, skin on
1 tablespoon grapeseed oil or
  another neutral-flavored oil
½ teaspoon kosher salt
¼ teaspoon freshly ground black
  pepper

Fava beans, also known as broad beans, are a staple ingredient in Mediterranean countries and are becoming more and more popular in North America. Their creamy texture and delicate flavor add a complexity to the dishes in which they are featured. In this recipe, the cooked fava beans are made into a lightly cooked puree (*favetta*) that serves as a lovely accompaniment to the velvety, perfectly cooked salmon and the crisp, bright endive slaw.

Preheat the oven to 400°F.

MAKE THE ENDIVE GARNISH: Cut the endive in half lengthwise through the core. Remove the core from both halves of the endive. On a cutting board, place 1 endive half cut-side down, then slice it lengthwise into very thin julienne strips. Repeat with the other endive half. In a small bowl, add the endive, lemon juice, olive oil, and salt. Toss well; set aside.

MAKE THE FAVA BEAN PUREE: In a large pot of boiling salted water, add the fresh (or frozen) shelled fava beans. Cook for 1 minute (or 2 minutes if frozen). In a colander, drain the beans, then rinse them under cold running water until cool. Using your fingers or a paring knife, carefully tear open the outer hull of each bean. Gently squeeze the fava beans into a small bowl; discard the hulls. In the work bowl of a food processor, add the fava beans, olive oil, water, thyme, and salt. Process until the mixture is smooth; set aside.

MAKE THE SALMON: Brush the top of each salmon fillet with grapeseed oil, then sprinkle with the salt and pepper. Heat a large ovenproof skillet over medium-high heat. Place the salmon fillets skin-side up into the hot skillet. Cook until the salmon flesh is brown and crusty, about 3 minutes. Gently turn each salmon fillet skin-side down. Place the skillet into the preheated oven. Bake until the salmon is firm but still slightly opaque in the center, 5 to 7 minutes.

In a medium skillet over medium heat, add the fava bean puree. Cook, stirring frequently, until the mixture is sizzling, about 4 minutes. Remove from the heat. Stir in the lemon juice. Taste and adjust seasoning as needed.

Place 1 portion of the puree near the center of each of 4 dinner plates, then place a salmon fillet alongside, overlapping slightly. Stir the endive garnish. Top each salmon fillet with an equal portion of the endive. Serve immediately.

Herb-Roasted Duck Breast with Carrot-Potato Mash and Chive Butter

COURTESY OF *EDIBLE RHODY* (RHODE ISLAND)
MAKES 4 SERVINGS

Chive Butter

3 tablespoons unsalted butter, room temperature

1 clove garlic, very finely chopped

1 tablespoon finely chopped fresh chives

1 teaspoon finely grated lemon zest

1 teaspoon freshly squeezed lemon juice

⅛ teaspoon kosher salt

Duck Breasts

1 tablespoon finely chopped assorted fresh herbs, such as parsley, sage, rosemary, or thyme

1 teaspoon kosher salt

¼ teaspoon freshly ground black pepper

2 teaspoons extra virgin olive oil

4 boneless duck breasts (6 to 8 ounces each), skin on

Carrot-Potato Mash

4 small carrots, cut into 1-inch lengths

4 Yukon gold potatoes, cut into 1½-inch cubes

3 tablespoons unsalted butter

½ cup buttermilk

1 teaspoon kosher salt, plus more if needed

¼ teaspoon freshly ground black pepper

The fresh chives in this recipe are essential and add a vibrant flavor. The elements of the plated dish work very well together, with the carrot-and-potato mash adding a colorful, homey touch to the plate. The skin on the duck breasts crisps up beautifully and the slices of duck fanned out on the mash create a very elegant presentation, but you can, of course, plate it more simply if you like.

MAKE THE CHIVE BUTTER: In a small bowl, stir together the butter, garlic, chives, lemon zest, lemon juice, and salt; set aside. (This compound butter can be made up to 2 days ahead, rolled into a log shape in plastic wrap, refrigerated, and sliced as needed.)

Preheat the oven to 400°F.

SEASON THE DUCK BREASTS: In a small bowl, stir together the fresh herbs, salt, pepper, and oil. Coat the duck breasts all over with the herb mixture; set aside.

MAKE THE CARROT-POTATO MASH: In a large pot of boiling salted water, add the carrots and potatoes. Return the water to a boil and cook until the carrots and potatoes are tender when pierced with a paring knife, 20 to 25 minutes. In a large colander, drain the vegetables. Return them to the pot and add the butter and buttermilk. Using a potato masher, mash the carrots and potatoes to the desired consistency (there's no need to get rid of all the lumps). Add the salt and pepper and mix well to combine. Taste and adjust seasoning as needed. Cover the pot to keep the mash warm.

Roast the duck breasts: Heat a large ovenproof skillet or sauté pan over medium-high heat. Place the duck breasts skin-side down into the skillet and cook until the skin is deeply browned, about 3 minutes. Using tongs to avoid pricking the skin, turn over each breast. Place the skillet into the preheated oven and cook to medium doneness (still pink inside; this is perfectly safe when cooking and eating duck), 6 to 8 minutes. Remove the breasts from the skillet and let rest for about 3 minutes.

Spoon some of the mash onto each plate. Cut each duck breast on the diagonal into ½-inch slices and fan the slices of each breast on top of the mash. Top each serving of duck with about a tablespoon of the chive butter. Serve immediately.

Side Dishes

Collard Tops with Parmigiano

COURTESY OF MELISSA PETERSEN/*EDIBLE MEMPHIS* (TENNESSEE)
MAKES 4 SERVINGS

Collard tops are the tops of young collard greens and include the blossoms and the young leaves. They look a bit like broccoli rabe, with a green, nubby flower, little leaves, and edible stalks. They are much more tender than mature collards and, combined with the other ingredients in this simple little casserole, are delightful as a late-spring or early-summer side dish.

Preheat the oven to 350°F. Have a large bowl of ice water ready. In a large saucepan of boiling salted water, blanch (partially cook) the collards until bright green and slightly tender, about 2 minutes. In a colander, drain the collards, then plunge the greens into the ice water. Drain well and squeeze dry; set aside.

In the same saucepan, melt the butter over medium-low heat. Add the garlic and cook until it is tender but not browned, about 2 minutes. Stir in the cream. Increase the heat to medium-high and cook until slightly thickened, 1 to 2 minutes.

Lightly grease a 1-quart casserole pan. In a medium bowl, combine the collards, cream mixture, cheese, salt, and pepper. Spread the mixture evenly into the baking pan. Cover with the lid or foil and bake until the cheese is melted, 15 to 20 minutes. Serve immediately.

1 bunch (about 1¼ pounds) collard tops or broccoli rabe (including flowers and stems), coarsely chopped
2 tablespoons unsalted butter
1 clove garlic, thinly sliced
½ cup heavy cream or half-and-half
⅓ cup freshly grated Parmigiano-Reggiano
½ teaspoon kosher salt
¼ teaspoon freshly ground black pepper

Asparagus with Morels and Tarragon

COURTESY OF KRISTEN LEE-CHARLSON/*EDIBLE MISSOULA* (MONTANA)
MAKES 6 SERVINGS

2 pounds asparagus, trimmed and
cut into 2-inch lengths
4 tablespoons unsalted butter, cut
into 1-tablespoon pieces
2 large shallots, finely chopped
¼ pound fresh morels, cleaned and
halved lengthwise if large, or
other exotic mushrooms
2 tablespoons finely chopped fresh
tarragon
½ teaspoon sea salt or kosher salt,
plus more if needed
1 tablespoon freshly squeezed
lemon juice

When local asparagus is in season, it's tempting to eat it at every meal. Asparagus is one of those vegetables that requires little adornment, and this dish fits the bill. If you can't find fresh morels or other exotic mushrooms, this recipe works wonderfully well with rehydrated dried morels, or a combination of various dried mushrooms.

Have a large bowl of ice water ready. In a large sauté pan with 3 inches of boiling, salted water, add the asparagus. Cook until just tender, 2 to 3 minutes. Using a slotted spoon, transfer the asparagus to the bowl of ice water. Once cool, transfer the asparagus to a plate lined with paper towels.

Empty the sauté pan and wipe dry. Heat 3 tablespoons of the butter over medium heat. When the foam subsides, add the shallots and cook, stirring frequently, until golden brown, 2 to 4 minutes. Add the morels and cook, stirring frequently, until tender, about 5 minutes.

Add the asparagus, 1 tablespoon of the tarragon, the salt, and the remaining tablespoon of butter and cook, stirring, until heated through, about 3 minutes. Remove the pan from the heat and stir in the lemon juice. Taste and adjust seasoning as needed.

Garnish with the remaining tablespoon of chopped tarragon. Serve immediately.

Desserts

Rhubarb Bread Pudding with Whiskey Sauce

COURTESY OF *EDIBLE VANCOUVER* (BC, CANADA)
MAKES 6 SERVINGS

This bread pudding is delicious on its own but is absolutely scrumptious when accompanied by the buttery whiskey sauce. The contrast between the puckery tartness of the rhubarb and the sweetness of the pudding that envelops it is heavenly. Although perfect for showcasing fresh local rhubarb, this dish can also be made year-round using frozen rhubarb. (You can also try using pitted fresh or tart cherries, peaches, plums, or apricots.) You might want to try serving it warm for breakfast, drizzled with pure maple syrup.

MAKE THE BREAD PUDDING: In a large bowl, whisk together the eggs, milk, half-and-half, ¼ cup of the sugar, the vanilla, and salt. Stir the bread into the egg mixture, cover the bowl, and refrigerate for at least 30 minutes or up to 2 hours, pushing the bread down into the liquid from time to time.

Preheat the oven to 375°F. Butter an 8-inch-square baking pan. In a medium bowl, combine the rhubarb, the remaining ¼ cup of sugar, and the cinnamon. Gently stir the rhubarb mixture into the bread mixture. Pour the mixture evenly into the prepared baking pan. Bake until golden brown and slightly puffed, 55 minutes to 1 hour 5 minutes. Remove from the oven and cool on a rack for about 30 minutes.

MAKE THE WHISKEY SAUCE, IF USING: In a small saucepan, melt the butter over medium heat. Whisk in the sugar, half-and-half, whiskey, and salt. Bring to a simmer and cook, stirring frequently, until the sauce is slightly thickened, 4 to 5 minutes. Remove from the heat.

To serve, spoon the warm bread pudding into serving bowls and drizzle with warm whiskey sauce.

Bread Pudding

4 large eggs
1 cup whole milk
1 cup half-and-half
½ cup granulated sugar
1 teaspoon pure vanilla extract
¼ teaspoon kosher salt
5 cups day-old cinnamon bread (with or without raisins), cut into ½-inch cubes
1 pound fresh rhubarb (about 6 hefty stalks), cut into ½-inch slices, or 4 cups frozen rhubarb
½ teaspoon ground cinnamon

Whiskey Sauce, optional

4 tablespoons unsalted butter
¼ cup granulated sugar
3 tablespoons half-and-half
2 tablespoons whiskey
Pinch of salt

The Best Strawberry Shortcakes

COURTESY OF CLAUDE MANN/*EDIBLE OJAI* (CALIFORNIA)
MAKES 8 SERVINGS

Macerated Strawberries

3 pints (6 cups) of the ripest, sweetest strawberries you can find, hulled and halved if small or quartered if large

2 tablespoons freshly squeezed lemon juice

1 tablespoon pure maple syrup, agave syrup, or granulated sugar, plus more if needed, optional

Shortcakes

2 cups all-purpose flour

¼ cup granulated sugar

1 tablespoon baking powder

½ teaspoon ground cinnamon, optional

½ teaspoon kosher salt

1¼ cups heavy cream

2 tablespoons butter, melted

Whipped Cream

2 cups heavy cream

1 tablespoon pure maple syrup or powdered sugar, or ½ tablespoon agave syrup, or to taste

¼ cup thinly sliced crystallized ginger, optional

One can toil for hours on more elaborate desserts without coming close to achieving the simple gratification of this almost effortless indulgence. Using cream instead of butter in the shortcake not only makes for lighter, more tender pastry, it also eliminates the step of cutting the butter into the flour. Consider doubling the shortcake recipe—shortcakes are great to have with morning coffee.

MACERATE THE STRAWBERRIES: In a large shallow-rimmed dish, mash about one-quarter of the strawberries with a fork. In a large bowl, toss together the mashed strawberries, unmashed berries, lemon juice, and maple syrup, if using. Taste and adjust sweetness as needed; set aside, stirring occasionally.

PREPARE THE SHORTCAKES: Preheat the oven to 425°F. Line a 9- by 13-inch rimmed baking sheet with parchment paper. In a large bowl, whisk together the flour, sugar, baking powder, cinnamon, if using, and salt. Using a wooden spoon or stiff spatula, stir in the cream. Mix until the mixture comes together in a sticky, crumbly mass.

Transfer the mixture onto a lightly floured work surface. Using floured hands, knead the dough only a few times until the mixture forms a soft dough. (For the lightest shortcakes, do not overknead.)

Divide the dough in half and shape each half into a 5-inch round. Cut each round into quarters. Place each quarter onto the prepared baking sheet, leaving a few inches between. Brush each quarter with melted butter. Bake until the tops of the shortcakes are golden, 12 to 16 minutes. Remove the shortcakes to a cooling rack to cool completely.

MAKE THE WHIPPED CREAM: In the bowl of a stand mixer (or in a large bowl using an electric hand mixer or by hand using a stiff whisk), combine the cream and maple syrup. Beat at medium-high speed until soft peaks form.

To assemble the shortcakes, split each shortcake in half crosswise. Place the bottom half of a shortcake on a plate. Spoon some of the macerated berries and a large dollop of whipped cream on top. Place the top half of the shortcake on top, and add more berries and their juices and whipped cream. Repeat with the remaining shortcakes. Garnish with the crystallized ginger, if using, and serve immediately.

FIRST COURSES

Pineapple Gazpacho   233

Arugula and Fennel Salad   234

Grilled Apricots with Blue Cheese and Hazelnuts   234

Fresh Spinach Salad with Hot Bacon Vinaigrette   235

Rich Corn Chowder   236

MAIN COURSES

Lobster Rolls   238

Poblanos Stuffed with Goat Cheese and Shrimp   241

Grilled Chicken and Peaches with Caramelized   242
    Onions and Goat Cheese

SIDE DISHES

Sautéed Spicy Green Beans and Tomatoes   243

Stir-fried Bok Choy with Caramelized Corn   244

Roasted Cauliflower with Golden Raisins and   247
    Pine Nuts

Double Corn Spoon Bread   248

Sweet Corn Fritters   248

DESSERTS

Frozen Maple Mousse   250

Blueberry Corn Bread   251

Caramel Ice Cream with Caramel Sauce and   252
    Fleur de Sel

Berry Ricotta Pie   253

Flaky Piecrust   254

summer

First Courses

Pineapple Gazpacho

ADAPTED FROM A RECIPE COURTESY OF GWEN ASHLEY WALTERS/*EDIBLE PHOENIX* (ARIZONA)
MAKES 4 SERVINGS

The answer is yes—this does taste as interesting as it sounds. And just so you don't forget that it is a Southwestern dish, it finishes with a tiny little kick of heat. Its lovely, pale yellow color with splashes of red and green from the peppers makes it almost as much of a delight to look at as to eat. Make the soup the day before you plan to serve it to give the flavors time to meld together.

MAKE THE GAZPACHO: In the work bowl of a food processor, add the pineapple, yellow bell pepper, onion, cucumber, vinegar, hot sauce, salt, white pepper, and brown sugar, if using. Process until the ingredients are pureed. Pour the gazpacho into a glass or stainless steel container. Cover and refrigerate for at least 2 hours or up to 24 hours.

MAKE THE PEPPER GARNISH: In a small bowl, stir together the red bell pepper, green bell pepper, cucumber, jalapeño, and cilantro, if using; set aside.

Prior to serving, stir the gazpacho. If it seems too thick, stir in the pineapple juice. Taste and adjust seasoning as needed. To serve, ladle the gazpacho into small bowls or cups. Sprinkle some of the pepper garnish on top of the gazpacho.

Gazpacho

1 ripe pineapple, peeled, cored, and cut into chunks

½ cup finely chopped yellow bell pepper

¼ cup finely chopped red onion

¼ cup peeled, seeded, and finely chopped cucumber

2 teaspoons rice wine vinegar, plus more if needed

½ teaspoon hot sauce, plus more if needed

¼ teaspoon kosher salt, plus more if needed

⅛ teaspoon ground white pepper

1 teaspoon light brown sugar, optional

¼ cup pineapple juice or water, if needed

Pepper Garnish

¼ cup very finely chopped red bell pepper

¼ cup very finely chopped green bell pepper

¼ cup seeded, very finely chopped cucumber

1 jalapeño pepper, cored, seeded, and very finely chopped

1 tablespoon finely chopped cilantro, optional

Arugula and Fennel Salad

COURTESY OF *EDIBLE OJAI* (CALIFORNIA AND THE WEST)
MAKES 6 SERVINGS

4 cups (about 5 ounces) lightly packed arugula

2 small fennel bulbs (about 1½ pounds)

2 tablespoons extra virgin olive oil

2 tablespoons freshly squeezed lemon juice (preferably from Meyer lemons), plus more if needed

½ teaspoon kosher salt, plus more if needed

¼ pound Pecorino Romano or Parmigiano-Reggiano

¼ teaspoon freshly ground black pepper

Enjoy this lovely salad as a starter or serve on a buffet table or even as a light lunch or dinner. The soft-textured, slightly peppery arugula combined with the mildly licorice-flavored, crunchy raw fennel makes for a perfectly satisfying salad.

In a large shallow salad bowl, arrange the arugula. Cut the stalks off of the fennel bulbs. Remove the fronds from the stalks and set aside. Cut each bulb in half lengthwise through the root. On a cutting board, place each half cut-side down, then cut in half lengthwise again. Cut each quarter into very thin slices crosswise and scatter the slices on top of the arugula. Cut the fennel stalks into thin slices on the diagonal and scatter on top of the salad.

Sprinkle the oil, lemon juice, and salt over the vegetables and toss gently. The salad should taste light and slightly lemony. Taste and adjust seasoning as needed.

Using a potato peeler or cheese slicer, cut ribbons of cheese and scatter them on top of the salad. Sprinkle with the pepper and top with the reserved fennel fronds. Serve immediately.

Grilled Apricots with Blue Cheese and Hazelnuts

COURTESY OF *EDIBLE SEATTLE* (WASHINGTON)
MAKES 6 SERVINGS

6 ripe firm apricots, halved through the stem and pitted

½ cup crumbled blue cheese

¼ cup chopped toasted hazelnuts

2 tablespoons liquid honey, plus more if needed

During the summer, planning a first course can be accomplished simply by walking from one end of a farmers' market to the other (and you may be similarly inspired by your own market.) This recipe was inspired by truly local Seattle ingredients—Estrella Family Creamery's Wynoochee River Blue, honey from Rockridge Orchards, and nuts from Holmquist Hazelnut Orchards. Choose ripe apricots that haven't gotten too soft. If you're in a rush, just skip the grilling step.

Preheat the grill on medium heat for 10 minutes. Grill the apricots cut-side down until the flesh is soft, 2 to 3 minutes.

Place the apricots on a plate cut-side up. Top each apricot with blue cheese and hazelnuts. Drizzle with honey. Serve warm.

Fresh Spinach Salad with Hot Bacon Vinaigrette

COURTESY OF MIKE CLEM, THE DRAKE RESTAURANT AT BURLINGTON, IOWA/*EDIBLE IOWA RIVER VALLEY* (IOWA)
MAKES 4 SERVINGS

A good old-fashioned warm spinach salad provides comforting fare with very little effort. We've all become accustomed to eating salads composed of delicate baby salad leaves, and this salad leaves those in the dust. There's something very satisfying about biting into mature spinach leaves that have been slightly warmed by a fairly zesty vinaigrette. This salad offers us one of those little trips back in time that makes us feel really good. And there's nothing wrong with that!

PREPARE THE SALAD: Place the spinach into a large salad bowl. Prepare the other salad ingredients and set aside.

MAKE THE VINAIGRETTE: In a small bowl, whisk together the vinegar, mustard, and wine; set aside. In a small saucepan, cook the sliced bacon over medium heat until golden brown. Add the onion and cook, stirring occasionally, until beginning to soften, about 2 minutes. Stir in the sugar, if using. Add the vinegar mixture, reduce the heat, and simmer for 3 minutes. Taste and adjust seasoning as needed.

Pour the hot vinaigrette over the spinach and toss to coat. Garnish with the sliced egg, mushrooms, and cooked bacon slices. Serve immediately.

Salad

8 cups (about ½ pound) trimmed fresh spinach leaves (not baby spinach)

2 hard-boiled eggs, sliced or chopped

¼ pound cremini or button mushrooms, sliced

4 slices cooked bacon

Vinaigrette

½ cup balsamic or sherry vinegar

2 tablespoons prepared yellow mustard

3 tablespoons white wine or water

3 slices raw bacon, thinly sliced

½ small onion, finely chopped

1 teaspoon granulated sugar, plus more if needed, optional

Rich Corn Chowder

COURTESY OF ROBIN McDERMOTT/*EDIBLE GREEN MOUNTAINS* (VERMONT)
MAKES 8 SERVINGS

Corn Broth, optional

4 medium ears corn
8 cups water

Chowder

4 slices thick-sliced bacon, cut
    into ¼-inch dice, optional, or
    2 tablespoons extra virgin olive oil
1 medium onion, finely chopped
1 carrot, finely chopped
¼ cup finely chopped celery root or
    celery
5 medium potatoes, chopped
4 cups corn broth (above), chicken
    broth, or vegetable broth
2 cups water
1 teaspoon kosher salt, plus more if
    needed
½ teaspoon freshly ground black
    pepper, plus more if needed
½ teaspoon freshly grated nutmeg
½ teaspoon dried thyme
1 bay leaf
1 cup heavy cream or half-and-half

It is not surprising that sweet corn frequently appears on Vermont menus during the few weeks it's in season. This luscious corn chowder uses the whole vegetable—cob and all—to create a dish that is satisfying and distinctive. If you choose to preserve some of the summer bounty for use throughout the year, frozen kernels (and cobs) work very well in this recipe.

MAKE THE CORN BROTH, IF USING: Stand an ear of corn up against a cutting board. Using a large sharp knife, and running the blade downward between the corn kernels and the corn cob, cut the corn kernels from the cob, rotating the cob until all kernels have been removed. Transfer the corn kernels to a medium bowl. Repeat with the remaining 3 ears of corn; set the corn kernels aside for making the chowder.

In a medium pot, add the water and the cobs from which the corn has been removed. Bring to a boil, partially cover the pot, reduce the heat, and simmer until the water has become rich and golden, about 1 hour 30 minutes. Set a fine-mesh strainer into a large bowl; strain the corn broth. Set the corn broth aside; discard the solids.

MAKE THE CHOWDER: In a large pot over medium heat, add the bacon, if using. Cook until the fat is rendered and the bacon is crisp, 7 to 10 minutes. Using a slotted spoon, transfer the bacon to a plate lined with paper towels and set aside. If not using the bacon, in a large pot, heat the oil over medium heat.

Add the onion and cook, stirring occasionally, for 3 minutes. Stir in the carrot and celery root and cook, stirring occasionally, until the vegetables soften, 3 to 5 minutes. Increase the heat to medium-high and stir in the potatoes, corn broth, water, salt, pepper, nutmeg, thyme, and bay leaf. Bring to a boil, cover the pot, reduce the heat, and simmer until the potatoes are soft, 15 to 20 minutes. Stir in the reserved corn kernels, bring the chowder back up to a simmer, and cook for 10 minutes.

Remove the bay leaf. Using an immersion blender or a potato masher, lightly break up some of the potatoes and corn in the chowder. Do not overprocess or you will lose the rustic texture of the chowder.

Stir in the cream and the reserved bacon. Taste and adjust the seasoning; you may need to add more salt to balance the sweetness of the corn broth and bring out the full flavor of this soup. Serve hot.

Main Courses

Lobster Rolls

MAYONNAISE RECIPE COURTESY OF *EDIBLE CAPE COD* (MASSACHUSETTS); LOBSTER RECIPE COURTESY OF
DOUG LANGELAND/*EDIBLE CAPE COD* (MASSACHUSETTS)
MAKES 4 SERVINGS; MAYONNAISE MAKES 1 CUP

Homemade Mayonnaise

1 large egg
1 large egg yolk
2 teaspoons Dijon mustard
2 teaspoons white wine vinegar
1 teaspoon kosher salt, plus more if
  needed
1½ cups vegetable oil or
  grapeseed oil
¼ teaspoon freshly ground black
  pepper, plus more if needed
2 teaspoons freshly squeezed lemon
  juice, plus more if needed

Lobster Rolls

4 Maine lobsters (1¼ pounds each)
½ cup Homemade Mayonnaise
  (above) or commercial
  mayonnaise, plus more if needed
8 top-sliced, pull-apart hot dog rolls
⅓ cup unsalted butter, melted

These lobster rolls are all about the lobster since they have no fillers or lettuce to detract from the succulence of the meat. We buy our lobsters from a lobsterman at the farmers' market; they are bursting with meat.

This recipe is very simple, with only a few ingredients. Accordingly, freshness and attention to small details make all the difference. You can use store-bought mayonnaise, but making your own in a food processor is very easy and adds a fresh richness that pushes these lobster rolls over the top. (This mayonnaise recipe is so easy to prepare and so foolproof, it will make you wonder why we use commercial mayonnaise at all.)

Adding about one-quarter teaspoon of hot sauce to the mayonnaise for the lobster is quite common, so try it if you like.

You can ask your fishmonger to steam and crack the lobsters and then you can remove the meat when you are constructing the rolls. Do not buy cooked lobster meat out of the shell: It dries out and is never as good.

MAKE THE MAYONNAISE: Place the egg, egg yolk, and mustard in the work bowl of a food processor. Process for 30 seconds and then, with the machine running, add the vinegar and salt and process for another 15 seconds. With the machine still running, begin to add the oil slowly, a few drops at a time. When the mixture starts to thicken, add the remainder of the oil in a slow, steady stream until it has been incorporated. Stop the machine. Add the pepper and lemon juice and pulse quickly to combine. Taste and adjust seasoning as needed, and pulse quickly to combine. Use immediately or store in the refrigerator in a sealed container for up to 2 days.

MAKE THE LOBSTER ROLLS: Fill a large pot at least 16 inches in diameter and 12 inches deep two-thirds full with water and bring to a rolling boil. Place the lobsters headfirst into the pot and cover with the lid. Return the water to a boil. Remove the lid and simmer the lobsters for about 11 minutes (see lobster-cooking notes, opposite).

Remove the lobsters from the pot using tongs and place them into a large bowl or the sink until cool enough to handle. Remove the lobster tails and claws. Using a lobster cracker, crack open the tails and claws and remove the meat. Roughly chop the meat and place it into a large bowl; set aside to cool completely.

Add the mayonnaise to the bowl with the lobster meat and stir to combine. Add additional mayonnaise if needed to achieve the desired consistency.

Heat a large skillet over medium-high heat for about 5 minutes. Lightly brush both sides of each hot dog roll with melted butter and place all the rolls into the

skillet. Cook the rolls until the bottoms are golden brown, 2 to 3 minutes. Turn the rolls over and them on the other sides until golden, again 2 to 3 minutes.

Remove the rolls from the skillet. Stuff each roll evenly with the prepared lobster filling. Serve 2 lobster rolls per person.

. . . .

NOTE ~ To figure the boiling time for live lobsters, after the cooking water has returned to a boil, a lobster should be simmered for 10 minutes for the first pound of weight of 1 lobster, plus 3 minutes for each additional pound. With this method, after the water has returned to a boil, a 1½-pound lobster would simmer for 10 minutes plus 1½ minutes, for a total of 11½ minutes, and a 2-pound lobster would cook for about 13 minutes.

Poblanos Stuffed with Goat Cheese and Shrimp

COURTESY OF *EDIBLE PHOENIX* (ARIZONA)
MAKES 8 FIRST-COURSE OR 4 MAIN-COURSE SERVINGS

Colorful and absolutely scrumptious, these stuffed peppers are a great first course or a luncheon entrée. You may get so hooked on them you'll want to try varying the filling by substituting cooked chicken or crabmeat for the shrimp.

ROAST AND PEEL THE POBLANOS AND RED BELL PEPPERS: Over an open gas flame (on the stove top or outdoor grill), roast the chiles and bell peppers, turning with tongs for even roasting, about 5 minutes each (you can roast 2 or 3 at a time on each gas burner). The chiles and bell peppers are done when they are soft, blackened, and blistered over most of their surfaces (it is not necessary to get every nook and cranny, and be careful not to overroast the chiles, which must remain intact for stuffing).

Place the hot chiles and bell peppers into 2 separate large bowls. Cover the bowls with plates or with plastic wrap; set aside for about 15 minutes. Using a paring knife, gently rub the skin off of the flesh of each chile and bell pepper. Wipe the surface of the flesh with paper towels to remove most of the excess skin and charred bits; discard the skin and set the chiles and bell peppers aside. (Never run roasted chiles or bell peppers under water to remove the skins; doing so removes flavorful natural oils.)

MAKE THE STUFFED POBLANOS: Preheat the oven to 350°F. Line a 9-by 13-inch rimmed baking sheet with parchment paper. Carefully slit each chile down one side and remove the seeds, leaving the stems attached.

In a medium bowl, combine the goat cheese, Panela cheese, shrimp, shallot, chopped bell pepper, cilantro, basil, salt, and black pepper; stir well. Taste and adjust seasoning as needed. Divide the cheese mixture into 8 equal portions. Place 1 portion into each chile, being careful not to overfill. Close each chile, overlapping the edges slightly. (These can be made a day ahead, covered, and refrigerated.) Transfer the stuffed poblanos to the baking sheet. Bake until just warmed through, about 10 minutes.

MAKE THE RED BELL PEPPER SAUCE: Cut open the roasted red bell peppers; remove and discard the stems and seeds. In a medium skillet, heat the oil over medium heat. Add the shallots, garlic, and serrano chile and cook, stirring occasionally, until the shallots are tender, about 3 minutes. Transfer the mixture to a blender. Add the roasted bell peppers, chicken broth, salt, and black pepper. Blend until smooth. Add more broth as needed to reach the desired consistency (it should not be too runny). Taste and adjust seasoning as needed. (The sauce can be made a day ahead and refrigerated.) Return the sauce to the skillet to warm slightly.

To assemble, place 1 or 2 stuffed poblanos onto each plate. Spoon sauce on and around the poblanos. Serve hot.

Roasted Poblanos and Red Bell Peppers

8 poblano chile peppers
2 large red bell peppers

Stuffed Poblanos

4 ounces mild goat cheese, room temperature
½ cup grated Panela or Monterey Jack cheese
½ pound cooked, peeled, and deveined shrimp, chopped
1 shallot, very finely chopped
¼ cup finely chopped red bell pepper
1 tablespoon finely chopped fresh cilantro leaves
1 tablespoon finely chopped fresh basil leaves
½ teaspoon kosher salt, plus more if needed
¼ teaspoon freshly ground black pepper, plus more if needed

Red Bell Pepper Sauce

1 tablespoon extra virgin olive oil
3 shallots, finely chopped
2 cloves garlic, finely chopped
1 serrano chile pepper, seeded and finely chopped
⅔ cup chicken or vegetable broth, plus more if needed
½ teaspoon kosher salt, plus more if needed
¼ teaspoon freshly ground black pepper

Grilled Chicken and Peaches with Caramelized Onions and Goat Cheese

COURTESY OF *EDIBLE CAPE COD* (MASSACHUSETTS)
MAKES 4 SERVINGS

Caramelized Onions

1 tablespoon extra virgin olive oil

1 tablespoon unsalted butter

2 large onions, halved and thinly sliced

¼ teaspoon kosher salt, plus more if needed

¼ teaspoon freshly ground black pepper, plus more if needed

1 tablespoon light brown sugar

Grilled Chicken and Peaches

2 medium peaches, peeled, pitted, and halved

¼ cup good brandy, such as cognac, optional

¾ teaspoon kosher salt

½ teaspoon freshly ground black pepper

4 boneless, skinless chicken breasts

Goat Cheese and Greens

2 cups local young mixed salad greens

2 tablespoons extra virgin olive oil

1 tablespoon freshly squeezed lemon juice, optional

¼ teaspoon kosher salt, plus more if needed

⅛ teaspoon freshly ground black pepper, plus more if needed

2 tablespoons liquid honey

1 goat cheese log (12 ounces), sliced into 12 equal rounds (see note)

This dish is emblematic of the delicious and creative flavor combinations that Joe Dunn, chef/owner of the Island Merchant and Islander restaurants, and creator of this recipe, devises. It takes a little time to caramelize the onions, but it's worth it as they are magical with the goat cheese. If you don't have cognac for marinating the peaches, you can use whatever is on hand (rum or port would be good) or omit the alcohol entirely.

Try serving a Grüner Veltliner with this fresh and delicious dish. The crisp, lean white wine goes amazingly well with a wide variety of foods and is in perfect harmony with the clean flavors of the peaches and the goat cheese.

MAKE THE CARAMELIZED ONIONS: In a large sauté pan, heat the oil and butter over medium heat. When the butter stops foaming, add the onions, salt, and pepper. Stir well and reduce the heat to medium-low. Cover the pan and cook the onions, stirring occasionally, for 10 minutes. Remove the cover from the pan. Stir the brown sugar into the onions and cook, stirring occasionally, until the onions are a deep golden brown, 30 minutes. Taste and adjust seasoning as needed. Place the onions into a bowl; set aside.

MAKE THE GRILLED CHICKEN AND PEACHES: If using the brandy, while the onions are cooking, place the peaches and brandy into a large bowl; toss well to combine. Preheat a gas grill on medium heat or prepare a moderately hot charcoal fire. Sprinkle ½ teaspoon of the salt and ¼ teaspoon of the pepper evenly over both sides of the chicken breasts. Lightly grease the grill rack. Place the chicken breasts on the rack and cook for 5 minutes. Turn each breast over and cook until the chicken is no longer pink inside, 3 to 5 minutes. Remove the chicken to a plate, tent the plate lightly with foil, and allow the chicken to rest for 5 minutes.

Remove the peaches from the brandy and pat dry with paper towels. Place the peaches cut-side down on the grill. Grill until browned, about 5 minutes. Remove the peaches from the grill. Sprinkle the grilled side of each peach half with the remaining ¼ teaspoon of salt and ¼ teaspoon of pepper; set aside.

MAKE THE GOAT CHEESE AND GREENS: In a medium bowl, toss together the salad greens, oil, lemon juice, if using, salt, and pepper. Taste and adjust seasoning as needed.

Place equal portions of the salad greens on 4 plates. Drizzle 1 tablespoon of the honey evenly over the greens. Place 3 slices of goat cheese over the greens on each plate. Slice the chicken breasts on the diagonal, keeping the slices from each breast together. Fan each chicken breast over the greens and cheese on each plate. Scatter the caramelized onions evenly over the chicken. Place the peach halves grilled-side up around the chicken and greens. Drizzle the remaining tablespoon of honey evenly over the components on each plate. Sprinkle each plate with a pinch each of salt and pepper, if desired.

. . . .

NOTE ~ A great way to slice rounds of goat cheese is with dental floss (unflavored, of course). It's less messy than using a knife, and the slices keep their shape.

Side Dishes

Sautéed Spicy Green Beans and Tomatoes

COURTESY OF *EDIBLE TORONTO* (ONTARIO, CANADA)
MAKES 4 SERVINGS

Fresh green beans must be properly cooked to be fully appreciated: Cooked too little and they're tough with little flavor; cooked too long and they become gray, mushy, and tasteless; but when cooked to the point where their color is a vibrant green and they have a bit of bite but no crunch, they're perfect. This simple recipe brings out the best of this common summer vegetable and the lightly cooked cherry tomatoes that accompany it.

. . . .

1 pound green beans, stem end trimmed
¼ cup slivered almonds or pine nuts
3 tablespoons extra virgin olive oil
1 small onion, thinly sliced
2 cloves garlic, very finely chopped
½ teaspoon ground cumin
½ teaspoon kosher salt
¼ teaspoon freshly ground black pepper
¼ teaspoon ground coriander
⅛ teaspoon ground cinnamon, optional
⅛ teaspoon ground cayenne, optional
15 cherry or grape tomatoes, halved

Fill a large bowl with water and ice; set aside. In a large saucepan of boiling salted water, add the green beans. Bring back up to a gentle boil and cook for 1 minute. In a colander, drain the beans, then plunge into the ice water. Remove the beans after 1 minute; drain and set aside.

In a large sauté pan or skillet, add the almonds and cook over medium heat, tossing often until fragrant and golden, 4 to 5 minutes. Place the almonds onto a plate; set aside. Wipe the pan clean.

In the same sauté pan or skillet, heat the oil over medium heat. Add the onion and cook, stirring occasionally, until slightly golden, 6 to 7 minutes. Stir in the garlic, cumin, salt, pepper, coriander, and the cinnamon and cayenne, if using, and cook for 1 minute. Add the green beans and stir to coat well with the onion and seasonings. Cook for 2 minutes, stirring occasionally. Add the tomatoes and cook, stirring occasionally, until softened, about 2 minutes.

Place the vegetables onto a serving dish. Sprinkle with the toasted almonds. Serve hot or at room temperature.

Stir-fried Bok Choy with Caramelized Corn

ADAPTED FROM A RECIPE COURTESY OF BETH COLLINS, THE ROSS SCHOOL/*EDIBLE EAST END* (NEW YORK)
MAKES 4 TO 6 SERVINGS

3 tablespoons vegetable oil or
   grapeseed oil

3 cups fresh corn kernels (cut from
   about 6 medium ears of corn) or
   frozen corn kernels (do not thaw)

1 tablespoon very finely chopped
   fresh ginger

2 cloves garlic, very finely chopped

6 cups very thinly sliced bok choy
   (not baby bok choy)

½ teaspoon kosher salt

¼ teaspoon freshly ground black
   pepper

2 tablespoons oyster sauce

You'll adore this easy side dish even if the combination of ingredients seems odd at first—and your kids will like it, too. Pan-roasting the corn kernels caramelizes their natural sugars, and the sweetness makes the dish irresistible. The bok choy provides juicy, crunchy elements if it's not overcooked, so go easy with it. Do not use baby bok choy in this recipe, as it lacks the texture of the mature vegetable.

This dish is great on its own or as a base for grilled tofu or fish.

In a large sauté pan or wok, heat 1 tablespoon of the oil over medium-high heat. Add the corn and cook, stirring occasionally, until lightly browned all over, 3 to 5 minutes. Remove the corn to a bowl; set aside.

In the same sauté pan, heat the remaining 2 tablespoons of oil over medium-low heat. Add the ginger and garlic and cook for 1 minute. Increase the heat to medium-high, add the bok choy, salt, and pepper, and cook, stirring frequently, until the bok choy is tender yet still crisp, 3 to 4 minutes.

Remove the pan from the heat. Stir in the caramelized corn and the oyster sauce. Serve hot or at room temperature.

Roasted Cauliflower with Golden Raisins and Pine Nuts

COURTESY OF MELISSA PASANEN AND RICK GENCARELLI/*EDIBLE GREEN MOUNTAINS* (VERMONT)
MAKES 4 TO 6 SERVINGS AS A SIDE DISH OR 4 SERVINGS OVER PASTA AS A MAIN COURSE

If you've never eaten roasted cauliflower, you've been missing out. The nutty flavor and slightly crispy texture of this locally grown summer vegetable will make memories of waterlogged white cauliflower blobs vanish immediately. It's the rare child who doesn't gobble up cauliflower when made this way. The cauliflower is also delicious tossed with a medium-sized shaped pasta like ziti or gemelli.

1 medium head (2 to 3 pounds) cauliflower, cored and cut into small florets

3 tablespoons extra virgin olive oil

1½ teaspoons kosher salt, plus more if needed

⅓ cup pine nuts

2 medium leeks, white and light green parts only, halved lengthwise and thinly sliced crosswise

¼ teaspoon freshly ground black pepper

¼ teaspoon freshly ground nutmeg or ground cardamom

⅛ teaspoon ground cayenne, optional

½ cup golden raisins, dried currants, or Thompson raisins

Preheat the oven to 400°F. Line a large rimmed baking sheet with parchment paper. Lightly grease the parchment paper.

Spread the cauliflower onto the baking sheet in a single layer. Drizzle the cauliflower with 2 tablespoons of the oil and sprinkle with 1 teaspoon of the salt. Bake for 15 minutes. Stir the cauliflower and bake until it is lightly browned and tender, 10 to 20 minutes.

In a large skillet or sauté pan, cook the pine nuts over medium heat, stirring frequently, until very lightly browned, about 2 minutes. Remove the pine nuts to a dish; set aside. In the same skillet, heat the remaining tablespoon of oil over medium heat. Add the leeks and cook, stirring frequently, until lightly browned, 3 to 5 minutes. Stir in the pepper, nutmeg, cayenne, if using, and the remaining ½ teaspoon of salt. Remove from the heat.

In a large bowl, toss the roasted cauliflower with the leek mixture, pine nuts, and raisins. Taste and adjust seasoning as needed. Great served hot or at room temperature.

Double Corn Spoon Bread

ADAPTED FROM A RECIPE COURTESY OF SAMANTHA IZZO, SIMPLY RED LAKESIDE BISTRO AT ITHACA, NEW YORK/*EDIBLE FINGER LAKES* (NEW YORK)
MAKES 6 SERVINGS

2 cups whole milk

⅓ cup cornmeal

2 cups fresh corn kernels (from 3 to 4 medium ears of corn)

1 large zucchini, finely chopped

1 tablespoon unsalted butter

2 teaspoons kosher salt, plus a pinch

¼ teaspoon freshly ground black pepper

4 large eggs, separated

3 scallions, thinly sliced

½ red bell pepper, seeded and finely chopped

1 jalapeño pepper, seeded and very finely chopped

There's nothing breadlike about this savory pudding. Light and fluffy, it showcases the vibrant colors and bright flavors of fresh, local corn and peppers. Make sure to pop it into the oven just before serving, because its soufflélike consistency will deflate and turn watery if left to rest too long.

Preheat the oven to 425°F. Butter a 1½- to 2-quart shallow casserole pan; set aside.

In a medium saucepan, combine the milk, cornmeal, corn kernels, zucchini, butter, salt, and pepper. Bring to a boil over medium heat, stirring frequently. Reduce the heat and simmer until thickened, 3 to 4 minutes. Remove the pan from the heat and transfer the mixture to a large bowl to cool completely. Whisk in the egg yolks. Stir in the scallions, bell pepper, and jalapeño.

In the bowl of a stand mixer (or a large bowl if using an electric hand mixer), beat the egg whites with a pinch of salt just until soft peaks form. Stir one-quarter of the beaten egg whites into the corn mixture. Using a rubber spatula, gently fold in the remaining egg whites in 2 additions.

Spread the mixture into the prepared pan. Bake until golden and puffed, about 15 to 20 minutes. Serve immediately, straight out of the oven.

Sweet Corn Fritters

COURTESY OF *EDIBLE OJAI* (CALIFORNIA)
MAKES 4 TO 6 SERVINGS

2 cups fresh corn kernels (from about 3 to 4 medium ears of corn)

2 tablespoons all-purpose flour

2 large eggs, separated

¼ cup finely chopped spring onions or scallions

½ teaspoon kosher salt, plus more for sprinkling, if desired

¼ teaspoon smoked paprika

⅛ teaspoon freshly ground black pepper

⅛ teaspoon ground cayenne

¼ cup extra virgin olive oil

1 tablespoon unsalted butter

Much lighter than hush puppies, these corn pancakes are perfectly seasoned and bring out the sweetness of corn kernels freshly cut from their cobs. You might want to consider doubling the recipe; these fritters disappear very quickly. Try serving these with some broiled tomatoes, sour cream, and a refreshing salsa made with chopped avocado, mango, lime, and cilantro, if desired.

In a large bowl, stir together the corn, flour, egg yolks, onions, salt, paprika, pepper, and cayenne. In the bowl of a stand mixer (or a large bowl if using an electric mixer), beat the egg whites until stiff peaks form. Stir one-quarter of the beaten egg whites into the corn mixture. Using a rubber spatula, gently fold the remaining egg whites into the corn mixture in 3 additions.

In a large skillet, heat the oil and butter over medium heat until the butter has melted. Carefully drop some of the corn mixture by tablespoons into the hot oil, taking care not to crowd the pan. Cook each fritter until browned, 2 to 3 minutes. Turn each fritter over and brown the other side, 1 to 2 minutes. Transfer the fritters to a platter lined with paper towels. Sprinkle lightly with salt, if desired. Repeat until all of the corn mixture has been used. Serve hot.

Desserts

Frozen Maple Mousse

COURTESY OF *EDIBLE GREEN MOUNTAINS* (VERMONT)
MAKES 8 TO 10 SERVINGS

1 cup pure maple syrup
  (see headnote)
4 large egg yolks
2 cups heavy cream
Toasted slivered almonds, optional

This is a great ice cream–like dessert that doesn't require the use of an ice cream maker. If you have a fondness for maple syrup, you will love this: It's got a very intense, concentrated maple flavor. For best results, use Grade B maple syrup; "B" just means darker, not inferior.

Pour the maple syrup into the upper bowl of a double boiler or into a large stainless steel or tempered-glass bowl. Place the egg yolks into a medium bowl; set aside.

In the lower pot of a double boiler or in a medium saucepan, add 2 inches of water. Bring up to a simmer. Place the bowl containing the maple syrup on top of the saucepan. Heat the maple syrup to hot (just barely simmering) but not boiling, 4 to 5 minutes. Remove the bowl of maple syrup from the heat.

While continuously whisking the egg yolks in their bowl, slowly add 2 tablespoons of the hot maple syrup to temper the egg yolks (so they will not curdle). Whisk the egg yolk mixture into the bowl of maple syrup.

Place the bowl of maple syrup and egg yolks on top of the saucepan. Cook the mixture, whisking continuously, until it is thick and smooth, 15 to 20 minutes. Remove from the heat. Place a piece of parchment paper directly onto the surface of the maple syrup mixture to prevent a skin from forming. Refrigerate until completely cooled, at least 1 hour.

Using a hand mixer or stand mixer, whip the cream until stiff peaks form. (The cream keeps its shape when you pick up the mixer beater from the bowl.) Stir 3 heaping spoonfuls of the whipped cream into the cooled maple syrup mixture. Gently fold one-third of the remaining whipped cream into the maple syrup mixture. Repeat until all the whipped cream has been folded in.

Pour the mixture into individual ramekins or a freezer-proof serving dish. Cover with plastic wrap and place in the freezer for 6 to 8 hours. (The mousse will keep well for up to 2 weeks in the freezer.)

To serve, garnish with toasted almonds, if using.

Blueberry Corn Bread

COURTESY OF JENNIFER KELLER, PECONIC BAKING COMPANY/*EDIBLE EAST END* (NEW YORK)
MAKES 16 SERVINGS

Corn Bread

1 cup yellow cornmeal
1 cup all-purpose flour
½ cup granulated sugar
3 teaspoons baking powder
¼ teaspoon kosher salt
1 cup whole milk
1 large egg, lightly beaten
4 tablespoons butter, melted
1 teaspoon pure vanilla extract
1 pint (2 cups) fresh blueberries

Honey Butter, optional

2 teaspoons melted butter
¼ cup liquid honey

Nothing can compare with the flavor of fresh blueberries in season. Put blueberries together with corn bread, and you're in for a treat. The corn bread is not too sweet, which allows the burst of blueberry goodness to shine through. Great for a light dessert, breakfast, or a snack, the squares are perfect for packing in your picnic basket.

MAKE THE CORN BREAD: Preheat the oven to 400°F. Grease an 8-inch-square baking pan; set aside. In a large bowl, whisk together the cornmeal, flour, sugar, baking powder, and salt; set aside.

In a medium bowl, whisk together the milk, egg, butter, and vanilla. Add the liquid ingredients to the large bowl containing the dry ingredients and stir with a rubber spatula until just combined. Gently fold in the blueberries.

Pour the mixture into the prepared pan. Bake until the corn bread is lightly browned and firm to the touch and a toothpick inserted into the center comes out clean, 30 to 40 minutes. Cool in the pan on a cooling rack.

MAKE THE HONEY BUTTER, if using: Whisk together the butter and honey in a small bowl. Brush all or some of the mixture onto the corn bread about 10 minutes after it is removed from the oven. Serve warm or at room temperature.

Caramel Ice Cream with Caramel Sauce and Fleur de Sel

COURTESY OF TRACEY RYDER/*EDIBLE COMMUNITIES*
MAKES 6 SERVINGS

Ice Cream

¼ cup plus 2 tablespoons
   granulated sugar

2 tablespoons water

½ teaspoon freshly squeezed lemon
   juice

1 cup heavy cream

5 large egg yolks

2 teaspoons fleur de sel sea salt,
   plus more for sprinkling

1½ cups whole milk

1 tablespoon pure vanilla extract

Caramel Sauce

½ cup water

1 cup granulated sugar

1 cup heavy cream

1 teaspoon pure vanilla extract

This is a dreamy custard-style ice cream that is not too sweet at all. The caramel sauce actually tastes more along the lines of a burnt caramel sauce so it adds depth of flavor instead of sweetness. The sprinkle of fleur de sel adds just the right amount of saltiness, which balances the whole dessert.

The recipe works best if you can make it at least one day ahead of when you plan to eat it.

MAKE THE ICE CREAM: In a heavy 2- to 4-quart saucepan, combine ¼ cup sugar, the water, and lemon juice. Cook over medium-high heat, stirring with a wooden spoon, until the sugar dissolves, 1 to 2 minutes. Stop stirring and continue cooking until the syrup is amber colored, 5 to 10 minutes. Swirl while cooking and watch closely to ensure the syrup doesn't burn.

Remove the pan from the heat and pour ¼ cup of the cream into the hot syrup (be careful not to burn yourself as it may splatter). Stir with a wooden spoon until smooth. Place over medium heat and cook until the mixture barely begins to boil, about 5 minutes. Remove from the heat, cover, and set aside.

In a medium bowl, combine the egg yolks, fleur de sel, the remainng 2 tablespoons of sugar, and the remaining ¾ cup of cream. Whisk until smooth, then stir in the milk.

Pour the milk mixture into the warm caramel syrup and cook over medium heat, stirring constantly with a wooden spoon and keeping the custard at a low simmer, until it lightly coats the back of a spoon, 4 to 8 minutes. Make sure not to let the custard boil. In a fine-mesh sieve set in a large bowl, strain the custard. Stir in the vanilla.

Allow the mixture to cool, then cover and refrigerate for at least 4 hours and up to 24 hours. Pour the custard into an ice cream maker and freeze according to the instructions. Transfer the ice cream to a covered container and freeze until firm, at least 3 hours.

MAKE THE CARAMEL SAUCE: In a large, heavy-bottomed saucepan, combine the water and sugar and cook over medium heat. Stir until the sugar dissolves completely and the syrup is clear. Stop stirring and continue cooking until the syrup turns a golden brown. Once the syrup begins turning amber colored, it will burn quickly, so watch it very closely. You want a medium-brown-colored syrup, but not burned.

Once you have the correct color, remove the pan from the heat and slowly stir in the heavy cream, a little at a time, trying to avoid splattering (to prevent getting burned).

Once the cream is incorporated, place the pan over low heat and stir until the caramel and cream are fully integrated. You may need to use a whisk to get it fully blended. Let it simmer over low heat for another minute. Remove from the heat and stir in the vanilla.

Just before serving, stir some of the caramel sauce (should be cooled to room temperature and stirred in without reheating) into the ice cream, adding a sprinkle of fleur de sel directly onto the ribbon of caramel sauce, then fold together with the ice cream so that the salt and sauce are loosely blended into the ice cream. Be careful not to overmix. Serve immediately, along with the rest of the sauce, either warm or at room temperature. The sauce can also be stored in a canning jar and refrigerated for up to a month.

Berry Ricotta Pie

COURTESY OF *EDIBLE JERSEY* (NEW JERSEY)
MAKES ONE 9-INCH PIE

This is traditionally an Italian Easter pie, but here it has been "Americanized" and "summerized" with the addition of berries—raspberries, blueberries, blackberries, or an assortment.

The Flaky Piecrust recipe makes two crusts, but this recipe calls for only one. You can halve the piecrust recipe, but if you're going to make a crust from scratch, you might as well make two, then freeze the other crust, tightly wrapped, for up to three months—or you can double the filling recipe to make two pies. (If you're short on time but don't want to purchase a store-bought dessert, there's nothing wrong with using a frozen pie crust instead of making one from scratch.)

1 piecrust, preferably Flaky Piecrust, page 254
2 large eggs
¼ cup plus 2 tablespoons granulated sugar
½ cup half-and-half
1½ cups ricotta cheese
1½ teaspoons finely grated orange zest
1½ tablespoons freshly squeezed lemon juice
½ teaspoon pure vanilla extract
1½ tablespoons all-purpose flour
¼ teaspoon kosher salt
1½ tablespoons Grand Marnier, optional
½ pint (1 cup) fresh berries, such as raspberries, blueberries, blackberries, or a mix

Preheat the oven to 350°F. On a lightly floured surface, roll 1 disk of the piecrust dough into a round, 12 inches in diameter. Transfer the dough to a 9-inch-diameter glass pie plate. Crimp the edge of the crust with your fingers or a fork.

In a medium bowl, add the eggs and sugar; whisk until well blended. Whisk in the half-and-half and ricotta. Add the orange zest, lemon juice, vanilla, flour, salt, and Grand Marnier, if using, and whisk well to combine. Pour the ricotta mixture into the piecrust. Scatter the berries evenly over the surface of the ricotta mixture.

Bake for 15 minutes. Reduce the oven temperature to 300°F. Bake until the center of the pie is just firm to the touch and no longer jiggles when the pan is gently shaken, 50 minutes to 1 hour 5 minutes more. Cool the pie completely on a rack before serving.

Flaky Piecrust

COURTESY OF GAIL GORDON OLIVER/*EDIBLE TORONTO* (ONTARIO, CANADA)
MAKES 2 PIE CRUSTS

2½ cups all-purpose flour
1 tablespoon granulated sugar
½ teaspoon kosher salt
10 tablespoons (1¼ sticks) cold unsalted butter, cut into ½-inch cubes
⅓ cup cold nonhydrogenated vegetable shortening or lard, divided into small chunks
½ cup ice-cold water

This is a wonderful all-purpose crust for both sweet and savory pies (just omit the sugar when using with savory fillings). Adding a bit of shortening along with the butter makes the dough easy to work with, while providing the rich flavor of an all-butter crust.

If only one crust is needed for a recipe, the second crust can be wrapped in plastic and then sealed in a plastic bag and frozen for up to three months. Transfer to the refrigerator twenty-four hours prior to rolling.

In the work bowl of a food processor fitted with a steel blade, add the flour, sugar, and salt. Pulse until combined. Add the butter and shortening. Cut in using a few short pulses until the mixture contains pea-sized lumps of butter and shortening. Add 6 tablespoons of the ice water and pulse, adding more water gradually if needed, just until the dough is moist enough to clump together when squeezed (it will still appear quite crumbly).

On a lightly floured flat surface, gently knead the dough into a ball. Cut the dough into 2 equal pieces. Flatten each piece into a disk about 4 inches in diameter. Wrap each disk in plastic wrap. Chill in the refrigerator for at least 2 hours or up to 3 days.

FIRST COURSES

Roasted Butternut Squash Soup   257

Smoked Trout Bruschetta with Romesco Sauce   258

MAIN COURSES

Bay-Scented Chicken with Figs   259

Halibut and Pancetta Stew   260

Pan-Seared Medallions of Pork with Apples   263

Chicken, Apple, and Butternut Squash Barlotto   264

Grilled Quail with Hazelnuts, Apricot Curry Sauce,   265
  and Wild Huckleberry Coulis

SIDE DISHES

Tomato and Ginger Chutney   266

Kohlrabi with Bacon   269

Mashed Sweet Potatoes with Candied Kumquats   270

Garlicky Brussels Sprouts Amandine   271

Creamy Pumpkin Grits with Brown Butter   272

Sausage and Rice Stuffing   274

DESSERTS

Triple Gingerbread with Brandied Apples   275

Double Chocolate Pear Cake   276

Grandmother's Apple Cake   277

Harvest Cake with Cider-Cinnamon Frosting   278

Lattice-Topped Apple Pie   280

Persimmon Rum Cake   283

fall

First Courses

Roasted Butternut Squash Soup

COURTESY OF GAIL GORDON OLIVER/*EDIBLE TORONTO* (ONTARIO, CANADA)
MAKES 8 SERVINGS

This is a thick puree of butternut squash and pumpkin, scented with nutmeg and thyme. You could use the flesh of a whole pumpkin for the soup, but the texture and flavor of pumpkins vary quite a bit, so using canned is an easy way to add richness. Roasting the squash intensifies its flavor as it softens and caramelizes in the oven.

1 butternut squash (3 to 4 pounds), peeled, seeded, and cut into ¾-inch chunks

¼ cup extra virgin olive oil

2 teaspoons kosher salt, plus more if needed

2 medium onions, chopped

3 medium carrots, chopped

2 stalks celery, chopped

¼ teaspoon freshly grated nutmeg

2 sprigs fresh thyme (tied together with kitchen twine) or ½ teaspoon dried thyme leaves

6 cups chicken broth or vegetable broth, plus more if needed

1 can (14 ounces) pure pumpkin puree (unsweetened)

¼ teaspoon freshly ground black pepper, plus more if needed

Heavy cream for drizzling, optional

2 tablespoons finely chopped chives

Preheat the oven to 425°F. In a large bowl, combine the butternut squash, 2 tablespoons of the oil, and ½ teaspoon of the salt. On a 9- by 13-inch rimmed baking sheet, spread the squash in a single layer. Bake until the squash is lightly browned and tender, 40 to 45 minutes.

In a large stockpot, heat the remaining 2 tablespoons of the oil at medium heat. Add the onions and cook, stirring occasionally, until softened, about 5 minutes. Add the carrots and celery and cook, stirring occasionally, for 5 minutes. Stir in the nutmeg and thyme. Add the broth, pumpkin puree, the remaining 1½ teaspoons of salt, and the pepper. Stir to combine. Bring to a boil. Reduce the heat, cover the pot, and simmer until the vegetables are tender, about 30 minutes.

Add the roasted squash to the stockpot, stirring well to combine. Return the contents to a boil, reduce the heat, cover the pot, and simmer for 10 minutes. If using fresh thyme, remove the sprigs.

Puree the soup in the pot until smooth using a handheld blender (or in very small batches using a countertop blender). Return to the pot if needed. Simmer for an additional 10 minutes. Taste and adjust seasoning as needed. (If the soup is too thick after it has finished cooking, you can add additional broth, preferably cooked with the soup for a couple of minutes to blend it properly. Adjust seasoning as needed.)

Serve hot in bowls, drizzled with heavy cream, if using, and sprinkled with chives.

Smoked Trout Bruschetta with Romesco Sauce

COURTESY OF WOODWARD'S GARDEN, SAN FRANCISCO/*EDIBLE SAN FRANCISCO* (CALIFORNIA AND THE WEST)
MAKES 6 SERVINGS; ROMESCO SAUCE MAKES ABOUT 2 CUPS

Romesco Sauce

½ cup whole hazelnuts

2 medium red bell peppers

6 sun-dried tomatoes (packed in oil) plus 2 tablespoons sun-dried-tomato oil

1 large clove garlic, chopped

1 canned chipotle chile pepper in adobo sauce, plus more if needed

1 cup lightly packed cilantro leaves or flat-leaf parsley leaves

2 teaspoons sherry vinegar or red wine vinegar

¼ cup extra virgin olive oil

½ teaspoon kosher salt, plus more if needed

¼ teaspoon freshly ground black pepper, plus more if needed

Bruschetta Toasts

1 baguette, sliced diagonally into ½-inch-thick pieces

¼ cup extra virgin olive oil

1 large clove garlic

Bruschetta Topping

1 teaspoon sherry vinegar

Pinch of kosher salt

Pinch freshly ground black pepper

2 teaspoons extra virgin olive oil

1½ cups coarsely chopped peppery greens, such as arugula, kale, watercress, or cilantro

½ pound smoked trout (bones and skin removed), broken into bite-sized pieces

Bell peppers are at their peak in early fall. Romesco, a classic Spanish sauce, illuminates their magnificence in a thick, nutty compound laden with hot chiles and garlic, the perfect foil for smoked trout and lightly dressed peppery greens. Serve these as a passed appetizer or as a plated course.

The leftover romesco sauce can be spread on chicken, then grilled or baked. It's also good with shrimp and pasta. Any leftover sauce can be stored in a sealed container in the refrigerator for up to one week.

MAKE THE ROMESCO SAUCE: Preheat the oven to 350°F. Place the hazelnuts on a rimmed baking sheet. Toast in the oven until fragrant and golden, 10 to 15 minutes. Place the nuts on a dish towel; cool slightly. Rub the nuts together in the towel until most of their skins come off. Cool completely.

Roast the bell peppers on a gas burner set to medium heat, turning occasionally, until their skins turn black and blister and the bell peppers begin to collapse, 8 to 10 minutes. (Alternately, preheat the oven to 450°F and roast the bell peppers directly on the middle oven rack, turning occasionally, until their skins darken and blister and the bell peppers begin to collapse, 20 to 30 minutes.) In a large bowl, place the bell peppers, cover with plastic wrap, and let rest for 15 minutes.

Using paper towels or a dish towel, peel the skins off the bell peppers, cut them in half, and remove the stems and seeds (do not run the peppers under running water to peel and seed; this will remove flavorful oils). Discard the skins, stems, and seeds. Set the bell peppers aside.

Place the hazelnuts into the work bowl of a food processor. Pulse on and off until the hazelnuts are very finely chopped. Add the sun-dried tomatoes and pulse until incorporated. Add the roasted bell peppers and pulse until incorporated. At this point, the mixture will have the consistency of a thick paste. Add the garlic, chipotle chile, cilantro, and vinegar and pulse until pureed. With the machine running, slowly add the sun-dried-tomato oil and olive oil. The sauce should be brightly flavored and spicy. Add the salt and pepper. Taste and adjust the seasoning as needed.

MAKE THE BRUSCHETTA TOASTS: Preheat the oven to 400°F. On a rimmed baking sheet, place the baguette slices in a single layer. Brush lightly with the olive oil. Toast in the oven until crisp and lightly golden, 8 to10 minutes, turning once. Rub each slice of bread with garlic. Set aside to cool.

PREPARE THE BRUSCHETTA TOPPING: In a small bowl, whisk the vinegar with the salt and pepper, then whisk in the olive oil. Toss the greens in the vinaigrette.

To assemble the bruschetta, spread each bruschetta toast generously with the romesco sauce. Top each toast evenly with some greens and one or two pieces of the trout. Serve immediately.

Main Courses

Bay-Scented Chicken with Figs

COURTESY OF *EDIBLE EAST BAY* (CALIFORNIA)
MAKES 4 SERVINGS

The enchanting scent that lingers in your memory after an autumn walk in the hills of East Bay, California, is likely to be from the leaves of the native bay tree. This recipe brings that scent to the dinner table in a perfect commingling with other local ingredients. Have fun with this recipe and play around with additional fresh or dried fruits or other flavorings instead of using the prunes and olives listed here. Serve with basmati rice or other grains, if you like; it will absorb the luscious sauce.

1 teaspoon kosher salt

½ teaspoon freshly ground black pepper

4 chicken legs or 1 chicken (about 3½ pounds), cut into quarters

2 tablespoons extra virgin olive oil

2 medium onions, halved and thinly sliced

2 cloves garlic, finely chopped

½ teaspoon ground cumin

2 tablespoons all-purpose flour

½ cup dry white wine

1½ cups chicken broth

6 fresh figs or 8 dried figs, cut into quarters

8 pitted prunes, cut into quarters, optional

½ cup drained green olives, pitted and halved, or ¼ cup drained and rinsed capers, optional

5 fresh bay leaves or 2 dried bay leaves

2 sprigs fresh thyme (tied together with kitchen twine) or ½ teaspoon dried thyme

Sprinkle ½ teaspoon of the salt and ¼ teaspoon of the pepper evenly over the chicken pieces. In a large sauté pan, heat the oil over medium-high heat. Add the chicken pieces skin-side down and cook until the skin is deeply browned, 3 to 5 minutes. Turn over each piece and brown the other side for about 2 minutes. Remove the chicken to a platter.

Reduce the heat to medium. Add the onions and cook, scraping the bottom of the pan and stirring occasionally, until softened, about 5 minutes. Add the garlic and cumin and cook, stirring, for 1 minute. Stir in the flour and cook, stirring, for 2 minutes. Whisk in the wine and cook, stirring, until the mixture is smooth, about 2 minutes. Slowly whisk in the chicken broth and cook, stirring, until smooth. Add the figs; prunes and olives, if using either or both; the bay leaves; thyme; and the remaining ½ teaspoon of salt and ¼ teaspoon of pepper, and stir well to combine. Add the chicken pieces and any juices in a single layer.

Bring the sauce to a boil, cover the pan, reduce the heat, and simmer until the chicken is tender and no longer pink inside, 40 to 45 minutes.

To serve, remove the chicken from the pan. Remove the bay leaves and thyme sprigs from the sauce with tongs and discard. Stir the sauce well and press down a bit on some of the figs and prunes to release some of their flavors into the sauce. Pour the sauce onto a shallow platter and place the chicken on top. Spoon some of the sauce over the chicken and serve immediately.

Halibut and Pancetta Stew

COURTESY OF EZRA TITLE, CHEZVOUS DINING IN TORONTO/*EDIBLE TORONTO* (ONTARIO, CANADA)
MAKES 6 SERVINGS

2½ pounds boneless, skinless wild Pacific halibut fillet or other firm-fleshed fish, cut into 1½-inch pieces

1 teaspoon kosher salt, plus more if needed

½ teaspoon freshly ground black pepper, plus more if needed

2 tablespoons extra virgin olive oil

1 tablespoon unsalted butter

¼ pound pancetta, cut into ½-inch pieces

1 medium onion, finely chopped

2 stalks celery, finely chopped

1 medium carrot, finely chopped

2 cloves garlic, very finely chopped

¼ teaspoon dried thyme

1 tablespoon all-purpose flour

2½ cups chicken broth or fish broth

⅔ cup amber ale

Juice and finely grated zest of 1 Meyer lemon or ½ traditional lemon

1 medium parsnip, cut into ¼-inch dice

1 medium sweet potato, cut into ¼-inch dice

¼ cup heavy cream

½ head escarole, cored and roughly chopped

This recipe was created by Ezra Title, chef and owner of Chezvous Dining in Toronto, who has developed numerous recipes containing beer for Ontario Craft Brewers. Ezra used Old Credit Amber Ale in developing this recipe, but you can try your own local amber ale. This is a beautifully satisfying dish that is elegant enough for a dinner party. Serve it in large soup bowls accompanied by crusty bread and provide your guests with soup spoons—they'll want to savor every last drop of the incredibly delicious sauce.

Pat the halibut pieces dry. Sprinkle with ½ teaspoon of the salt and ¼ teaspoon of the pepper. In a large sauté pan, heat 1 tablespoon of the oil and 1½ teaspoons of the butter over medium-high heat. Add half of the halibut pieces and cook until lightly browned on the bottom, about 3 minutes. Turn the pieces and cook until lightly browned, 1 to 2 minutes (do not cook through). Remove the halibut to a platter. Repeat with the remaining tablespoon of oil, 1½ teaspoons of butter, and the halibut. Set aside.

Reduce the heat to medium. In the same sauté pan, add the pancetta and cook, stirring frequently, until browned, about 5 minutes. Pour off all but 2 tablespoons of the fat in the pan. Add the onion and the remaining ½ teaspoon of salt and ¼ teaspoon of pepper and cook, stirring occasionally, for 3 minutes. Add the celery and carrot and cook, stirring occasionally, for 4 minutes. Stir in the garlic and thyme and cook for 1 minute. Add the flour and stir for 3 minutes.

Slowly stir in the broth, ale, and lemon juice. Bring to a boil. Reduce the heat and simmer for 5 minutes. Stir in the parsnip and sweet potato and cook until tender, 10 to 15 minutes. Add the cream and escarole and cook, stirring, until the escarole is slightly wilted.

Return the halibut and any juices to the pan. Cover the pan, reduce the heat, and simmer gently until the halibut is barely cooked through, 4 to 6 minutes. Taste and adjust seasoning as needed. Garnish with lemon zest and serve immediately.

Pan-Seared Medallions of Pork with Apples

COURTESY OF IOWA CITY'S NEW PIONEER CO-OP/*EDIBLE IOWA RIVER VALLEY* (IOWA)
MAKES 4 SERVINGS

October is National Pork Month, according to the National Pork Board. Although pork is big business in Iowa, there are a lot of small farmers doing great things with pork the all-natural way and without conventional confinement. One is Grass Run Farms in Dorchester, Iowa, which raises heritage varieties of pork without antibiotics or hormones. Farmers Ryan and Kristine Jepsen also raise grass-fed beef and humanely raised veal. In their spare time, the Jepsens are actively working to create a strong local food system in northeast Iowa through the Northeast Iowa Food & Farm Coalition.

This recipe combines pork with apples, two local flavors that demonstrate the beauty of a simple classic.

- 1 pork tenderloin (about 1 pound)
- 4 tablespoons unsalted butter
- 4 medium firm-fleshed apples, such as Granny Smith or Cortland, peeled, halved, cored, and cut into thin slices
- 1 teaspoon granulated sugar
- ½ teaspoon kosher salt, plus more if needed
- ¼ teaspoon freshly ground black pepper, plus more if needed
- 1 tablespoon extra virgin olive oil
- 2 large shallots, very finely chopped
- 1 tablespoon chopped fresh thyme leaves or 1 teaspoon dried thyme
- ½ cup apple brandy, such as Calvados
- 1 cup heavy cream
- ¼ cup apple cider or juice

With a large, sharp knife, cut the tenderloin into 4 equal lengths. Cut each length lengthwise again into 3 slices. On a clean counter or work surface, lay out a 12-inch sheet of plastic wrap or parchment paper. Place the pork slices cut-side up on the plastic wrap or parchment paper, leaving a 2-inch space between them. Cover the slices with another 12-inch sheet of plastic wrap or parchment paper. Using a mallet, pound each slice to a thickness of ¼ inch.

In a 10-inch skillet, melt 2 tablespoons of the butter over medium-high heat. Add the apple slices and sugar and cook until the underside is golden brown, 3 to 4 minutes. Turn and cook until the other side is golden brown, 3 to 4 minutes. Place the apple slices into a shallow dish; cover and set aside. Using a dry paper towel or dish towel, carefully wipe the pan clean.

Sprinkle the salt and pepper evenly over both sides of the pork medallions. In the same skillet used to cook the apple slices, heat the oil and 1 tablespoon of the butter over medium-high heat. Add 6 of the pork medallions and cook until lightly browned on both sides and slightly pink inside when cut slightly with a knife, 1 to 2 minutes per side. Transfer the medallions to a plate and make a tent with foil around them to keep the meat warm. Repeat with the remaining 6 pork medallions, adding them to the plate, then re-covering with the foil.

In the same skillet, melt the remaining tablespoon of butter over medium heat. Add the shallots and thyme and cook, stirring occasionally, until softened, about 2 minutes.

Add the apple brandy and cook, scraping up any browned bits, until the liquid is slightly reduced and thickened, about 1 minute. Stir in the cream and cider. Increase the heat to medium-high and cook, stirring occasionally, until the sauce is slightly thickened and coats the back of a spoon, 4 to 6 minutes. Remove from the heat. Taste and adjust seasoning as needed.

To serve, arrange 3 pork medallions on each plate. Spoon the sauce over the pork. Top generously with sautéed apples. Serve hot.

Chicken, Apple, and Butternut Squash Barlotto

COURTESY OF BRENDAN VESEY, THE BOOT IN NORFOLK, VIRGINIA/*EDIBLE CHESAPEAKE* (MARYLAND/D.C.)
MAKES 4 TO 6 SERVINGS

1 whole chicken (3½ to 4 pounds),
cut in eighths

2 teaspoons kosher salt, plus more
if needed

½ teaspoon freshly ground black
pepper, plus more if needed

2 tablespoons grapeseed oil or
another neutral-flavored oil

1 medium onion, finely chopped

1 small butternut squash (about
2 pounds), peeled, seeded, and cut
into 1-inch chunks, or
2 medium sweet potatoes, peeled
and cut into 1-inch chunks

2 Stayman or other firm-fleshed
apples, peeled, cored, and cut into
1-inch chunks

½ teaspoon freshly grated nutmeg

5 cups chicken broth, plus more if
needed

1 cup apple cider or 1 additional cup
chicken broth

2 cups pearl barley

2 sprigs fresh rosemary

2 tablespoons unsalted butter

⅓ cup grated firm local sheep's milk
cheese or Pecorino Romano or
Parmigiano-Reggiano

This is a great one-pot meal that showcases the flavors of fall and will make your kitchen smell incredibly good. Barlotto is a risotto-style dish in which the short-grain rice is replaced by pearl barley, which does not require as much tending as rice does when cooking risotto: In this recipe, there's no standing over a pot, ladling in broth, and stirring for twenty minutes. Pearl barley is available at most supermarkets or natural foods stores. The barlotto minus the chicken would be a great side dish on your Thanksgiving table.

This works beautifully with free-range chickens from Full Quiver Farm in Suffolk, Virginia, and Double A Farm in Yale, Virginia, but use the best, freshest chicken you can find. Piedmont cheese from Everona Dairy in Rapidan, Virginia, is perfect in this recipe, but Pecorino Romano or Parmigiano-Reggiano will work if you can't find local cheese.

Preheat the oven to 400°F. Sprinkle each side of the chicken pieces with ½ teaspoon of the salt and ⅛ teaspoon of the pepper. In a large ovenproof sauté pan or Dutch oven with a capacity of at least 5½ quarts, heat the oil over medium-high heat. Place 4 pieces of the chicken in the pan and brown well on both sides, a total of 7 to 8 minutes. Remove the chicken pieces to a plate. Repeat with the remaining 4 pieces of chicken. Set aside.

Pour off and discard all but 2 tablespoons of the oil remaining in the sauté pan. Reduce the heat to medium, add the onion to the pan, and cook, scraping the bottom of the pan and stirring occasionally, for 3 minutes. Stir in the squash, apples, nutmeg, and the remaining 1 teaspoon of salt and ⅛ teaspoon of pepper and cook, stirring occasionally, for 3 minutes.

Stir in the chicken broth, apple cider, barley, and rosemary and bring to a boil. Boil gently for 5 minutes. Place the chicken pieces and any juices on top, skin-side up, in a single layer if possible. Turn off the heat. Cover the pan loosely with foil or parchment paper. Carefully transfer the pan to the oven and bake until the chicken is browned and the juices run clear when pricked with a fork or knife, about 1 hour.

Remove the pan from the oven and place on the stove top. Turn off the oven. Transfer the chicken pieces to a plate. Add the butter and cheese to the hot barlotto in the pan, stirring until the butter is melted. There should still be quite a bit of liquid with the barlotto. If not, add a little chicken broth or water. Taste and adjust seasoning as needed.

To serve, place the barlotto into a large shallow serving bowl and top with the chicken pieces. Serve hot.

Grilled Quail with Hazelnuts, Apricot Curry Sauce, and Wild Huckleberry Coulis

ADAPTED FROM A RECIPE COURTESY OF DALE RASMUSSEN, THE RESORT ON THE MOUNTAIN AT MOUNT HOOD/ *EDIBLE PORTLAND* (OREGON)
MAKES 6 SERVINGS

This quail dish might seem complicated, but it truly isn't, and each component is very versatile. The sauces can be made ahead of time and reheated before serving, and the marinated quail takes just minutes to grill up. What's more, your guests will truly savor the crisp-skinned herbed quail and the two spicy fruit sauce accompaniments. The quail is also fabulous on its own or with only one of the sauces, while the apricot curry sauce is wonderful with chicken and pork, and the coulis can be used with other savory dishes or even as a drizzle for cheesecake, ice cream, or pound cake.

MARINATE THE QUAIL: In a large shallow container, whisk together the oil, garlic, thyme, sage, lemon juice, salt, and pepper. Add the quail and, using your hands, evenly coat the quail with the marinade. Cover the container and place into the refrigerator for at least 1 hour or overnight.

MAKE THE WILD HUCKLEBERRY COULIS: In a small saucepan, add the huckleberries, sugar, water, ginger, cinnamon, and cloves. Bring to a boil, lower the heat, and simmer until the huckleberries are soft, about 20 minutes. Remove the mixture from the heat and allow to cool for about 10 minutes. In a blender, add the huckleberry mixture and blend until smooth. Taste and adjust sweetness as needed; set aside.

MAKE THE APRICOT CURRY SAUCE: In a medium saucepan, heat the oil over medium heat. Add the apricots, shallots, and garlic and cook, stirring occasionally, for 5 minutes. Stir in the curry powder, paprika, salt, Riesling, and cider, and bring to a boil. Reduce the heat and simmer until the apricots are soft, about 15 minutes. Stir in the lemon juice. Remove from the heat and allow to cool for about 10 minutes. Add the apricot mixture to a blender, cover, and blend until smooth. Return the sauce to the saucepan over low heat, stirring occasionally.

Grill the quail: Preheat a grill over medium heat. Remove the quail from the marinade and place skin-side down on the grill. Cook until the skin is well browned, about 10 minutes. Turn the quail over and continue to cook until the meat is cooked through, about 5 minutes.

Just before serving, stir the melted butter into the apricot curry sauce. Taste and adjust seasoning as needed.

To serve, spoon some of the apricot curry sauce onto each plate. Place 2 grilled quail over the sauce. Lightly drizzle the huckleberry coulis over the quail. Garnish with the chopped hazelnuts. Serve immediately.

Quail

1 cup extra virgin olive oil

2 cloves garlic, finely chopped

3 tablespoons finely chopped fresh thyme leaves

3 tablespoons finely chopped fresh sage leaves

2 tablespoons freshly squeezed lemon juice

1 teaspoon kosher salt

¼ teaspoon freshly ground black pepper

12 quail, semiboneless or bone-in, butterflied

½ cup chopped roasted Oregon hazelnuts

Wild Huckleberry Coulis

1 pound huckleberries or blueberries

¼ cup granulated sugar, plus more if needed

1 cup water

1 teaspoon ground ginger

½ teaspoon ground cinnamon

½ teaspoon ground cloves

Apricot Curry Sauce

2 teaspoons extra virgin olive oil

1 cup chopped dried apricots

2 shallots, finely chopped

2 cloves garlic, smashed

2 teaspoons curry powder

1 teaspoon smoked paprika

¼ teaspoon kosher salt, plus more if needed

1 cup Riesling, such as Willamette Valley

1 cup apple cider

1 tablespoon freshly squeezed lemon juice

4 tablespoons unsalted butter, melted

Side Dishes

Tomato and Ginger Chutney

COURTESY OF *EDIBLE BOSTON* (MASSACHUSETTS)
MAKES 6 TO 8 SERVINGS

8 plum tomatoes
3 tablespoons extra virgin olive oil
1 medium onion, finely chopped
3 cloves garlic, very finely chopped
1 serrano chile pepper or 2 jalapeño
   peppers, cored, seeded, and very
   finely chopped
1 (2-inch) knob of ginger, peeled and
   very finely chopped
2 teaspoons ground cumin
1 teaspoon ground coriander
1 teaspoon kosher salt, plus more if
   needed
¼ teaspoon freshly ground black
   pepper, plus more if needed
1 cinnamon stick, optional
¼ cup rice vinegar or cider vinegar
2 teaspoons granulated sugar
¼ cup chopped fresh cilantro leaves
1 tablespoon freshly squeezed lime
   juice, plus more if needed

Here is a brightly flavored relish that makes good use of an abundance of locally grown tomatoes in early fall. It packs a generous ginger punch. Of course, as with any cooking (as opposed to baking) recipe, you can eliminate or add many ingredients at will. If ginger's not your thing, just leave it out. This chutney is great served with lamb, chicken, rice, or bean dishes.

Bring a medium saucepan filled halfway with water to a boil; reduce the heat to a simmer. Have a large bowl of ice water ready. Cut out the stem end of each tomato (a tomato coring tool is ideal for this). Make a small, shallow X in the skin at the other end of each tomato. Using a slotted spoon, gently lower 2 tomatoes into the simmering water. Cook the tomatoes until the skin around the X begins to peel away from the flesh when prodded with a paring knife, 30 to 45 seconds. Using the slotted spoon, remove the tomatoes to the bowl of ice water. Allow them to cool for about 1 minute, then remove from the water. Using a paring knife, peel the skin from each tomato, beginning at the end with the X. Repeat with the remaining tomatoes.

Cut each tomato in half lengthwise. (Note: Regular tomatoes, as opposed to plum, would be cut crosswise.) Using your fingers, remove the seeds from each tomato half; discard the skin and seeds. Cut the tomatoes into ¼-inch dice. Place in a small bowl and set aside.

Drain and wipe dry the saucepan used to blanch the tomatoes. Heat the oil in the saucepan over medium heat. Add the onion and cook, stirring occasionally, until softened, about 4 minutes. Stir in the garlic, serrano chile, ginger, cumin, coriander, salt, pepper, and cinnamon stick, if using, and cook, stirring, for 2 minutes.

Stir in the vinegar, sugar, and reserved tomatoes and bring to a boil. Reduce the heat and simmer the chutney until the tomatoes are soft and the chutney is the desired consistency, 15 to 25 minutes. Depending on the size of your pan and the juiciness of your tomatoes, you might need to add some water if the chutney becomes too thick. Transfer the chutney to a bowl and let cool.

Stir in the cilantro and lime juice. Taste and adjust seasoning as needed. If the chutney is too acidic, add a pinch of sugar to help balance the flavors. Place the chutney in a sealed glass jar and store in the refrigerator for up to 2 weeks.

Kohlrabi with Bacon

ADAPTED FROM A RECIPE COURTESY OF CRISS ROBERTS, *BURLINGTON HAWK EYE/*
EDIBLE IOWA RIVER VALLEY (IOWA)
MAKES 4 SERVINGS

Many people are often stumped by kohlrabi. It looks like a root vegetable, but, in fact, it's part of the cabbage family. (Its German name translates to "cabbage turnip.") The larger the kohlrabi, the tougher it is, so seek out small ones that can be grated raw and used in a slaw or eaten in a salad. Kohlrabi is popular in Eastern Europe and Asia, as well as Central Michigan; Livingston County, Michigan, has even proclaimed itself the Kohlrabi Capital of the World.

This recipe is adapted from an old Shepherd's Seeds cookbook and can be served any time of day.

2 tablespoons unsalted butter

1 tablespoon extra virgin olive oil

1 medium onion, finely chopped

4 kohlrabi bulbs (about 2½ pounds), outer rind removed, cut into ½-inch dice

2 cloves garlic, very finely chopped

½ cup chicken broth

½ teaspoon kosher salt, plus more if needed

¼ teaspoon freshly ground black pepper

2 slices pork or turkey bacon, cooked and crumbled, optional

¼ cup sour cream

In a large sauté pan, heat the butter and oil over medium heat. Add the onion and cook, stirring occasionally, for 2 minutes. Stir in the kohlrabi and cook, stirring occasionally, until lightly browned, about 10 minutes. Stir in the garlic and cook for 1 minute. Add the chicken broth, salt, and pepper. Increase the heat to medium-high and cook, stirring occasionally, until the kohlrabi is tender and the broth has been absorbed, 3 to 4 minutes.

Stir in the bacon, if using. Taste and adjust seasoning as needed. Serve hot, with sour cream on the side.

Mashed Sweet Potatoes with Candied Kumquats

COURTESY OF JESSE GRIFFITHS/*EDIBLE AUSTIN* (TEXAS)

MAKES 6 SERVINGS

5 medium sweet potatoes, peeled and cut into large chunks

¼ cup granulated sugar

1 cup water

12 kumquats, thinly sliced and seeds removed

4 tablespoons unsalted butter

½ cup half-and-half or whole milk, warmed

½ teaspoon kosher salt, plus more if needed

½ teaspoon freshly grated nutmeg, plus more if needed

For traditional Thanksgiving dinners, the flavors remain the same: bird, spice, pumpkin, fruit, and sage. This combination comes about not by chance or whimsy, but through an agrarian imperative—one of the last vestiges of countrywide seasonal eating left in our society. Preserving this connection is now our prerogative. A perfect pairing for Central Texas late-fall dinners is sweet potatoes and kumquats, the tree fruit that matures in Texas in late November, just in time for the local Thanksgiving feast.

In a large saucepan, place the sweet potatoes and cover with cold water. Bring to a boil, lower the heat, and boil gently until tender, 20 to 25 minutes.

In a small saucepan, combine the sugar, 1 cup water, and kumquats. Bring to a boil and continue to boil, stirring occasionally, until the liquid is the consistency of syrup, 10 to 15 minutes. Set aside.

When the sweet potatoes are tender, drain them well in a colander and return them to the pot. Mash them using a potato masher. Stir in the butter, half-and-half, salt, and nutmeg. Taste and adjust seasoning as needed.

In a heatproof serving dish, place the mashed sweet potatoes and scatter the candied kumquats and syrup on top. Serve hot. (This can be made the day before. Cover and refrigerate, then reheat uncovered in a 350°F oven for about 30 minutes; a nice little crust will form on top.)

Garlicky Brussels Sprouts Amandine

COURTESY OF *EDIBLE NUTMEG* (CONNECTICUT)
MAKES 4 TO 6 SERVINGS

You'd never know you were eating Brussels sprouts with this recipe. Shredded like a slaw, and then sautéed with garlic and slivered almonds, the result is a pleasant amalgam of sweet and savory. Because they are a member of the cruciferous vegetable family, Brussels sprouts are loaded with calcium and are also powerful cancer fighters. Of course, they taste best when purchased locally, fresh from the farmers at the market or farm stand.

2 tablespoons slivered almonds

1½ pounds Brussels sprouts, trimmed

2 tablespoons extra virgin olive oil

6 cloves garlic, thinly sliced

1 tablespoon maple syrup

¼ cup water

1 teaspoon kosher salt, plus more if needed

¼ teaspoon freshly ground black pepper, plus more if needed

1 tablespoon cider vinegar, optional

⅓ cup dried cranberries or cherries, optional

In a large sauté pan or skillet, toast the almonds over medium heat, stirring frequently, until very lightly browned, about 2 minutes. Remove the almonds to a dish; set aside. Reserve the pan for later use.

In the work bowl of a food processor fitted with the slicing disk, process the Brussels sprouts in stages until they are all shredded.

In the reserved sauté pan, heat the oil over medium heat. Add the garlic and cook, stirring frequently, until lightly golden, 2 to 3 minutes. Add the Brussels sprouts, increase the heat to medium-high, and cook, stirring occasionally, until the Brussels sprouts begin to turn brown, 2 to 3 minutes. Stir in the maple syrup, water, salt, and pepper. Cover the pan, reduce the heat to medium-low, and cook until the Brussels sprouts are lightly wilted, about 5 minutes.

Remove the cover, stir in the cider vinegar, if using, and cook, stirring occasionally, for 2 minutes. Stir in the dried cranberries, if using, and the almonds. Taste and adjust seasoning as needed. Serve immediately.

Creamy Pumpkin Grits with Brown Butter

ADAPTED FROM A RECIPE COURTESY OF MELISSA PETERSEN/*EDIBLE MEMPHIS* (TENNESSEE)
MAKES 6 TO 8 SERVINGS

Brown Butter

½ cup (1 stick) unsalted butter

3 tablespoons fresh thyme or sage leaves, finely chopped

Grits

3 tablespoons unsalted butter

1 medium onion, very finely chopped

2½ cups water

3 cups whole milk

1¼ teaspoons kosher salt, plus more if needed

¼ teaspoon freshly ground black pepper, plus more if needed

¾ cup stone-ground grits

1½ cups canned pure pumpkin puree or sweet potato puree (unsweetened)

½ cup heavy cream, half-and-half, or whole milk

½ cup finely grated Parmigiano-Reggiano

Grits are rather bland on their own, which is why they are so often overloaded with cheese, cream, and butter to add some flavor. This recipe was inspired by a treatment for risotto, bumping up the flavor with the sweetness of pumpkin, a touch of pungent thyme, and more modest amounts of butter, cream, and cheese. You can even use half-and-half or milk instead of the cream. The grits will still be creamy and flavorful.

MAKE THE BROWN BUTTER: In a 10-inch skillet, melt the butter over medium heat. Cook, stirring occasionally, until the foaming subsides and the butter has turned golden brown, 3 to 4 minutes. Add the thyme and cook for 1 minute, stirring. Pour the butter into a heatproof bowl; cover and set aside.

MAKE THE GRITS: In the same skillet, melt the 3 tablespoons butter over medium-low heat. Add the onion and cook, stirring occasionally, until softened, about 8 minutes; set aside.

In a 4-quart heavy pot, bring the water, milk, salt, and pepper to a boil over high heat. Slowly add the grits to the pot in a thin stream while whisking to blend them into the liquid. Reduce the heat and cook the grits at a bare simmer (adjusting heat as necessary), stirring frequently with a long-handled whisk and scraping the bottom and sides of the pot to prevent scorching, until the grits are thickened to the consistency of porridge, 30 to 35 minutes. If the grits become too dry, add more water or some milk.

Add the cooked onion and the pumpkin puree and cook, stirring continuously, for 3 minutes. Remove from the heat. Stir in the cream and cheese. Taste and adjust seasoning as needed. Spoon into individual cereal or soup bowls and serve immediately, drizzled with the brown butter.

Sausage and Rice Stuffing

COURTESY OF JESSE GRIFFITHS/*EDIBLE AUSTIN* (TEXAS)

MAKES 6 TO 8 SERVINGS

1 or 2 tablespoons rendered duck fat, extra virgin olive oil, or grapeseed oil

½ pound fresh sausage, such as Peach Creek pan sausage, casings removed

½ medium onion, finely chopped

¼ cup chopped fresh sage, rosemary, or thyme leaves, or a combination, or 1 teaspoon dried sage, rosemary, or thyme

2 cups organic brown Texmati rice or brown basmati rice

½ cup dry white wine

4 cups chicken broth or water

½ teaspoon kosher salt, plus more if needed

¼ teaspoon freshly ground black pepper, plus more if needed

¼ pound duck livers or chicken livers, optional

Grace your holiday table with this intensely delicious side dish stuffing that combines the best local artisanal sausages, in this case from Peach Creek Fram, in String Valley, Texas, and Texas-grown rice with duck liver, if you like, and fresh herbs. The perfect accompaniment for roast duck or turkey, this recipe can easily be doubled for a big crowd.

In a large saucepan or Dutch oven, heat 1 tablespoon of the duck fat over medium heat. Add the sausage, breaking it apart with a wooden spoon. Cook the sausage, stirring occasionally, until browned, about 5 minutes. Stir in the onion and herbs and cook until the onion is softened, about 5 minutes. Add the rice, stir well to coat with the other ingredients and cook, stirring occasionally, for 2 minutes.

Increase the heat to high. Stir in the wine and cook until it has completely evaporated. Stir in the chicken broth, salt, and pepper. Bring to a boil. Reduce the heat, cover the pot with the lid, and simmer until the rice is tender and the liquid has been absorbed.

If using the livers, in a small pan, heat 1 tablespoon of duck fat over medium-high heat. Add the livers and cook until browned, 1 to 2 minutes. Turn them over and cook the other side until browned, about 1 minute. Cool slightly, then coarsely chop them; set aside.

Stir the livers into the rice. Taste and adjust seasoning as needed. Serve hot.

Desserts

Triple Gingerbread with Brandied Apples

COURTESY OF LOLA WYKOFF, THE CAFÉ AT ROSEMONT, LAMBERTVILLE, NEW JERSEY/
EDIBLE JERSEY (NEW JERSEY)
MAKES 6 TO 8 SERVINGS

This is a family recipe that's been tweaked with the addition of candied and fresh ginger. For many people, the fragrance of gingerbread baking always signifies the start of autumn. This is a special treat, with or without the brandied apples, and it is a crowd-pleaser topped with ice cream or freshly whipped cream. (The recipe is easy to double.)

MAKE THE GINGERBREAD CAKE: Preheat the oven to 350°F. Butter and sugar an 8-inch-square baking pan. In the bowl of a stand mixer (or a large bowl if using an electric hand mixer), cream the butter and brown sugar for 3 to 4 minutes. Add the molasses, corn syrup, egg, and grated ginger and beat until well blended.

In a medium bowl, whisk together the flour, baking soda, ground ginger, and salt. Add the dry ingredients alternately with the buttermilk to the molasses mixture in 3 additions until blended. Stir in the candied ginger. Pour the batter into the prepared pan.

Bake until the center of the cake springs back when gently pressed and a toothpick inserted into the center comes out clean, 35 to 40 minutes. Cool on a rack for about 15 minutes before removing the cake from the pan. Continue to cool the cake on a rack.

MAKE THE BRANDIED APPLES: In a large saucepan, heat the butter, applejack, brown sugar, and salt over medium heat until the butter has melted and the mixture is bubbling. Stir in the apples. Bring back up to a gentle boil, reduce the heat, and simmer, stirring very gently after 4 minutes, until the apples soften but are not mushy, 8 to 9 minutes.

To serve, spoon some of the brandied apples (warm or at room temperature) around each piece of cake.

Gingerbread Cake

½ cup (1 stick) unsalted butter, room temperature

½ cup firmly packed dark brown sugar

¼ cup unsulphured molasses

¼ cup dark corn syrup

1 large egg

1 (2-inch) knob of ginger, peeled and grated

1½ cups all-purpose flour

1 teaspoon baking soda

1 tablespoon ground ginger

½ teaspoon kosher salt

½ cup buttermilk

⅓ cup finely chopped candied ginger

Brandied Apples

2 tablespoons unsalted butter

¼ cup applejack, apple brandy (such as Calvados), or brandy

3 tablespoons dark brown sugar

⅛ teaspoon kosher salt

3 cooking apples, such as Rome or Granny Smith, peeled, cored, and thinly sliced

Double Chocolate Pear Cake

COURTESY OF *EDIBLE TORONTO* (ONTARIO, CANADA)
MAKES 16 SERVINGS

1½ cups all-purpose flour

⅔ cup granulated sugar

1 teaspoon baking powder

1 teaspoon baking soda

⅛ teaspoon kosher salt

¼ cup unsweetened cocoa powder

¾ cup semisweet chocolate chips

3 ripe pears, such as Bosc or an heirloom variety, peeled, cored, and chopped

1 tablespoon freshly squeezed lemon juice

1 large egg

¾ cup whole milk

⅓ cup vegetable oil or grapeseed oil

1 teaspoon pure vanilla extract

Banana chocolate chip cake is a classic that achieves its moist texture from mashed bananas. This recipe was created using local Ontario pears to create that same fruity moistness. That, along with cocoa and chocolate chips for superb fudginess, makes this cake a winner, especially when served with vanilla ice cream from a local dairy.

Preheat the oven to 350°F. Lightly grease an 8-inch-square baking pan. Line the bottom of the pan with parchment paper; set aside.

In a large bowl, combine the flour, sugar, baking powder, baking soda, and salt. Sift in the cocoa powder and whisk to combine it with the other ingredients. Stir in the chocolate chips; set aside.

In a large shallow dish, combine the pears and lemon juice. Mash the pears until smooth. Whisk in the egg, milk, oil, and vanilla.

Add the liquid ingredients to the bowl of dry ingredients. Stir just until blended. Spread the batter evenly into the prepared pan.

Bake until the center of the cake springs back when lightly touched (or a toothpick inserted into the center comes out just barely moist), 35 to 40 minutes Let cool on a rack for 15 minutes. Remove the cake from the pan to cool completely before serving.

Grandmother's Apple Cake

COURTESY OF *EDIBLE GREEN MOUNTAINS* (VERMONT)
MAKES 12 SERVINGS

Adapted from a recipe handed down by a beloved grandmother, this moist cake filled with apples and accented with warm spices takes advantage of one of Vermont's best-stored fruits. Prepare it with the glaze when you want to impress or finish a meal with finesse, without the glaze for a wonderful addition to a brunch menu or an indulgent breakfast.

MAKE THE APPLE CAKE: Preheat the oven to 350°F. Grease a 9-inch tube pan. Dust with flour, shaking out any excess flour; set aside.

In a medium bowl, whisk together the flour, cinnamon, baking soda, and salt; set aside.

In a large bowl, whisk together the sugar and oil. Whisk in the eggs and vanilla until well blended. Using a rubber spatula, fold in one-half of the dry ingredients until just blended. Repeat with the remaining dry ingredients. Fold in the apples. The batter will be very thick and sticky. Spoon the batter evenly into the prepared pan. Using the back of a metal spoon, smooth the surface.

Bake until dark golden brown and very firm (not springy) to the touch, 1 hour 5 minutes to 1 hour 10 minutes. Let cool in the pan on a rack for 20 minutes. If using the glaze, place a sheet of wax or parchment paper underneath the rack to catch drips.

MAKE THE CARAMEL GLAZE, if using: While the cake is cooling, in a small saucepan, combine the brown sugar, butter, and cream. Bring to a boil, stirring continuously. Boil for 2 minutes, stirring continuously. Remove from the heat and stir in the vanilla. Set aside.

Turn out the cake onto a flat plate. Invert it onto the rack so the cake is topside up.

If using the glaze, immediately drizzle the hot glaze over the warm cake. Let the cake cool completely before serving.

Apple Cake

3 cups all-purpose flour

1½ teaspoons ground cinnamon

1 teaspoon baking soda

½ teaspoon salt

1½ cups granulated sugar

1 cup grapeseed oil or vegetable oil

3 large eggs

1 teaspoon pure vanilla extract

4 or 5 large apples, such as Rome or Granny Smith, peeled, cored, and cut into ½-inch chunks (to make 4 cups)

Caramel Glaze, optional

½ cup firmly packed light brown sugar

4 tablespoons unsalted butter

2 tablespoons heavy cream

½ teaspoon pure vanilla extract

Harvest Cake with Cider-Cinnamon Frosting

COURTESY OF *EDIBLE RHODY* (RHODE ISLAND)
MAKES 16 SERVINGS

With spices, a hint of brown sugar, and a seriously addictive frosting, this cake is sweet enough to qualify as dessert, but with all those vegetables, you don't need as much oil as you might with regular carrot cake. You may suspect there are too many vegetables, but they'll all blend in fine.

MAKE THE HARVEST CAKE: Preheat the oven to 350°F. Grease a 9-inch-square baking pan. Line the bottom of the pan with parchment paper; set aside.

In a medium bowl, toss together the carrots, parsnip, zucchini, and apple; set aside.

In another medium bowl, whisk together the all-purpose flour, whole wheat flour, baking soda, salt, cinnamon, and ginger; set aside. In a large bowl, whisk together the eggs, granulated sugar, and brown sugar until light and frothy. Add the oil and vanilla, and whisk until blended. Add the flour mixture to the sugar mixture and stir using a rubber spatula until just combined. Add the shredded vegetables and apple and the pecans, if using, and stir until they are completely coated with the batter. Spread the batter evenly into the prepared pan.

Bake on the middle oven rack until the cake is uniformly brown and quite firm when lightly touched in the center, and a toothpick inserted into the center comes out clean, 45 to 55 minutes. Let cool on a cooling rack for 15 minutes, then invert the cake onto the cooling rack. Peel off the parchment paper and invert the cake back onto the rack to continue cooling for at least 1 hour.

MAKE THE CIDER-CINNAMON FROSTING: In a small bowl (or the bowl of a stand mixer), add the butter and cream cheese. Using a hand mixer (or a stand mixer fitted with the paddle attachment), whip the butter, cream cheese, and apple cider together on medium speed until very smooth, about 3 minutes. At low speed, slowly add the powdered sugar and cinnamon and beat until blended. Taste the frosting and add more powdered sugar or cinnamon as needed.

Spread the frosting evenly over the top of the cake, and on the sides if desired. Sprinkle lightly with cinnamon and the chopped pecans, if using. Cover the cake in plastic wrap and refrigerate for at least 1 hour. Serve chilled. Store in a covered container in the refrigerator.

Harvest Cake

2 large carrots, finely shredded or grated

1 large parsnip, finely shredded or grated

1 medium zucchini, finely shredded or grated

1 tart apple, peeled, cored, and finely shredded or grated

1¼ cups all-purpose flour

½ cup whole wheat flour

1½ teaspoons baking soda

¾ teaspoon kosher salt

1 teaspoon ground cinnamon

½ teaspoon ground ginger

3 large eggs

1 cup granulated sugar

¼ cup firmly packed light brown sugar

½ cup grapeseed oil or another neutral-flavored oil

1 teaspoon pure vanilla extract

¾ cup chopped pecans or walnuts, optional

Cider-Cinnamon Frosting

2 tablespoons unsalted butter, softened

¾ cup cream cheese, room temperature

2 teaspoons apple cider

1 cup powdered sugar, plus more if needed

Pinch of ground cinnamon, plus more if needed, and ¼ teaspoon for garnish

¼ cup chopped pecans or walnuts, optional

Lattice-Topped Apple Pie

COURTESY OF *EDIBLE RHODY* (RHODE ISLAND)
MAKES 8 SERVINGS

Pie Dough

½ teaspoon kosher salt

½ cup ice water

3 cups all-purpose flour

2½ teaspoons granulated sugar

9 tablespoons cold unsalted butter,
cut into ¼-inch cubes

6 tablespoons cold leaf lard, cut into
¼-inch cubes

Apple Filling

3 pounds apples (about 7 large),
preferably 3 varieties, peeled,
cored, and thinly sliced

2 tablespoons freshly squeezed
lemon juice

1½ teaspoons potato flour (potato
starch) or all-purpose flour

½ teaspoon ground cinnamon

¼ teaspoon freshly grated nutmeg

¼ teaspoon kosher salt

½ cup granulated sugar

1 tablespoon unsalted butter

Artisan baker Paul Bergeron, of Rhode Island's Sakonnet River Pie, has perfected his piecrust with a time-honored ingredient—leaf lard, the purest form of lard. It is trans fat free and is actually higher in unsaturated fat than butter. A little leaf lard in the pie dough and you can shape, weave, and crimp to your heart's content, and your crust won't brown too quickly either. The potato flour may seem unusual, but it thickens without gumminess. All-purpose flour could also work.

If creating a lattice top seems like too much effort for you, just divide the dough into two equal portions and use one to create a regular top crust. Remember to cut slits in the top before baking to allow steam to escape.

If you prefer to make a vegetarian pie dough, use the Flaky Piecrust (page 254).

MAKE THE PIE DOUGH: In a small bowl, dissolve the salt in the water; set aside.

In the work bowl of a food processor, add the flour and sugar and pulse a few times to combine. Add the butter and lard. Use a few rapid, short pulses just until the mixture is the consistency of pea-sized lumps. Add the reserved saltwater. Pulse just until the dough comes together.

Transfer the dough to a lightly floured surface. Form the dough into a ball. Cut off two-thirds of the dough. Shape it into a ball, flatten it slightly, and wrap it tightly in plastic wrap. Repeat with the remaining one-third of the dough. Refrigerate overnight for best results.

Position the rack in the lowest third of the oven. Preheat the oven to 400°F.

MAKE THE APPLE FILLING: In a large bowl, combine the apples and lemon juice, tossing the apples to coat well. In a small bowl, whisk together the potato flour, cinnamon, nutmeg, and salt, using your fingers to break up any clumps of potato flour. Whisk in the sugar. Add the potato flour mixture to the apples in the large bowl and toss the apples to coat well (your hands are the best tool for this task).

Roll out the dough: On a lightly floured surface, roll the smaller disk of the dough into a round, 12 inches in diameter. Transfer the dough to a 9-inch-diameter glass pie plate. Fold the edge under and form a high rim. Stir the apple filling and carefully pour it, including all juices, into the crust, filling up the sides to within ½ inch of the top edge of the crust and mounding the apples up toward the center of the pie. Dot the filling evenly with the butter. Set aside.

On a lightly floured surface, roll out the larger disk of dough into a round, 13 inches in diameter. Cut the dough into 10 equal-width strips. Arrange 5 strips evenly across the pie, using the longer strips in the center and the shorter strips nearer the edges. Form a lattice by weaving the other 5 strips of dough in and out across the first strips, using the longer strips in the center and the shorter strips nearer the edges. Using a sharp knife, cut the ends of the dough strips to within ½ inch of the outside of the rim of the bottom crust. Gently press the ends of the dough strips onto the outside of the bottom crust. Crimp the edges with your fingers or a fork.

Bake the pie for 15 minutes. Reduce the oven temperature to 375°F and continue to bake until the crust is deep golden (cover the edges of the piecrust with foil if the crust is browning too quickly) and the juices are bubbling thickly, 45 to 55 minutes. Cool on a rack for at least 1 hour before serving.

Persimmon Rum Cake

COURTESY OF *EDIBLE AUSTIN* (TEXAS)
MAKES 8 SERVINGS

Before moving back to Austin, Jessica Maher worked as pastry chef at Savoy in New York City, a busy restaurant with a focus on seasonal and sustainable products. When she created this cake for chef Jesse Griffiths's all-local Thanksgiving feast for *Edible Austin,* Jessica featured persimmons, which are plentiful in Central Texas in the fall season. According to Griffiths, there's no better way to celebrate the "only food holiday" (the day of the year when food is center stage—no presents, no egg hunts, no fireworks) than with food from your own community and a group of people you like, love, or are related to by blood.

Jessica suggests that you enjoy the simple efficiency of the wire whisk when making this recipe or others. You may dismiss it as hopelessly low-tech, but a wire whisk is easy to use, is less complicated to set up and clean than an electric mixer, and takes up little storage space.

Serve the cake as is or with crème fraiche and sliced kumquats.

- 5 to 8 ripe persimmons or 4 to 5 mangoes (if available), peeled and pitted
- 2 tablespoons freshly squeezed lemon juice
- ⅔ cup dried currants
- ½ cup golden raisins
- ¾ cup dark rum
- 1¾ cups walnut halves
- 1½ cups bread flour
- 1½ teaspoons baking soda
- 1 teaspoon kosher salt
- ½ teaspoon ground cloves
- ½ teaspoon freshly grated nutmeg
- 2 cups granulated sugar
- 1 tablespoon grapeseed oil or another neutral-flavored oil
- 1 teaspoon finely grated ginger
- ½ teaspoon finely grated lemon zest
- 1½ teaspoons pure vanilla extract
- ¾ cup whole milk

Preheat the oven to 350°F. Grease and flour a 9-inch-round cake pan or a Bundt or tube pan; set aside.

In a blender or food processor, puree the flesh of 5 persimmons (or 4 mangoes) with 1 tablespoon of the lemon juice. Place the pureed fruit into a 4-cup measuring cup. Process more fruit as needed to measure 2½ cups of puree. Pass the fruit through a fine-mesh strainer over a bowl to remove excess fibers; set aside.

In a small bowl, combine the currants, raisins, and rum; set aside.

Spread the walnut halves on a baking sheet. Bake until toasted, about 10 minutes. Remove the walnuts and chop; set aside. Reduce the oven temperature to 325°F.

In a large bowl, sift together the bread flour, baking soda, salt, cloves, and nutmeg. In a medium bowl, whisk together the persimmon puree, the remaining 1 tablespoon of lemon juice, the sugar, oil, ginger, lemon zest, and vanilla.

Add the puree mixture to the flour mixture. Whisk until just combined. Using a rubber spatula, fold in the milk, the currant mixture, and the walnuts until just combined; do not overmix. Pour the batter into the prepared pan.

Bake until the center of the cake is firm and a toothpick inserted into the center comes out clean, 1 hour 15 minutes to 1 hour 30 minutes. Cool the cake completely in the pan on a cooling rack. When cool, slice and serve.

FIRST COURSES

Mushroom Soup au Gratin   285

Beet Borscht   286

Bubby's Cabbage Borscht   287

Sea Bass Ceviche with Avocado   288

Caramelized Onion Tart   289

The Golden Egg   290

MAIN COURSES

Hoppin' John Supreme   293

Squash, Mushroom, and Sage Strata   294

Seared Pollock with a Ragout of Mussels and   296
    Brussels Sprout Leaves

Slow-Cooked Maple-Cider Brisket   297

Braised Pomegranate Chicken with Walnuts   299

Gingersnap-Crusted Lamb Loin Medallions   300
    with Brandied Fig Sauce

Brew-Braised Lamb Shanks with Apple Butter   301
    and Sauerkraut

Chile-Braised Roasted Meat   302

Elk Steaks in Red Wine Sauce   303

SIDE DISHES

Southern Corn Bread   304

Southern Cooked Greens   305

Roasted Root Vegetables   307

DESSERTS

A Honey of a Cake   308

Chocolate–Brown Ale Cake with Cream   309
    Cheese Icing

winter

First Courses

Mushroom Soup au Gratin

COURTESY OF *EDIBLE TORONTO* (ONTARIO, CANADA)
MAKES 4 SERVINGS

The rich earthiness of mushrooms makes them a prime ingredient for dishes in cooler weather; they're comforting, satisfying, and full of flavor (a boon when there are fewer produce options). Mushrooms are grown in Ontario all year-round, which inspired Gail Gordon Oliver, the publisher of *Edible Toronto*, to make this simple, luscious, and flavorful soup. It's prepared like French onion soup but has the richness of mushrooms instead of onions. Almost a meal in itself, just add a salad, and dinner is ready. The soup's mushroom flavor is more intense the day after it's made, so you might want to cook it ahead and reheat it before finishing it in the oven.

- 2 tablespoons extra virgin olive oil or grapeseed oil
- 1 small onion, halved and very thinly sliced
- ¾ pound assorted fresh mushrooms, such as button, cremini, portobello, shiitake, or oyster, thinly sliced (remove chewy or tough stems)
- 1 teaspoon kosher salt, plus more if needed
- 1 clove garlic, very finely chopped
- ¼ teaspoon dried thyme
- ¼ teaspoon freshly grated nutmeg
- ¼ teaspoon freshly ground black pepper
- 6 cups beef broth, chicken broth, or vegetable broth
- ½ teaspoon finely grated lemon zest
- 4 slices (each ½ inch thick) French bread, lightly toasted
- ¼ pound grated or sliced Swiss, Gruyère, or Emmentaler cheese

In a medium pot, heat the oil over medium heat. Add the onion and cook, stirring occasionally, for 2 minutes. Add the mushrooms and ½ teaspoon of the salt, increase the heat to medium-high, and cook, stirring occasionally, until the mushrooms are golden brown, about 4 minutes. Stir in the garlic, thyme, nutmeg, and pepper and cook for 1 minute. Stir in the beef broth, lemon zest, and the remaining ½ teaspoon of salt. Bring to a boil. Reduce the heat, cover the pot with the lid, and simmer for 25 to 30 minutes. Taste and adjust seasoning as needed.

Place the oven rack about 8 inches from the broiler. Preheat the broiler. Place four 12-ounce ovenproof bowls onto a rimmed baking sheet or the broiler pan.

Ladle the soup evenly into the bowls. Float 1 slice of toast over the soup in each bowl. Top each bowl evenly with the cheese. Place the pan with the soup bowls under the broiler and broil until the cheese is lightly browned and bubbling. Serve immediately.

Beet Borscht

COURTESY OF *EDIBLE IOWA RIVER VALLEY* (IOWA)
MAKES 8 SERVINGS

¾ pound beef short ribs (flanken), each strip cut in half

½ medium onion, finely chopped

½ medium carrot, thinly sliced

¼ cup dried lima beans (soaked in water overnight), optional

8 cups water

5 medium beets (about 2 pounds), peeled

1 medium apple, such as Rome or Granny Smith, peeled, quartered, cored, and sliced

2 tablespoons granulated sugar, plus more if needed

2 teaspoons kosher salt, plus more if needed

¼ cup freshly squeezed lemon juice, plus more if needed

Sour cream, optional

Beet borscht was a signature dish of *Edible Iowa River Valley* publisher Wendy Wasserman's grandmother, whose recipe came straight from her Russian roots and made its way into her family's heart. The recipe was shrouded in secrecy, however, until the day Wendy's father sat his mother down to crack the borscht code. When beets are fresh and flavorful in Iowa (where Wendy had been editor of *Edible Iowa River Valley*) and in the Washington, D.C., area where she now lives, this recipe brings a little bit of Wendy's Russian heritage, and fond memories, into her current life.

When working with beets, take steps to avoid splattering juices—whether that's wearing an apron or gloves, working in the sink, or other measures.

In a large saucepan or Dutch oven, place the short ribs in a single layer and add the onion, carrot, lima beans, if using, and water, making sure the short ribs are completely submerged (add more water if necessary). Bring to a boil, partially cover the pot with the lid, lower the heat, and simmer for 1 hour, occasionally skimming scum from the surface of the liquid with a slotted spoon.

Add the whole beets. Bring the mixture back up to a boil, partially cover the pot, reduce the heat, and boil gently until the beets are crisp-tender when pierced with a paring knife, about 30 minutes. Turn off the heat.

Remove the beets and place them on a plate to cool slightly for 15 minutes. Grate the beets using a food processor or a box grater. Return the grated beets to the pot and stir in the apple slices, sugar, and salt. Bring to a boil, cover the pot, reduce the heat, and simmer for 30 minutes. (Add water as needed if the borscht is too thick.)

Remove the short ribs and any loose bones from the pot. Separate the meat from the bones and membrane; discard the bones and membrane. Shred or cut the meat into bite-sized pieces, and return the meat to the pot.

Stir in the lemon juice. Taste and adjust seasoning as needed. Serve hot, with a dollop of sour cream, if using.

Bubby's Cabbage Borscht

COURTESY OF *EDIBLE TORONTO* (ONTARIO, CANADA)
MAKES 8 SERVINGS

Cabbage is a common base for borscht, although beets are better known. Gail Gordon Oliver's grandmother, Debbie Chodos, who immigrated to Canada from Lithuania as a child, made delicious soups, and her cabbage borscht was a favorite. It took Gail a bit of time to replicate the specific flavors of her version, acting from memory and taste-testing alone. Her grandmother used "sour salt" (citric acid crystals) instead of lemon juice, and chuck instead of short ribs. And she often eliminated the stewing meat altogether, placing raw meatballs into the simmering borscht instead, where they'd soak up the soup's flavors as they cooked.

This borscht features not only cabbage instead of the beets and apple of the previous recipe but also tomatoes and onions, for a very different but irresistible soup. This can be a meal in itself, served with fresh, crusty kimmel bread (seeded rye).

In a large pot or Dutch oven, combine the beef, the roughly chopped onion, carrots, celery, garlic, bay leaf, and water, making sure the beef is well submerged in the water (add more water if needed). Bring to a boil. Reduce the heat and simmer, partially covered, for 1 hour 30 minutes, occasionally removing scum from the surface of the liquid with a slotted spoon.

Using a slotted spoon, remove the beef from the pot and place it in a bowl. In a fine-mesh strainer set in a large bowl, strain the broth; discard the vegetables, bay leaf, and any loose bones. Separate the beef meat from the bones and membrane; discard the bones and membrane. Cut or shred the meat into bite-sized pieces; set aside. (Note: At this stage, you may wish to refrigerate the beef broth overnight and remove the congealed fat before proceeding with the recipe. Refrigerate the meat in a separate container.)

In the same large pot, combine 5 cups of the strained beef broth, the cooked beef, cabbage, the finely chopped onions, tomatoes and their liquid, tomato juice, sugar, salt, and pepper. Stir well, lightly breaking up the tomatoes, and bring to a boil. Reduce the heat, partially cover the pot, and simmer, stirring occasionally, until the cabbage is tender, 1 hour 10 minutes to 1 hour 30 minutes.

Stir in the lemon juice. Taste and adjust seasoning as needed. Serve hot.

2 pounds beef short ribs (flanken), each strip cut in half

1 large onion, roughly chopped

2 large carrots, roughly chopped

2 stalks celery, roughly chopped

1 clove garlic

1 bay leaf

8 cups water, plus more if needed

1 small head green cabbage, halved, cored, and cut into ½-inch chunks

2 medium onions, finely chopped

1 large can (28 ounces) whole tomatoes

3 cups tomato juice

2 tablespoons granulated sugar or light brown sugar, plus more if needed

1 teaspoon kosher salt, plus more if needed

¼ teaspoon freshly ground black pepper, plus more if needed

2 tablespoons freshly squeezed lemon juice, plus more if needed

Sea Bass Ceviche with Avocado

COURTESY OF CLAUD MANN/*EDIBLE OJAI* (CALIFORNIA)
MAKES 6 TO 8 SERVINGS

¾ pound very fresh boneless, skinless sea bass, Pacific halibut, or other firm-fleshed fish, cut into very small dice

3 tablespoons freshly squeezed lime juice

3 tablespoons freshly squeezed lemon juice

2 tablespoons extra virgin olive oil

1 teaspoon dried oregano, preferably Mexican

¼ cup drained pickled, sliced jalapeño peppers (sometimes labeled "Nacho Jalapeños"), very finely chopped, plus 2 tablespoons of the juice

½ medium sweet onion, very finely chopped

¾ cup grape tomatoes, quartered, or 1 medium firm-ripe tomato, cut into very small pieces

½ medium cucumber, peeled, halved lengthwise, seeded, and cut into very small pieces

⅓ cup finely chopped pitted green olives (preferably not brined in vinegar; if they are, rinse well and drain before using)

½ cup (about 3 ounces) very finely crumbled cotija (firm Mexican cheese) or feta cheese

1 serrano chile pepper, very finely chopped

2 tablespoons finely chopped fresh cilantro leaves

Kosher salt, as needed

1 firm-ripe avocado

Thick tortilla chips

Mexican hot chili sauce, such as Cholula

Much of Southern California cuisine is influenced by Mexican flavors, and this *ceviche de cabrilla,* a refreshing marinated fish dish, is wonderful when lemons and avocados are in season in the Ojai Valley. Although the ingredients list is long, this is very simple to make and packs a lot of flavor. Feel free to substitute any fresh, firm, white-fleshed fish if sea bass or halibut are not available.

In a medium bowl, combine the fish, 2 tablespoons of the lime juice, and 2 tablespoons of the lemon juice. Stir well. Cover and refrigerate for at least 3 hours or up to 6 hours, stirring occasionally. In a large colander, drain the fish. Discard the juices.

In a large bowl, whisk together the oil, oregano (rubbed together between your palms first to help release its flavor and aroma), and jalapeño juice. Add the drained fish and stir to combine the ingredients. Add the pickled jalapeños, onion, tomatoes, cucumber, olives, cheese, serrano chile, cilantro, and the remaining 1 tablespoon of lime juice. Toss gently and thoroughly to combine ingredients. Taste and adjust seasoning with salt as needed.

Peel and pit the avocado and cut it into ½-inch cubes. In a small bowl, toss the avocado gently with the remaining 1 tablespoon of lemon juice. Add to the bowl of ceviche and toss gently to combine. Serve with tortilla chips and hot chili sauce.

Caramelized Onion Tart

COURTESY OF *EDIBLE FRONT RANGE* (COLORADO)
MAKES 8 TO 10 SERVINGS

This caramelized onion tart is a classic southern French dish called *pissaladière* (sort of a thick pizza without the tomatoes and cheese), and dates back to the time of the Avignon Papacy. Delectable and versatile, it can be served as an appetizer, brunch item, or with a salad for a light lunch or supper. It's often made with a puff pastry base, so if you don't have time to make the yeast dough, frozen puff dough will work just fine.

MAKE THE CRUST: In a small bowl, add the warm water. Sprinkle with the yeast and sugar. Stir to blend. Let stand until foamy, about 10 minutes.

In the work bowl of a food processor, add the flour and salt; pulse until blended. Add the yeast mixture and 2 tablespoons of the oil; pulse until the dough clumps together, adding more flour by tablespoonfuls if the dough is sticky. Process until a shiny ball forms, about 1 minute. On a lightly floured work surface, turn the dough out and knead until smooth and elastic, 3 to 5 minutes.

Coat a large bowl with the remaining 1 tablespoon of oil. Add the dough to the bowl and turn it to coat with oil. Cover with plastic wrap, then a kitchen towel. Let rise in a warm, draft-free area until doubled in volume, about 1 hour 30 minutes. Punch down the dough; cover and let rise until puffed and almost doubled, about 1 hour. (Now is a good time to make the filling.) Punch down the dough and allow it to relax for 5 to 10 minutes before pressing it into the baking pan.

MAKE THE FILLING: While the dough is in its second rise, in a large skillet or sauté pan, heat the oil over medium-high heat. Add the onions and reduce the heat to medium-low. Cook the onions slowly, stirring occasionally and reducing the heat to low if there is any sign of burning, until the onions are cooked down and very lightly caramelized, 45 to 55 minutes. Add the garlic, salt, pepper, and thyme, and cook, stirring, for 1 minute. Remove the pan from the heat.

Preheat the oven to 450°F. Lightly grease a 9- by 13-inch rimmed baking sheet. Press the dough evenly into the baking pan. Spread the onion filling evenly over the dough, leaving a 1-inch border uncovered around the outside edge. Arrange the anchovy fillets and the olives in a decorative pattern over the onions.

Bake until the bottom and edges of the crust are golden brown, 15 to 20 minutes. Remove from the oven, let cool a bit on a wire rack, and serve warm, drizzled with extra virgin olive oil.

Crust

1 cup warm water (105°F to 115°F)
1 tablespoon active dry yeast
1 teaspoon granulated sugar
2¾ cups (or more) all-purpose flour
1 teaspoon kosher salt
3 tablespoons extra virgin olive oil

Filling

¼ cup extra virgin olive oil, plus
   more for drizzling
3 pounds yellow onions, halved and
   thinly sliced
3 large cloves garlic, very finely
   chopped
½ teaspoon kosher salt
¼ teaspoon freshly ground black
   pepper
1½ teaspoons very finely chopped
   fresh thyme leaves
10 oil-packed anchovy fillets, drained
8 Niçoise or kalamata olives,
   drained, pitted, and halved

The Golden Egg

ADAPTED FROM A RECIPE COURTESY OF ALAIN PASSARD/*EDIBLE SAN FRANCISCO* (CALIFORNIA)
MAKES 6 SERVINGS

6 tablespoons crème fraîche

6 large farm-fresh eggs

6 pinches sea salt

6 pinches freshly ground black pepper

12 drops sherry vinegar

6 heaping teaspoons very, very finely chopped fresh chives

6 teaspoons pure maple syrup

Alain Passard has been making "the golden egg" since 1999, when he first heard cookbook author Patricia Wells describe it in a radio interview. It is a simmered egg topped with vinegar, chives, crème fraîche, and a little maple syrup. It is tasty, but the biggest thrill is in the presentation.

Passard says: "I was so inspired by Wells's description ('an appetizer that properly awakens your palate with a jolt of surprise and a clap of acclamation') that for a millennium celebration high in the Swiss Alps, I hauled (by snowmobile) enough ingredients to make three dozen of the eggs. While blizzardlike winds and snow howled outside, we welcomed the year 2000 with a dip into the golden egg.

"It is easy enough to do at home, and I've since sawed the tops off hundreds of eggs, much to the delight of dinner guests. I use a knife when cutting the tops off the eggs, but a standard egg topper does a somewhat admirable job. Restaurants use a fancy tool called a *toque oeuf* that you can order online."

While ordinary grocery store eggs will suffice, a farm-fresh pastured egg, with its luxuriously rich yolk, raises this dish to the realm of culinary nirvana.

You will need the following tools: a very sharp, thin-bladed slicing knife (preferably not a chef's knife) or an egg topper (*toque oeuf*); sharpening steel; rock salt; one 4-quart saucepan; and six demitasse spoons.

In a small bowl, whip the crème fraîche until smooth. Cover and refrigerate until ready to use.

On a cutting board, gently hold 1 egg with the wider end down. Slowly turn the egg and, sawing back and forth with your knife, carve a groove around the shell about ½ inch from the top. Continue the motion until you hear a light crack. Stop. This signals that you've broken through the shell at this one point. Rotate the shell a bit and continue. Each time you hear a crack, stop and turn the egg. Very slowly and gently, cut your way through the shell until it slices off cleanly. It usually takes 2 to 3 minutes per egg, depending on the thickness of the shell (farm eggs sometimes have very thin shells). Be sure to hone your knife after topping each shell.

Tip the topped egg into a bowl so that the white runs out, all the while keeping the yolk in the shell. Depending on the size of the hole you've made, you can also spill the yolk into the palm of your hand, letting the whites slip through your fingers, and then carefully slide the yolk back into the shell.

Line an empty egg carton with plastic wrap. Gently wipe off the sides of the egg with a damp paper towel and return the egg to the egg carton. Repeat with the remaining 5 eggs. Reserve the topped eggs in the refrigerator, tightly covered, for up to 1 day before serving.

Bring a medium saucepan with 3 inches of water to a simmer. Season each egg with a pinch each of sea salt and pepper, and set the shells in the water. (Don't worry—they float upright.) Cook until the edges of the yolks begin to set, about 3 minutes. Pick up the eggs with your fingers and arrange them upright on a rock salt–lined platter.

With your thumb over the top of a bottle of sherry vinegar, drizzle a couple drops, no more, into each egg. Add chopped chives to the eggs—a heaping teaspoon per egg (Passard measures the amount of chives with a small melon ball scoop). Spoon whipped crème fraîche into each egg until it reaches the top of the shell.

Drizzle each filled egg with maple syrup and serve immediately, being sure to pass diners a demitasse spoon so they can dig right in.

Main Courses

Hoppin' John Supreme

COURTESY OF GIBSON THOMAS/*EDIBLE MARIN & WINE COUNTRY* (CALIFORNIA)
MAKES 6 SERVINGS

Hoppin' John is traditionally served in many parts of the South on New Year's Day. The black-eyed peas are said to bring you good luck in the coming year. This gorgeous and delicious dish consists of several components that are cooked separately and then served together. There are many versions around the South; this is the one that *Edible Marin & Wine Country*'s publisher Gibson Thomas's aunt Carol on the Eastern Shore of Mobile Bay in Alabama "fixes." Gibson considers it to be the most "supreme."

The Southern Cooked Greens (see page 305), which almost always accompany hoppin' John, are said to bring you money in the coming year. The Southern Corn Bread (page 304) is for sopping up the delicious "pot likker" from the greens.

When purchasing the smoked ham hock, look for a naturally smoked hock, not one cured with chemical smoke flavoring. Crisp bacon strips make a delicious garnish, if desired. Happy New Year!

1 pound dried black-eyed peas, picked over and rinsed

1 meaty smoked ham hock (about 10 ounces)

9 cups water

1 large white onion, finely chopped

¼ teaspoon crushed red chile flakes

2½ teaspoons kosher salt, plus more if needed

¾ teaspoon freshly ground black pepper, plus more if needed

2 cups long-grain white rice (not instant)

½ pound smoked ham, roughly chopped into small pieces

2 large tomatoes, seeded and chopped, or ¾ cup halved cherry tomatoes

½ cup Homemade Mayonnaise (page 238) or commercial mayonnaise

1 bunch scallions, white and light green parts only, thinly sliced on the diagonal

6 strips bacon

In a large saucepan or Dutch oven, add the black-eyed peas, ham hock, and water. Bring to a boil; boil for about 3 minutes, continuously skimming off any foam that rises to the surface. Stir in the onion, chile flakes, 1 teaspoon of the salt, and ¼ teaspoon of the pepper. Reduce the heat, cover the pot, and simmer until the peas are barely tender, 25 to 30 minutes.

Using a ladle, transfer 3½ cups of the broth into a medium saucepan. Cover the pot containing the peas and simmer until they are tender, about 10 minutes. Remove the ham hock (remove and reserve the meat for another use). Taste and adjust seasoning as needed.

Bring to a boil the 3½ cups of broth in the saucepan. Add the rice and the remaining 1½ teaspoons of salt and ½ teaspoon of pepper. Return to a boil, cover the pot, reduce the heat, and simmer until the liquid is absorbed and the rice is tender, 20 to 30 minutes. Sauté the bacon strips until crispy. Slice into thin pieces and reserve on a dry paper towel.

To serve, spoon a portion of rice onto each plate. Top with black-eyed peas and enough of the broth to moisten the rice. Scatter diced ham and tomatoes on top of the peas. Top with a large dollop of the mayonnaise and sprinkle with the sliced scallions and crispy bacon. Serve immediately.

Squash, Mushroom, and Sage Strata

COURTESY OF *EDIBLE ASPEN* (COLORADO)
MAKES 4 TO 6 SERVINGS

1 butternut squash (about 2 pounds)

5 large eggs, beaten

2 cups whole milk or half-and-half

2 tablespoons unsalted butter or extra virgin olive oil

1 medium onion, halved and thinly sliced

¼ pound assorted mushrooms, thinly sliced

2 teaspoons kosher salt

2 cloves garlic, very finely chopped

2 tablespoons finely chopped fresh sage leaves

½ teaspoon freshly grated nutmeg

1 teaspoon curry powder or ground cumin

½ teaspoon crushed red chile flakes

¼ cup dry sherry, white wine, or water

¼ cup finely chopped drained sun-dried tomatoes (oil-packed), optional

¼ teaspoon freshly ground black pepper

½ cup crumbled goat cheese

¼ cup crumbled blue cheese, optional

4 cups (1-inch cubes) day-old sourdough, whole wheat, or white bread (about ½ pound)

¼ cup freshly grated Parmigiano-Reggiano

Baked egg casseroles are often called stratas, from the Italian. (The word *strata* refers to layers, either literally to layers of ingredients or, in this case, figuratively to the layers of flavor from the different ingredients.)

Stratas are a delicious way to use up bread and all sorts of other ingredients, many of which are readily found in your pantry or fridge. This recipe combines the sweetness of roasted butternut squash with the earthiness of mushrooms and a variety of other flavor components that cook up together to create a wonderful, crusty-topped dish that's perfect for breakfast, brunch, lunch, or dinner. You can even assemble the whole thing ahead of time in an ovenproof glass baking dish, refrigerate it overnight, and pop it into the oven first thing in the morning or whenever you plan to serve it.

Preheat the oven to 400°F. Cut the squash in half lengthwise. Using a spoon, scoop out the seeds and discard them. Place the squash halves cut-side down on a baking sheet lined with parchment paper. Bake until the squash skin can be easily pierced with a fork, about 45 minutes. Allow the squash to cool for about 30 minutes. (Note: You can complete these steps up to 2 days before making the strata; wrap the roasted squash halves in foil and refrigerate until needed.) Peel the squash and cut the flesh into cubes about ¾ inch wide; set aside.

Lower the oven temperature to 350°F. Grease a 9- by 13-inch baking pan; set aside. In a small bowl, whisk together the eggs and milk; set aside.

In a large skillet or sauté pan, melt the butter over medium heat. Add the onion and cook, stirring occasionally, for 3 minutes. Add the mushrooms and ½ teaspoon of the salt, increase the heat to medium-high, and cook, stirring frequently, until the mushrooms turn golden, about 2 minutes. Stir in the garlic, sage, nutmeg, curry powder, and chile flakes and cook for 1 minute. Add the sherry, stirring for 1 minute to scrape up brown bits from the bottom of the pan.

In a large bowl, add the mushroom mixture; the cubed roasted squash; sun-dried tomatoes, if using; the remaining 1½ teaspoons of salt; the pepper; goat cheese; and blue cheese, if using. Stir gently to combine. Stir in the cubed bread, then add the egg mixture and stir to combine well.

Pour the mixture evenly into the prepared baking pan. Sprinkle with the grated cheese. Bake until the strata is puffed and golden, 50 to 55 minutes. Let stand for about 15 minutes before serving.

Seared Pollock with a Ragout of Mussels and Brussels Sprout Leaves

. . . .

COURTESY OF *EDIBLE RHODY* (RHODE ISLAND)

MAKES 4 SERVINGS

8 large Brussels sprouts

1 pound fresh mussels, beards removed and scrubbed well

1 cup dry white wine

3 sprigs fresh thyme

2 cloves garlic, thinly sliced

1 shallot, thinly sliced

2 tablespoons heavy cream

6 tablespoons unsalted butter, cut into small cubes

1 tablespoon finely chopped flat-leaf parsley

1 teaspoon freshly squeezed lemon juice, if needed

4 pollock fillets (about 8 ounces each) or other thin-skinned, firm-fleshed fish fillets

1 teaspoon kosher salt for the fish, plus more if needed for the sauce

¼ teaspoon freshly ground black pepper

2 tablespoons grapeseed oil or another neutral-flavored oil

Pollock is a member of the cod family and has a similar rich taste. Also called blue cod, it is available in New England year-round. It has a thin skin and no pin bones. It's divine when paired with mussels in this light cream sauce. The Brussels sprout leaves add a bright splash of color, flavor, and texture to this very special dish, which is perfect for an elegant dinner party. Feel free to substitute other seasonal vegetables, such as asparagus or fiddleheads, for the Brussels sprout leaves.

. . . .

On a cutting board, place 1 Brussels sprout on its side. Using a paring knife, cut an inverted V at the outer edge of the core, extending about ¼ inch into the flesh of the Brussels sprout. Repeat with the remaining sprouts. Using your fingers and a paring knife, gently pry the outer green leaves off of each Brussels sprout. You should have about 1 cup of bright green leaves.

Have ready a medium bowl of ice water and a tray of towels or paper towels. In a medium pot of boiling salted water, cook the Brussels sprout leaves for 1 minute. Using a slotted spoon, remove the leaves and place them into the bowl of ice water. After 1 minute, remove the leaves and drain on the towels; set aside.

In a large saucepan, add the mussels, wine, thyme, garlic, and shallot. Cover and bring the liquid to a boil. Cook until the mussels have opened, 4 to 6 minutes.

Using a slotted spoon, remove the mussels to a large plate, discarding any unopened mussels. Remove the mussels from their shells and place them into a bowl; discard the shells.

With a fine-mesh strainer set into a small saucepan, strain the cooking liquid; discard the solids. Cook the liquid over medium-high heat until it is reduced to about 3 tablespoons, about 5 minutes. (The measure doesn't have to be exact, but tilt the pan to spoon out a sample measure, if you like.) Remove from the heat.

Whisk in the heavy cream and butter, about 1 tablespoon at a time, adding another portion of butter only after the first has melted. Stir in the parsley. Taste the sauce and add the lemon juice or some salt as needed. Cover the pan and set aside.

Using a sharp knife, cut a few shallow lengthwise slits about ½ inch apart through the skin of each pollock fillet. Sprinkle the fillets evenly with the 1 teaspoon salt and the pepper. In a large sauté pan or skillet, heat the oil over medium-high heat. Place the fish fillets skin-side up in the pan. Allow the fish to cook until the flesh is brown and crisp on one side and no longer sticks to the pan, 4 to 5 minutes. Carefully turn over each fillet and cook until the skin is brown and crisp and the fish is just barely cooked through, 4 to 5 minutes.

When the fish is almost cooked, add the Brussels sprout leaves and the cooked mussels to the sauce in the saucepan. Heat very gently over medium-low heat for about 2 minutes. Place each fish fillet on a plate. Spoon the sauce, along with the Brussels sprout leaves and mussels, evenly around each fillet. Serve immediately.

Slow-Cooked Maple-Cider Brisket

ADAPTED FROM A RECIPE COURTESY OF COURTNEY CONTOS, INN AT ESSEX, VERMONT/
EDIBLE GREEN MOUNTAINS (VERMONT)
MAKES 6 SERVINGS

The aroma of this brisket—accented with apple cider vinegar, maple syrup, and bacon—will attract everyone into the kitchen while it's cooking, and then to the table, where it's sure to be gobbled up in no time. The flavorful sauce is delightful served over mashed rutabagas or potatoes and a side of Brussels sprouts completes the meal.

1 beef brisket (4 to 5 pounds)
2 cloves garlic, cut into thin slivers
3 tablespoons bacon drippings, vegetable oil, or grapeseed oil
2 onions, halved and thinly sliced
3 cloves garlic, very finely chopped
1 tablespoon kosher salt
1 teaspoon dried oregano
¾ teaspoon freshly ground black pepper
¼ teaspoon ground cayenne
2 tablespoons tomato paste
1 cup strong brewed coffee
¾ cup apple cider vinegar
¾ cup maple syrup, preferably Grade B
½ cup chicken broth
1 tablespoon Dijon mustard
½ pound Vermont maple-smoked bacon, cooked and crumbled, optional

Preheat the oven to 350°F. Using a paring knife, cut small slits all over the brisket, inserting a sliver of garlic into each slit as you cut it. Place the brisket into a large Dutch oven or roasting pan fitted with a lid.

In a large sauté pan or saucepan, heat the bacon drippings over medium heat. Add the onions and cook, stirring occasionally, until golden, 6 to 7 minutes. Add the garlic, salt, oregano, black pepper, and cayenne and stir for 1 minute. Add the tomato paste and cook, stirring continuously, for 1 minute. Stir in the coffee, vinegar, maple syrup, chicken broth, and mustard. Bring the ingredients to a boil.

Pour the contents of the sauté pan over the brisket in the Dutch oven. Cover the pan with the lid and place it into the oven. Bake for 30 minutes. Decrease the heat to 300°F and bake, basting the meat with the pan sauce once or twice, until the brisket is fork tender, about 3 hours. Allow the meat to rest for about 15 minutes.

Slice the meat across the grain using an electric knife or sharp carving knife. Place the sliced meat into a large ovenproof serving pan with a lid. Remove the fat from the surface of the sauce. Pour the sauce over and around the meat. Cover the pan with the lid. (At this point, you can store the brisket, covered, in the refrigerator overnight, if desired. Reheat the brisket in a preheated 350°F oven until the sauce is bubbling, 30 to 45 minutes.)

Place the pan with the brisket into the oven and bake for 30 minutes. Garnish with the crumbled bacon, if using. Serve immediately.

Braised Pomegranate Chicken with Walnuts

COURTESY OF CHERYL KOEHLER/*EDIBLE EAST BAY* (CALIFORNIA)

MAKES 4 SERVINGS

Locally grown walnuts, pistachios, pomegranates, and lemons are in abundance in California in the wintertime, so that's the season to enjoy this variation on a traditional Persian dish. If you prefer a thicker sauce (the sauce here is quite thin), you can use a greater quantity of nuts or add two tablespoons of flour to the onion and garlic mixture prior to adding the pomegranate juice. Serve with basmati rice to round out the meal.

- 1 teaspoon kosher salt, plus more if needed
- ½ teaspoon freshly ground black pepper, plus more if needed
- 1 whole chicken (about 3½ pounds), cut into 8 pieces, or 4 chicken quarters of your choice
- 2 tablespoons extra virgin olive oil or grapeseed oil
- 1 medium onion, sliced
- 2 cloves garlic, very finely chopped
- ½ teaspoon ground cardamom or cinnamon
- 2 cups pure pomegranate juice (unsweetened)
- 1 tablespoon granulated sugar, optional
- 1 tablespoon finely grated lemon zest
- 1 tablespoon freshly squeezed lemon juice, plus more if needed
- ½ cup unsalted walnuts or pistachios
- Pomegranate seeds, optional

Sprinkle the salt and pepper evenly over all sides of the chicken pieces. In a large sauté pan, heat the oil over medium-high heat. Place 4 of the chicken pieces in the pan and brown well on both sides, a total of 3 to 4 minutes. Remove the chicken pieces to a plate. Repeat with the remaining 4 pieces of chicken. Set aside.

Pour off and discard all but 2 tablespoons of the liquid remaining in the pan. Reduce the heat to medium, add the onion to the sauté pan, and cook, stirring occasionally, until golden brown, 7 to 8 minutes. Add the garlic and cardamom and cook, stirring continuously, for 1 minute. Stir in the pomegranate juice; sugar, if using; lemon zest; and lemon juice. Cook for 2 minutes, scraping up any brown bits from the bottom of the pan.

Add the chicken pieces and any juices back into the pan in a single layer, spooning some sauce over the top. Bring the liquid in the pan to a boil. Reduce the heat, cover the pan with a lid, and simmer until the chicken is tender and no longer pink inside, 35 to 40 minutes.

In a small skillet, toast the walnuts over medium heat, tossing frequently until they are just barely beginning to brown, 2 to 3 minutes. Remove from the heat. Coarsely chop the nuts using a mini food processor or on a sturdy surface with a mallet. Place 2 tablespoons of the nuts into a small dish; set aside. Finely chop the remaining walnuts, placing them in a separate small dish; set aside.

When the chicken is cooked, remove the chicken pieces to a serving platter. Cover with foil to keep warm. Add the 2 tablespoons reserved walnuts to the cooking liquid in the pan, stir well, and simmer for 5 minutes. Pour the sauce over the chicken and sprinkle with the remaining reserved chopped walnuts and pomegranate seeds, if using. Serve immediately.

Gingersnap-Crusted Lamb Loin Medallions with Brandied Fig Sauce

ADAPTED FROM A RECIPE COURTESY OF CATHERINE WILKINSON/*EDIBLE PHOENIX* (ARIZONA)
MAKES 6 SERVINGS

Roast Lamb

1 teaspoon kosher salt

¼ teaspoon freshly ground black pepper

3 boneless lamb loin medallions (about 1 pound each), silver skin removed, or lamb sirloins (see headnote)

1 tablespoon liquid honey

1 tablespoon Dijon mustard

½ teaspoon dried rosemary or dried thyme

1 cup crushed gingersnap cookies

Brandied Fig Sauce

1 teaspoon grapeseed oil or another neutral-flavored oil

1 large shallot, finely chopped

1½ cups chicken broth

1 cup brandy

½ cup freshly squeezed orange juice

1 cup thinly sliced dried Calimyrna figs

1 tablespoon light brown sugar, plus more if needed

½ teaspoon dried rosemary or dried thyme

½ teaspoon kosher salt, plus more if needed

¼ teaspoon freshly ground black pepper, plus more if needed

This recipe was inspired by the winning dish of the Best American Lamb Family Recipe Contest in Denver. The gingersnap crust provides a wonderful, sweet-and-spicy counterpart to the lamb, which is best when cooked no further than medium-rare. The brandied fig sauce is divine, and can also be used as an accompaniment to beef, pork, and poultry dishes.

This recipe is also great using lamb sirloins (about one pound each). If using lamb sirloins, increase the roasting time to twenty-five to thirty-five minutes.

MAKE THE ROAST LAMB: Preheat the oven to 425°F. Have ready a large roasting pan fitted with a rack. Sprinkle the salt and pepper on all sides of the lamb medallions.

In a small bowl, combine the honey, mustard, and rosemary. Using a pastry brush, brush the honey mixture evenly over all sides of the lamb. On a rimmed baking sheet, spread the crushed gingersnaps. Place the lamb medallions one at a time onto the crushed gingersnaps, coating all sides and pressing firmly to adhere. Place the lamb onto the rack in the roasting pan.

Bake until the gingersnap crust is lightly browned and a meat thermometer inserted into the thickest part of one lamb medallion reads 145°F for medium-rare, 16 to 18 minutes, depending on thickness. Allow the lamb to rest for 10 minutes before slicing.

MAKE THE BRANDIED FIG SAUCE: While the lamb is roasting, in a medium saucepan, heat the oil over medium heat. Add the shallot and cook, stirring occasionally, until lightly golden, 1 to 2 minutes. Add the chicken broth, brandy, orange juice, figs, brown sugar, rosemary, salt, and pepper. Stir well, then bring to a boil. Reduce the heat and simmer until the figs are soft, about 20 minutes. Cool for 5 minutes.

In the work bowl of a food processor, pour the mixture and process until the figs are pureed. In a fine-mesh strainer set into a medium bowl, press the fig puree using a ladle or whisk to press the liquid through. Discard the solids. Taste the sauce and adjust the seasoning as needed.

To serve, slice the lamb across the grain to the desired thickness, keeping the slices of each medallion together. Spoon some of the sauce onto the center of each of 6 plates. Fan one-half of the slices from each medallion over the sauce. Spoon some more sauce over the top of the lamb slices. Serve immediately.

Brew-Braised Lamb Shanks with Apple Butter and Sauerkraut

COURTESY OF *EDIBLE TORONTO* (ONTARIO, CANADA)
MAKES 6 SERVINGS

Lamb shanks are a perfect main-course dish for a cold winter day. Braising bone-in meats contributes a huge amount of flavor, as well as natural gelatin for thickening. Gail Gordon Oliver of *Edible Toronto* added red lentils to this recipe instead of flour as a thickening agent (as well as for extra flavor and nutrition), a great tip whenever you're braising, stewing, or making soups. The recipe highlights the interplay of sweet, salty, and tangy elements, using local apple butter, sauerkraut, and canned tomatoes to create a scrumptious mélange of homegrown ingredients. This recipe also works well with beef short ribs and oxtail. Serve with mashed potatoes, if you like.

- 6 lamb shanks (¾ pound to 1 pound each)
- 2 teaspoons kosher salt
- ½ teaspoon freshly ground black pepper
- 2 tablespoons grapeseed oil or another neutral-flavored oil
- 2 medium onions, finely chopped
- 3 large carrots, cut into 1-inch lengths
- 2 stalks celery, cut into 1-inch lengths
- 3 cloves garlic, very finely chopped
- ½ teaspoon ground cayenne
- 1 bottle (12 ounces) dark beer
- 2 cups beef broth or chicken broth
- 1 large can (28 ounces) whole tomatoes, preferably organic
- ½ cup sauerkraut juice (drained from a jar or can of sauerkraut)
- 1 cup drained sauerkraut
- ½ cup apple butter
- 1 small rutabaga (about 1 pound), peeled and cut into 1-inch chunks
- ⅓ cup dried red lentils
- 5 sprigs fresh thyme (tied together with kitchen twine) or 1 teaspoon dried thyme
- 1 teaspoon dried juniper berries, lightly crushed, optional
- 3 bay leaves

Preheat the oven to 325°F. Dry the lamb shanks well. Sprinkle the lamb shanks on all sides with the salt and pepper. In a large sauté pan, heat the oil over medium-high heat. Cook 3 of the lamb shanks until deeply browned on all sides, about 6 minutes. Repeat with the remaining 3 lamb shanks, lowering the heat a bit if necessary to prevent burning. Remove the lamb shanks to a plate. Discard any remaining oil from the pan.

Return the pan to the heat; reduce to medium. Add the onions and cook, stirring frequently and scraping the bottom of the pan, for 3 minutes. Add the carrots and celery and cook, stirring frequently, for 2 minutes. Add the garlic and cayenne and cook for 1 minute. Increase the heat to high. Add the beer and cook, stirring occasionally and scraping the bottom of the pan, until the beer is reduced by half, 4 to 5 minutes.

Add the broth, tomatoes with their liquid, sauerkraut juice, sauerkraut, and apple butter. Stir well to combine, lightly breaking up the tomatoes with a wooden spoon. Bring to a boil. Stir in the rutabaga; lentils; thyme; juniper berries, if using; and bay leaves. Return to a boil.

Transfer the contents of the pan to a roasting or braising pan large enough to hold the lamb shanks in a single layer. Add the lamb shanks and any juices to the pan, nestling them in among the vegetables and spooning over some of the liquid. Cover tightly with the pan's lid or with foil.

Bake in the oven until the lamb is fork tender, about 2 hours. Discard the bay leaves and thyme sprigs. Remove the lamb shanks to a platter. Spoon off and discard any visible fat from the sauce, then stir the sauce well. Serve the lamb hot, smothered in sauce and vegetables.

Chile-Braised Roasted Meat

COURTESY OF *EDIBLE CHICAGO* (ILLINOIS)
MAKES 6 TO 8 SERVINGS

Chile Paste

1 head garlic, separated into cloves
  (do not remove skins)
4 dried whole ancho chile peppers
3 dried whole pasilla, Anaheim, or
  New Mexico chile peppers
1 dried whole chipotle chile pepper,
  optional
1 cup chicken broth, beef broth, or
  water

Roast

1 beef chuck, boneless lamb, or pork
  shoulder roast (5 to 6 pounds)
1 teaspoon kosher salt, plus more if
  needed
½ teaspoon freshly ground black
  pepper
2 tablespoons vegetable oil or
  grapeseed oil, plus more if needed
2 medium onions, finely chopped
3 large carrots, cut into 1-inch
  lengths
3 stalks celery, cut into 1-inch
  lengths
1 tablespoon ancho chili powder
2 teaspoons dried oregano
2 teaspoons ground cinnamon
1½ cups dry red wine
1 cup chicken or beef broth, or water
1 can (14.5 ounces) diced tomatoes
1 tablespoon light brown sugar
4 sprigs fresh thyme (stems tied with
  kitchen twine) or 1 teaspoon dried
  thyme
3 bay leaves

Beef is big in Chicago (and the Midwest), and there's a large community of native Mexicans in the region, hence the compbination of beef and chiles in this recipe. The flavor base is derived from three varieties of dried chiles, creating a very dark and slightly bitter paste, which—after roasting with the meat juices, the vegetables, and the braising liquid of red wine and tomatoes—creates an earthy, complex, spicy-sweet sauce.

Try this dish with Southern Corn Bread (page 304).

MAKE THE CHILE PASTE: In a large skillet, toast the garlic cloves in their skins over medium-high heat, stirring frequently, until brown, 4 to 5 minutes; set aside. In the same skillet, add the dried whole chiles and toast, turning frequently, until lightly browned, about 5 minutes. In a large bowl of very hot water, immerse the chiles until soft, about 15 minutes; drain.

Remove the stem from each chile, cut each chile in half, and remove the seeds and membrane. Discard the seeds and membranes. Remove the skins from the toasted garlic cloves. In a blender, add the chiles, garlic, and 1 cup broth. Puree until smooth; set aside.

MAKE THE ROAST: Preheat the oven to 325°F. Sprinkle the meat on all sides with the salt and pepper. In a large Dutch oven or ovenproof casserole dish, heat the oil over medium-high heat. Add the meat and brown well on all sides, adding more oil if needed and reducing the heat if necessary to prevent scorching. Remove the meat to a platter; set aside.

Reduce the heat to medium. In the same pot, add the onions and cook, stirring occasionally and scraping the bottom of the pan, until softened, about 3 minutes. Add the carrots and celery and cook, stirring occasionally, for 3 minutes. Stir in the ancho chili powder, oregano, and cinnamon and cook, stirring, for 1 minute. Add the chile paste mixture and stir, coating the vegetables, for 1 minute. Add the wine, increase the heat to high, and cook, stirring continuously until the wine is reduced by half, about 3 minutes. Stir in 1 cup of broth, the tomatoes, brown sugar, thyme, and bay leaves.

Return the meat to the pot, nestling it in among the vegetables and pouring some of the liquid over the top. Bring the liquid to a boil and cover the pot with the lid. Place the pot in the oven and roast until the meat is very tender, about 3 hours.

Remove the meat from the pan; set aside to rest for about 20 minutes. Skim excess fat from the surface of the sauce. Discard the thyme sprigs and bay leaves.

Serve the sauce as is, or you can puree all or some using an immersion or standard blender. The sauce will be coarse and rustic in texture. Taste and adjust seasoning as needed. Slice the meat across the grain and serve smothered with sauce.

Elk Steaks in Red Wine Sauce

COURTESY OF GAIL GORDON OLIVER/*EDIBLE TORONTO* (ONTARIO, CANADA)
MAKES 4 SERVINGS

Elk is a wonderfully flavorful, though not overly gamy, meat that is quite low in fat and contains slightly lower levels of cholesterol than most other red meats. This is a very simple yet elegant preparation featuring a red wine sauce that balances the sharpness of whole grain mustard with the tangy sweetness of red currant jelly. Elk is very lean, so take care not to cook it beyond medium-rare or you'll risk toughening up the meat.

If you would like or need to choose a substitute for the elk, try venison or beef steaks in this lovely red wine sauce.

4 elk, venison, or beef steaks or medallions (about ½ pound each)
½ teaspoon kosher salt, plus more if needed
¼ teaspoon freshly ground black pepper, plus more if needed
2 tablespoons grapeseed oil or another neutral-flavored oil
2 shallots or ½ small onion, very finely chopped
1 cup dry red wine
½ cup beef broth or chicken broth
1 tablespoon grainy mustard
2 tablespoons red currant jelly
2 tablespoons cold unsalted butter, cut into small cubes

Pat the elk steaks dry. Sprinkle evenly with the salt and pepper. In a large sauté pan or skillet, heat the oil over medium-high heat. Add the steaks and allow them to cook until a nice brown crust develops and the steaks no longer stick to the pan, about 3 minutes. Turn the steaks and continue to cook to medium-rare, about 2 minutes. Remove the steaks to a plate; set aside to rest.

Reduce the heat to medium. In the same pan, add the shallots. Cook, stirring, about 2 minutes. Add the red wine, increase the heat to medium-high, and cook, scraping up the brown bits from the bottom of the pan, until the wine is reduced by about two-thirds, about 3 minutes. Whisk in the broth, mustard, and red currant jelly. Bring to a boil and cook until reduced slightly, about 2 minutes. Remove the pan from the heat.

Whisk in the butter, 2 or 3 cubes at a time, adding another portion of butter only after the first has melted. Taste and adjust seasoning as needed. Slice the steaks across the grain to the desired thickness. Spoon the sauce evenly over or around the steaks and serve immediately.

Side Dishes

Southern Corn Bread

COURTESY OF GIBSON THOMAS/*EDIBLE MARIN & WINE COUNTRY* (CALIFORNIA)
MAKES 6 SERVINGS

1 cup fine or extra-fine ground white cornmeal (stone ground is best, as it is processed less and has fewer additives)

2 teaspoons baking powder

¼ teaspoon baking soda

½ teaspoon kosher salt

1 cup buttermilk

1 large egg, lightly beaten

3 tablespoons unsalted butter, melted, plus butter for serving

If you have a well-seasoned cast-iron pan shaped like ears of corn, by all means, use that for this tasty, traditional dish. If not, you can use a six- to seven-inch cast-iron skillet or muffin tin. It is very important to remember to heat the greased pan in the oven before adding the batter. If you forget, your corn bread will likely stick and you will lose the delicious crunchy goodness on the bottom of each piece.

Southern Corn Bread is traditionally served with Hoppin' John Supreme (page 293) on New Year's Day.

Preheat the oven to 450°F. Generously grease a 6- to 7-inch cast-iron pan with 1 tablespoon room-temperature butter. Place the empty pan into the preheated oven.

In a large bowl, whisk together the cornmeal, baking powder, baking soda, and salt. In a small bowl, whisk together the buttermilk and egg. Add the buttermilk mixture to the dry ingredients in 3 additions, stirring to blend after each addition. Stir in the melted butter.

Remove the hot pan from the oven. Immediately (and carefully, as it may splatter) pour the batter evenly into the pan. Return the pan to the oven and bake until the corn bread is browned on top and a toothpick inserted into the center comes out clean, 25 to 35 minutes. (For corn sticks or muffins, bake for 15 to 20 minutes.) Serve warm with butter.

Southern Cooked Greens

COURTESY OF GIBSON THOMAS/*EDIBLE MARIN & WINE COUNTRY* (CALIFORNIA)
MAKES 6 SERVINGS

Thomas's Southern family has always eaten turnip greens, and they still do, even though some of them live in California now. You can substitute collard greens or mustard greens, or a combination of two or all three—whatever is local and convenient. If you use collards, they should have the entire stem and central rib cut from the leaf and be sliced crosswise into strips about an inch thick. By creating the rich pork stock before adding the greens, the leaves are able to take on these flavors while retaining their toothsome texture and preserving their many nutrients.

When purchasing the ham hock, look for a naturally smoked hock, not one cured with chemical smoke flavoring.

1 meaty smoked ham hock (about 10 ounces)

1 large white onion, quartered

3 quarts water

2 tablespoons apple cider vinegar, plus more if needed

1 tablespoon dark brown sugar

1 tablespoon kosher salt, plus more if needed

¼ teaspoon freshly ground black pepper, plus more if needed

3 pounds fresh turnip greens, collard greens, or mustard greens, or a combination

In a Dutch oven or stockpot, add the ham hock, onion, water, vinegar, brown sugar, salt, and pepper. Bring to a boil. Reduce the heat, cover the pot, and simmer for 1 hour. Remove the ham hock (you may remove and reserve the meat for another use), and add the greens a handful at a time, allowing each addition to wilt before adding the next, so that all the greens are submerged in the meat stock.

Simmer the greens uncovered, stirring occasionally, until the greens are tender but not completely limp, 25 to 30 minutes. Taste and adjust seasoning as needed (a splash of additional cider vinegar gives it an extra kick). To serve, use a slotted spoon to dish out the greens, but do include some of the delicious "pot likker" juices.

Roasted Root Vegetables

COURTESY OF GAIL GORDON OLIVER/*EDIBLE TORONTO* (ONTARIO, CANADA)
MAKES 4 SERVINGS

Any combination of root vegetables would work well in this recipe. The list includes, but is not limited to, sweet potatoes, parsnips, potatoes, carrots, fennel, turnips, rutabaga, beets, kohlrabi, and onion wedges. Each of these vegetables contains natural sugars that caramelize when roasted, intensifying their flavor and sweetness.

If you decide to make this dish with red beets, use a separate bowl to toss them with oil, salt, and herbs, if using, to prevent their red juices from bleeding onto the other vegetables. They can be roasted on the same pan, alongside but not mixed with the other vegetables.

Preheat the oven to 425°F. Line the bottom of a 9- by 13-inch rimmed baking sheet with parchment paper. Set aside.

In a large bowl, combine the vegetables. Add the oil, salt, and thyme, if using. Using your hands, toss the vegetables to coat well with the oil and seasonings. Transfer the vegetables in a single layer to the prepared baking sheet.

Bake until vegetables such as potatoes and sweet potatoes are soft, and other vegetables such as parsnips and beets are tender but still slightly firm, when pierced with a paring knife, about 35 to 45 minutes.

Transfer the roasted vegetables to a serving bowl or platter. Add the vinegar, if using, and use salad servers to gently toss the vegetables to coat. Taste and adjust seasoning as needed. Serve warm or at room temperature.

2 pounds assorted root vegetables, cleaned, peeled, and cut into 1-inch chunks

2 tablespoons extra virgin olive oil or grapeseed oil

1 teaspoon kosher salt, plus more if needed

½ teaspoon dried thyme or oregano, optional

1 tablespoon sherry vinegar or balsamic vinegar, plus more if needed, optional

Desserts

A Honey of a Cake

....

COURTESY OF *EDIBLE TORONTO* (ONTARIO, CANADA)
MAKES 10 TO 12 SERVINGS

3 cups all-purpose flour, plus 1
    tablespoon, optional
2 teaspoons baking powder
1 teaspoon baking soda
1 teaspoon ground cinnamon
½ teaspoon kosher salt
½ teaspoon ground ginger
¼ teaspoon ground allspice
3 large eggs
1 cup granulated sugar
1 cup grapeseed oil or vegetable oil
1 cup strong brewed coffee, cooled
    to room temperature
1 cup liquid honey
½ cup raisins, optional

Winter is prime time for honey. Try to purchase your honey directly from local honey producers who are selling their products at farm stands and farmers' markets to ensure you're getting a 100 percent local product.

This is a recipe from *Edible Toronto*'s Gail Gordon Oliver's grandmother, who baked it for the Jewish High Holidays, when honey is a significant ingredient, and also year-round when Gail was growing up. It's delicious when freshly baked, but it becomes moister and richer the next day and keeps well.

....

Preheat the oven to 350°F. Grease and flour a 9-inch-diameter tube pan; set aside.

In a medium bowl, whisk together the 3 cups flour, baking powder, baking soda, cinnamon, salt, ginger, and allspice; set aside.

In the work bowl of a stand mixer (or a large bowl if using an electric hand mixer), add the eggs and sugar and beat until fluffy. Gradually beat in the oil, coffee, and honey.

Add the flour mixture to the batter in 3 additions, mixing until just combined after each addition. If using raisins, coat them with the 1 tablespoon flour (to prevent them from sinking) in a small bowl, shaking off the excess flour, and stir them into the batter.

Pour the batter into the prepared pan. Bake until the top of the cake springs back when lightly touched in the center and a toothpick inserted into the center of the cake comes out barely clean, 55 minutes to 1 hour 5 minutes. Allow the cake to cool on a rack for about 10 minutes before removing it from the pan. Serve warm or at room temperature or store covered in the refrigerator for up to a week.

Chocolate–Brown Ale Cake with Cream Cheese Icing

COURTESY OF *EDIBLE AUSTIN* (TEXAS)
MAKES ONE DOUBLE-LAYER CAKE, 8 OR 9 INCHES IN DIAMETER

Bakers Brett Anderson and Andrea VanScoy have a flair for the dramatic and know that people love whimsical desserts. In their home kitchen, they converted a classic Barr Mansion (Austin, Texas's certified organic reception and events center) wedding cake into a stunning holiday or party centerpiece. Although somewhat time-consuming to prepare, it's a worthy project to dedicate yourself to on a dull winter's day—and just wait until you see your family and friends' faces when they see this cake! The ale is a great secret ingredient too; it adds richness and moisture, but the cake won't taste like beer.

Andrea's cocoa dots, while not an essential part of the cake, really makes it eye-catching.

MAKE THE CHOCOLATE–BROWN ALE CAKE: In a medium saucepan, add the ale, butter, and granulated sugar. Cook over medium heat, stirring occasionally, until the mixture begins to bubble. Simmer, stirring occasionally and reducing the heat if necessary to prevent boiling, for 5 minutes. Remove the pan from the heat and whisk in the cocoa powder. Allow the mixture to cool until it feels similar in temperature to a hot, delicious, chocolaty bath.

Preheat the oven to 325°F. Grease 2 round baking pans (8 or 9 inches in diameter) and swirl a handful of flour or cocoa powder into each, giving them a thin but even coating.

In a large bowl, whisk together the eggs and yogurt until they are well blended. Whisk the cooled beer mixture into the egg mixture. In a medium bowl, whisk together the flour, baking soda, and salt. Sift about one-quarter of the flour mixture into the wet mixture, whisking briefly to combine. Repeat with the remaining flour mixture in 3 additions.

Pour the batter evenly into the prepared pans. Sprinkle ½ cup of the chocolate chips on top of the batter in each pan. If the chocolate chips do not sink into the batter, tap them slightly with the whisk until they dip below the surface of the batter.

Bake until the cakes begin to pull away from the edges of the pans and a toothpick inserted into the center of the cake comes out just barely clean, 30 to 45 minutes. Transfer the cake pan to a rack to cool for about 15 minutes. Carefully remove the cakes from the pans and allow to cool top-side up completely.

continued

Chocolate–Brown Ale Cake

1⅓ cups Independence Bootlegger Brown Ale or other ale local to your community

¾ pound (3 sticks) unsalted butter

3 cups plus 1 tablespoon granulated sugar

1 cup plus 2 tablespoons Dutch-process cocoa powder, sifted

3 large eggs

½ cup plus 1 tablespoon whole-milk yogurt

2½ cups whole wheat flour

2¼ teaspoons baking soda

1 teaspoon kosher salt

1 cup semisweet chocolate chips

Cream Cheese Icing

12 ounces full-fat cream cheese

¾ cup (1½ sticks) unsalted butter

6 cups sifted powdered sugar

½ teaspoon kosher salt, plus more if needed

Drop of peppermint or almond flavoring, plus more if needed, optional

Andrea VanScoy's Cocoa Dots, optional

7 ounces dark chocolate (see note, page 310)

¼ cup organic light corn syrup or rice syrup, plus more if needed

MAKE THE CREAM CHEESE ICING: In the bowl of a stand mixture (or in a large bowl using an electric hand mixer), add the cream cheese and butter and beat at medium-high speed until smooth. Scrape down the bowl and continue to mix at low speed. Add 1 cup of the powdered sugar, mixing at low speed and adding another cup when the last has been incorporated, until all of the powdered sugar has been used. Scrape the bowl before each addition of powdered sugar. Add the salt and the flavoring, if using. Taste and adjust salt and flavoring as needed.

Frost the cake: Place 1 of the cooled cake layers onto a turntable or a large platter fitted with a cake base board the same size as the cake. (Alternately, for a cake base, you can cut out a disk of cardboard and wrap it in aluminum foil.) Place a dollop of icing onto the center of the cake layer. Center the second cake layer on top, over the dollop of icing, which will secure it. Drop another dollop of icing onto the center of the cake and spread the frosting with a metal spatula (an offset spatula is best for spreading icing) until the top is covered. Press down, moving slowly and firmly so the frosting really adheres to the cake. Scrape the spatula on the side of an empty bowl and wipe it with a cloth from time to time to prevent crumbs from getting into your frosting.

Continue adding frosting to the top. Take the frosting in and out of the fridge as necessary to make sure it is not too cold (stiff) or too runny (loose) to be controllable. With each dollop, as you reach the edge of the cake, move the frosting slowly over the side of the cake. As it begins to fall, turn the spatula handle to the ceiling and press the frosting around the sides and between the layers of the cake. You will turn the cake in one direction while pressing the spatula in the opposite direction. At some point it will seem natural to scrape and clean your spatula and grab a spatula-full of frosting and pull or push it around the cake. Pull the spatula across the top edge so that it is pretty square. The desired effect is the flat sealant layer of frosting called a "crumb coat." It is okay if you can see the cake through this sheer layer.

Refrigerate the cake at least 20 minutes.

Pull the cake out of the fridge and repeat the frosting step until you can't see the cake through the frosting. (It can help to refrigerate again.) Keep your spatula clean and hot by dipping it in a glass of hot water and drying it on a clean cloth. Use the warm moisture and use broad endless strokes to create the cleanest, smoothest surface possible. Avoid getting the cake wet. Clean up the base of the cake.

MAKE ANDREA VAN SCOY'S COCOA DOTS, if using: First, to make modeling chocolate, in the top of a double boiler, melt the chocolate, stirring until smooth. Whisk in the syrup. Transfer the mixture into a bowl lined with parchment paper. Cover the bowl with parchment paper or plastic wrap secured with a rubber band. Put the bowl into the refrigerator until it has just set, 10 to 20 minutes.

After the modeling chocolate has set, turn it out onto a clean work surface dusted with cocoa powder or nonstick cooking spray to prevent sticking. Cut the modeling chocolate into 4 pieces. Gently knead each piece. Place each piece between 2 sheets of parchment paper and use a rolling pin to spread the chocolate into very thin rectangles. Cut out dots (and ribbons, if you like) for adorning the frosted cake. Refrigerate the dots for at least 20 minutes.

If adding cocoa dots to the cake, do so before putting the cake into the refrigerator to set. Remove the dots from the fridge and apply to the cake in a creative way.

Refrigerate the cake for at least 4 hours to allow it to set up well. On the big day, avoid letting the cake sit on display at room temperature for more than 2 hours before serving.

. . . .

NOTE ~ The higher percentage of cacao, the more intense the chocolate flavor, so the more syrup is required to balance it.

Recipes by Region

NORTHEAST

First Courses
Bubby's Cabbage Borscht	287
Mushroom Soup au Gratin	285
Rich Corn Chowder	236
Roasted Butternut Squash Soup	257
Strawberry Arugula Spring Salad	209
Vermont Cheddar Ale Soup	211

Main Courses
Brew-Braised Lamb Shanks with Apple Butter and Sauerkraut	301
Elk Steaks in Red Wine Sauce	303
Grilled Chicken and Peaches with Caramelized Onions and Goat Cheese	242
Halibut and Pancetta Stew	260
Herb-Roasted Duck Breast with Carrot-Potato Mash and Chive Butter	226
Lobster Rolls	238
Seared Pollock with a Ragout of Mussels and Brussels Sprout Leaves	296
Slow-Cooked Maple Cider Brisket	297

Sides
Double Corn Spoon Bread	248
Garlicky Brussels Sprouts Amandine	271
Roasted Cauliflower with Golden Raisins and Pine Nuts	247
Roasted Root Vegetables	307
Sautéed Spicy Green Beans and Tomatoes	243
Stir-fried Bok Choy with Caramelized Corn	240
Tomato and Ginger Chutney	266

Desserts
A Honey of a Cake	308
Berry Ricotta Pie	253
Blueberry Corn Bread	251
Double Chocolate Pear Cake	276
Flaky Piecrust	254
Grandmother's Apple Cake	277
Harvest Cake with Cider-Cinnamon Frosting	278
Lattice-Topped Apple Pie	280
Triple Gingerbread with Brandied Apples	275

SOUTHEAST

First Courses
A Spring Pan Roast of Oysters	212

Main Courses
Broiled Shad Roe with Pancetta	216
Chicken, Apple, and Butternut Squash Barlotto	264
Kudzu Quiche in Puff Pastry	219
Sullivan's Island Shrimp Bog	207

Sides
Collard Tops with Parmigiano	227
Creamy Pumpkin Grits with Brown Butter	272

SOUTHWEST

First Courses
Pineapple Gazpacho	233

Main Courses
Aspen Tri-Tip Roast	213
Caramelized Onion Tart	242
Gingersnap-Crusted Lamb Loin Medallions with Brandied Fig Sauce	300
Poblanos Stuffed with Goat Cheese and Shrimp	241
Squash, Mushroom, and Sage Strata	294
Wild Onion and Spinach Tart	218

Sides
Mashed Sweet Potatoes with Candied Kumquats	270
Sausage and Rice Stuffing	274

Desserts
Chocolate–Brown Ale Cake with Cream Cheese Icing	309
Persimmon Rum Cake	283

CALIFORNIA AND THE WEST

First Courses
Sea Bass Ceviche with Avocado	288
Poke	210
Smoked Trout Bruschetta with Romesco Sauce	258
The Golden Egg	290

Main Courses
Bay-Scented Chicken with Figs	259
Braised Pomegranate Chicken with Walnuts	299
Glazed Lamb Chops	214
Hoppin' John Supreme	293

Sides
Arugula and Fennel Salad	234
Asparagus with Morels and Tarragon	228
Southern Cooked Greens	305
Southern Corn Bread	304
Sweet Corn Fritters	248

Desserts
The Best Strawberry Shortcakes	230

NORTHWEST

First Courses
Grilled Apricots with Blue Cheese and Hazelnuts	234

Main Courses
Egg Noodles with Fresh Spring Vegetables	223
Grilled Quail with Hazelnuts, Apricot Curry Sauce, and Wild Huckleberry Coulis	265
Linguine with Clams	217
Wild Salmon with Fava Bean Puree	224

Desserts
Rhubarb Bread Pudding with Whiskey Sauce	229

MIDWEST

First Courses
Beet Borscht	286
Fresh Spinach Salad with Hot Bacon Vinaigrette	235

Main Courses
Chile-Braised Roasted Meat	302
Pan-Seared Medallions of Pork with Apples	263

Sides
Kohlrabi with Bacon	269

Desserts
Frozen Maple Mousse	250

Edible Communities Publications

Edible Communities, Inc.
Cofounders, Tracey Ryder &
    Carole Topalian
369 Montezuma Avenue, #577
Santa Fe, NM 87501
Telephone: (505) 989-8822
info@ediblecommunities.com
www.ediblecommunities.com

NORTHEAST

Edible Allegheny
Jack Tumpson, Publisher
1501 Reedsdale Street, Suite 202
Pittsburgh, PA 15233
(412) 431-7888
info@edibleallegheny.com
www.edibleallegheny.com

Edible Boston
Ilene Bezahler, Publisher
288 Washington Street, #363
Brookline, MA 02445
(617) 278-9114
ilene@edibleboston.net
www.edibleboston.net

Edible Brooklyn
Brian Halweil
Stephen Munshin, Publishers
P.O. Box 779
Sag Harbor, NY 11963
(631) 537-4637
brian@ediblebrooklyn.net
stephen@ediblebrooklyn.net
www.ediblebrooklyn.net

Edible Buffalo
Lisa Tucker, Publisher
P.O. Box 1772
Williamsville, NY 14231
(716) 565-2306
info@ediblebuffalo.com
www.ediblebuffalo.com

Edible Cape Cod
Doug and Dianne Langeland, Publishers
P.O. Box 515
Cummaquid, MA 02637
(508) 375-9883
info@ediblecapecod.com
www.ediblecapecod.com

Edible East End
Brian Halweil
Stephen Munshin, Publishers
P.O. Box 779
Sag Harbor, NY 11963
(631) 537-4637
brian@edibleeastend.com
stephen@edibleeastend.com
www.edibleeastend.com

Edible Finger Lakes
Michael Welch, Publisher
P.O. Box 207
Ithaca, NY 14851
(607) 272-2510
michael@ediblefingerlakes.com
www.ediblefingerlakes.com

Edible Green Mountains
Deborah Schapiro, Publisher
150 Dorset Street, PMB 297
South Burlington, Vermont 05403
(802) 651-1030
info@ediblegreenmountains.com
www.ediblegreenmountains.com

Edible Hudson Valley
Eric Steinman, Editor
Nancy Brannigan Painter, Publisher
P.O. Box 650
Rhinebeck, NY 12572
(845) 688-6880
info@ediblehudsonvalley.com
www.ediblehudsonvalley.com

Edible Jersey
Nancy Brannigan Painter, Publisher
P.O. Box 279
Maplewood, NJ 07040
(973) 763-6691
nancy@ediblejersey.com
www.ediblejersey.com

Edible Manhattan
Brian Halweil
Stephen Munshin, Publishers
P.O. Box 779
Sag Harbor, NY 11963
(631)537-4637
info@ediblemanhattan.com
www.ediblemanhattan.com

Edible Nutmeg
Robert Lockhart, Publisher
P.O. Box 308
Washington Depot, CT 06794
(860) 868-2730
info@ediblenutmeg.com
www@ediblenutmeg.com

Edible Philly
Nancy Brannigan Painter, Publisher
31 Woodland Road
Maplewood, NJ 07040
(973) 763-6691
www.ediblephilly.net

Edible Pioneer Valley
Melissa Weinberger, Publisher
19 Hill Avenue
Easthampton, MA 01027
(718) 781-4763
info@ediblepioneervalley.com
www.ediblepioneervalley.com

Edible Queens
Leah McLaughlin, Publisher
4-75 48th Avenue, #1402
Long Island City, NY 11109
(347) 738-4330
info@ediblequeensmagazine.com
www.ediblequeensmagazine.com

Edible Rhody
Genie McPherson Trevor, Editor
John Schenck, Publisher
P.O. Box 9243
Providence, RI 02940
(401) 588-1926
info@ediblerhody.com
www.ediblerhody.com

Edible South Shore
Laurie Hepworth
Michael Hart, Publishers
15 Evergreen Street
Kingston, MA 02364
(781) 582-1726
Michael@ediblesouthshore.com
Laurie@ediblesouthshore.com
www.ediblesouthshore.com

Edible Toronto
Gail Gordon Oliver
P.O. Box 85528
Toronto, Ontario M5N 0A2
(416) 481-7474
info@edibletoronto.com
www.edibletoronto.com

Edible Vineyard
Sam and Ali Berlow, Publishers
4 State Road, 2nd Floor, Suite 2
P.O. Box 1838
Vineyard Haven, MA 02568
(508) 693-2425
info@ediblevineyard.com
www.ediblevineyard.com

Edible White Mountains
KC Wright, Publisher
P.O. Box 249
Elkins, NH 03233
(603) 526-9081
kc@ediblewhitemountains.com
www.ediblewhitemountains.com

SOUTHEAST

Edible Blue Ridge
Steve Russell, Publisher
Natalie Russell, Editor
1614 Brandywine Drive
Charlottesville,VA 22901
(434) 296-2120
steve@edibleblueridge.com
natalie@edibleblueridge.com
www.edibleblueridge.com

Edible Lowcountry
Fred Thompson
Belinda Ellis
2144 Hamrick Drive
Raleigh, NC 27615
(919) 847-0074
info@ediblelowcountry.com
www.ediblelowcountry.com

Edible Memphis
Melissa and Kjeld Petersen, Publishers
P.O. Box 3091
Memphis TN 38173
(901) 552-4742
info@ediblememphis.com
www.ediblememphis.com

Edible Metro & Mountains
Maria Klouda, Publisher
P.O. Box 4186
Canton, GA 30114
(678) 910-4975
maria@ediblemetroandmountains.com
www.ediblemetroandmountains.com

Edible New Orleans
Rachel Arons, Publisher
1503 Tchoupitoulas Street
New Orleans, LA 70130
(917) 660-0886
info@ediblenewneworleans.com
www.ediblenewneworleans.com

Edible Orlando
Kendra Lott, Publisher
1325 Lee Road
Orlando, FL 32810
(407) 687-0828
kendra@edibleorlando.com
www.edibleorlando.com

Edible Piedmont
Fred Thompson, Publisher
7474 Creedmoor Road, #315
Raleigh, NC 27613
(919) 847-0074
info@ediblepiedmont.com
www.ediblepiedmont.com

Edible Sarasota
Tracy and John Freeman, Publishers
Matthew and Tina Bossy-Freeman
4781 Country Manor Drive
Sarasota, FL 34233
(941) 927-4409
info@ediblesarasota.com
www.ediblesarasota.com

Edible South Florida
Katie Sullivan, Publisher
540 Minorca Avenue
Coral Gables, FL 33134
(646) 284-7025
katie@ediblesouthflorida.com
www.ediblesouthflorida.com

SOUTHWEST

Edible Aspen
Lisa Houston, Publisher
P.O. Box 11510
Aspen, CO 81611
(970) 925-6000
lisa@edibleaspen.com
www.edibleaspen.com

Edible Austin
Marla Camp, Publisher
Jenna Noel, Associate publisher
Kim Lane, Editor
1415 Newning Avenue
Austin, Texas 78704
(512) 441-3971
info@edibleaustin.com
www.edibleaustin.com

Edible Dallas & Fort Worth
Nanci Taylor
Karen McCullough, Publishers
P.O. Box 180127
Dallas, TX 75218
(214) 327-5577
info@edibledallasfortworth.com
www.edibledallasfortworth.com

Edible Front Range
Lynne Eppel, Publisher
3033 Third Street
Boulder, CO 80304
(303) 449-4383
lynne@ediblefrontrange.com
www.ediblefrontrange.com

Edible Phoenix
Pamela Hamilton, Publisher
P.O. Box 9519
Phoenix, AZ 85068
(602) 361-7363
info@ediblephoenix.com
www.ediblephoenix.com

Edible Santa Fe
Kate Manchester, Publisher
551 West Cordova Road, #511
Santa Fe, NM 87505
(505) 212-0791
kate@ediblesantafe.com
www.ediblesantafe.com

MIDWEST

Edible Chicago
Ann Flood
Rebecca J. Liscum, Publishers
159 North Marion Street, #306
Oak Park, IL 60301
(708) 386-6781
info@ediblechicago.com
www.ediblechicago.com

Edible Columbus
Tricia Wheeler, Publisher
2338 Abington Road
Columbus, OH 43221
(614) 296-5053
info@ediblecolumbus.com
www.ediblecolumbus.com

Edible Grande Traverse
Charlie Wunsch
Barb Tholin, Publishers
P.O. Box 930
Traverse City, MI 49685
(231) 360-3663
info@ediblegrandetraverse.com
www.ediblegrandetraverse.com

Edible Iowa River Valley
Kurt Michael Friese
Kim McWane Friese, Publishers
River Valley Press, LLC
22 Riverview Drive NE
Iowa City, Iowa 52240
(319) 321-7935
www.edibleiowa.com

Edible Louisville
Steve Makela, Publisher
P.O. Box 4820
Louisville, KY 40204
(502) 299-1096
steve@ediblelouisville.com
www.ediblelouisville.net

Edible Madison
Jamie Johnson, Publisher
51420 Johnstown Road
Soldiers Grove, WI 54655
(608) 735-4106
jamie@ediblemadison.com
www.ediblemadison.com

Edible Twin Cities
Carol and Chuck Banks
Michelle and Ken Hueser
2136 Ford Parkway, #292
St. Paul, MN 55116
(612) 229-0498
info@edibletwincities.net
www.edibletwincities.net

Edible WOW
Kate and Robb Harper, Publishers
P.O. Box 257
Birmingham, Michigan 48012
(248) 731-7578
kate@ediblewow.com
robb@ediblewow.com
www.ediblewow.com

PACIFIC NORTHWEST

Edible Portland
Deborah Kane, Publisher
Ecotrust
721 NW Ninth Avenue, Suite 200
Portland, OR 97209
(503) 227-6225
dkane@ecotrust.org
www.edibleportland.com

Edible Seattle
Alex Corcoran, Publisher
1752 NW Market Street, #131
Seattle, WA 98107
(206) 605-9005
alex@edibleseattle.net
www.edibleseattle.net

Edible Vancouver
Phillip Solman
Debbra Mikaelsen, Publishers
1038 E. 11th Avenue
Vancouver, BC V5T 2G2 Canada
(604) 812-9652
info@ediblevancouver.com
www.ediblevancouver.com

CALIFORNIA AND THE WEST

Edible Bozeman
Kali Gillette, Publisher
111 South Grand Avenue, Suite 219
Bozeman, MT 59715
(406) 219-3945
kali@ediblebozeman.com
www.ediblebozeman.com

Edible East Bay
Cheryl Koehler, Publisher
5245 College Avenue, #836
Oakland, CA 94618
(510) 225-5776
cheryl@edibleeastbay.com
www.edibleeastbay.com

Edible Hawaiian Islands
Gloria Cohen, Publisher
P.O. Box 753
Kilauea, Hawaii 96754
(808) 828-1559
gloria@ediblehawaiianislands.com
www.ediblehawaiianislands.com

Edible Los Angeles
Liz Silver, Publisher
Mike and Jenny Brady
1040 North Las Palmas Avenue
Building 10
Los Angeles, CA 90038
(323) 645-1027
info@ediblela.com
www.ediblelosangeles.com

Edible Marin & Wine Country
Gibson Thomas, Publisher
160 Summit Avenue
Mill Valley, CA 94941
(415) 515-4456
gibson@ediblemarinandwinecountry.com
www.ediblemarinandwinecountry.com

Edible Missoula
Kristen Lee-Charlson, Publisher
P.O. Box 9350
Missoula MT 59807
(406) 541-3999
editor@ediblemissoula.com
www.ediblemissoula.com

Edible Ojai & Ventura County
Jane Handel, Claud Mann, and
    Perla Batalla, Publishers
P.O. Box 184
Ojai, CA 93024
(805) 646-6678
info@edibleojai.com
www.edibleojai.com

Edible Reno-Tahoe
Amanda Burden, Publisher
7641 Autumn Ridge Circle
Reno, NV 89523
(775) 746-1462
amanda@ediblerenotahoe.com
www.ediblerenotahoe.com

Edible Sacramento
Jennifer and Daren Cliff, Publishers
1904 5th Street
Sacramento, CA 95811
(916) 444-7175
ediblesacramento@gmail.com
www.ediblesacramento.com

Edible San Diego
Riley Davenport, Publisher
3643 Voltaire Street
San Diego, CA 92106
(619) 222-8267
info@ediblesandiego.com
www.ediblesandiego.com

Edible San Francisco
Bruce Cole, Publisher
236 West Portal Avenue, #191
San Francisco, CA 94127
(415) 242-0260
ediblesanfrancisco@gmail.com
www.ediblesanfrancisco.com

Edible San Luis Obispo
Bob Banner, Publisher
2500 Oakview Drive
Templeton, CA 93465
(805) 434-3950
info@ediblesanluisobispo.com
www.ediblesanluisobispo.com

Edible Santa Barbara
Krista Harris
Steve Brown, Publishers
1710 Calle Cerro
Santa Barbara, CA 93101
(805) 898-9612
info@ediblesantabarbara.com
www.ediblesantabarbara.com

Edible Shasta-Butte
Earl Bloor
Candace Byrne, Publishers
7 Hidden Brooke Way
Chico, CA 95928
(530) 345-9509
info@edibleshastabutte.com
www.edibleshastabutte.com

Index

Page numbers in *italics* indicate photographs.

A

Abbondanza Farms (Colorado), 112
African food traditions, 58
Agave, 82
Agricultural Land Reserve (ALS), 167
Aidells, Bruce, 117
Akiwenzie's Fish & More (Ontario),
    34–35, *35*
Albers, Celeste, 70, 71, 77
Albers, George, 77
Albright, Lee, 16
Albuquerque (New Mexico), Joe S. Sausage,
    97–98, *98*
Al Forno restaurant (Providence), 52
Alger, John and Linda, 150
Alger Vineyards (California), 150
Allandale Farm (Boston), *13*, 13–15
Allegheny Mountain region, 46
Amagansett (New York), Quail Hill Farm,
    20–24, *21*, *23*
American Livestock Breeds Conservancy,
    78, 85, 86
American Tuna (San Diego), 149
Amish farming, 50
Anderson, Brett, 309
Andiario, Tony, 103, 104
Angeli Caffé (Los Angeles), 139, 141
Ann Arbor (Michigan), Eve's Table,
    198–199, *199*
Anson Mills (South Carolina), 77
Anson Restaurant (Charleston), 70
Apple(s). *See also* Cider
    Brandied, 275
    Butter, Brew-Braised Lamb Shanks
        with Sauerkraut and, 301
    Cake, Grandmother's, 277
    Chicken, and Butternut Squash
        Barlotto, 264
    orchards, 24–28, *25*, *26*, 76
    Pan-Seared Medallions of Pork with,
        262, *263*
    Pie, Lattice-Topped, 280–281, *281*
    varieties of, 26, 27–28, 76, 147, 204
Apricot(s)
    Curry Sauce, 265
    Grilled, with Blue Cheese and
        Hazelnuts, 234
Arizona, 84, 112–113
    Greg LaPrad—Quiessence Restaurant
        (Phoenix), 102–104, *103*
    Janos restaurant (Tucson), 105–106,
        106, 110
    Native Seeds/SEARCH (Tucson), 82,
        84, 105, 106, 108–110, *109*
    Phoenix Public Market, 99–101, *100*
Aronoff, Eve, 198–199
Arugula
    and Fennel Salad, 234
    Strawberry Spring Salad, 209, *209*
Asparagus with Morels and Tarragon, 228
Aspen (Colorado), 111

Astoria (Queens, New York), 51
Atlanta (Georgia), 77
Austin (Texas), 84, 111
    Boggy Creek Farm, 89
Avery, David and Liesbeth, 156, 166–169, *167*
Avocado
    Ceviche, Sea Bass, with, 288
    Poke, Ahi-Ono-, 210

B

Bacon
    drippings, in Southern cuisine, 58
    Kohlrabi with, *268*, 269
    Vinaigrette, Hot, 235
Bajema, Ramona, 1
Bakeries, 29, 47, 49, 53, 147, 280
    Le Petit Outre bakery (Missoula), 136,
        137, 138, 148
Ballantyne, Dayna, 202
Banchet, Jean, 70
Bankston, Jailyn, 108
Barbecue, 56
Barber, Dan, 49
Barber, Dave, 174
Barker, Ben and Karen, 78
Barlotto, Chicken, Apple, and Butternut
    Squash, 264
Bayless, Rick, 192
Beans. *See also* Fava bean(s)
    Green, and Tomatoes, Sautéed Spicy, 243
    squash, and corn (Three Sisters), 10, 130
Beard, James, 156
Beef. *See also* Livestock; Ranchers
    in Beet Borscht, 286
    Brisket, Maple-Cider, Slow-Cooked, 297
    in Cabbage Borscht, Bubby's, 287
    in Chile-Braised Roasted Meat, 302
    Tri-Tip Roast, Aspen, 213
Beer
    breweries, 112, 148, 149, 150, 156,
        176, 203
    Cheddar Ale Soup, Vermont, *211*, 211
    Chocolate–Brown Ale Cake with Cream
        Cheese Icing, 309–310
    in Halibut and Pancetta Stew, 260, *261*
    Lamb Shanks, Brew-Braised, with Apple
        Butter and Sauerkraut, 301
    Sixpoint Brownstone, 47
Beet Borscht, 286
Bell pepper(s)
    in Gazpacho, Pineapple, 233
    Red, and Roasted Poblanos, 241
    Red, in Romesco Sauce, 258
    Red, Sauce, *240*, 241
Bergeron, Paul, 280
Berkeley (California), Eccolo restaurant,
    132–133, *133*
Berry, Wendell, 174
Berry Ricotta Pie, 253
"Best of the Midwest" show, 190
Bezahler, Ilene, 16
Bi-Rite Market (San Francisco), 149
Bison, 92–94, *93*, 113, 180
Bistro Campagne (Chicago), 180
Bjelland, Leif, 136, 138
Black Diamond Farm (New York), 27

Black-eyed peas, in Hoppin' John Supreme,
    292, 293
Blankenship, Melanie, 150
Blueberry
    Corn Bread, 251
    farmers—Alvin and Shirley Harris
        (Tennessee), 59–61, *60*
Blue Cheese, Grilled Apricots with Hazelnuts
    and, 234
Blue Ridge (Virginia), 76
Boetticher, Taylor, 132–133
Boggy Creek Farm (Texas), 89
Boggy Meadow Cheese (New Hampshire), 53
Bok Choy, Stir-fried, with Caramelized Corn,
    244, *245*
Borscht
    Beet, 286
    Cabbage, Bubby's, 287
Boskydel Vineyard (Michigan), 184–185,
    185, *186*, 186, 187
Boston (Massachusetts), 46
    Allandale Farm, *13*, 13–15
Boulder (Colorado)
    Community Roots, 90–91, *91*
    farmers' market, 90, 112
Bozeman (Montana), 146
Brait, Andrew, 131
Bread(s). *See also* Bakeries
    Corn, Blueberry, 251
    Corn, Southern, 304, *305*
    Spoon, Double Corn, 248
Bread Pudding, Rhubarb, with Whiskey
    Sauce, 229
Bremner's Juice (British Columbia), 177
Bresnick, Paul, 22
Breweries, 112, 148, 149, 150, 156, 176, 203
Bricks-Wells, Bridgette, 150
Brisket, Maple-Cider, Slow-Cooked, 297
British Columbia (Canada)
    Forstbauer Farm, 159–161, *160*
    Lotusland Vineyards, 166–169, *167*
    Vancouver, 177
Broccoli, post-harvest handling of, 125–126
Brodeur, Tasha, 32
Broken Arrow Ranch (Texas), 111
Brooklyn (New York City), 46–47
Bruschetta, Smoked Trout, with Romesco
    Sauce, 258
Brussels Sprout(s)
    Amandine, Garlicky, 271
    Leaves, Ragout of Mussels and, with
        Seared Pollock, 296
Buffalo (New York), 47
    Massachusetts Avenue Project, 38–43,
        39, *41*
Burgerville restaurant chain (Oregon), 156
Burwell, Sloane, 99
Butchers
    Belmont Butchery (Virginia), 68–69, *69*
    charcuterie, 68, 132–133, *133*
    Fleisher's Meat (New York), 49
    Marlow & Sons (Brooklyn), 47
Butter
    Apple, 301
    Brown, 272
    Chive, 226
    Honey, 251

Butternut squash
    Chicken, and Apple Barlotto, 264
    Mushroom, and Sage Strata, 294, *295*
    Soup, Roasted, *257*, 257
Byrd, William, II, 56

C

Cabbage Borscht, Bubby's, 287
Café Manna (Brookfield, Wisconsin), 181
Cake(s)
    Apple, Grandmother's, 277
    Chocolate–Brown Ale, with Cream
        Cheese Icing, 309–310
    Chocolate Pear, Double Chocolate, 276
    Gingerbread, with Brandied Apples,
        Triple, 275
    Harvest, with Cider-Cinnamon Frosting,
        278, *279*
    Honey of a, 308
    Persimmon Rum, *282*, 283
    Strawberry Shortcakes, The Best,
        230, *231*
Calder, John, 182, 183
Calder Dairy Farm (Michigan), 182–183, *183*
California, 114–150
    charcuterie (East Bay), 132–133, *133*
    Edible Communities publications in, 315
    Evan Kleiman—Angeli Caffé (Los
        Angeles), 139–142, *140*
    Food for Thought Ojai, 142–145, *145*
    Full Belly Farm, 130–131
    geography of, 115
    local food production in, 116–118
    Ojai Pixie tangerine, 120–124, *121*,
        122–123
    organic food movement in, 125–129
    people, places, things, 146–151
    produce delivery to San Francisco, 126,
        127, 128–129
    recipes by region, 312
Camp, Marla, 84
Camp, Megan, 29, 32, 34
Canada. *See* British Columbia; Ontario
Candia Vineyards (New Hampshire), 53
Capay Valley Grown (Sacramento), 149
Cape Cod (Massachusetts), 47
    Coonamessett Farm, 16–20, *17*, *18*
Cape Land and Sea Harvest (CLASH), 47
Caramel
    Glaze, 277
    Ice Cream, with Caramel Sauce and
        Fleur de Sel, 252–253
    Sauce, 252-253
Carmona, Oscar, 150
Carolina Plantation Rice (South Carolina),
    62–65, *63*, *64*
Carpenter's Grist Mill (Rhode Island), 51
Carrot-Potato Mash, 226
Casey Farm (Rhode Island), 52
Caswell, Seth, 162, 163
Catapano Goat Farm (New York), 48
Cato Corner Cheese (Connecticut), 50
Cauliflower, Roasted, with Golden Raisins
    and Pine Nuts, *246*, 247
Cauthen, Tanya, 68–69, *69*
Cecchini, Dario, 132

Center for Whole Communities, 23
Central Coast Brewing (California), 150
Certified Farmers Market, 122
Certified Naturally Grown (CNG)
    program, 61
Charcuterie, 68, 132–133, *133*
Charleston (South Carolina), 76–77
    FIG restaurant, 70–71, *71*
Chaskey, Scott, 20–24, *21*
Chateau Grand Traverse (Michigan), 185
Cheddar, 10, 29
    Ale Soup, Vermont, *211*, 211
Cheese makers, artisanal, 29, 48, 49, 50, 51,
    53, 112, 149, 151, 264
Cheese steak, Philly, 50
Chenel, Laura, 148
Chesapeake Bay, 56, 76
Chewning, Ted, 71
Chicago (Illinois), 203
    Bistro Campagne, 180
    Farm-in-the-Zoo, 192
    Green City Market, 189–193, 203
Chicken. *See also* Poultry
    Apple, and Butternut Squash
        Barlotto, 264
    with Figs, Bay-Scented, 259
    Label Rouge standards, 85–87
    and Peaches, Grilled, with Caramelized
        Onions and Goat Cheese, 242–243
    Pomegranate, Braised, with Walnuts,
        298, 299
    rustic hybrids, 86
    Wholesome Harvest, 98
Chile Paste, 302
Chile(s)
    festival (Colorado), 112
    Meat, -Braised Roasted, 302
    Poblanos Stuffed with Goat Cheese
        and Shrimp, *240*, 241
    varieties of, 82, 113
Chive Butter, 226
Chocolate
    –Brown Ale Cake with Cream Cheese
        Icing, 309–310
    Cocoa Dots, Andrea VanScoy's, 309, 310
    Pear Cake, Double, 276
Chodos, Debbie, 287
Chotzinoff, Robin, 94
Chowder, Corn, Rich, 236, *237*
Christensen, Roxanne, 87
Churchill, Jim, 120–124, 143
Chutney, Tomato and Ginger, 266, *267*
Ciccone, Silvio T., 186
Cider, 14–15, 205
    -Cinnamon Frosting, 278, *279*
    -Maple Brisket, Slow-Cooked, 297
Cider Hill Farm (Massachusetts), 46
CitySeed (New Haven), 43–45, *44*
City Slicker Farms (Oakland), 146
Clams
    Bonac clam pie, 48
    fried, 46
    Linguine with, *217*, 217
    Quahogs, 52
    Razor, 176
Clem, Mike, 235
Cleverdon, David, 191

Cocoa Dots, Andrea VanScoy's, 309, 310
Coffee roasters, 78, 156
Cohlmeyer, David, 52
Collard
    in Southern Cooked Greens, 305
    Tops with Parmigiano, *227*, 227
Collins, Beth, 244
Colonial food traditions, 10, 12, 52, 56, 58
Colorado, 111, 112
    Community Roots (Boulder), 90–91, *91*
    Jack Rabbit Hill Estate Winery, 95,
        96, 97
    Peak Spirits distillery, *95*, 95–97, 111
    SPIN (Small Plot Intensive) farming,
        90–91
Coming Home to Eat: *The Pleasures and
    Politics of Local Foods* (Nabhan), 1
Common Market (Philadelphia), 50
Community Alliance with Family Farmers
    (Sacramento), 149
Community Food Security Coalition, 108
Community gardens, 47, 77
    Massachusetts Avenue Project (Buffalo),
        38, *39*, 40, *41*, 42
Community Involved in Sustaining
    Agriculture (CISA), 51
Community Roots (Boulder), 87, *88*, 88
Community Sponsored Market (CSM), 45
Community Supported Agriculture (CSA),
    12, 22, 46, 77, 90, 106, 131, 157, 201
Compost, 22, 77
Connecticut, 50
    CitySeed (New Haven), 43–45, *44*
Connington, Karen, 97
Contos, Courtney, 211, 297
Coohill, Tom, 70
Cookstown Greens (Ontario), 52
Coonamessett Farm (Massachusetts), 16–20,
    17, *18*
Corn
    beans, and squash (Three Sisters), 10, 130
    Broth, 236
    Caramelized, Stir-fried Bok Choy with,
        244, *245*
    Chowder, Rich, 236, *237*
    Fritters, Sweet, 248–249, *249*
    Hopi Blue, 130, *131*, 131
    native seeds, 110
    and organic farming, 15
    in Southwest food culture, 82
    Spoon Bread, Double, 248
Corn Bread, 56
    Blueberry, 251
    Southern, 304, *305*
Cornell Geneva Experiment Station (New
    York), 27
Cowgirl Creamery (California), 149
Cowpeas, 65
Cox, John, 135
Coxe, Campbell, 62–65, *63*
Crabs, blue, 76
Cranberry growers, 47, 52
Cream Cheese
    Frosting, Cider-Cinnamon, 278, *279*
    Icing, 309–310
Cristofolo, Pat, 102–104
Crowell, Amy, 218

Cucunato, Joseph C., Jr. (Joe S. Sausage), 97–98, *98*
Curry, Erica, 32
Curry Sauce, Apricot, 265

D

Dabrowski, Bob, 53
Dahl, Kevin, 110
Dai Due Supper Club (Austin), 111
Dailey, Maya, 99, 103, 104
Dairy farms, 49, 52, 53, 151
    Calder Dairy (Michigan), 182–183, *183*
    Everona Dairy (Virginia), 264
    Mecox Bay Dairy (New York), 48
Daley, Vi (alderman), 189–190, 192
Daley, Richard M., 189, 192, 193, 203
Dallas (Texas), 112
Davis, Peter, 46
DeBettencourt, Gina, 53
Decorah (Iowa), Seed Savers Exchange, 179–180, 200–201
Delaty, Simone, 201, 202
Delehanty, Tom, 85–87, *87*
DeMaria, Michael, 102
Desert Harvesters, 84
Desert Weyr (Colorado), 111
Destiny Produce (Georgia), 77
Devotay restaurant (Iowa City), 180, 204
Dine' be' Iiná, Inc. (The Navajo Lifeway), 84
Distillery, Peak Spirits (Colorado), *95,* 95–97, 111
Donnie's Smokehouse (New York), 41
Dooley, Beth, 197
Dott, Tom, 20
Double A Farm (Virginia), 264
Dow, Nuna, 99
Dowd, Laura, 201–202, *202*
Dromgoole, John, 111
Dry Rub, Aspen, 213
Duck Breast, Herb-Roasted, with Carrot-Potato Mash and Chive Butter, 226
Duguid, Naomi, 139
Dupree, Nathalie, 58
Durham, T. R., 198

E

East Bay (California), 146
East End Food Co-Op (Pennsylvania), 46
East New York Farms, 47
Eccles, Beth and Brent, 191
Eccolo restaurant (Berkeley), 132–133, *133*
Eckhouse, Herb and Kathy, 188–189
Ecology Center (Berkeley), 146
Ecotrust Food & Farms program (Portland, Oregon), 173–175, *175*
Edge, John T., 74
Edible Aspen, 95–97, 213, 294, 314
Edible Austin, 84, 89, 92–94, 107–108, 218, 270, 274, 283, 309, 314
Edible Boston, 13–15, 266, 313
Edible Buffalo, 38–43, 313
Edible Cape Cod, 2–3, 16–20, 209, 238, 242, 313
Edible Chesapeake, 68–69, 216, 264, 314

Edible Chicago, 189–192, 193, 302, 314
Edible Communities, Inc. (ECI)
    founding of, 1–2
    Local Hero Awards, 6
    publications of, 2–4, 313–315
Edible East Bay (California), 132–133, 259, 299, 315
Edible East End (New York), 244, 313
Edible Finger Lakes (New York), 24–28, 248, 313
Edible Front Range (Colorado), 87–88, 289, 314
Edible Grand Traverse (Michigan), 184–187, 314
Edible Green Mountains (Vermont), 29–34, 211, 236, 247, 250, 277, 297, 313
Edible Hawaiian Islands, 134–135, 212, 214, 315
Edible Iowa River Valley, 188–189, 200–202, 235, 263, 269, 286, 314
Edible Jersey (New Jersey), 253, 275, 313
Edible Los Angeles, 139–142, 315
Edible Low Country (South Carolina), 62–65, 70–71, 314
Edible Marin & Wine Country (California), 293, 304, 305, 315
Edible Memphis, 59–61, 72–73, 219, 227, 272, 314
Edible Missoula, 136–138, 228, 315
Edible Nutmeg (Connecticut), 43–45, 271, 313
Edible Ojai (California), 1, 2, 120–124, 142–145, 230, 234, 248, 288, 315
Edible Phoenix, 99–106, 108–110, 233, 241, 300, 314
Edible Piedmont (North Carolina), 66–67, 74–75, 212, 220, 314
Edible Portland, 157–158, 164–165, 169–171, 173–175, 223, 224, 265, 315
Edible Rhody (Rhode Island), 36–37, 226, 280, 296, 313
Edible San Francisco, 125–131, 258, 290, 315
Edible Santa Fe, 85–87, 97–98, 314
Edible Seattle, 162–163, 172–173, 217, 234, 315
Edible Toronto, 34–35, 243, 254, 257, 260, 276, 285, 287, 301, 303, 307, 308, 313
Edible Twin Cities (Minnesota), 193–197, 315
Edible Vancouver, 159–161, 166–169, 229, 315
Edible WOW (Michigan), 182–183, 198–199, 315
Education programs
    CitySeed (New Haven), 45
    Farm-in-the-Zoo (Chicago), 192
    on farms, 16, 19–20, 21, 22, 31–32
    Farm to School (Boston), 46
    Massachusetts Avenue Project (Buffalo), 38, 40, 42–43
    Permaculture Guild (Arizona), 101
Egg(s)
    The Golden, 290–291
    in Kudzu Quiche in Puff Pastry, 219
    in Onion, Wild, and Spinach Tart, 218
    Strata, Squash, Mushroom, and Sage, 294, *295*
Eisenhart, John, 224

Ela, Steve, 96
Elk Steaks in Red Wine Sauce, 303
Emory University, 77
Erwin, Kelley, 46
Estrada family, of Friend's Ranches (California), 120, 122
Evans, Amy, 67
Evans, Julie, 109
Eve: Contemporary Cuisine—Methode Traditionnelle (Aronoff), 199
Everona Dairy (Virginia), 264
Eve's Table (Ann Arbor), 198–199, *199*

F

Fairview Gardens (Santa Barbara), 150
Farmer D Organics (Georgia), 77
Farmers' markets
    Berkeley (California), 133
    Boulder (Colorado), 90, 112
    Buffalo (New York), 42
    Chicago (Illinois), 189–193
    Detroit (Michigan), 204
    Hollywood (California), 140–141
    Ithaca (New York), 48
    Los Angeles (California), 147
    Mount Pleasant (South Carolina), 77
    New Haven (Connecticut), 43–44, *44,* 45
    New York City, 27, 50, 74
    Phoenix (Arizona), 99–101, *100*
    Portland (Oregon), 176
    San Francisco (California), 133
    Santa Fe (New Mexico), 87
Farm Fresh Rhode Island, 51
Farm-in-the-Zoo (Chicago), 192
Farmstead at Mine Brook (Massachusetts), 51
Farm-to-school programs. *See* School lunch programs
Farm Winery Act of 1976, 48
Fatted Calf (East Bay, California), 132–133
Fava bean(s)
    in Egg Noodles with Fresh Spring Vegetables, *222,* 223
    Puree, Wild Salmon with, 224, *225*
Feast!, 76
Fennel and Arugula Salad, 234
Ferroni, Lara, 173
Fields, Steve, 143
Fig(s)
    Chicken with, Bay-Scented, 259
    Sauce, Brandied, 300
FIG restaurant (Charleston), 70–71, *71*
Filberts (Hazelnuts), 176
    Apricots, Grilled, with Blue Cheese and, 234
Finger Lakes (New York), 48
Fischer, Mark, 111
Fish. *See also* Fisheries; Salmon
    Halibut and Pancetta Stew, 260, *261*
    Poke, Ahi-Ono-Avocado, 210
    Poke, Sesame-Ahi, with Maui Onions, 210
    Pollock, Seared, with a Ragout of Mussels and Brussels Sprout Leaves, 296

Sea Bass Ceviche with Avocado, 288
Shad, 50
Shad Roe, Broiled, with Pancetta, 216
Trout, Smoked, Bruschetta with
    Romesco Sauce, 258
Fisheries
    Akiwenzie's Fish & More (Ontario),
        34–35, 35
    American Tuna (San Diego), 149
    Cape Cod, 47
    Chesapeake Bay, 56
    Lummi Island Wild Preserves
        (Washington), 162–163, 163
Fitzsimmons, Hugh, 92–94
Fleisher's Meat (Kingston, New York), 49
Fleur de Sel, Caramel Ice Cream with
    Caramel and, 252
Flowers, Bob, 93, 94
Food Bank Farm (Massachusetts), 51
"Food for Growth" report, 42, 47
Food Lifeline (Seattle), 176
Food Share (Ojai, California), 148
FoodShare (Toronto), 52
Food System Economic Partnership
    (Michigan), 205
Food for Thought Ojai (California), 142–145,
    145, 148
Foraging, 117
Forrester, Jill and Keith, 77
Forstbauer, Mary, 159–161, 160
Forstbauer Farm (British Columbia), 159–
    161, 160
Fort Worth (Texas), 112
Four Town Farm (Massachusetts), 37
Franklin Cider Mill (Michigan), 105
Friend, Elmer, 120
Friend's Ranches (Ojai, California), 120–124,
    121, 122–123
Friese, Kurt, 188, 201, 202
Fritters, Sweet Corn, 248–249, 249
Frosting, Cider-Cinnamon, 278, 279
Fujita, Marty, 142–145, 148
Full Belly Farm (California), 130–131
Fuller, Bill, 46
Full Quiver Farm (Virginia), 264

G

Gaining Ground Farm (Oregon),
    157–158, 158
Gallatin Valley Botanical (Montana), 146
Garden City Harvest (Missoula), 148
Garden Gate Vineyards (North Carolina),
    66–67, 67
Gardner, Benjamin, 44
Garmo, Peter de, 169–171, 170
Garten, Ina, 194, 195
GAVA (New Haven, Connecticut), 44
Gazpacho, Pineapple, 233
Gencarelli, Rick, 32, 33–34, 247
Geneva (New York), Red Jacket Orchards,
    24–28, 25, 26
Gentry, Cindy, 99, 101
George, Randy, 49
Georgia, 58, 77
Georgia Organic Growers Association, 70

Germon, George, 52
Gin, Peak Spirits, 111
Ginger
    in Gingerbread, Triple, with Brandied
        Apples, 275
    and Tomato Chutney, 266, 267
Gingerbread with Brandied Apples,
    Triple, 275
Ginger Gold apples, 76
Gingersnap-Crusted Lamb Loin Medallions
    with Brandied Fig Sauce, 300
Glass Onion restaurant (Charleston), 76
Glynwood Cold Spring, 49
Gnose, Brock, 136
Goat Cheese
    artisanal, 48, 148, 151
    Chicken and Peaches, Grilled, with
        Caramelized Onions and, 242–243
    Poblanos Stuffed with Shrimp and,
        240, 241
Golden Fig Fine Foods (Minnesota), 193–
    195, 194
Good Food, 139
Good Harbor Vineyards (Michigan), 186
Good Life Garden (California), 149
Good Loaf, The (New Hampshire), 53
Goose Island Brewery (Chicago), 203
Grand Traverse (Michigan), 203
Granville Island (Vancouver), 177
Grass Run Farms (Iowa), 263
Greeley, Alexandra, 69
Green Beans and Tomatoes, Sautéed
    Spicy, 243
Green City Market (Chicago), 189–193, 203
Greene, Ken, 49
Greenfield Free Harvest Supper
    (Massachusetts), 51
Greenmarkets (New York City), 27, 50, 74
Green Mountains (Vermont), 48
Greens, Southern Cooked, 305
Griffin, Andy, 125–129
Griffiths, Jesse, 111, 270, 283
Grist mill, 51
Grits, 58
    Pumpkin, Creamy, with Brown Butter,
        272, 273
GrowMemphis Community Gardens, 77
GRUB (Growing Resourcefully, Uniting
    Bellies, 150
Gullah cooking, 58
Gutekanst, Rita, 190

H

Halibut and Pancetta Stew, 260, 261
Ham
    country, 56, 58
    in Greens, Southern Cooked, 305
    in Hoppin' John Supreme, 292, 293
    La Quercia (Iowa), 188
Hamilton, Pamela, 84
Hamren, Nancy, 154
Handel, Jane, 1
Hanson, Lance and Anna, 95–97
Hardy, Ryan, 111
Harris, Alvin and Shirley, 59–61, 60, 77

Harris, Will, 77
Harrison, Alex, 183, 199
Hawaii 2050 Sustainability Task Force, 147
Hawaiian Islands, 119, 146–147
    Ocean Vodka, 134–135, 135
Hawthorne Valley Farm (New York), 12
Haynes, Anne Gatling, 43
Hazelnuts. See Filberts
Healy, Allen, 53
Heartlands restaurant (St. Paul), 181
Henderson, Elizabeth, 23, 48
Henrietta's Table (Cambridge), 46
Herbst, Bob, 184–185
Hines, Maria, 172, 172–173
Hitt, Alex, 78
Hodge, Frank, 90
Hohokam, irrigation system of, 84
Holcomb Farm (Connecticut), 50
Holden, Megan, 171
Hollomon, Zoe, 40
Honey
    in Apricots, Grilled, with Blue Cheese
        and Hazelnuts, 234
    Butter, 251
    of a Cake, A, 308
Honey Brook Organic Farm (New Jersey), 49
Hood, Kristi, 22
Hopi, corn growing of, 82
Hoppin' John Supreme, 292, 293
Howell, G. Stanley, 186
Huckleberry Coulis, Wild, 265
Hudson, Cindy, 165
Hudson Valley (New York), 49
Hughes, Chris, 111
Huppert, Andrew, 2

I

Ice Cream, Caramel, with Caramel Sauce
    and Fleur de Sel, 252–253
Icing, Cream Cheese, 309–310
Illinois. See Chicago
Immigrant cuisine, 12, 180
Institute for Agriculture and Trade
    Policy, 197
Interim Restaurant (Memphis), 77
Iowa, 203–204
    Local Foods Connection, 201–201
    Motley Cow Café (Iowa City), 180–181
    La Quercia Prosciutto Americano, 188,
        188–189
    Seed Savers Exchange (Decorah), 179–
        180, 200–201
Iowa State University, 204
Island Creek Oysters (Massachusetts), 52
Ithaca Farmers Market (New York), 48
Izzo, Samantha, 248

J

Jack Rabbit Hill Estate Winery (Colorado),
    95, 96, 97
Jackson, Jeff, 149
Jacobo, Joaquina, 130–131
Jacobson, Mike, 185
James Beard Foundation, 199

Jamestown settlement, 56
Janos restaurant (Tucson), 105–106, 110
Jefferson, Thomas, 28, 76
Jepsen, Ryan and Kristine, 263
Joffe, Darron, 77
Johnson, Pete, 48
Josinsky, Aaron, 32
Junta (New Haven), 44
Jutz, Susan, 201, *202*, 202

K

Kalchik, Chuck, 185
Karney, Rick, 53
Kay, Vina, 195
Keller, Jennifer, 251
Kelly, Harold, 62–63, 65
Kennedy, Jamie, 52
Kesey, Chuck, 154
Kettlehouse brewery (Missoula), 148
Kildeer Farm (Vermont), 48
Killeen, Johanne, 52
Kitchen tips, 207
Kleiman, Evan, 139–142, *140*
Knoll, Rick and Kristie, 146
Koehler, Cheryl, 299
Kohlrabi with Bacon, *268*, 269
Koizim, Harvey, 43
Kramer, Jackson, 77
Kroeker, Arlene, 169
Kudzu, *72*, 72–73
    Quiche in Puff Pastry, 219
Kumquats, Candied, with Mashed Sweet
    Potatoes, 270

L

Label Rouge chickens, 85–87, *87*
Laity, Carole, 223
Lake Erie Concord Grape Belt, 47
Lamb
    in Chile-Braised Roasted Meat, 302
    Chops, Glazed, 214, *215*
    Churro, 112
    Loin Medallions, Gingersnap-Crusted,
        with Brandied Fig Sauce, 300
    Shanks, Brew-Braised, with Apple Butter
        and Sauerkraut, 301
Lambert, Paula, 112
La Montanita Cooperative (New
    Mexico), 113
Land Stewardship Project (Minnesota), 204
Langeland, Dianne, 2, 3
Langeland, Doug, 2, 3, 238
LaPrad, Greg, 102–104, *103*
Larry's Beans (North Carolina), 78
Lata, Mike, 70–71, *71*, 78
Law, Jim, 190, 192
Lawrence, Edward, 14
Leavey, Rich, 130
Lee, Christopher, 132–133, *133*
Lee, Fred, 23
Lee, John, 14–15, *15*, 16
Lee-Charlson, Kristen, 228
Leelanau Peninsula wine region (Michigan),
    184–187, *185*, *186*

Leelanau Wine Cellars, Ltd. (Michigan),
    185–186
Leibrock, Susan, 108
Lenegar, Michael and Charline, 77
Let's Be Frank hot dogs, 149
Levaux, Ari, 138
Leverette, Racine and Ellis, 41
Linguine with Clams, *217*, 217
Liscum, R. J., 192
Lively Run Goat Cheese (New York), 48
Livestock. *See also* Ranchers
    Midwest, 180, 263
    Northeast, 49, 52
    Southeast, 77, 78
Lobster Rolls, 238–239
Local Foods Connection (Iowa), 201–202
Long Island (East End), 48
Longoria, Freddie, 93
Los Angeles, 147
    Evan Kleiman—Angeli Caffé,
        139–142, *140*
Lotusland Vineyards (British Columbia),
    166–169, *167*
Love, Ken, 147
Lowcountry (South Carolina), 76–77
Lucia's Restaurant (Minneapolis), 196–197,
    197
Lummi Island Wild Preserves (Washington),
    162–163, *163*

M

Mâche, 36
Madison, Deborah, 91
Mad River Valley Localvores (Vermont), 48
Maggie's Mercantile (Pennsylvania), 46
Magnolia Brewpub (San Francisco), 149
Magnolia Grill (Durham), 78
Maher, Jessica, 283
Malloy, Pat McCart, 143
Manchester, Kate, 84
Mandel, Abby, 189–193
Mandel (Abby) Charity Foundation, 192
Manhattan (New York City), 49–50
Mann, Claude, 230, 288
Manning, Ivy, 158
Maple
    -Cider Brisket, Slow-Cooked, 297
    Mousse, Frozen, 250, *251*
Maple syrup, 47
Maple Wind Farm (Vermont), 49
Marcuvitz, Sheldon, 223
Marin County (California), 147–148
Marionberry, 176
Marshall, Bob, 148
Martha's Vineyard (Massachusetts), 53
Marvin, David, 31
Maryland, Chesapeake Bay, 56, 76
Massachusetts
    Allandale Farm (Boston), *13*, 13–15
    Community Sponsored Agriculture
        (CSA) in, 12
    Coonamessett Farm (Cape Cod), 16–20,
        17, *18*
    people, places, things, 46, 47, 50–51,
        52, 53

tax laws on agricultural land, 14
Massachusetts Avenue Project (Buffalo, New
    York), 38–43, *39*, *41*
Mattera, Chris, 68–69, *69*
Mawby, Larry, 186
Mawby (L.) Vineyards (Michigan), 186
Mayonnaise, Homemade, 238, *239*
McCann Crowell, Laurie, 193–195, *194*
McClendon, Bob, 112
McDermott, Robin, 48, 236
McGarry, Joe, 162
McGowan, Dan, 36
McGuire, Oogie, 111
McNiff, Patrick, 52
McTiernan, Jennifer H., 43, 44–45
Meat. *See also* Beef; Butchers; Lamb;
    Livestock; Pork; Ranchers
    bison, 92–94, *93*, 94, 113, 180
    charcuterie, 68, 132–133, *133*
    Chile-Braised Roasted, 302
    cured, 56, 132, 188–189
    Elk Steaks in Red Wine Sauce, 303
    humanely raised and processed, 49,
        77, 263
    locally sourced, 69
Mecox Bay Dairy (New York), 48
Meeder, Jesse, 40
Memphis (Tennessee), 77
Merwin, Ian, 27–28
Mesquite, 82
Mesquite flour, 82
Meyer, Danny, 50
Michielssen, Eric, 150
Michigan, 203, 204–205
    Calder Dairy Farm, 182–183, *183*
    Eve's Table (Ann Arbor), 198–199, *199*
    Leelanau Peninsula wine region, 184–
        187, *185*, *186*
Michigan Grape and Wine Industry Council
    (MGWIC), 186, 187
Michigan State University, 186
Midwest, 178–205
    agricultural regions of, 180
    Calder Dairy Farm (Michigan),
        182–183, *183*
    Edible Communities publications in,
        314–315
    Eve's Table (Ann Arbor), 198–199, *199*
    food traditions of, 180–181
    Golden Fig Fine Foods (St. Paul,
        Minnesota), 193–195, *194*
    Leelanau Peninsula wine region
        (Michigan), 184–187, *185*, *186*
    Local Foods Connection (Iowa),
        201–201
    Lucia's Restaurant (Minneapolis),
        196–197, *197*
    people, places, things, 203–205
    La Quercia Prosciutto Americano (Iowa),
        180, *188*, 188–189
    recipes by region, 312
    restaurants, 180–181
    Seed Savers Exchange (Iowa), 179–180,
        200–201, 204
Mikaelsen, Debra, 161
Milestone Specialty Produce
    (Pennsylvania), 46

Miller, Henry and Ila, 202
Milwaukee (Wisconsin), Meritage restaurant, 181
Minneapolis (Minnesota), 204
 Lucia's Restaurant, 196–197, *197*
Minnesota, 204
 Golden Fig Fine Foods (St. Paul), 193–195, *194*
 Heartlands restaurant (St. Paul), 181
 Lucia's Restaurant (Minneapolis), 196–197, *197*
Missoula (Montana), 148
 Le Petit Outre bakery, 136, *137*, 138
Money, Elizabeth Linhart, 131
Montana, 146, 148
 Le Petit Outre bakery (Missoula), 136, *137*, 138
Morels, Asparagus with Tarragon and, 228
Morgan, Steve, 90
Motley Cow Café (Iowa City), 180–181
Mount Pleasant Farmers Market (South Carolina), 77
Mousse, Maple, Frozen, 250, *251*
Mozzarella Company (Texas), 112
Muir, John, 116
Muller, Paul, 131
Mushroom(s)
 in Egg Noodles with Fresh Spring Vegetables, *222*, 223
 Morels, Asparagus with Tarragon and, 228
 Soup au Gratin, *285*, 285
 Squash, and Sage Strata, 294, *295*
Mussels and Brussels Sprout Leaves, Ragout of, Seared Pollock with, 296
Mustard greens, in Southern Cooked Greens, 305
Mylan, Tom, 47

N

Nabhan, Gary Paul, 1, 84
Nachu, Minnie, 110
Nahabedian, Carrie, 193
Nash, Kipp, 87–88, *88*
National Energy Lab of Hawaii Authority (NELHA), 134
National Fiery Foods and Barbecue Show (Albuquerque), 97
Native American agriculture, 10, 82, 84, 113
Native American food tradition, 10, 12
Native Harvest Wild Rice (Minnesota), 204
Native Seeds/SEARCH, 82, 84, 105, 106, 108–110, *109*
Nature's Harmony Farm (Georgia), 77
Nelson, Suzanne, 109, 110
Nelson Farms (New Hampshire), 53
Nemirow, Adam, 70
Neola Farms Black Angus Beef (Tennessee), 77
New Belgium Brewery (Colorado), 112
New Hampshire, 53
New Haven (Connecticut), CitySeed, 43–45, *44*
New Jersey, 10, 49
New Mexico, 84, 113

Joe S. Sausage (Albuquerque), 97–98, *98*
Pollo Real chicken ranch (Santa Fe), 85–87, *87*
New Mexico Acequia Association, 113
New Mexico Farmers Marketing Association, 113
New Pioneer Co-op (Iowa City), 263
New Rivers restaurant (Providence), 36–37
New York City
 greenmarket system, 27, 50, 74
 people, places, things, 46–47, 49–50, 51
New York State
 people, places, things, 46–47, 48
 Quail Hill Farm (Amagansett), 20–24, *21*, *23*
 Red Jacket Orchards (Geneva), 24–28, *25*, *26*
Nicholson, Brian and Mark, 25, 27-28
Noodles, Egg, with Fresh Spring Vegetables, *222*, 223
North Carolina, 78
 Garden Gate Vineyards (Mocksville), 66–67, *67*
Northeast, 8–53
 Akiwenzie's Fish & More (Ontario), 34–35, *35*
 Allandale Farm (Massachusetts), *13*, 13–15
 Bruce Tillinghast—New Rivers restaurant (Providence), 36–37
 CitySeed (New Haven, Connecticut), 43–45, *44*
 colonial farm settlements in, 10, 12
 Coonamessett Farm (Massachusetts), 16–20, *17*, *18*
 Edible Communities publications in, 313–314
 food traditions of, 9–10, 12
 Massachusetts Avenue Project (Buffalo), 38–43, *39*, *41*
 people, places, things, 46–53
 Quail Hill Farm (New York), 20–24, *21*, *23*
 recipes by region, 312
 Red Jacket Orchards (New York), 24–28, *25*, *26*
 Shelburne Farms (Vermont), 12, 29–34, *30*, *33*
Northeast Iowa Food & Farm Coalition, 263
Northeast Organic Farmers Association (NOFA), 20–21, 23, 24
North Valley Farms (California), 151
Northwest. *See* Pacific Northwest
Nuestras Raices (Holyoke, Massachusetts), 51
Nurseries, organic, 150

O

O-Bread Bakery (Vermont), 29
Ocean Vodka (Hawaii), 134–135, *135*
Ojai (California), 148
 Food for Thought Ojai, 142–145, *145*
 Pixie tangerine, 120–124, *121*, *122–123*, 148
Ojai Vineyard (California), 148
O'Keefe, Ed, 185
O'Kelley, Sarah, 71

Oliver, Gail Gordon, 254, 257, 285, 287, 301, 303, 307, 308
Olmsted, Frederick Law, 29
Olson, Shanan, 112
Oman, Don, 169–170, 171
Onion(s)
 Caramelized, Chicken and Peaches, Grilled, with Goat Cheese and, 242–243
 Maui, Sesame-Ahi Poke with, 210
 Tart, Caramelized, 289
 Wild, and Spinach Tart, 218
Ontario (Canada), 52
 Akiwenzie's Fish & More, 34–35, *35*
Orange orchards, California, 122–124, *121*, *122–123*
Orchards
 apple, 24–28, *25*, *26*, 76
 orange, 122–124, *121*, *122–123*
Oregon
 Ecotrust Food & Farms program (Portland), 173–175, *175*
 Gaining Ground Farm, 157–158, *158*
 Pastaworks (Portland), 169–171, *170*
 Portland, 176
 Sokol Blosser Winery, 164–165, *165*
 Willamette Valley, 154
Organic certification
 Certified Naturally Grown (CNG) program, 59, 61
 USDA, 15, 24, 61, 165, 172
Organic Farming Research Foundation, 96
Osentowski, Jerome, 111
Ouellette, Cheryl, 176
Oysters
 Cape May Salt/Delaware Bay, 49
 Island Creek, 52
 Spring Pan Roast of, A , 212

P

Pacific Northwest, 152–177
 agricultural regions of, 154, 156
 Ecotrust Food & Farms program (Portland, Oregon), 173–175, *175*
 Edible Communities publications in, 315
 food and beverages of, 156
 food resources of, 153–154
 Forstbauer Farm (British Columbia), 159–161, *160*
 Gaining Ground Farm (Oregon), 157–158, *158*
 Lotusland Vineyards (British Columbia), 166–169, *167*
 Lummi Island Wild Preserves (Washington), 162–163, *163*
 Maria Hines—Tilth restaurant (Seattle), *172*, 172–173
 Pastaworks (Portland, Oregon), 169–171, *170*
 people, places, things, 176–177
 recipes by region, 312
 Sokol Blosser Winery (Oregon), 164–165, *165*
Paine, Michael and Jill, 157–158
Pasanen, Melissa, 34, 247
Passard, Alain, 290

Pasta
    Joe S. Sausage (Santa Fe), *98*, 98
    Linguine with Clams, *217*, 217
    Pastaworks (Portland, Oregon), 169–171, *170*
Pastaworks (Portland, Oregon), 169–171, *170*
Patel, Raj, 139
Paul Maui Vodka (Hawaii), 135
Peaches and Chicken, Grilled, with Caramelized Onions and Goat Cheese, 242–243
Peak Spirits distillery (Colorado), *95*, 95–97, 111
Pear Cake, Double Chocolate, 276
Peconic Land Trust (New York), 21, 48
Pecoraro, Rich, 112
Pedersen, Tom, 111
Pedi, Jewel, 148
Peet, Alfred, 156
Penn-Romine, Carol, 72–73, 142
Penn's Corner Farm Alliance (Pennsylvania), 46
Pennsylvania, 46, 50
Peppers. *See* Bell Pepper(s); Chile(s)
Peregine Farms (North Carolina), 78
Permaculture Guild (Arizona), 101
Permaculture Institute (Colorado), 111
Persimmon Rum Cake, *282*, 283
Pertuset, Jenni, 163
Petersen, Melissa, 219, 227, 272
Peterson Specialty Produce (San Diego), 149
Pete's Greens (Vermont), 48
Le Petit Outre bakery (Missoula), 136, *137*, 138, 148
Petrini, Carlo, 171
Philadelphia (Pennsylvania), 50
Phillips, Liz, 61
Phoenix (Arizona), 112–113
    Greg LaPrad—Quiessence Restaurant, 102–104, *103*
    Public Market, 99–101, *100*
Picard, Diane, 38, 42
Pie(s). *See also* Quiche
    Apple, Lattice-Topped, 280–281, *281*
    Berry Ricotta, 253
Piecrust(s)
    Flaky, 254, *255*
    Lard, 280
Piedmont (North Carolina), 78
Pierce, Kim, 112
Pineapple Gazpacho, 233
Pinsof, Jeanne, 192
Piper, Odessa, 189
Pissaladiere, 289
PlacerGROWN (Sacramento), 149
Plimoth Plantation (Massachusetts), 52
Plow to Plate (New Milford, Connecticut), 50
Plumfield Plantation (South Carolina), 62–65, *63*, *64*
Poblanos Stuffed with Goat Cheese and Shrimp, *240*, 241
Poke
    Ahi-Ono-Avocado, 210
    Sesame-Ahi, with Maui Onions, 210
Pollan, Michael, 139
Pollock, Seared, with a Ragout of Mussels and Brussels Sprout Leaves, 296

Pollo Real chicken (New Mexico), 85–87, *87*
Polly's Pancake Parlor (New Hampshire), 53
Polyface Farm (Virginia), 76, 85
Pomegranate Chicken, Braised, with Walnuts, *298*, 299
Pork. *See also* Bacon; Ham; Sausage
    barbecue, Southern, 56
    charcuterie, 68, 132–133, *133*
    in Chile-Braised Roasted Meat, 302
    cured and smoked, 56, 58
    Medallions of, Pan-Seared, with Apples, *262*, 263
    La Quercia Prosciutto Americano (Iowa), 180, *188*, 188–189
    Shelburne Farms (Vermont), 32–33
    small-production, 180
    Wholesome Harvest (Iowa), 98
Porter, Jay, 149
Portland (Oregon), 176
    Ecotrust Food & Farms program, 173–175, *175*
    Pastaworks, 169–171, *170*
Potager Restaurant (Colorado), 112
Potato(es)
    -Carrot Mash, 226
    varieties, 111, 176
Poultry
    backyard, 87, 118
    humane slaughter, 53
    Label Rouge standards, 85–86
    Pollo Real (Santa Fe), 85–87, *87*
    in Southeast, 77, 264
Practical Farmers of Iowa, 204
Prosciutto, La Quercia (Iowa), *188*, 188–189
Providence (Rhode Island), 52
    Bruce Tillinghast—New Rivers restaurant, 36–37
Pudding, Bread, Rhubarb with Whiskey Sauce, 229
Pumpkin Grits, Creamy, with Brown Butter, 272, *273*

Q

Quahogs, 52
Quail, Grilled, with Hazelnuts, Apricot Curry Sauce, and Wild Huckleberry Coulis, 265
Quail Hill Farm (New York), 20–24, *21*, *23*
Quail Hill Farm Cookbook, 22
Queens (New York City), 51
La Quercia Prosciutto Americano (Iowa), 180, *188*, 188–189
Quiche(s)
    Kudzu, in Puff Pastry, 219
    Onion, Wild, and Spinach Tart, 218
Quiessence Restaurant (Phoenix, Arizona), 102–104, *103*

R

RAFT (Renewing America's Food Traditions), 53, 82, 84, 108
Rahr & Sons Brewery (Texas), 112
Raja, Samina, 42, 47
Ramos, Steve, 36

Ranchers
    in California, 117
    and heritage breeds, 82
    sustainable commercial production by, 82
    in Texas, 92–94, *93*, 111
Raphael, Maggie, 46
Rasmussen, Dale, 265
Realmuto, Joe, 22
Red Bell Pepper(s). *See* Bell Pepper(s), Red
Redfeather, Nancy, 147
Red Hen Bakery (Vermont), 49
Red Hook (Brooklyn, New York), 47
Red Jacket Orchards (Geneva, New York), 24–28, *25*, *26*
Redmond, Judith, 131
Red Wine Sauce, Elk Steaks in, 303
Rhode Island, 51–52
    Bruce Tillinghast—New Rivers restaurant (Providence), 36–37
Rhubarb Bread Pudding with Whiskey Sauce, 229
Ricci, James, 186
Rice
    Carolina Plantation (South Carolina), 62–65, *63*, *64*
    in Hoppin' John Supreme, *292*, 293
    production, in South, 58
    and Sausage Stuffing, *274*, 274
    in Shrimp Bog, Sullivan's Island, 220, *221*
Rice flour, 65
Richards, Keith, 59
Richmond (Virginia), Belmont Butchery, 68–69, *69*
Ricotta Berry Pie, 253
Rink, Bernard C., 184, 185, *186*, 186, 187
Rink, Jim, 187
Ripperto, Teri, 112
Rivers, Dru, 131
Roberts, Criss, 269
Roberts, Glenn, 77
Rodale Institute, 61, 131
Romesco Sauce, 258
Roos, John, 198
Rothenberg, Peter, 43, 45
Rowley, Jon, 176
Rupf, Jorg, 96
Rutgers University Agricultural Experiment Station, 49
Ryder, Tracey, 1–5, 143, 252, 313

S

Sabo, Jenny, 146
Sakonnet River Pie (Rhode Island), 280
Salad(s)
    Arugula and Fennel, 234
    Spinach, Fresh, with Hot Bacon Vinaigrette, *235*, 235
    Strawberry Arugula Spring, *209*, 209
Salatin, Joel, 76, 85
Salmon
    candy, 177
    Chinook, 176
    Lummi Island Wild Preserves (Washington), 162–163

Wild, 153–154
Wild, with Fava Bean Puree, 224, *225*
Salomon, Sharon, 101, 104
San Diego (California), 149
San Francisco (California), 149
    produce delivery to, 126, *127,* 128–129
    Veritable Vegetable, 126
San Luis Obispo (California), 150
Santa Barbara (California), 150
Santa Fe (New Mexico), 113
    Pollo Real chicken ranch, 85–87, *87*
Satzewich, Wally, 90
Sauce(s)
    Apricot Curry, 265
    Caramel, 252–253
    Fig, Brandied, 300
    Red Bell Pepper, *240,* 241
    Red Wine, 303
    Romesco, 258
    Whiskey, 229
Sausage
    Belmont Butchery (Richmond), 68–69, *69*
    half-smokes, 76
    Joe S. Sausage (Albuquerque), 97–98, *98*
    and Rice Stuffing, *274,* 274
Savoring the Seasons of the Northern Heartland (Watson), 197
Sayle, Carol Ann, 89
Scallops, 48, 53
Schmidt, Michael, 52
Schneider, Derrick, 133
School gardens, 144, *145,* 150, 174
School lunch programs
    Davis Joint Unified School District (California), 149
    Ecotrust (Portland), 174, *175*
    Edible Schoolyard (California), 143
    Food for Thought Ojai, 142–145, *145*
    Healthy Lunch and Lifestyle (California), 150
Schwemm, Amy, 109–110
Sea Bass Ceviche with Avocado, 288
Seafood. *See* Fish; Shellfish
Seattle (Washington), 156, 176
    Maria Hines—Tilth restaurant, *172,* 172–173
Seed Savers Exchange (Iowa), 179–180, 200–201, 204
Seed saving
    Native Seeds/SEARCH, 82, 84, 105, 106, 108–110, *109*
    Seed Savers Exchange, 179–180, 200–201, 204
    Southern Exposure Seed Exchange, 76
Seed Time (Chaskey), 21–22
Seychew, Christa Glennie, 43
Shad, 50
    Roe, Broiled, with Pancetta, 216
Shalhoub, Tony, 144
Shamlian, Randy, 98
Sharkey, Erin, 38
Sharma, Neelam, 147
Shasta-Butte (California), 150–151
Sheiffele, Judy, 43
Shelburne Farms (Vermont), 12, 29–34, *30, 33*

Shellfish. *See also* Oysters; Clams; Shrimp
    Lobster Rolls, 238–239
    Mussels, Ragout of Brussels Sprout Leaves and, with Seared Pollock, 296
    in Northeast, 47, 52, 53
    in Southeast, 56, 76
Shellfish Promotion and Tasting (SPAT), 47
Sherman, Stuart, 51
Sherr, Holly, 190, 192
Shields, John, 216
Shortcakes, Strawberry, The Best, 230, *231*
Shortt, Lynda, 53
Shrimp
    Bog, Sullivan's Island, 220, *221*
    and grits, 58
    Poblanos Stuffed with Goat Cheese and, *240,* 241
    side stripe, and spot prawns, 177
Silverton, Nancy, 147
Simpson, Bruce, 186
Sixpoint Brownstone Beer, 47
Slow Food movement, 53, 88, 171, 175, 198
Smith, Bob and Diane, 51
Smith, Sam, 31–32, 33
Smith, Shay, 134, 135
Smith Island (Chesapeake Bay), 76
Smolowitz, Ron, 16, 17, 19, 20
Smoot, Carey, 97
Sokol Blosser, Susan, 164–165, *165*
Sokol Blosser Winery (Oregon), 164–165, *165*
Soto, Hernando de, 56
Soup(s)
    Beet Borscht, 286
    Butternut Squash, Roasted, *257,* 257
    Cabbage Borscht, Bubby's, 287
    Cheddar Ale, Vermont, *211,* 211
    Corn Chowder, Rich, 236, *237*
    Gazpacho, Pineapple, 233
    Mushroom, au Gratin, *285,* 285
South Carolina, 58, 76–77
    Carolina Plantation Rice, 62–65, *63, 64*
    FIG restaurant (Charleston), 70–71, *71*
    Wadmalaw Island Farm, 70
Southeast, 54–79
    Belmont Butchery (Richmond, Virginia), 68–69, *69*
    Carolina Plantation Rice (South Carolina), 62–65, *63, 64*
    Edible Communities publications in, 314
    FIG restaurant (Charleston, South Carolina), 70–71, *71*
    food traditions of, 55–56, 58
    Garden Gate Vineyards (North Carolina), 66–67, *67*
    Harris, Alvin and Shirley (Tennessee), 59–61, *60*
    kudzu in, *72,* 72–73
    people, places, things, 76–78
    recipes by region, 312
    Southern Foodways Alliance, 74–75, *75*
Southeastern Massachusetts Agricultural Partnership (SEMAP), 52
Southern Exposure Seed Exchange (Virginia), 76
Southern Foodways Alliance, 74–75, *75*
Southern Sustainable Farming, 59
Southwest, 80–113

Boggy Creek Farm (Texas), 89
Community Roots (Boulder, Colorado), 90–91, *91*
Edible Communities publications in, 314
food sources of, 81–82, 84
Greg LaPrad—Quiessence Restaurant (Phoenix, Arizona), 102–104, *103*
irrigation in, 84
Jack Rabbit Hill Estate Winery (Colorado), 95, 96, 97
Janos restaurant (Tucson, Arizona), 105–106, *106,* 110
Native Seeds/SEARCH (Arizona), 82, 84, 105, 106, 108–110, *109*
Peak Spirits distillery (Colorado), 95, 95–97, 111
people, places, things, 111–113
Phoenix Public Market (Arizona), 99–101, *100*
Pollo Real chicken (Santa Fe, New Mexico), 85–87, *87*
ranches in, 82
recipes by region, 312
SPIN (Small Plot Intensive) farming (Colorado), 90–91
Sprouting Healthy Kids project (Texas), *107,* 107–108
Souza, Flavio and Marcia, 53
SPIN (Small Plot Intensive) farming, 90–91
Spinach
    Salad, Fresh, with Hot Bacon Vinaigrette, *235,* 235
    and Wild Onion Tart, 218
Spoon Bread, Double Corn, 248
Sprouting Healthy Kids project (Austin, Texas), *107,* 107–108
Squash
    Butternut, Chicken, and Apple Barlotto, 264
    Butternut, Soup, Roasted, *257,* 257
    corn, and beans (Three Sisters), 10, 130
    Mushroom, and Sage Strata, 294, *295*
    native seeds, 110
Stackhouse, Nate, 185–186
Stadtländer, Michael, 52
Starks, Riley, 162
Star Route Farm (Bolinas, California), 125, 126
Staub, Clark, 150
Stegner, Sarah, 191
Stern, Trudy, 41
Steves, Harold, 177
Stone Barns Center for Food and Agriculture (New York), 12, 49
Stone Brewing (San Diego), 149
Stop, The (Toronto, Ontario), 52
St. Paul (Minnesota), 204
    Golden Fig Fine Foods, 193–195, *194*
    Heartlands restaurant, 181
Strata, Squash, Mushroom, and Sage, 294, *295*
Strawberry
    Arugula Spring Salad, *209,* 209
    Shortcakes, The Best, 230, *231*
Stuffing, Sausage and Rice, *274,* 274
Sustainable Farm Products (New Hampshire), 53

Sustainable Food Center (Austin), *107*, 107–108

Sweet Potatoes, Mashed, with Candied Kumquats, 270

T

Tangerine, Ojai Pixie, 120–124, *121*, *122–123*, 148

Tart(s)
Caramelized Onion, 289
Wild Onion and Spinach, 218

Tataki Sushi (San Francisco), 149

Taza Chocolates, 46

Tennessee, 77
Harris, Alvin and Shirley, 59–61, *60*, 77

Terry, Bryant, 146

Texas, 84, 111, 112
Boggy Creek Farm (Austin), 89
Sprouting Healthy Kids project (Austin), *107*, 107–108

Thacher, Tony, 120, *122*

Thacher family, of Friend's Ranches (California), 120, 122–123

Thomas, Craig, 150

Thomas, Gibson, 293, 304, 305

Thompson, Fred, 75, 212, 220

Thunder Heart Bison (Texas), 92–94, *93*

Tillinghast, Bruce, 36–37, *37*

Tilth restaurant (Seattle), *172*, 172–173

Title, Ezra, 260

Tohono O'odham Community Action (Phoenix, Arizona), 113

Tolmach, Adam, 148

Tomato(es)
and Ginger Chutney, 266, *267*
and Green Beans, Sautéed Spicy, 243
varieties of, 24, 49

Topalian, Carole, 1, 2, 3, 313

Toronto (Ontario), 52

Town Green (New Haven, Connecticut), 44

Trevor, Genie McPherson, 37

Tri-Tip Roast, Aspen, 213

Tritto, Michael, 42

Trotter's Cafe and Bakery (St. Paul), 204

Trout, Smoked, Bruschetta with Romesco Sauce, 258

Tru-Teas, 41

Tucson (Arizona)
Janos restaurant, 105–106, 110
Native Seeds/SEARCH, 82, 84, 105, 106, 108–110, *109*

Tuna
Ahi-Ono-Avocado Poke, 210
Sesame-Ahi Poke with Maui Onions, 210

Turnip, Macomber, 52

Turnip greens, in Southern Cooked Greens, 305

Tuscon (Arizona)
Janos restaurant, 105–106, *106*
Native Seeds/SEARCH, 82, 84, 105, 106, 108–110, *109*

The '21' Club (New York City), 50

U

Union Square Greenmarket (New York), 27, 50

University of California Davis, 149

Urban agriculture
Community Roots (Boulder), 90–91, *91*
Massachusetts Avenue Project (Buffalo), 38, *39*, 40, *41*, 42
rooftop gardens, 203
SPIN (Small Plot Intensive) farming, 90–91
Youth Farm and Market Project (Minnesota), 197

Urban Hens, 90

Urban Roots (Austin, Texas), 111

USDA organic certification, 15, 24, 61, 165, 172

V

Valley Shepherd Creamery (New Jersey), 49

Vancouver (British Columbia), 177

Van En, Robyn, 48

VanScoy, Andrea, 309

Veal, humanely-raised, 263

Veritable Vegetable (San Francisco), 126

Vermont, 48–49
Shelburne Farms, 12, 29–34, *30*, *33*

Vesey, Brendan, 264

Vestal, Beau, 37

Vinaigrette, Bacon, Hot, 235

Vineyards. *See* Wineries

Vintage Virginia Apples, 76

Vinton, Sherri Brooks, 45

Virginia, 56, 76
Belmont Butchery (Richmond), 68–69, *69*

Virginia Junior League Cookbook, 56

Vodka, 77, 96
Ocean Vodka (Hawaii), 134–135, *135*

W

Wadmalaw Island Farm (South Carolina), 70

Wagner, Phil, 184

Wajswol, Eran, 49

Walker, Seth, 175

Walpole, Ben, 62

Walpole, Ford, 65

Walters, Gwen Ashley, 106, 110, 233

Washington State
Lummi Island Wild Preserves, 162–163, *163*
Maria Hines—Tilth restaurant (Seattle), *172*, 172–173
Seattle, 156, 176
Yakima Valley, 156

Wasserman, Wendy, 286

Water, deep-sea bottled, 134–135

Waters, Alice, 105, 143, 146, 189, 192

Watson, Lucia, 196–197, *197*

Weavers Way Food Cooperative Farm (Philadelphia), 50

Webb family, of Shelburne Farms (Vermont), 29, 31

Welch, Michael, 28

Weld, William Fletcher, 13

West. *See also* California; Pacific Northwest
Edible Communities publications in, 315
food traditions of, 116
local food production in, 119
people, places, things, 146–151
Le Petit Outre bakery (Missoula, Montana), 136, *137*, 138
recipes by region, 312

Western Sustainability Exchange, 146

Westville Village Renaissance Alliance (Connecticut), 44

Whealy, Diane Ott, 200

Whiskey Sauce, 229

Whitaker, Bo and Sonya, 66–67

White Oak Pastures (Georgia), 77

Whitton Flowers and Produce (Tennessee), 77

Wholesome Harvest (Iowa), 98

Wicks, Judy, 50

Widmer Brothers Brewery (Portland), 176

Wiemer, Hermann J., 48

Wilcox, Jessica, 146

Wilder, Janos, 105–106, *106*, 110

Wilkinson, Catherine, 300

Willamette Valley (Oregon), 154

Wineries
California, 147, 148, 150
Garden Gate Vineyards (North Carolina), 66–67, *67*
Jack Rabbit Hill Estate (Colorado), 95, 96, 97
in Leelanau Peninsula (Michigan), 184–187, *185*
Lotusland Vineyards (British Columbia), 166–169, *167*
Northeast, 10, 47, 48, 53
Pacific Northwest, 156
Sokol Blosser (Oregon), 164–165, *165*

Wolfert, Paula, 139

Wong, Alan, 147

Woodman, "Chubby," 46

Woodman's of Essex (Boston), 46

Woodward, Henry, 62

Woodward's Garden (San Francisco), 258

World-Wide Opportunities on Organic Farms (WWOOFers), 168

Wykoff, Lola, 275

Y

Yakima Valley (Washington), 156

Yee, Larry, 2

Yoder, Calvin and Judy, 202

Young, Tim and Liz, 77

Youth development programs, 38, 40, 111, 147, 197

Youth Farm and Market Project (Minnesota), 197

Z

Zingerman's (Michigan), 204